India in the Chinese Imagination

ENCOUNTERS WITH ASIA

Victor H. Mair, Series Editor

Encounters with Asia is an interdisciplinary series dedicated to the exploration of all the major regions and cultures of this vast continent. Its time frame extends from the prehistoric to the contemporary; its geographic scope ranges from the Urals and the Caucasus to the Pacific. A particular focus of the series is the Silk Road in all of its ramifications: religion, art, music, medicine, science, trade, and so forth. Among the disciplines represented in this series are history, archeology, anthropology, ethnography, and linguistics. The series aims particularly to clarify the complex interrelationships among various peoples within Asia, and also with societies beyond Asia.

A complete list of books in the series is available from the publisher

INDIA IN THE CHINESE IMAGINATION

MYTH, RELIGION, AND THOUGHT

EDITED BY
JOHN KIESCHNICK AND MEIR SHAHAR

PENN

UNIVERSITY OF PENNSYLVANIA PRESS

PHILADELPHIA

Published by
University of Pennsylvania Press
Philadelphia, Pennsylvania 19104-4112
www.upenn.edu/pennpress

Printed in the United States of America
on acid-free paper

10 9 8 7 6 5 4 3 2 1

Library of Congress Cataloging-in-Publication Data

India in the Chinese imagination / edited by John Kieschnick
and Meir Shahar. — 1st ed.
p. cm. — (Encounters with Asia)
Includes bibliographical references and index.
ISBN 978-0-8122-4560-8 (hardcover : alk. paper)
1. China—Civilization—Indic influences. 2. China—
Relations—India. 3. India—Relations—China. I. Kieschnick,
John, 1964– I. Shahar. Meir, 1959– III. Series: Encounters
with Asia.
DS721.I59 2014
303.48'251054—dc23 2013022777

In Memory of
John R. McRae

Contents

India in the Chinese Imagination

Figure 1. Liu Songnian's *arhat* (*luohan*), c. 1155–1218. Courtesy the National Palace Museum Taiwan, Republic of China.

Introduction

Liu Songnian's (ca. 1155–1218) *Arhat* is considered a masterpiece of Chinese portraiture (Figure 1). The renowned court painter depicted in it an Indian Buddhist saint (*arhat*) as he had imagined him to appear. Liu likely never met an Indian in person. In order to render one he merely exaggerated the facial features the Chinese had long associated with foreigners from the west: prominent nose, bushy eyebrows, bulging eyes, and a bearded chin. He even furnished his fanciful Indian subject with pirate-like earrings. The whimsical effect notwithstanding, Liu's arhat is deeply moving. Gazelles grazing at his feet and gibbons frolicking overhead, the Indian saint is in complete harmony with the surrounding nature. His concentrated gaze is directed far into space—or into the recess of his own soul. Having shed all worldly concerns, he has achieved transcendence.

Liu's *Arhat* might furnish a convenient introduction to the twin aspects of this book: the Indian impact on the Chinese creative imagination and the Chinese imaginings of India. Beginning in the first century CE, the Buddhist faith brought to China Indian saints and gods, demons and ghouls that were to change forever the Chinese mental landscape. The Buddhist arhats (Chinese: *luohan*), for example, became a favorite topic of Chinese fiction and visual arts, celebrated in statues, paintings, and novels down to modern times. At the same time, the Buddhist influx of Indian philosophy and mythology, art and material culture led inquisitive Chinese minds to ponder their source. For almost two millennia, Chinese thinkers and novelists, artists and architects have been recreating India within their own borders. Paintings such as Liu Songnian's reveal to us India and its inhabitants as fancied by the Chinese: India in the Chinese imagination.

India's impact on Chinese civilization has been the subject of intensive research. Generations of scholars have revealed to us the indebtedness of Chinese culture to Indian precedents. Beginning in the first centuries CE, India contributed—largely through the vehicle of Buddhism—to all aspects of Chinese religious, cultural, artistic, and material life. Chinese notions of transcendence had been radically transformed by the Buddhist notion of liberation, just as the Chinese heavens and hells had been populated by gods and demons of Indian descent. Chinese paintings and sculptures drew heavily on the Indian—no less than the Central Asian and Greco-Buddhist—techniques by which the Buddha had been visually rendered, and the Chinese performing arts—storytelling and drama—adopted the Indian modes of the *chantefable* (alternating prose and verse) that had been common in the Indian subcontinent. Chinese philosophy had been forever altered by the substance and style of Indian epistemological and ontological discourse, and the Chinese diet was transformed by the adoption of the sugar and the rice gruel that had been consumed by Indian Buddhist missionaries. Even Chinese furniture had been fashioned after Indian precedents. Prior to the advent of Buddhism, the Chinese sat on mats, whereas following the example of Indian monks they began sitting on chairs.[1]

This volume differs from the extensive scholarship that inspired it in paying particular attention to three related aspects of the Indo-Chinese encounter. The first is the impact of Indian religion and literature on the Chinese creative imagination broadly conceived. Buddhism brought to China creatures of the Indian imagination, and metaphysical products of the Indian mind, that were to shape Chinese religion, literature, and philosophical discourse all through the modern period. The following chapters survey Indian gods and demons, no less than philosophical concepts of life, death, and rebirth that inspired Chinese authors far beyond the confines of the Buddhist monastic establishment. The Chinese imagining of India is the second topic. The two civilizations being separated by a daunting geographical gap, only a tiny fraction of the Chinese population had ever been in direct contact with Indian people or things. Hence the Chinese were forced to strain their imagination to conceive of the land to which they were so deeply indebted. The chapters reveal the often surprising ways in which Chinese authors—lay and clerical alike—sought to comprehend India, applying to it Chinese intellectual tools. Closely related is the third topic: the Chinese recreation of India within its own borders. Here the contributors examine some of the ways Chinese monarchs and priests rethought and reinvented Indian philosophy and Indian institutions.

Granting the tremendous influence India exerted over medieval China (largely through Buddhism), it is well to note that the two civilizations had been interacting for the most part indirectly. Prior to modern times, communication and exchange between India and China were conducted largely via intermediaries. Intensive and prolonged *direct* contact originated no earlier than the twentieth century, when it sometimes took a hostile turn. In 1962, after a series of border skirmishes, Chinese and Indian troops clashed in what later became known as the "Sino-Indian War," a brief but costly conflict fought in harsh conditions over disputed territory. The war had far-reaching implications for Chinese-Indian relations in the latter half of the twentieth century, but it is also remarkable as the first military confrontation between the two cultures in over a thousand years.[2] The war marked a new era of direct contact—in this case sadly violent—between India and China; despite the long history of influence and exchange, for approximately two thousand years, relations between India and China had been almost always conducted via neighboring countries and peoples.

We might easily lose sight of the layers of mediation that lay between India and China, given the rich history of trade between the two regions. In medieval times, each was well aware of the other's existence, exchanging all manner of goods and even a series of political embassies. Beginning in roughly the first century, a vibrant trade between India and China flourished, with the establishment and expansion of the Silk Route. India supplied precious gems and aromatics, medicinal plants, spices, cotton, and Buddhist devotional objects; China sent porcelain, gold, camphor, and, above all, silk.[3] The goods came through various routes—most famously through the oasis kingdoms of Central Asia, but also by sea and along passages through Tibet and Burma. But while there are records of Indian traders in China and Chinese traders in India, trade for the most part took place through middlemen.[4] Much of what came to China from India arrived through the efforts of Sogdians, Parthians, and later Arabs. Hence, while many Chinese had seen Indian cotton, or consumed sugar that had been refined by techniques transmitted from India, few would have ever met an actual Indian. The same was true for Indians, who may have been familiar with Chinese silks, but would probably have purchased them from other Indians or from Central Asian merchants.

Records of embassies from India to China and from China to India demonstrate that a select few *did* interact with their counterparts, but such exchanges were the exception rather than the rule. The same was true even for Buddhism, India's most famous and successful import to China. From the first century to the thirteenth, some intrepid Indian monks did make their way to China, and on the Chinese side, pilgrims went to India, came back to China, and wrote about their experiences, most notably Faxian (337–ca. 422), Xuanzang (602–664), and Yijing (635–713). But these pilgrims are famous in part because they were exceptional. Even among the most accomplished Chinese monks, few ever even expressed an intention of making the trip to the land of the Buddha; the journey was considered too treacherous, the obstacles—including the Taklamakan desert, the Himalayas, and the sea—too great. Indeed, the three great Chinese pilgrims were known as much for making the trip itself as for what they saw and learned in India. And while the accounts of India by Faxian, Xuanzang, and Yijing remain valuable for understanding India in the medieval period, they were written for a particular Chinese audience and reflect the way these three talented Chinese pilgrims wanted their trips to be perceived in China.[5] In other words, as sources for literate Chinese to understand India, the travel accounts of the Chinese pilgrims provided only indirect access to India, tied up with preconceptions of both the authors and what the authors assumed their Chinese readers wanted to know. From the second century to the eleventh, a handful of Indian monks were active in China, but their numbers were overshadowed by monks from Central Asia—Sogdiana, Bactria, Parthia, Kucha, Khotan and the Kushan empire—who bridged the gap that separated India and China.

The work of virtually all these foreign monks centered on the translation of scripture. For well over half a millennium, Buddhists in China carried out perhaps the greatest, and certainly the best organized, long-term translation project in the history of the world. Working in teams, under imperial auspices, monks and laymen translated a massive body of Buddhist writings from Indian languages—for the most part Sanskrit—into Chinese. Hence, if most Chinese did not have access to India through travel or contact with merchants or monks, they could at least read books from India. Granted, Indian books were largely limited to Buddhist scriptures—references to non-Buddhist Indian writings are extremely rare in Chinese history. Nonetheless, reams of accurate, carefully rendered translations of Buddhist scripture at least seem to have provided Chinese with direct access to Indian Buddhism. But even here, knowledge of India was mediated through the Chinese language. Translators, attempting to present Buddhist writings in elegant, sophisticated Chinese, chose Chinese terms with resonance in the Chinese tradition, inevitably leading to shades of meaning and associations not present in the original.[6] The number of Chinese monks with any facility at all in Sanskrit was severely limited; the study of Sanskrit was not part of standard monastic training even for the most advanced monks in China. And the massive body of literature on lay interest in Buddhism yields rare examples—if any—of Chinese literati learning Sanskrit.[7] The relationship between India and China was hence markedly different from that between, for example, China and Japan or Korea. From medieval times to the twentieth century, educated Japanese read widely in Chinese writings—not just Buddhist works—in the original language. Korean monks not only traveled to China, but even became famous within China, composing works in Chinese, attracting Chinese disciples, and contributing directly to the development of Chinese Buddhism. In contrast, the only recorded attempt by a Chinese monk to compose a work in Sanskrit was when the emperor commanded Xuanzang to oversee a Sanskrit translation of the *Dao de jing*.[8]

But even for those Chinese who could not read Sanskrit, travel to India, or meet any who had, the accounts of pilgrims and merchants, precious foreign objects, and, above all, the rich Buddhist literature in Chinese translation were more than enough to inspire speculation about various facets of Indian life. And the picture of India in the Chinese imagination rapidly filled in gaps in knowledge, as fragments of information trickling into China from India took on lives of their own.

Take, for instance, the place of the great Indian king Aśoka in Chinese history. It is unlikely that Aśoka had any significant impact, even indirectly, on China during his third-century BCE rule. But when, centuries later, the story of his rule reached China in Buddhist texts, the *idea* of Aśoka occupied Chinese minds for centuries. Chinese Buddhists claimed that any number of finds were remains of stūpas and relics that had been distributed "throughout the world" by the great Indian king.[9] And more important still, medieval Chinese emperors like Sui Wendi and Empress Wu drew on the story of Aśoka, imitating his supposed distribution of Buddhist relics to legitimate their own position as "Buddhist rulers."[10] Just as some Buddhist texts that had only limited circulation in India became enormously successful in China and some texts purporting to be translations from Sanskrit originals were in fact composed in China, biographies of Indian figures grew or were invented entirely in China.[11]

If Chinese rulers might draw on ideas from India, at times no doubt as much for reasons of political expediency as piety, Chinese monks were in equal parts inspired and haunted by India. Inspired, because they saw in the sacred land of the Buddha possibilities of perfection; haunted, because the China that surrounded them could never equal the India they imagined. Tansen Sen describes the Chinese anxiety over India's perfection as a "borderland complex." Although most Chinese assumed that China, the "Middle Kingdom" (*zhongguo*), was the center of the world, Chinese monks often reserved the term middle kingdom for India. And since travel to India was impractical for all but a select few Chinese monks, many traveled to India in their imaginations, witnessing elaborate Indian Buddhist monasteries in visions or discovering that famous relics or even Buddhist deities had left India to take up residence in China.[12] And while Chinese Buddhists described the Indians of their imagination as spiritually accomplished and honest, rivals to Buddhists at court conjured an image of Indians as a devious and pernicious race.[13]

Scholarship on the role of the image of India in Britain—during a time when contacts between India and Britain were much more intimate than those between India and China—underline the importance of imagination even when contact is by displaying his own extraordinary penis. Yamabe carefully traces the sources for elements in these stories, demonstrating the way Buddhists in Central Asia patched together motifs and concepts, making an array of adjustments as they adapted Buddhist lore for a new, Chinese audience.

Part II, "India in Chinese Imaginings of the Past," explores how Chinese authors, deeply concerned with history, attempted to fit Indian history—and particularly Indian Buddhist history—into their conception of the past. In "From Bodily Relic to Dharma Relic Stūpa: Chinese Materialization of the Aśoka Legend in the Wuyue Period," Shi Zhiru reconstructs one of the least well understood episodes in the remarkable history of Aśoka's rule in the Chinese political imagination when, in the tenth century, Chinese rulers imitated an act they believed Aśoka had carried out, purportedly manufacturing 84,000 miniature stūpas, each containing woodblock printed scriptures along with other precious objects, leaving behind both documents describing the event and a rich archaeological record, most of which has only come to light in recent years. In "'Ancestral Transmission' in Chinese Buddhist Monasteries: The Example of the Shaolin Temple," Ye Derong draws on the unparalleled wealth of epigraphical material from the Shaolin Temple to elucidate how major monasteries in premodern China constructed monastic family lines stretching back ultimately to India, in this way creating for generations of monks identities and loyalties to individual monasteries, lineages, and Buddhism as a whole. When Chinese Buddhists attempted to link the Chan tradition back to India, they focused considerable attention on the figure of Bodhidharma as a key link tying the early Chan lineage back to India and eventually the Buddha himself. Chan scholars have, over the past hundred years, demonstrated just how weak this link was. In "The Hagiography of Bodhidharma: Reconstructing the Point of Origin of Chinese Chan Buddhism," John McRae returns to the legends of Bodhidharma and suggests that we should not be too quick to dismiss the value of early legends of Bodhidharma for understanding the earliest strands of Chan, and that it is possible to perceive connections between these early strands and Buddhism of the same period in other parts of Asia.

Finally, in Part III, "Chinese Rethinking of Indian Buddhism," three scholars take different approaches to the question how to assess the relationship between Chinese and Indian Buddhism. In "Is Nirvāṇa the Same as Insentience?" Robert Sharf examines historically unrelated and on the surface entirely distinct doctrinal debates, two in India and one in China, and asks whether these apparently arcane and unrelated debates might in fact stem from fundamental concerns—personal identity, ethical responsibility, sentience, and death—that continue to occupy philosophers today, though now in radically different "thought experiments." In the final two contributions to the volume, Christine Mollier and Stephen Bokenkamp explore the manifestations of Indian elements not in the more obvious realm of Chinese Buddhism, or even in popular religion, but in Daoism. Mollier, in "Karma and the Bonds of Kinship in Medieval Daoism: Reconciling the Irreconcilable," shows how, as the doctrine of karma swept across Asia, Daoists gradually appropriated and reinterpreted it in their own scriptures. Finally, Bokenkamp, in "This Foreign Religion of Ours: Lingbao Views of Buddhist Translation," argues that beyond the more obvious appropriation of terms and concepts, Daoists were also inspired by the Chinese encounter with Sanskrit to conceive "celestial scripts," a sublime form of writing in which Daoist scriptures, and even, much earlier, some Buddhist scriptures, were composed before being translated into more mundane and more easily decipherable writing for followers of the Dao in our world.

Taken together, the ten chapters presented here reveal both the depth and the subtlety of the encounter between India and China: depth in that they disclose Indian connections in the realms of Chinese gods, conceptions of the underworld, the past, and language as Chinese negotiated problems in family relations, cosmology, literary convention, and the exploration of consciousness; subtle, in that the lives of Indian images, texts, concepts, and gods took on new forms in China and, fueled by a febrile and fertile imagination, over the course of centuries, developed in circuitous and unpredictable ways.

The editors wish to express their gratitude to Moshe Peterburg (Peter), President of Peterburg Holdings, whose generosity made this book possible. We are similarly thankful to the Tel Aviv University Department of East Asian Studies and the Tel Aviv University Confucius Institute. Tansen Sen and Jonathan Silk took an interest in the manuscript early on, and we are grateful for their comments. We are likewise grateful to our students Ron Atazky, Or Biron, Ernest Kuzin, and Oded Paporisch, for their dedication to the project.

John McRae participated in the conference, but died during the preparation of the volume. It is to his memory that we dedicate this book.

PART I

Indian Mythology and the Chinese Imagination

ji is the foundational collection of this genre. What Jones discovers is that certain techniques were deliberately and consistently employed, first, to maintain the pretense that the entire contents of the narrative were true, and, second, to advance the narrative from incident to incident.

> Because of the "paratactic structure" of many classical Chinese narratives, the problems of transitions between scenes and plot development in general were usually manipulated by categories . . .[2] and, where absolutely necessary, by conjunctions such as *nai* ("so"), *zhi* ("arriving [at some time or place]"), *hou* ("later"), or *yushi* ("thereupon").[3]

These mechanisms for advancing the narrative, which continued into the Tang period (618–907) in the classical tales known as *chuanqi* ("transmission of the strange") include conspicuous use of terms that mean "suddenly, instantly, quickly" and so forth, or references to dreams, drinking of alcoholic beverages, and the appearance of ghosts and spirits. Because these devices can be used to justify (if only superficially) almost any transition from one situation or state to another, they permit even the most extravagant scenarios. In other words, they enable the author to construct what is essentially a fictional narrative in all but name and ontological assumptions.

As a matter of fact, *zhiguai* and related genres in the Six Dynasties were regarded (even by their own authors) almost as journalistic newsgathering.[4] With *zhiguai*, there was no conscious fictionalization, but rather an attempt to record strange or supernatural events that the official historians had overlooked, yet that were considered important for the complete historical record. It is no wonder that *Sou shen ji* was often referred to by later scholars as *yushi* ("leftover history"). As Karl Kao has put it so well:

> In Western literature, the supernatural and the fantastic, as their association with the term *fantasy* suggests, are conceived mainly from the angle of creative perception (the author's projection of his vision) rather than from that of the reality represented. Within the Chinese context, the opposite orientation is assumed: Six Dynasties *chih-kuai* [*zhiguai*] particularly are considered as the "records" of facts and observable natural phenomena (or hearsay).[5]

Speaking of "hearsay," an even earlier forerunner of fiction in China is what was called *xiaoshuo* ("small talk"). A peculiar phenomenon that goes back to the *ji* is the foundational collection of this genre. What Jones discovers is that certain techniques were deliberately and consistently employed, first, to maintain the pretense that the entire contents of the narrative were true, and, second, to advance the narrative from incident to incident.

> Because of the "paratactic structure" of many classical Chinese narratives, the problems of transitions between scenes and plot development in general were usually manipulated by categories . . .[2] and, where absolutely necessary, by conjunctions such as *nai* ("so"), *zhi* ("arriving [at some time or place]"), *hou* ("later"), or *yushi* ("thereupon").[3]

These mechanisms for advancing the narrative, which continued into the Tang period (618–907) in the classical tales known as *chuanqi* ("transmission of the strange") include conspicuous use of terms that mean "suddenly, instantly, quickly" and so forth, or references to dreams, drinking of alcoholic beverages, and the appearance of ghosts and spirits. Because these devices can be used to justify (if only superficially) almost any transition from one situation or state to another, they permit even the most extravagant scenarios. In other words, they enable the author to construct what is essentially a fictional narrative in all but name and ontological assumptions.

As a matter of fact, *zhiguai* and related genres in the Six Dynasties were regarded (even by their own authors) almost as journalistic newsgathering.[4] With *zhiguai*, there was no conscious fictionalization, but rather an attempt to record strange or supernatural events that the official historians had overlooked, yet that were considered important for the complete historical record. It is no wonder that *Sou shen ji* was often referred to by later scholars as *yushi* ("leftover history"). As Karl Kao has put it so well:

> In Western literature, the supernatural and the fantastic, as their association with the term *fantasy* suggests, are conceived mainly from the angle of creative perception (the author's projection of his vision) rather than from that of the reality represented. Within the Chinese context, the opposite orientation is assumed: Six Dynasties *chih-kuai* [*zhiguai*] particularly are considered as the "records" of facts and observable natural phenomena (or hearsay).[5]

Speaking of "hearsay," an even earlier forerunner of fiction in China is what was called *xiaoshuo* ("small talk"). A peculiar phenomenon that goes back to the

Chapter 1

Transformation as Imagination in Medieval Popular Buddhist Literature

Victor H. Mair

From its very beginnings, Chinese civilization has been preoccupied with record-keeping and history-making.[1] No other civilization on earth can match the sustained dedication to the enterprise of writing down for posterity the main events of each dynasty and reign that has transfixed China for two millennia and more. The monumental twenty-five official histories, impressive though they may be, constitute but a small part of the remarkable Chinese commitment to historiography.

By the same token, however, the perennial obsession with history has put fiction on the defensive in China. Naturally, as with all other civilizations, the Chinese have felt the impulse to create fiction. However, due to the extreme admiration for chronicles, annals, documents, and other written accounts of what transpired in the enactment of government institutions, as well as the policies and the actions of rulers and officials on a day-by-day basis, fictionalizing was considered intellectually suspect. Consequently, would-be authors of fiction had to resort to various stratagems and justifications when writing their stories (and later, novels).

Let us take, for example, the *zhiguai* ("tales of anomalies") of the Six Dynasties (220–589), the first major Chinese genre of what might be thought of by modern literary historians as fictional narrative. In a profoundly important but little known paper on "The Poetics of Uncertainty in Early Chinese Literature," Andrew Jones investigates the mechanisms whereby the narratives of the tales of anomalies in *Sou shen ji* (Records of Investigations on Spirits) were constructed. Compiled by Gan Bao (fl. 320) during the first half of the fourth century, *Sou shen*

PART I

Indian Mythology and the Chinese Imagination

late Warring States and Han period (roughly fourth century BCE to second century CE), *xiaoshuo* was supposedly gathered from what the populace was saying in the villages and lanes, hence it served as a sort of premodern opinion-gathering mechanism. The great twentieth-century short-story writer and essayist Lu Xun (1881–1936) begins his *Brief History of Chinese Fiction* thus: "*Hsiao-shuo* [*xiaoshuo*], the name for fiction, was first used by Chuang Tzu [Zhuang Zi], who spoke of 'winning honour and renown by means of *hsiao-shuo*.' All he meant by this expression, as a matter of fact, was chit-chat of no great consequence."[6] It is curious that the Modern Standard Mandarin term for "fiction" is simply a calque upon *xiaoshuo*.[7] Already by the Tang period (618–907), though, *xiaoshuo* could refer to various types of miscellaneous records, and in the Song it signified storytelling.

The relationship between storytelling and fiction is absolutely crucial for the history of the latter. Indeed, storytelling lies at the foundation of both vernacular fiction and drama in China,[8] and its traces are evident even in highly developed short stories and novels. One of the most obvious signs of the oral storytelling background of vernacular fiction in China is what Patrick Hanan calls its "simulated context."[9] That is to say, the narrator of a work of fiction adopts the simulacrum of a storytelling session, even when creating a work *ab novo* or thoroughly refashioning the materials from earlier versions of his story. After a series of studies in which he demonstrated that the corpus of extant vernacular short stories from the Qing period (1644–1912) and earlier are primarily written literature,[10] Hanan went on to account for the apparent marks of orality. His definition of this concept is as follows:

> "Simulated context" means the context or situation in which a piece of fiction claims to be transmitted. In Chinese vernacular fiction, of course, the simulacrum is that of the oral storyteller addressing his audience, a pretense in which the author and reader happily acquiesce *in order that the fiction can be communicated*.[11]

This resort to a simulated storytelling context in fiction may have been done partly out of habit, yet even so it reveals two fundamental features of vernacular fiction in China. First, it really did evolve from storytelling. Second, the author's unwillingness to take credit for making up the story that he is relating (he would rather pretend [and in most cases it was true] that he was simply writing something down that had been bequeathed to him by the oral tradition). Even for the modern Chinese literary critic Henry Zhao, the image of "reality" in a fictional text is distorted. No wonder, then, that throughout the Chinese tradition of fiction, the narrator has always been "uneasy." It is as though the narrator of fiction in China is uncomfortably aware he is telling a lie.[12]

In a 1985 paper entitled "The Narrative Revolution in Chinese Literature," I argued that Buddhist ontological presuppositions injected into the Chinese literary scene a totally new approach to fictionalizing, one that had none of the hang-ups about reality and historicity that have always dogged Chinese authors of short stories and novels.[13] Because Buddhist philosophy holds that the perceived universe is empty (*śūnyatā*) and illusory (*māyā*), a product of mentation, there is nothing to prevent an author from regarding whatever comes into his mind as having equal status and authority with "things" that he perceives. But how does an author, a creator, present what he imagines in his own mind to an audience, so that it seems as "real" to them as it does to him?

The key to this act of mental creation is "transformational manifestation." This is a concept that is rather difficult to grasp, but it is central to the Buddhist approach to literary creation that had such a tremendous impact on fiction writing in China, beginning gradually in the Six Dynasties,[14] and becoming irresistible during the Tang and later. While—even to this day—transformational manifestation has never completely liberated mainstream Chinese fiction writers from the bond and burden of history, it certainly has loosened and lightened them.

The doctrinal basis for transformational manifestation is the *nirmāṇa-kāya*, the Emanation/Created Body or physical embodiment of a Buddha, also called the *rupa-kāya* (Form/Material Body). The *nirmāṇa-kāya* is one of the three bodies of a Buddha, the other two being his *dharma-kāya* (Truth Body) and *saṃbhoga-kāya* (Enjoyment Body).[15] It is a common trope in Buddhist scriptures for the Buddha to manifest himself through transformation (*nirmāṇa*; *bianhua*) and other transcendental faculties or powers (e.g., *abhijñā*; *shentong*). Thus, in the *Da fang guang fo huayan jing ([Buddha]avataṃsakasūtra)* translated by Buddhabhadra (359–429) we find: "All the Buddhas emanate transformational bodies to fill up all the dharma worlds" (T. no. 278 , 683bc). The same text, as translated by Śikṣānanda (652–710), in another passage has the following vivid description: "All the Buddhas produce transformations from every single one of their pores" (384a). There are numerous other Sanskrit terms that were rendered by *bian* and that would have colored the Chinese understanding of transformation: *vikāra* ("change of form or nature, modification"), *pariṇāma* ("alteration, evolution, development"), *prātihārya* ("jugglery, working miracles"), and so on.

Once it is established that the Buddhas can project or emanate transformational manifestations, this makes it conceivable for other individuals of advanced ability to do likewise. Transformational manifestations may occur in several modalities. The individual (i.e., character in a narrative) performing the transformation may (1) change one thing into another thing; (2) change him/herself or part(s) of him/herself into something else; (3) cause the projection or emanation of something from his/her mind. It is the third type that is quintessentially Buddhist in nature and that enables the fictionalizer to create extraordinarily vivid universes and sub-universes parallel to the ones we perceive in the course of our daily lives. Buddhist transformations are by nature highly visual, even if one is only describing them in words, not actually depicting them through art. This innate visuality of transformational manifestation leads to a ready acceptance of pictorial and other illustrative aids on the part of the narrator/storyteller, or at least the eager adoption of graphic metaphors.

For instance, there exists a popular Buddhist narrative from Dunhuang, the "Xiang mo bianwen" (Transformation Text on the Subduing of Demons), that perfectly embodies what transpires in the act of performing transformational manifestations. The story is about a contest of magical powers between Śāriputra, a favorite disciple of the Buddha, and Raudrākṣa, leader of the heretics.[16] Both men are able to produce, through powerful mental processes, seemingly palpable manifestations, but Śāriputra wins each of the six rounds and is declared the victor (the king is a prominent witness to this exciting competition). As a result of this victory, the Buddhists are able to build Prince Jeta's monastery garden (*vihāra*), the famous Jetavana. Such thaumaturgical abilities are a commonplace in Buddhist lore: "To a certain extent, all Buddhist saints are possessed of magical powers, and these frequently prove efficacious in gaining converts."[17] Yet the contest of miraculous apparitions between Śāriputra and Raudrākṣa recorded in "Transformation Text on the Subduing of Demons"—spectacular and exciting though it undoubtedly is—bespeaks greater reliance on mental abilities than, say, the resort to the sheer necromancy of a Fotucheng (Buddhacinga; d. 348), who practiced his wonder-working in Luoyang starting from 310.

By sheer good fortune, not only do we have the "Transformation Text on the Subduing of Demons," we also possess a unique, illustrated scroll that would actually have been used by a *bian* ("transformation") storyteller in performance. That is the inestimably precious manuscript P4524 in the Bibliothèque Nationale (Paris). It is because of this illustrated scroll that we not only can understand what went on in a transformation storytelling performance, but we can actually see on the scroll what transformational manifestations (in essence, conjurations) look like and can gain an idea of how they were produced.

We know that, before Śāriputra engaged in his fierce struggle of psychic prowess with Raudrākṣa, he meditated intensely beneath a banyan tree. And we can see in each scene on the scroll that Śāriputra is accompanied by his so-called *dhyāni* ("transcendent; produced by meditation") Buddha of inspiration who sits on a cloud above his head. P4524 and its accompanying *bianwen* ("transformation text") is thus the paradigmatic substantiation of both the picture storytelling genre and the Buddhist concept of transformational manifestation that inspired it. At the same time, P4524 is arguably the single most important artifact for the study of the oral-visual background of Chinese popular literature.[18] In P4524, both Śāriputra and the Six Heterodox Masters led by Raudrākṣa are said to *huachu* ("conjure up" through transformation) various manifestations; less often, the competing conjurors are said to *xian* ("cause to appear" or "manifest") their spectacles. A fuller appreciation of the significance of P4524 for the development of vernacular fiction and drama in China may be gained through a reading of *Painting and Performance*, which is an extended explication of the historical background and cultural milieu of this singular scroll, as well as a study of its offshoots in China and parallels throughout in Asia and the rest of the world.[19]

Elsewhere, I have shown that the device of transformational manifestation around which the narrative of the Dunhuang Śāriputra story is structured served as the organizational principle for a major episode in the plot of "Zhang Daoling qi shi Zhao Sheng" (Zhang Daoling Seven Times Tests Zhao Sheng). Furthermore, I demonstrated how the ultimate antecedents for the contest of supernatural powers in both was to be found in the 48th story (the 9th story in the 10th scroll) of the *Xianyu jing* (*Sūtra of the Wise and the Foolish*), T. no. 202, vol. 4, p. 418b–420c, titled "Xuda qi jingshe" (Sudatta Raises a Monastery).[20]

Yet the most celebrated practitioner of *bian* in Chinese literature is not Śāriputra, but Monkey (Sun Wukong [Monkey Enlightened About Emptiness]), the simian hero of the famous late Ming novel, *Xiyou ji* (Journey to the West). That the later folk Buddhist tradition took delight in the spectacular and dazzling quality of supernatural manifestations in and of themselves is evident from this typical passage featuring Monkey:

> Seeing that the demon[21] was becoming savage, Monkey now used the method called Body Outside the Body. He plucked out a handful of hairs, bit them into small pieces and then spat them out into the air, crying "Change!" [*bian*] The fragments of hair changed into several hundred small monkeys, all pressing round in a throng. For you must know that, when anyone becomes an Immortal, he can project his soul, change his shape, and perform all kinds of miracles. Monkey, since his Illumination,

could change every one of the 84,000 hairs of his body into whatever he chose.[22]

It is interesting to observe that, although Monkey here employs the transformational modality of changing parts of his body (hairs) into something else—namely, small monkeys (i.e., in effect multiplying himself)—he also clearly raises the possibility of other modalities, including the simplest one of merely changing his shape and the highest one of "project[ing] his soul" (i.e., his mind). All together, Monkey is said to possess seventy-two transformations (*qishi'er bian[hua]*), but this is purely a magic number that is widespread throughout Eurasia.[23] Although *Journey to the West* includes conspicuous Taoist (especially Quanzhen [Complete Perfection]) and other elements, the overall framework and basic sources of the narrative are Buddhist, and Monkey's flamboyant, playful *bian* transformations are clearly inspired by Buddhism.

Already in *Da Tang Sanzang qu jing shihua* (Poetic Tale of Tripitaka Fetching Sūtras), a thirteenth-century forerunner of *Journey to the West*, Monkey is intimately associated with transformational (*bian*) powers at that stage in the development of the narrative. In this charming novella, Monkey Pilgrim displays his ability to bring about transformation virtually at will. In chapter 3, for example, he changes a beautiful woman into a bundle of grass and then back again. Indeed, in chapter 6, he is able to transform his golden-ringed staff into a gigantic demon (*yakṣa*). This manipulation of his staff, of course, becomes a key motif in *Journey to the West*.[24] Such transformational exuberance pervades Buddhist and Buddho-Taoist popular literature in medieval and late imperial times, and even seeps into sectarian texts such as *baojuan* ("precious scrolls").[25] We may fairly say that, from the introduction of Buddhism into East Asia at the end of the Han period to the late imperial period, *nirmāṇa* and related concepts of transformational manifestation grew from being an alien presence to an integral component of Chinese popular literature.

Conclusion

Telling a story is a natural human activity. Stories told about the gods are myth, stories about real people of the past are history or legend, and so forth. The presence (or absence) of fictional narrative in a given culture is not something that we should necessarily take for granted as a universal phenomenon, since fiction requires certain ontological presuppositions that may not be shared by all cultures.

native psychological, social, and religious tensions. These, however, will not be exhausted in this brief chapter. The following pages highlight only those aspects of the Chinese Nezha myth that can be traced back to India. As we will see, Sanskrit literature had associated the boyish Nalakūbara with the awesome child-god Kṛṣṇa (Bāla-Kṛṣṇa). It is possible, therefore, that two of the greatest Asian story-cycles—the Indian legends of the baby Kṛṣṇa, and the Chinese myths of the infant Nezha—are not unrelated.

The figure of Nezha/Nalakūbara was brought to China by Tantric ritual masters who had harnessed the powers of the Hindu gods to fight evil spirits ranging from the demons of disease to foreign armies. Hence, the history of the impish Nezha might illustrate the significance of Tantric Buddhism (also known as esoteric Buddhism) as an agent for the Indian gods' impact upon the Chinese imagination. Tantric Buddhism had served as a vehicle for the transmission of the Indian pantheon of divinities into China. In this respect, this chapter joins recent scholarship that has demonstrated the tremendous influence of esoteric Buddhism on medieval China.

Whereas Nalakūbara's Indian history has received no scholarly attention, Nezha's Chinese career has been investigated. In the following pages I draw upon the discoveries of Liu Ts'un-yan, Chen Xiaoyi, Hok-Lam Chan, Xiao Dengfu, and other scholars who have surveyed the Chinese sources on the enfant terrible.[2]

The Chinese Nezha

Xifeng's allusion to Nezha was not exceptional. By late imperial times, the Indian-born god had become a Chinese household name. The fiendish child-god had captured the imagination of Chinese believers to such an extent that he ranked among their most popular divinities. To be sure there are numerous measures for the popularity of Chinese gods: Some have temples dedicated to them, whereas others commonly figure as ancillary divinities on the altars of other deities. Some occupy prominent positions in the heavenly bureaucracy, whereas the hagiographies of others are recorded in Daoist, or Buddhist, scriptures. The scope of the Nezha cult may be briefly gauged by the number of temples dedicated to him (in Taiwan, with over a hundred to his name, he is among the most widely worshiped gods), by his prominence in spirit-medium cults, and by his role in Daoist rituals, in which he is titled "The General of the Middle Altar" (Zhongtan yuanshuai).[3] Clearly, by late imperial times, the rebellious child had emerged as one of the most widely recognized divinities in the pantheons of the popular religion and of the Daoist faith alike.

As impressive as the numbers associated with the Nezha cult may be, the true measure of the mischievous god's significance in Chinese culture is provided by the prevalence of his myth. As early as the thirteenth century, Nezha's adventures were celebrated in a large body of Yuan-period *zaju* plays. During the late-Ming he figured in two of the most influential novels on the supernatural, *The Journey to the West* (1592) and the *Investiture of the Gods* (ca. 1620), and by the eighteenth and nineteenth centuries he became the subject of a vast body of oral literature and drama in a wide range of regional dialects. More recently, the unruly child's exploits were taken up by the modern media—cinema and television—which in some instances have colored the young revolutionary with a socialist aura. A cursory survey of the cartoon shelves in any Chinese bookstore—whether on the mainland, in Taiwan, or elsewhere—reveals that the naughty child's reputation is rivaled only by that of the mischievous simian Sun Wukong.

Present-day versions of the Nezha myth derive for the most part from the early seventeenth-century *Investiture of the Gods* (*Fengshen yanyi*). The novel elaborates over several chapters the dramatic career of the rebellious child-god, which may be briefly summarized as follows:

> Nezha was the son of General Li Jing. His mother had been ominously pregnant for three years, before giving birth to a ball of flesh. Considering it monstrous, the alarmed father hacked the ball with his sword, whereupon a tiny child, armed with a magic ring, and wrapped in a red sash, emerged from within. Shortly thereafter, the Daoist immortal Taiyi arrived on the scene, and named the newborn Nezha.
>
> When he was seven years old (and six feet tall) the child went bathing in a river. Laundering his girdle, he caused the water to boil all the way to the underwater palace of the dragon king, who dispatched his son to check the cause of the disturbance. In the ensuing fray, Nezha killed the dragon prince, making a belt from its tendons.
>
> Playing in the garden, Nezha came upon a bow that—unbeknown to him—no one but the mythic Yellow Emperor of old had been able to bend. The child effortlessly drew the bowstring, shooting an arrow that killed the acolyte of the rock spirit Shiji Niangniang. Blaming Nezha's father, the ogress attacked the boy, who was narrowly rescued by the immortal Taiyi.
>
> The enraged dragon king demanded reparations for his lost offspring

> from Nezha's father, who blamed Nezha for bringing a disaster upon the family. A murderous conflict between father and son issued, at the height of which the child committed suicide, thereby returning to his parents the body he had owed them. The child's disembodied soul sought help from his master Taiyi, who fashioned for him fresh limbs from a lotus flower. Equipped with a new body, Nezha was reborn into the world, no longer recognizing his father as such. Attempting to avenge his suicide by patricide, he was thwarted by divine intervention, which led to an uneasy compromise—but no sincere truce—between father and son.[4]

The legend is remarkable for its visceral rendering of Chinese family tensions. The narrative pivots upon the life-and-death struggle between father and son, whose mutual hatred originated at the very moment of the latter's birth, when Li Jing aimed his sword at him. The brutal family conflict lasts through the son's disavowal of his parents, his spiteful return of his body to them, and the climax of his rebirth and attempted patricide. In a society that highlighted the primacy of filial piety (*xiao*) as a supreme ethical value, it is striking that the child shows no signs of remorse for trying to kill his father. The myth should be explored, therefore, against the background of the Confucian ideology that it so brazenly violates. The applicability of a Freudian Oedipal interpretation is similarly intriguing, especially as all versions of the myth highlight Nezha's strong emotional ties with his mother, who defends him from her husband, and in whose dreams he repeatedly appears.[5]

The seventeenth-century *Investiture of the Gods* is oriented toward Daoism. The novel's principal protagonists are invariably identified as Daoist gods, immortals, or, at the very least, adepts. Nezha's master, for example, is the Daoist Perfected (*zhenren*) Taiyi, from Golden Gleam Cave on Qianyuan Mountain. Taiyi functions as Nezha's godfather: He bestows on him his name and, after the child's climactic suicide, resurrects his disembodied soul. Contrary to this Daoist bias, earlier versions of the myth are firmly rooted in Buddhism. Ming-period (1368–1644) encyclopedias of the gods, no less than the celebrated *Journey to the West* (1592), identify Nezha's savior as the Buddha, who mercifully fashions for him a new body made from the religion's principal symbol of the lotus.[6] The legend's Buddhist context is similarly attested by the appearance of the Pagoda-Bearer Heavenly King Vaiśravaṇa as Nezha's father. We will return to the Buddhist guardian deity below. Here suffice it to note that the legend provides an etiological explanation to the pagoda (*stūpa*) that he had wielded in Asian art as early as medieval times (see Figure 2): The pagoda was bestowed upon Vaiśravaṇa

Figure 2. Vaiśravaṇa, Tenth-century painting on silk from Dunhuang. © The Trustees of the British Museum, Stein painting 138.

by the Buddha—the Nezha myth has it—as a secret weapon that would enable him to control his rebellious son. When the father recites a spell, the *stūpa* entraps and burns his offspring, not unlike the metal ring with which Xuanzang disciplines his impish novice Sun Wukong.

The earliest full version of the Nezha myth survives in *The Comprehensive Collection of the Three Religions' Origins and Deities* (*Sanjiao yuanliu soushendaquan*), which although dating from the Ming period, is believed by most scholars to derive from a Yuan (1279–1368) source.[7] The hagiographic encyclopedia weaves together the myth of Nezha's Oedipal conflict with his heroic exploits as dragon-tamer. At the tender age of five days, Nezha overcomes the ocean's dragon lords, killing their king. His murder of the aquatic god implicates his father, leading to the family feud. The late Ming novels *Journey to the West* and *Investiture of the Gods* elaborate in great detail on the infant Nezha's battle with the water monster, from whose sinews he makes himself a belt. The divine apparel has contributed to the diversity of the naughty child's cult. As the producer of a magically potent belt, Nezha became the tutelary divinity of the Sash and Girdle Guilds. Eighteenth-century Beijing belt-makers dedicated a temple to Nezha near the city's Black-Dragon Pool (Heilongtan).[8]

Nezha's role of dragon-tamer was related to his significance as the tutelary deity of Yuan-period Beijing (then Dadu). According to a fourteenth-century legend, the Mongol capital had been fashioned in the image of the rebellious child, its eleven gates corresponding to his three heads, six arms, and two feet. As Hok-Lam Chan has suggested, the infant-god had been assigned the post of the capital's guardian because of his successful record as dragon-queller. Yuan-period Dadu, no less than present-day Beijing, had suffered from acute water shortages—as well as occasional flooding—that were attributed to the Dragon King. It was Nezha's ability to control the aquatic monster that had earned him the role of the capital's heavenly protector. Thus, Nezha's birthday in the second month coincided with the festivities of the Dragon Raising Its Head, when the capital's residents beseeched the water god for fine weather.[9]

Before we proceed to examine Nezha's Indian origins, we may summarize his salient traits: He is a child; he is divinely powerful; he is locked in conflict with his parents (especially his father); he draws a mighty bow that no one has been able to bend; and he is a dragon-tamer.

Nezha, Nalakūbara, and Vaiśravaṇa

In Spring 841, Ennin (793–864) visited the Tang capital Chang'an, participating in the festivities of the Buddha Śākyamuni's tooth, which had been treasured at the Chongsheng Monastery. The sacred relic, the Japanese monk reported, had been bestowed upon the Chang'an monk Daoxuan (596–667) by Prince Nazha—"Heir-apparent of the Heavenly King Vaiśravaṇa."[10]

The identification of Nezha (then Nazha) as Vaiśravaṇa's son had been shared by contemporaneous Chinese sources. With the exception of one writer who described the rebellious child as the Heavenly King's *grandson*, medieval texts invariably identified him as the Indian deity's son.[11] Indeed, the divine child's Indian identity of Vaiśravaṇa's offspring is suggested also by the etymology of his name: Nezha is not a Chinese word; it is the shortened—and slightly corrupted—transcription of the Sanskrit name born by the Heavenly king's son: Nalakūbara.

Buddhist sūtras that survive in the Sanskrit original and in Chinese translation prove the identity of Nalakūbara and Nezha, revealing the gradual process of the latter's formation.[12] The *Great Peacock-Queen Spell* (*Mahāmāyūrīvidyārājñī*) is an early Tantric text that invokes the divine child's name to fight snakebites. The sūtra enjoyed great popularity throughout Asia, surviving in several short and long Sanskrit recensions as well as in at least six successive Chinese translations. Nalakūbara figures in three of the latter, each variously rendering his name: Saṅghabhara's sixth-century version had Naluojiupoluo; Yijing's (635–713) seventh-century translation had Naluojubaluo; and several decades later Amoghavajra (705–774) chose Nazhajuwaluo.[13] In other writings of his, the great Tantric master dispensed with the ending *juwaluo*, giving Vaiśravaṇa's son the Chinese name Nazha.[14] The latter was only slightly altered—some seven centuries later—by the addition of the mouth radical, producing the modern pronunciation Nezha.

Amoghavajra's Nazhajuwaluo (followed by the shortened Nazha) might seem far removed from Nalakūbara, but it might have derived from one of the latter's original variants. Different Sanskrit, and Prakrit, texts variously give the divine child's name as Nalakūvara, Nalakūvala, Narakuvera, and Naṭakuvera (for which Nazhajuwaluo would be an accurate transcription, as the Sanskrit retroflex *ṭa* had been transliterated in medieval Chinese as *zha*).[15]Another possible variant, Nartakapara (literally: "The Best of Dancers") is suggested by the Tibetan translation of the infant's name: Gar-mkhan mchog.[16]

Thus, Nezha's Chinese fame derived from his father's Indian renown. Vaiśravaṇa (Chinese: Pishamen, or Duowen Tian), also known as Kubera, had been among the most venerable Indian deities. He had figured in Sanskrit literature from its Vedic origins, and by the time the great epics were composed—around the middle of the first millennium BCE—his position of a principal deity had been established. In the *Rāmāyaṇa*, Vaiśravaṇa is the Warden of the North, the Lord and Giver of Wealth (Dhanapati, Dhaneśvara, or Dhanada), and the king of the semi-divine semi-demonic *yakṣas*, who inhabit the waters. His northern connection was inherited by Buddhist authors, who had adopted him as a guardian deity. Vaiśravaṇa became the Heavenly King of the North, one of the four Buddhist Lokapālas (World Rulers) associated respectively with the cardinal points. The martial god presides over the northern slopes of the mythic Mount Meru, whence he leads his awesome *yakṣa* armies in defense of the Buddhist faith.[17]

Vaiśravaṇa's Chinese cult had been localized through the identification of the Indian god with a historical Chinese warrior. Li Jing (571–649) was a renowned general, who had led the Tang armies to numerous victories in China and Central Asia. Shortly after his death, the heroic warrior became the object of a religious cult, which flourished into the Song period (960–1279). The general's military exploits were celebrated in a large body of oral and written fiction, which gradually associated him with the Indian god. Storytellers and playwrights merged the Tang general with the martial Heavenly King.[18] Thus, the historical general—who might well have been a Vaiśravaṇa devotee—was identified with the object of his cult.

Nalakūbara and Tantric Buddhism

Our brief etymological analysis of the name Nezha (Nazha) has yielded references to Tantric texts and authors. We have traced the Chinese name Nezha to its Sanskrit origin Nalakūbara through the successive translations of the proto-Tantric *Great Peacock-Queen Spell* (*Mahāmāyūrī vidyārājñī*), and we have noted the key role played by the influential Tantric master Amoghavajra (705–74) in determining the god's Chinese name. The Tantric connection betrays the school's significance in the history of the rebellious child. Tantric Buddhism (or esoteric Buddhism; Chinese: Mijiao) had served as a vehicle for the transmission of the Nalakūbara cult from India to China.

The Tantric sūtras that feature Nezha are ritual texts endowing the practitioner with the supernatural strength to combat enemies from the demons of disease to military foes. They include detailed instructions for harnessing the power of the gods, thus gaining victories in warfare, politics, and love. The manuals disclose the secret formulas for summoning the gods into a ritual arena called *maṇḍala*, activating their divine might by means of hand-gestures (*mudrās*) and oral incantations. Tantric sūtras are often self-styled collections of spells (Sanskrit: *dhāraṇī*; Chinese: *tuoluoni*), in which the bulk of text is made of an oral incantation. Aiming to preserve the potency of the Sanskrit original, the translators are usually careful to transcribe the spell rather than translate it. The typical *dhāraṇī* sūtra is thus a Sanskrit incantation written down in Chinese characters.[19] For our purpose, the significance of this liturgical body lies in its reliance upon the Hindu pantheon of divinities. Tantric masters adopted each and every Indian supernatural being, from the *deva* gods to the *asura* demons, from the *nāga* dragons to the *rākṣasa* ghouls. Their esoteric literature brought to China striking creatures of the Indian mythological imagination, such as the Horse-Headed Avalokiteśvara (Guanyin) and the Oedipal pair of Śiva and his elephantine offspring Gaṇeśa. The gods of esoteric Buddhism exercised deep influence upon the Chinese imagination. A growing body of scholarship is revealing that they penetrated the popular religion, leaving their mark on fiction and drama alike.[20]

Tantric masters summoned Nalakūbara as the commander of his father's army of demonic *yakṣas*. The son of the martial *yakṣa* king Vaiśravaṇa was imagined as a heroic *yakṣa* general. Several versions of the *Great Peacock-Queen Spell*, as well as at least one edition of the esoteric *Amogha-pāśa* (which is dedicated to Avalokiteśvara's Tantric cult), give Nalakūbara the title "Great Yakṣa General" (Sanskrit: *mahā-yakṣa-senāpati*; Chinese: *Da-yaocha-jiang* or *yaocha dajiang*).[21] In these sūtras, the rebellious child shares the exalted rank with numerous other demon officers. However, there is evidence that he figured in medieval China as the object of an individual cult as well. The titles of esoteric ritual texts dedicated to Nalakūbara are preserved in the Chinese canon. Huilin's (737–820) bibliographic dictionary lists two Tantric manuals that featured him as their principal protagonist: *Prince Nalakūbara's Dhāraṇī Sūtra of Accomplishments* (*Nazha Taizi qiu chengjiu tuoluoni jing*) and *The Sūtra of Nalakūbara's Accomplishments* (*Nazhajuboluo qiu chengjiu jing*). The terms *dhāraṇī* and *siddhi* (literally: "accomplishment") indicate the Tantric orientation of the two now-lost Nalakūbara sūtras. Even though they figure elsewhere in Buddhist literature, their occurrence in titles is typical of esoteric scriptures. Similar texts dedicated to the child's esoteric cult made it also to Japan, for they are listed in the fourteenth-century Tantric encyclopedia *Byakuhō kushō* (Selections from the Oral Transmission of White Treasures).[22]

Were the now-lost Nalakūbara sūtras compiled in China, or were they translated from the Sanskrit? A likely answer is provided by corresponding Tibetan texts. The *Derge Kanjur* canon includes two esoteric manuals of the rebellious child's cult: *The Yakṣa Nartakapara's Tantra*, and *The Great Yakṣa General Nartakapara's Tantric rituals*.[23] Complete with elaborate *dhāraṇīs*, the two Tibetan Tantras had been translated from the Sanskrit, evincing that Nalakūbara's esoteric cult had been well-established in medieval India. The Chinese sūtras of the *yakṣa* prince—like the Tibetan ones—were most likely rendered from the Sanskrit. The Tantric cult of Vaiśravaṇa's son originated in medieval India, whence it spread throughout Asia.

The Nalakūbara *tantras* are preceded in the Tibetan canon by ritual texts dedicated to another *yakṣa* general, his brother Maṇibhadra (or Maṇigrīva).[24] The two siblings, Ananda Coomaraswamy suggests, had served as the commanders of their father's army as early as Vedic times.[25] The esoteric literature dedicated to the "Great *Yakṣa* Maṇibhadra" had enjoyed tremendous popularity throughout Asia. Manuscript fragments of his Sanskrit spells—dating from the first centuries CE—have been found along the Silk Road in today's Xinjiang Province. Unlike Nalakūbara's Chinese sūtras (now lost), a Maṇibhadra ritual manual is extant in the Chinese canon. The numerous Maṇibhadra texts sometimes identify the "Great Yakṣa" as Vaiśravaṇa's son (and Nalakūbara's brother) and sometimes celebrate him independently of them.[26]

The prodigious Amoghavajra (705–774) contributed to the Chinese cult of the *yakṣa* brothers. Enjoying the successive patronage of three Chinese emperors, the Indian (or possibly Sogdian) Tantric master had produced over a hundred and sixty esoteric scriptures, many of which are not translations strictly speaking. As Michel Strickmann has suggested, they are rather adaptations of Indian materials that were likely composed by the influential Tantric master himself.[27] Within his voluminous writings, Amoghavajra provides the earliest extant ritual prescriptions for the drawing of Nalakūbara's image, as well as a clear definition of his role as guardian of the state. Appearing in one of the scriptures dedicated to his father (or, as Amoghavajra has it, grandfather) Vaiśravaṇa, Nazha declares: "I enforce the Buddha's dharma, wishing to subdue the hateful people and snuff out the evil mind. Day and night I would stand guard, protecting the king, the grand ministers, and the hundred officials. I would kill the devils and the like. I, Nazha, would use the *vajra* club to stab their eyes and heart . . . I would in the future subdue and destroy to ashes all the evil humans, protecting the kingdom's borders."[28]

The semi-demonic semi-divine *yakṣas* fascinated Chinese audiences. Nalakūbara and his brother Maṇibhadra were not the only specimens to penetrate Chinese lore. Rather, the entire class of aquatic warriors was to figure prominently in Chinese popular fiction. Originally transcribed as *yaocha* and later as *yecha*, the *yakṣas* had been celebrated in Chinese literature all through the late imperial period. In seventeenth- and eighteenth-century fiction they are usually described as minions in the underwater administration of the dragon kings. In the *Investiture of the Gods*, Nezha—whose own origins were forgotten—kills a *yakṣa* (before proceeding to murder the dragon king's son).[29] The Indian warriors also inspired Chinese martial artists. The renowned Shaolin Temple warriors named two of their Ming-period fighting techniques Big Yakṣa and Small Yakṣa.[30]

The identity of the Indian gods was defined by their myths (oral or written) no less than by their visual images. Tantric Buddhism played a major role in bringing to China the characteristic iconography of the multi-headed and multi-armed Hindu divinities. The voluptuous imagining of the gods was especially apparent in their wrathful manifestations (Chinese *fennu*, or *weinu*; Sanskrit: *krodha*). Each Tantric deity has a cultivated and dignified mien side by side with an awful apparition that he assumes—out of compassion to those who obstruct him—terrorizing them into the correct path.[31] The latter revealed to Chinese artists the scope of Indian fantasies of the supernatural. Wielding assorted weaponry, the wrathful Tantric deities came to China equipped with a multiplicity of bodily organs and bedecked by abundant divine ornaments.

As a proper Tantric divinity, the *yakṣa*-infant Nalakūbara featured a wrathful manifestation, which must have been terrifying indeed, for it is frequently mentioned in Song-period literature. The recorded sayings of Chan masters—who employed the child's suicide as the topic of *gong'an* dialogues—describe him as the "Wrathful Nazha" (Fen'nu Nazha). Like the *asura* devils, the terrifying Nazha sported three heads and six arms (or, according to some sources, eight arms).[32] Shanzhao's (947–1024) recorded sayings allude, for example, to the "Wrathful Nazha striking the emperor's bell; three-headed and six-armed he shakes heaven and earth."[33] The twelfth-century *Blue-Cliff Records* (*Biyan lu*), uses the well-known image of the monstrous Nazha to describe a prototypical eccentric saint:

> At times idly sitting in a grass-strewn hut atop a lonely peak,
> At others barefoot roaming the bustling city centers.
> One minute, like a Wrathful Nazha, displaying three heads and six arms,
> Another, like the moon's or the sun's face, beaming rays of universal
> compassion.[34]

Song-period art might have left us visual evidence of the "Wrathful Nazha." The renowned thirteenth-century Quanzhou Pagodas (constructed between 1228 and 1250) feature two adjacent engravings that—I suggest—might represent the

benevolent and malevolent aspects of the child-god respectively (see Figures 3 and 4). The former shows Nazha riding the subdued dragonking, holding in his left hand the belt he had made from its son's sinews. In his right hand, the child-warrior is wielding the bow that no one but he and the Yellow Emperor have been able to draw. Even though he is clad in armor, the god's facial expression is appropriately childish. The awesome three-headed and six-armed apparition in the opposite sculpture belongs most likely to the Wrathful Nazha. Interestingly, it is grasping the sun and the moon, as described in at least one text to be discussed below. Previous scholarship has suggested that the three-headed six-armed monster is an *asura* devil. However, I believe his appearance side by side with the (likely) Nazha indicates that he is none other than his wrathful manifestation.[35]

The Wrathful Nazha has held such a grip on the imagination of the Chinese that they envisioned their capital in his image. According to a fourteenth-century legend, Beijing (then Dadu) had been fashioned in the Tantric warrior's shape. The city's designers, graced by the divine epiphany of the child warrior, drew its walls in his likeness. Beijing's eleven gates corresponded to the wrathful god's three heads, six arms, and two feet. Hence, the capital of the Yuan empire was referred to in popular lore as Nalakūbara City (Nazha Cheng). That the Chinese named their sacred metropolis after an Indian deity is as succinct an indication as any of the two civilizations' interpenetration.[36]

Nalakūbara in Indian Lore

Those who enforce the law and those who violate it sometimes come from the same background. We are told that in certain families one brother may become a police officer and another a criminal. Whether this folklore reflects social reality or not, it does describe the Indian gods, who often transcend legal boundaries.[37] Take the *yakṣas* for example: In the *Rāmāyaṇa* the water spirits fight along with the gods against the cannibalistic *rākṣasa*s, who are none other than their cousins, for the *yakṣa* king and the protector of the gods' wealth Vaiśravaṇa is the half-brother of the arch-evil Rāvaṇa, leader of the *rākṣasa* hordes.

The description of Nalakūbara in Sanskrit literature should begin therefore with his troubled family background. The *yakṣa* was incorporated as a guardian deity into the Buddhist pantheon precisely because of his personal familiarity with the powers of evil. His very uncle was the vicious Rāvaṇa who had kidnapped the most beloved Indian heroine Sītā. Indeed, the earliest extant Nalakūbara episode concerns his sexual, and generational, competition with his uncle. In Vālmīki's *Rāmāyaṇa*, the evil *rākṣasa* rapes his nephew's lover, the attractive courtesan Rambhā. In consequence of his sexual crime, Rāvaṇa is unable to force himself upon Sītā, for he had been cursed by Nalakūbara never to lie with a woman against her will. The story might have been added to the epic as an afterthought, explaining Sītā's emergence unblemished from her captivity in Rāvaṇa's hands.[38]

In the *Rāmāyaṇa*, Nalakūbara is defeated by his evil uncle, who rapes his lover. In a Buddhist Jātaka tale, he emerges victorious in sexual competition with a Garuḍa Bird. The beautiful Queen Kākātī—wife of the king of Benares—had been kidnapped by the divine bird. The king informs his court musician Naṭakuvera (Nalakūbara) of her disappearance. Naṭakuvera hides within the rich plumage of the Garuḍa King, who carries him to his love nest. There, Naṭakuvera himself copulates with the kidnapped woman. When the Garuḍa King realizes he has been duped, he sends Kākātī in disgust to her lawful husband. The bird is left to lament his own role in bringing Naṭakuvera to its sweetheart:

Out upon the foolish blunder,
What a booby I have been!
Lovers best were kept asunder,
Lo! I've served as go-between.[39]

The best-known Nalakūbara tale similarly portrays him as a sexual trickster. Belonging to the celebrated Kṛṣṇa story-cycle, the episode has enjoyed tremendous popularity in oral, and written, fiction no less than in visual art. Nalakūbara and his brother Maṇigrīva, it goes, were frolicking with naked women in the waters of the Ganges, unmindful of the approaching sage Nārada. Enraged by their impropriety, the sage cursed the *yakṣa* brothers, transforming them into twin Arjuna-trees. After a hundred celestial years, the baby Kṛṣṇa who had been tied by his mother to a mortar (as a punishment for childish mischief) crawled between the two trees. Easily uprooting them, he brought the two brothers back to life. The story concludes with the twin *yakṣas'* hymns of praise to the baby-god.[40]

The three episodes alike portray Nalakūbara as a lover, which role he has continued to play in Indian regional literatures. In Piṅgaḷi Sūranna's Telugu novel *The Sound of the Kiss* (*Kaḷāpūrṇodayamu*) (ca. 1600), for instance, Nalakūbara is not only the most handsome man in the world, but also the richest (being the son of the god of wealth Vaiśravaṇa).[41] Does this image accord with his depiction in Chinese fiction? Is the image of the Indian Nalakūbara related to the character of the Chinese Nezha?

On the most general level, the demonic aspects of the Chinese enfant terrible derive from his *yakṣa* origins. Nezha's violence is rooted in his dubious identity of god *and* demon. His outrageous behavior echoes his familial ties with the arch-evil *rākṣasa* ghouls. Furthermore, the child's conflict with his father might have been prefigured in Nalakūbara's generational conflicts with his uncle Rāvaṇa and the sage Nārada respectively. Nevertheless, key elements of the Chinese myth are missing from the Indian legend. Nalakūbara neither kills a dragon nor lifts a magic bow. His family discords notwithstanding, he does not attempt to murder his father as his Chinese incarnation does. Even if Nezha's personality is indebted to Nalakūbara's, it is impossible to trace the plot of his Chinese story to the latter's. Nezha's Chinese adventures seem to have been fashioned after a different model.

There is also a certain age difference. Whereas Nalakūbara is invariably portrayed as a young man, his Chinese manifestation is a child, even a baby. Indeed, childishness is such a defining trait of Nezha that, to this day, toys are the most common sacrifice offered him. His devotees consider Nezha an infant, for which reason they present him with balls, marbles, dolls, and various games.[42]

Kṛṣṇa

The story of Nalakūbara's punishment by the sage Nārada does feature an infant. This is of course the great god Viṣṇu, incarnated as the baby Kṛṣṇa. Turning our attention from the tale's secondary protagonist (the *yakṣa* Nalakūbara) to its principal one (the divine savior Kṛṣṇa), we are struck by the similarities to the Chinese Nezha myth. Kṛṣṇa, like Nezha, is first and foremost a baby. His story pivots upon the concealment of a great god under a child's fragile appearance. The infant Kṛṣṇa, like the baby Nezha, kills a dragon (Sanskrit: *nāga*). Kṛṣṇa's childhood, like Nezha's, is marked by Oedipal tensions, culminating in the murder of a surrogate father-figure (King Kaṃsa). Furthermore, Kṛṣṇa foreshadows Nezha's martial feat, drawing a divine bow that no one has been able to bend. In the following paragraphs I will not attempt to cover the literature or history of the great god Kṛṣṇa (Viṣṇu). I will merely sketch a few aspects of his myth that might be relevant to the emergence of the Nezha cycle.

The child Kṛṣṇa (Bāla-Kṛṣṇa) is among the most important Indian gods. Viṣṇu's babyish incarnation has been the subject of countless literary and visual works of art, being a central figure of the *bhakti* devotional movement. The baby Kṛṣṇa cycle had originated—likely independently of the Viṣṇu figure—during the first millennium BCE. However, by the first centuries CE their legends were firmly intertwined. The *Harivaṃśa* supplement to the *Mahābhārata* contains the principal feats of the divine infant, including the subjugation of the dragon Kāliya and the defeat of the ogress Pūtanā. His story-cycle was subsequently enlarged in the *Viṣṇu Purāṇa* (ca. fifth century) and the *Brahma Purāṇa*, receiving its canonical Sanskrit form in the ninth, or early tenth, century *Bhāgavata Purāṇa* (which reflected the influence of the South-Indian *bhakti* movement). The latter had served as a source for an enormous body of drama and song in regional languages. To this day, the pranks of the playful Kṛṣṇa are lovingly sung throughout the subcontinent. His divine exploits have been similarly celebrated in visual art: from Gupta-period sculpture, through early modern court painting, down to contemporary gaudy posters, the baby god has been among the most widely portrayed in Indian art.[43]

Kṛṣṇa, like Nezha, is first and foremost a baby. The delight of his literature derives from the suspense of concealment, the might of the great god being hidden in a baby's fragrant body. Mother Yaśodā's futile attempts to discipline her mischievous Kṛṣṇa result in displays of his supernatural strength. Indeed, it is as an illustration of the divine child's might that the protagonist of this chapter—Nalakūbara (Nezha)—makes his appearance in the Kṛṣṇa cycle: Unable to control her playful son, Yaśodā ties him to a heavy mortar. The infant effortlessly carries it around and, rubbing it against the twin Arjuna trees, releases the *yakṣa* brothers Nalakūbara and Maṇigrīva, who become his devotees.

The child Kṛṣṇa is a butter thief. His innovative pilfering methods are the subject of numerous stories, in which he breaks into his mother's (and her neighbors') pantries. His butter-theft exploits have made the child-god a favorite figure of contemporary dairy advertisements. They also occasion an enchanting episode in which the god as the totality of the universe is revealed to his mother. Suspecting her son of stealing butter yet again, Yaśodā orders him to open his mouth, only to behold within it the entire cosmos, including her native Braj County, and within it her own village, and she herself gazing into Kṛṣṇa's mouth:

> She then saw in his mouth the whole eternal universe, and heaven, and the regions of the sky, and the orb of the earth with its mountains, islands, and oceans; she saw the wind, and lightning, and the moon and stars, and the zodiac; and water and fire and air and space itself; she saw the vacillating senses, the mind, the elements, and the three strands of matter. She saw within the body of her son, in his gaping mouth, the whole universe in all its variety, with all the forms of life and time and nature and action and hopes, and her own village, and herself.[44]

Figure 5. Kṛṣṇa atop Kāliya (Quanzhou remains of a thirteenth-century Hindu temple). Photo Meir Shahar.

Figure 6. Drawing the mortar, Kṛṣṇa releases Nalakūbara from underneath the Arjuna tree Quanzhou remains of a thirteenth-century Hindu temple. Photo Meir Shahar.

mighty god has been able to draw the awesome weapon, yet Prince Rāma easily bends it to the breaking point.[52] Thus, the three divinities that have tamed a similar water monster also wield an identical instrument. Kṛṣṇa, Viṣṇu (Rāma), and Nezha alike successfully draw a magic bow.

The Supreme Secrets of Naṇa Deva

Among the most important Indian gods, evidence of the Child-Kṛṣṇa's renown comes from as far as China. The thirteenth century witnessed the construction of one, or possibly, two Brahmanical temples in the Southern Chinese port of Quanzhou (Fujian Province). Fashioned by Tamil merchants in the South Indian Chola Style, their remains have survived to this day.[53] They include two votive pillars decorated with images from Viṣṇu's life. Two scenes are particularly relevant to our discussion. They show the child-god playing the flute atop the conquered Kāliya dragon (recognizable by his five hoods), and his uprooting of the Arjuna tree, releasing the imprisoned Nalakūbara and his brother (see Figures 5, 6).[54]

The Quanzhou images of the Indian child-god evince his Asian renown. The Kṛṣṇa legend had spread along the maritime trade routes throughout South Asia. Even though the extant images likely played no role in the emergence of the Chinese Nezha—they were carved too late for that—it is not impossible that the creators of the Chinese myth were familiar with the antics of the Indian dragon-tamer Kṛṣṇa. It is noteworthy that the southern Chinese port of Quanzhou has yielded one of the earliest surviving Nezha icons. Recall the thirteenth-century Quanzhou pagodas featuring the mighty infant atop the vanquished dragon (see above, Figures 3, 4).

We possess a textual hint—it is no more than that—of a possible connection between the two Asian child-gods. A Chinese esoteric text features a deity called Naṇa, whose name and attributes appear to be a hybrid of Nalakūbara and Kṛṣṇa. The *Scripture of the Supreme Secrets of Naṇa Deva* (*Zuishang mimi Nana tian jing*) suggests the possibility that Tantric masters have colored Nalakūbara in the hues of his divine savior Kṛṣṇa. The scripture might support the hypothesis that the Chinese Nezha was created by the merging of the Indian Nalakūbara with Kṛṣṇa.

The *Scripture of the Supreme Secrets of Naṇa Deva* belongs to what could be described as the second wave of Chinese Tantric translations. If we consider Amoghavajra and his eighth-century colleagues as representatives of the first stage, the second phase included translations that were conducted under the patronage of the Northern Song (960–1127). Some of the most important Tantric sūtras—including the Guhyasamāja and the Hevajra—were rendered into Chinese during this latter phase. The *Supreme Secrets of Naṇa Deva* was translated by the prolific Kashmiri monk Tianxizai (Devaśāntika?) (?–1000) who, after arriving in China in 980, had worked for twenty years in the imperially sponsored Institute for the Translation of the Sūtras. Devaśāntika was responsible for rendering some of the most outrageous sexual, even necrophilic, Tantric manuals. His *Rituals of the God Vināyaka Explicated by Vajrasattva* guides the practitioner in the production of zombie sexual slaves. More pertinently for our purpose, he had translated a *dhāraṇī sūtra* of Nalakūbara's brother Maṇibhadra (Maṇigrīva).[55]

Like other *dhāraṇī sūtras* of its kind, the *Supreme Secrets of Naṇa Deva* opens with a great gathering of Indian divinities headed by the Buddha. The congregation has assembled at Vaiśravaṇa's Palace, where a charming youth named *Naṇa* makes his appearance.[56] After being empowered by the Buddha, the young god reveals the Supreme Secret Spell that occupies the bulk of the text. Naṇa is described as follows:

> At that time there was a Deva called Naṇa. His appearance was exceptionally handsome, and his face beamed with a gentle smile. He was holding the sun, the moon, and various weapons. His numerous treasures and abundant jewelry shone more brightly than the sun and the moon. He made himself a *luoye* robe[57] from the dragons Nanda (Nantuo) and Upananda (Wuponantuo), and a belt from the dragon Takṣaka (Dechajia).[58] He possessed the same immense strength as Nārāyaṇa (Naluoyan) [i.e.,Viṣṇu]. He too came to the assembly and sat down facing the Buddha. . . .
>
> At that time the Buddha emanated great light from his Dharma-body of meditation. The light covered the entire Buddha Universe, reaching all the great evil *yakṣas*, the various types of *rākṣasas* (*luocha*) and *piśācas* (*pishezuo*),[59] and all the evil dragons (*nāgas*) (*long*) as far as the heavenly constellations. When the Buddha's light shone upon them they all awoke to the truth.
>
> The Buddha's light returned to him and, after encircling him three times, entered his head. It then reissued in seven colors from his brow, entering Naṇa Deva's head.
>
> When the Buddha light penetrated his head, Naṇa Deva displayed an enormous body like Mt. Sumeru. His facial expression alternated between terrifying anger and a broad smile. He had a thousand arms, and he was

> holding a skull (*kapāla* [*geboluo*])[60] and numerous weapons. He was handsomely adorned with a tiger-skin robe and skulls. He emanated blazing light, possessing immense strength.
>
> When Naṇa Deva displayed this [divine] body, the great earth shook, and all who beheld him were terrified.[61]

The mysterious Naṇa's connection to the Chinese Nazha (Nezha) is unmistakable. The two young divinities share similar names, and an identical residence (Vaiśravaṇa's Palace). They are also equally adept in the subjugation of dragons, which Naṇa, like Nezha, uses as a belt. Recall that the Chinese god has become the patron deity of the Sash and Girdle Guild because of his expert fabrication of a dragon-sinews belt. Furthermore, the *Supreme Secrets of Naṇa Deva* predates all extant Nezha sources associating the child-god with a dragon. Thus, the Tantric sūtra might have been the textual source of the legend portraying Nezha as a dragon-tamer.

At the same time Naṇa differs from Nazha. Their names are not identical and, more significantly, their titles differ. Whereas Tantric literature has invariably identified Nazha as a *yakṣa*, the *Supreme Secrets of Naṇa Deva* describes him as a god (*deva*). Naṇa's divine standing is therefore higher than Nazha's. Significantly, even as he makes his appearance in Vaiśravaṇa's palace, Naṇa is not identified as his son. Indeed, his position is much more elevated than the Heavenly King's, so much so that at least one scholar has considered the *Supreme Secrets of Naṇa Deva* irrelevant to the Nazha (Nezha) saga.[62]

From another angle the charming Naṇa is perhaps reminiscent of an Indian *deva*—the mighty Viṣṇu incarnated as the bewitching child Kṛṣṇa. Firstly, he is as powerful. We are told that Naṇa "possessed the same immense strength as Nārāyaṇa," the latter being a common appellation of Viṣṇu.[63] Second, he is equally charming. The *sūtra* highlights the allure of its divine protagonist: "His appearance was exceptionally handsome, and his face beamed with a gentle smile." Even when assuming his fearful form, Naṇa's "facial expression alternates between terrifying anger and a broad smile." Thus, it is not impossible that Devaśāntika—or his Indian sources—have had an impression of the beloved Kṛṣṇa in mind when they created the enchanting dragon-tamer Naṇa (who was to influence the Chinese Nazha). Kṛṣṇa might have played a role in the eventual emergence of the Chinese Nezha.

Conclusion

Nezha and the Kṛṣṇa incarnation of Viṣṇu share significant similarities. The two gods are toddlers, and their respective myths pivot upon the concealment of divine might under a misleadingly fragile appearance. The two child-gods are motivated by similar Oedipal urges, performing identical heroic feats. At the tender age of seven, Nezha and Kṛṣṇa alike subdue a dragon. Furthermore, the two youthful gods equally draw a divine bow no one else has been able to bend.

The Nezha legend and the Kṛṣṇa myth are related. Nezha is none other than Nalakūbara who figures as a secondary character in the lore of the Indian child-god. It is not impossible that Nalakūbara has acquired some traits of his story's principal protagonist. The Tantric masters that brought the *yakṣa* to China might have colored him in the hues of his savior, the divine-child Kṛṣṇa. Admittedly, this hypothesis cannot be proven. However, some support for it might be furnished by the *Scripture of the Supreme Secrets of Naṇa Deva*, which appears to celebrate a fusion of the two divinities. The god Naṇa might be a mixture of Nalakūbara and Kṛṣṇa.

Whether the Chinese Nezha has been fashioned after Nalakūbara *and* Kṛṣṇa or after the former only, his myth demonstrates the impact of Tantric Buddhism upon the Chinese supernatural. Nezha was brought to China by Tantric missionaries, whose rituals had harnessed the powers of each and every Indian god. His illustrious career illustrates the role of esoteric Buddhism in bringing Indian mythology to bear upon the Chinese imagination of divinity.

Chapter 3

Indic Influences on Chinese Mythology: King Yama and His Acolytes as Gods of Destiny

Bernard Faure

Indian influence on Chinese culture is usually seen through the prism of Buddhism. For all its foreignness, Buddhism was probably one of the aspects of Indian thought and culture that was easiest to adopt by and adapt to Chinese consciousness. Indeed, as a philosophical and moral teaching, it had some obvious Chinese counterparts (and potential rivals).[1] However, as Rolf Stein and Michel Strickmann have argued, an important aspect of Buddhism's appeal for the Chinese was its mythology, and in particular its demonology.[2] The latter was also its most "Indic" characteristic, although it has been largely ignored by Buddhist scholarship.

It is well known, of course, that Indian Buddhism borrowed much of its pantheon from Brahmanism and Hinduism. This is even more true in the case of Tantric Buddhism, which developed in India during the sixth and seventh centuries, and was imported to China in the eighth century, then to Japan during the ninth century. Indeed, Strickmann has argued that Tantrism had a much deeper influence on Chinese religion than earlier studies, too dependent on Japanese views, have acknowledged. He went so far as claiming that much of Daoism, as well as popular Chinese rituals such as the "Land and Water Assemblies," cannot be understood without Tantric Buddhism.[3] So, in a sense, Tantric Buddhism is probably that place where Indian influence is the most visible—it is, as it were, the most "Indianized" (in the sense of "Hinduized") form of Buddhism—inasmuch as Buddhism was also a reaction against Vedic-Brahmanic religious culture.

We have become more aware of the danger of a teleological approach that takes Japanese Buddhism as its goal (*telos*). This teleological approach, however, may also have some advantages: since cultural influence is essentially a selective process, the image of later developments in a different culture—inasmuch as they are no longer seen as a *telos*—also reveals what has *not been* selected, and suggests how things could have been otherwise. It also allows us to counter another type of teleological history based on the current state of Chinese Buddhism, a modernist view that tends to reject the ritualistic and "magical" aspects of Buddhism as "superstitions."

The case at hand, the cult of King Yama (Yanluo wang), provides a good illustration of this model of "roads taken and not taken." Its evolution in Japan, on the other hand, shows us the resilience, in medieval esoteric texts, of certain aspects that were all but erased from the Chinese records. In the case of Japanese esoteric Buddhism in particular, we are fortunate to have a large commentarial literature, whereas the canonical literature in the Taishō edition of the Buddhist canon practically stops with Yixing (683–727), Vajrabodhi (662–732), and Amoghavajra (705–774).

The logic of Tantric ritual is that of worldly benefits obtained by bringing deities into the ritual arena. It usually implies that the beneficiary is still alive, and differs in this respect from funerary rituals that imply a departed beneficiary and a ritual journey to the other world (for instance to "break the gates of Hell" and deliver the damned). Thus, its main tendency is quite different from that found in texts on funerary rituals, which are looking at a post-mortem situation and trying to alleviate Yama's judgment and the ensuing punishment. In this "worldly" conception, the main punishment is the shortening of a person's lifespan, and the ritual aims consequently at extending his or her life. Of course, the two approaches are not mutually exclusive, and a concern for "hungry ghosts" (Skt. *pretas*) can also be found in Chinese Tantric texts.[4] Indeed, much of the discourse on Yama is about the afterlife and the most popular texts dealt with the story of the Arhat Mulian (Skt. Maudgalyāyana) rescuing his mother or with the Ghost Festival (Yulanpen hui).[5] As Stephen Teiser has shown, the Yulanpen literature spares us no details about the horrors of the Buddhist Hells. Tantric texts, on the other hand, are more concerned with Death itself, and they insist on the judicial function of Yama and his acolytes. But the first mention of these acolytes (as "companion deities") is really about ritually rescuing the dying from Death itself, from Yama's grip, rather than alleviating death's aftermath.[6] It is this "this-worldly" version of that religious system that I want to consider here.

Figure 7. Yama-deva, rom *Bukkyō zuzō shūsei*. Courtesy of Kyoto shiritsu geijutsu daigaku.

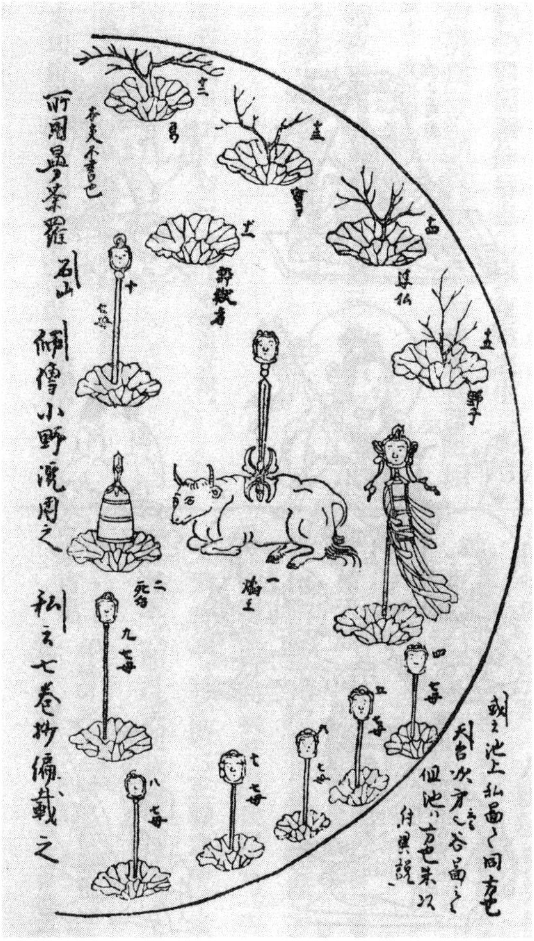

Figure 8. Yama's Wind-altar, from *Kakuzenshō*, in *Dai Nihon bukkyō zensho*, *Taishō shinshū daizōkyō zuzōbu* edition.

The Wind-Altar is in fact a *samaya* mandala, in which Yama and his retinue are represented in the form of symbols ("Seals")—such as small heads on the top of daṇḍa-staffs or swords). It includes Yama and his two consorts, his assistant Citragupta, the Seven Mothers, and four kinds of animals (vultures, crows, *basu* birds, and jackals or foxes) that form their retinue. This type of mandala is visually dominated by the Mothers and scavenger animals. Some sources, even more detailed, mention other bloodthirsty demons like the piśacas and piśacīs, demons that devour the human spirit.[27]

Another popular type of medieval Japanese mandala can probably be traced back to Chinese models. It contains eleven deities.[28] It is already a hybrid mandala, reflecting a compromise or a transition between the Indian and Chinese conceptions of Yama. The god and his immediate retinue are represented as Indian devas, whereas his assistant Citragupta is replaced by (or merges with) the Chinese god of Taishan, Taishan Fujun, and his assistants—all dressed in official Chinese garb. This type of mandala seems to have appeared in China around the sixth century, and to have been imported to Japan in the ninth century.[29] Yama is represented at the center riding a buffalo, and flanked by two consorts. On his right is a boar-headed demoness called Camuṇḍa, on his left a long-haired ḍākinī. Above (or behind) him is Taishan Fujun, holding a daṇḍa-staff and writing on a register. On either side are a divine youth called Siddha-vidyādhara (Chengjiu xian, "Perfected [Mantra-holding] Ascetic"), and the elephant-headed Vināyaka (J. Shōten). Below Yama is the Great God of the Five Paths (Wudao dashen), a.k.a. General of the Five Paths (Wudao Jiangjun), flanked by his assistants, Siming (Officer of the Lifespan) and Silu (Officer of the Registers).

Yama is actually at the center of two groups, composed respectively of Indian and Chinese deities, which represent two different conceptions of death—"magical" and karmic. The first group, demonic in nature, represent the dark powers that attack people and steal their vital essence. The second represents the judicial (and karmic) processes that can shorten (or lengthen) their lifespan. This mandala was used in life-prolonging rituals, not funerary rituals.

The Death Function

Among Yama's two consorts, Queen Death (Mṛtyu) is Death personified, and in that sense she is perceived as identical with one aspect of Yama. Kālarātrī ("Black Night") rules over the dark realm of the forests and cemeteries, a realm haunted by bloodthirsty beings like the ḍākinīs.[30] The term *ḍākinī* originally refers to a kind of ghoul that haunts charnel grounds and feeds on human flesh and blood. In the *Mahāvairocana sūtra*, they are said to be tamed by Mahākāla.[31] In the Womb Realm mandala, three of them are depicted, eating human flesh next to a corpse.

In Figure 9, however, we see a single ḍākinī, who holds a bag in one hand, and is no longer devouring corpses (while she still steals people's vital essence). The ḍākinīs are closely related to the Seven Mothers (Saptamātṛka, Ch. Qimutian). According to Yixing's *Commentary on the Mahāvairocana-sūtra*, the latter are attendants of King Yama.[32] The Mothers were originally animal-faced or bird-faced demonesses.[33] As they were progressively integrated into the official

Figure 9. Yama-deva mandala, from *Bukkyō zuzō shūsei*. Courtesy of Kyoto shiritsu geijutsu daigaku.

Although the translation "companion deities" implies that there are two of them—unless we take it to mean that the deity is the twin of the individual—this was not always the case. Sometimes there was only one protecting spirit, at other times they might be five or more, or even legions. In the Sanskrit *Bhaiṣajyaguru-sūtra*, we seem to be dealing with one single spirit who reports the good and evil deeds of humans to Yama, whereas in Chinese, the companion deities become two spirits contrasted in various ways (above all by gender).[55]

The duality motif can be traced back to the couple formed by Yama and his sister Yamī. Yama and Yamī are indeed "deities born together"—and there is only one step from them to the "companion deities." The image of the companion deities as assistants of Yama was greatly developed in China under the influence of various Chinese notions regarding individual destiny. It is also in China that the fusion (or confusion) between the companion deities on the one hand, Tongsheng and Tongming on the other, took place. Most Japanese sources combine these two sources (*Avataṃsaka-sūtra* and *Bhaiṣajyaguru-sūtra*). The companion deities were sinicized and gradually identified with the Chinese deities Siming and Silu. One further step is taken when they become the talking head(s) represented on the daṇḍa staff of King Yama—which is, as we have seen, a replication, not only of the companion deities, but also of Yama himself.

The *Avataṃsaka-sūtra*'s notion of the companion deities as protectors is still found in the *Mohezhiguan* by the Tiantai master Zhiyi: "The Devas Tongsheng and Tongming are spirits who protect the body. The body is like a citadel. When the citadel is solid, its protectors are strong. When the mind is strong, the body-spirits are strong too."[56] In this text, Tongsheng and Tongming are simply protective spirits born along with the individual, and nothing is said of their gender or of their judiciary function. These features appear in a commentary on the *Wuliangshou jing* by Jizang (549–623): "All beings each have gods called *Tongsheng* and *Tongming*. Tongsheng is a female who stands over the right shoulder [of the person] and records evil deeds, Tongming a male who stands over his left shoulder and records good deeds."[57] Here, Tongsheng is a female spirit who records *evil* acts, Tongming a male spirit who records *good* acts. Just the contrary is true, however, in the case of the apocryphal *Sūtra of the Ten Kings*, according to which all beings have two companion deities, a male one who records *evil* acts and looks like a demon (*rakṣasa*), and a female one who records good acts and looks like the goddess Lakṣmī (Śrī).[58]

In popular imageries of hell, although the paired nature of the companion deities was preserved, the gender difference was lost: all infernal functionaries are male, and they are represented as functionaries or warriors. The female figure, however, was preserved in the daṇḍa staff. The notion of companion deities seems to have fused with the traditional Chinese belief in two vital spirits (*hun* and *po*) that constitute the person. It was also influenced by the Chinese belief in stellar deities like Siming and Silu, who keep records of people's actions and adjust their date of death accordingly. Siming was already worshiped independently in early China, and in some Dunhuang manuscripts, he is feared for the calamities he can cause.[59] It is only around the fourth and fifth centuries that he came to be paired with Silu, perhaps, in turn, on the model of the companion deities.

In the administrative conception of the Other World that characterizes Chinese religion, the companion deities lost their protective function and turned into yet another pair of officials in charge of recording all good and evil deeds and of presenting their registers to King Yama at the time of judgment. While allegedly neutral in their testimony, they take on an increasingly prosecutor-like aspect. This perception has dominated Chinese (and Japanese) representations of them—in particular iconographic representations. Thus, we have gradually shifted from the register of protection to that of punishment. Although these guardians were initially morally ambivalent, and in principle neutral, they tended to polarize into malevolent and benevolent spirits.

Conclusion

The Indian Yama is a multifunctional deity. He is not just a deva or a Dharma king, but also a demon-king who is said to "cut off the root of life" of humans. In this role, he is structurally identical to Skanda and Vināyaka (two deities related to the Seven Mothers) on the one hand, to Mahākāla (himself related to the ḍākinīs) on the other. As "panoptical" judge and god of destiny, Yama was close to deities like Brahmā and Indra, but also, more important, the "companion deities."

In Chinese Buddhism, the Yama mandalas constituted an "arena of contention," in which various Indian and Chinese deities vied for recognition. The disappearance of the ḍākinīs and other "Mothers" corresponds to the sinicization of Yama and his retinue, but it may also reflect the fact that, in Japanese Tantrism at least, some of these deities (Dakiniten, Shōten, etc.) continued to develop independently, eventually ascending to the summit of the pantheon.[60] In China, however, with the development of the cult of Kṣitigharba (Dizang) and of the Ten Kings, Yama himself was essentially reduced to his juridical and inquisitorial functions, and his realm limited to the afterlife. The departure of his demonic one of the reasons I examined the *Ocean Sūtra* in detail in my dissertation and tried to clarify its background.[4]

I cannot cover all my arguments in the limited space of this chapter,[5] so here let me simply state the conclusion of my dissertation. In spite of Ono Genmyō's and Alexander Soper's arguments for the Gandhāran origin of the *Ocean Sūtra*,[6] I believe that Central Asia, especially the Turfan area, is the likely place of origin of this sūtra. There must have been significant interactions between the Chinese and non-Chinese peoples in Central Asia, and I believe the *Ocean Sūtra* could have been produced only in such a milieu.

The four very peculiar stories about the Buddha's male organ contained in the seventh chapter of the *Ocean Sūtra*, entitled "The visualization of [the Buddha's] hidden male organ,"[7] are typical examples of such cross-cultural interactions. As is well known, in the standard hagiography of Buddhism, the Buddha's male organ is said to have been concealed and invisible from the outside.[8] Sometimes this matter is touched on in the standard Buddhist canon,[9] but it is not the type of topic that receives major attention in Buddhist scriptures. The *Ocean Sūtra* is quite exceptional in that it has a chapter that is exclusively devoted to this topic, and as I said, the stories contained therein are very strange. Since these types of unusual elements are often helpful in assessing the nature of the text that contains them, I would like to examine these stories carefully in this chapter. Since I have discussed the first and the fourth of these stories elsewhere,[10] I would like to focus here on the second and the third stories. In what follows, I shall first summarize these stories and then attempt to clarify their textual background.

Stories About the Buddha's Hidden Organ in the *Ocean Sūtra*

The second story goes as follows:

> A large ring of prostitutes came to Śrāvastī from Mathurā and were doing many evils. Three sons of a rich merchant Rulüda[11] frequented their place and wasted their father's money. Worrying about this, Rulüda went to King Prasenajit and asked him to execute all the prostitutes. However, the King kept Buddhist vows and did not want to kill people. Therefore, the King went to the Buddha and asked him to admonish the prostitutes.
>
> The Buddha informed Sudatta that he would teach the prostitutes at a <u>debate hall</u> (*shichang*) in seven days. When the day came, the King beat a

golden drum and made all debaters in the country come to the debate hall. All members of the sangha and the prostitutes were also summoned.

Then each of the great disciples of the Buddha created his own vehicle, such as a cave, nāgas, and a jewel tree, and, performing miracles in concentration, flew to the debate hall. Finally, the Blessed One led Ānanda and, walking in space, came to the debate hall.

The Buddha took a seat and briefly taught about suffering, emptiness, impermanence, and the perfections (*pāramitā*) to the assembly, but the women did not accept [his teaching].

Among the group of women, a prostitute, Lovable (Keai) by name, said to the women: "The ascetic Gautama has no desire by nature, and people say that he is impotent. That is why he denounces desire in public. If his bodily parts are complete, he should clearly show us that he has this mark like the Jains did.[12] [If he does so], we will become his disciples. If he does not have this mark, he denounces impurity in vain. This person without an organ has no desire by nature; why would he not preach that desire is impure?"

[The prostitute] having thus spoken, the Tathāgata magically created an elephant. A white lotus emerged between the legs of the elephant and touched the ground. Having seen this, the women burst into laughter. They said to one another: "The ascetic is good at conjuration."

The Buddha also magically created an image of a horse king, who extended his retracted organ. It hung like a beryl cylinder and reached his knees. Having seen it, the women said even more that it was conjuration.

After that, the Buddha dismissed the entire audience and confronted the prostitutes by himself. The women laughed loudly and said: "Ascetic, do you have the bodily part or not?" The Buddha said: "I have a complete male body. I am a sound man."

At that time, the Blessed One opened his undergarment (*nihuanseng*, *nivāsana*). [The women] saw the Buddha's body, [which was] entirely flat. Then, [his organ] gradually emerged like that of a horse king. When it first appeared, it was like the bodily organ of an eight-year-old boy, and it gradually grew into the shape of that of an adolescent. Seeing this, all the women rejoiced. Then the hidden organ gradually grew [and became] like a cylindrical banner of lotus flowers. In each layer there were ten billion lotuses; each lotus had ten billion jewel colors; each color had ten billion emanation Buddhas; and each emanation Buddha was served by ten billion bodhisattvas and a boundless assembly.

Then the emanation Buddhas unanimously criticized the faults of the bad desires of the women. Upon hearing this, the prostitutes were overcome by shame and submitted to the Buddha's teaching. Listening to the Buddha's sermon, they reached spiritual attainments of various degrees.[13]

The third story is as follows:

There was a brothel in Vāranasī, in which a prostitute *Sumanās (Miaoyi) resided. Leading Nanda and Ānanda, the Buddha went there to beg. The woman had no respect for the Buddha but developed an attachment to Nanda and Ānanda.

[Knowing this,] the Blessed One one day magically created three handsome boys, all of whom were fifteen years of age. Having seen them, the woman rejoiced and prostrated to the young emanation boy. She said: "If you fulfill my wish, I will not spare any offering."

The emanation man did not object. She approached [him] according to [her] own wish. On the first day and night her mind was not tired. On the second day, her amorous mind was gradually put to rest. On the third day she said: "Great man, you can rise up to eat and drink." The emanation man rose up [but] did not stop. The woman developed aversion and regret. The emanation man said: "My way [of making love, which I have been following] from previous lives, is that, whenever I have intercourse with a woman, I take a rest [only] after twelve days."

When she heard these words, she was like a person whose throat is blocked by food and who cannot spit out or swallow it. Her body hurt as if pounded by a pestle. On the fourth day, it was as if she had been run over by a cart. On the fifth day, as if an iron ball had entered her body. On the sixth day, all her joints ached as if an arrow had entered her heart.

The woman thought: "I have heard that the Buddha saves suffering people. Today, why does he not come and save me?"

Having thought thus, she blamed herself: "From now on, I will never indulge myself in sexual desire. I would rather stay in the same cave with tigers, wolves, lions, and other beasts than indulge in sexual desire and experience such pain."

Then she stood up and ate, but whether she walked or sat, [he was] with her. The emanation man was also angry: "Damn, this bad woman impedes my business. I would rather die than be ashamed." The woman said: "If you want to die, do as you will."

At that time, the emanation man took a sword and thrust it into his neck. Blood gushed out and smeared the woman's body. On the second day after his death, blue pus [began to] stink. On the third day, [his corpse] swelled up. On the fourth day, it was rotten; feces, urine, bad worms, as well as blood, and pus were smeared on her body. She was extremely disgusted, but she could not escape. On the fifth day, the skin and flesh gradually became rotten. On the sixth day, all his flesh had fallen off. On the seventh day, only his stinking bones remained, which stuck to her body like glue or lacquer.

The woman made a vow: "If deities, sages, or the Buddha can remove my suffering, I shall donate everything I have."

When she thus thought, the Buddha [came] to her house. When she saw the Buddha, she was embarrassed, but there was nowhere to hide the bones. [So] she took a white blanket and boundless perfume to conceal the stinking bones, but the smell was as strong as before. When she saluted to the Buddha, suddenly the stinking bones appeared on her back. She was extremely embarrassed and said with tears: "If you can save me from this suffering, I will become [your] disciple."

[Then] due to the power of the Buddha, the stinking bones disappeared. Greatly rejoicing, she said: "Blessed One, I shall now donate everything I treasure to you." The Buddha prayed for her in a fluent pure voice, and she attained the stage of stream-entrant (*srota-āpanna*).[14]

Indian Myth and Chinese Imagination

The story lines of these two narratives are of course different, but both have strongly sexual content, the ambience of which is very different from that of standard Buddhist texts. We know that some Tantric texts have highly sexual elements, but now we are dealing with a text from the fifth century, which is a bit too early for it to be a full-fledged Tantric text. We should also recall that the *Ocean Sūtra* was probably an apocryphal sūtra composed by Chinese. It seems very unusual for Chinese people to discuss these sorts of topics openly in a religious text. If so, where did these stories come from?

On this matter, it is difficult for me to believe everything was the product of the Chinese imagination. At least some elements have a strongly Indian flavor, and I suspect the core elements of these stories came from India. Thus, the stories may well be good examples of "Indian myth transformed in a Chinese apocryphal text." Let us discuss these elements one by one.

Liṅga

First of all, we have to discuss the most eye-catching element, the enormous glorification of the male organ. This extraordinary glorification of the male organ seems alien to the Buddhist tradition. The motif of the Buddha's hidden organ itself is of course authentically Buddhist, but when it is discussed, it is usually treated in a very indirect and implicit way.[15] This is not something that the Buddha would triumphantly show off. Therefore, it would be reasonable to suspect that this element came from some non-Buddhist tradition, and a natural guess would be that it was influenced by Shaivite *liṅga* worship, as Soper has already suggested.[16]

I cannot locate an exactly corresponding story in Shaivite literature, but the notion of a huge organ reaching heaven[17] resonates, if not directly, in the following story in summary:

> In the beginning of the Cosmos, Viṣṇu was sleeping in the middle of the primordial ocean. Then resplendent Brahmā approached him, and they began a quarrel over which of them created the world. Thereupon, a huge *liṅga* in the shape of a pillar of fire covered with a garland of flames appeared in front of the two deities. Brahmā and Viṣṇu flew upwards and downwards respectively to find the end of this *liṅga*, but neither of them found it in a hundred years.
>
> Then the two astounded and confused deities began to praise Śiva. In response, Śiva showed himself and revealed that, in fact, both deities had been created from the limbs of Śiva.[18]

Figure 10 is a statue representing this scene (from Tamil Nadu, ca. twelfth century). Note that Brahmā, as a wild gander, is flying upward and Viṣṇu, as a wild boar (Varāha), is flying downward.[19]

It would not be too far-fetched to suspect that the imagery of the boundless *liṅga*, the ends of which not even Viṣṇu and Brahmā could find, and which was blazing in garlands of flame, was connected to the Buddhist imagery of the golden body of the Buddha and became the origin of the cosmic golden organ covered with lotus flowers.

Figure 10. Liṅgodbhavamūrti, from Mudiyanur, South Arcot, Tamilnadu, ca. twelfth century. © American Institute of Indian Studies, Accession No. 81209. By permission of the Government Museum, Chennai, which stores the original artifact.

Furthermore, one might also note that the Buddha himself is sometimes represented in India as a fiery pillar.[20] I do not, of course, mean that the fiery pillar image of the Buddha had in its origin anything to do with *liṅga*. Nevertheless, probably both the fiery pillar and the cosmic *liṅga* had the implication of *axis mundi*,[21] and thus it would not have been unnatural for these two images to be associated in somebody's mind.

Paintings of Ithyphallic Maheśvara

Even if we can observe a strong influence of Indian *liṅga* worship here, this does not solve all the problems. If the *Ocean Sūtra* were an authentic Indian text, it would be easy to explain such a Shaivite influence. However, as I said above, I find it difficult to maintain an Indian origin for this sūtra. If so, how can we explain the Shaivite influence on a Chinese apocryphal text?

Maheśvara himself is frequently mentioned in Chinese versions of Buddhist texts, but there are very few texts that specifically mention the phallic aspect of this deity.[22] We should also note that a record of Xuanzang's (602–664) travel in the *Xu gaoseng zhuan* (T. no. 2060, vol. 50, 449b3–7) describes how Indian people worship *liṅga* without feeling shame. Apparently, to the author Daoxuan (596–667) this was something novel, and he could not presuppose his readers' prior knowledge of the matter. Probably *liṅga* worship was little known in China. If so, how did the Chinese author(s)[23] of the *Ocean Sūtra* become acquainted with Shaivite phallicism?

I cannot quote any text that both was demonstrably available in the Chinese cultural area and could have been the direct source of the *Ocean Sūtra* in this regard. There are, however, some suggestive pieces of art.

In India, understandably Śiva (or Maheśvara) is often represented as an ithyphallic figure. Figure 11 is an example (from Kauśāmbī area, third–fourth century).

Figure 12 is Maheśvara with his consort Umā (fourth century). Here, he has three heads and an erect *liṅga*, and he rides a bull. Above him appear two other figures.

A similar representation of Maheśvara is found in Central Asia also. There is a painting of Maheśvara with his consort brought from Qizil. He has three heads, rides a bull, and is ithyphallic. He also seems to have more than two arms.[24]

Similar figures were also found at Dandān-Oilik (in the Khotan area).[25] Figure 13 is one example. This figure has three heads, four arms, two of which hold the

Figure 11. Ithyphalic Śiva, said to come from Kauśāmbī area, third-fourth century. After J. C. Harle, *Gupta Sculpture: Indian Sculpture of the Fourth to the Sixth Centuries A.D.* (New Delhi: Munshiram Manoharlal, 1996), plate 54. Los Angeles County Museum of Art. © Mumshiram Manoharlal.

Figure 12. Umā-Maheśvara, from Rang Mahal, fourth century. © American Institute of Indian Studies, by permission of the Gaṅgā Government Museum, Bikaner, which stores the original artifact.

Figure 13. Ithiphalic Maheśvara, from Dandān-Uiliq (in the Khotan area), sixth century? © Trustees of the British Museum, museum number 1907, 1111.71/ See also Roderick Whitfield, *The Art of Central Asia* (Tokyo: Kōdansha, 1984), plate 70-1 [D. VII. 6].

sun and the moon, rides bulls, and is ithyphallic (sixth century?).[26] Thus the image of the ithyphallic Maheśvara was definitely well known in Chinese Central Asia.

Let us now turn to Dunhuang. Figure 14 shows a painting of Maheśvara in Mogao Cave 285. This black figure has three faces and six arms, two of which hold the sun and the moon. He rides a bull.[27] Thus the painting clearly inherits the styles of Maheśvara in Khotan and Qizil. However, we should note one difference. Something triangular is jutting out from the upper hem of the waistcloth, but its meaning is not immediately clear. The painter was influenced by the iconography of Maheśvara from farther west, but apparently he could not understand, or perhaps did not even expect, that a deity should have an erect organ.[28] This suggests that the painter had a strongly Chinese mindset. The cave containing this painting has dated inscriptions from the early sixth century,[29] so the paintings can also be fairly safely dated to the same period.

Furthermore, the relief of Maheśvara in Yungang Cave 8 (Figure 15) is dated to the fifth century (ca. 471–96),[30] so it is even earlier than the Dunhuang painting. Accordingly, it is certain that the basic iconographic features of Maheśvara were already known in China in the fifth century. If so, it would be a safe assumption that the iconography of this deity was well known in Central Asia before that period. Thus, when the *Ocean Sūtra* was composed in the fifth century, the necessary information about Maheśvara must have been available in Central Asia, if not in a textual form.

On the other hand, we should note that, although this Yungang relief inherits other traits of Maheśvara,[31] there is nothing that suggests an upright *liṅga*. This probably indicates that a phallic image was too alien to Chinese sensibilities and that people hesitated to display it openly in a religious site, or perhaps the relevant information was not even available in this area. This is one of the reasons I consider the composition of the *Ocean Sūtra* in China proper unlikely.

On the other hand, if we assume that this sūtra was composed in Chinese Central Asia, the matter becomes much easier to understand. As we have seen, the standard iconography of Maheśvara (Śiva), including the erect *liṅga*, was probably well known in Central Asia around the time the *Ocean Sūtra* was composed. In addition, cultural restrictions that would hinder the expression of this motif must have been much weaker in Central Asia than in China proper.

All things taken together, I think the most likely scenario is that the Chinese authors of the *Ocean Sūtra* in Central Asia obtained information about Shaivite phallicism through oral communication with people from further western areas and transformed it in their own imagination.

Figure 14. Maheśvara in Mogao Cave 285, sixth century. Detail of Tonkō Bunbutsu Kenkyūjo, ed., *Chūgoku sekkutsu Tonkō Bakkōkutsu* (Chinese Caves, Dunhuang Mogao Caves), Vol. 1 (Tokyo: Heibonsha, 1980), plate 119. © Cultural Relics Press.

Figure 15. Maheśvara in Yungang Cave 8, ca. 471–96 or slightly later. Detail of Tonkō Bunbutsu Kenkyūjo, ed., *Chūgoku sekkutsu Tonkō Bakkōkutsu*, plate 183. © Cultural Relics Press.

The Elephant and the Horse

Now, let us look at other elements of these stories. In the second story, when the Buddha confronted the prostitutes, he first created an elephant and a horse and made them extend their symbolic organs. But the significance of these small episodes is not very clear in the context of the *Ocean Sūtra*.

The significance of this passage becomes much more understandable if we refer to the following passages from the *Da zhidu lun* (Treatise on the Great Perfection of Wisdom, hereafter *Treatise*):

> The tenth is the mark of the hidden male organ, which is like [those of] a well-tamed elephant-treasure and a horse-treasure.
>
> Question: When the bodhisattva attains the supreme awakening (*anuttarasamyaksaṃbodhi*), in what situation do the disciples see the mark of the hidden male organ?
>
> Answer: He shows the mark of the hidden male organ in order to resolve people's doubt.
>
> Other people say: The Buddha magically creates an elephant-treasure and a horse-treasure and, showing them to his disciples, he says: "The mark of my hidden male organ is like those."[32]

Many expressions in the descriptions of the Buddha's bodily marks in the *Ocean Sūtra* are apparently based on the *Treatise*.[33] Here also, the *Treatise* is a likely source of the *Ocean Sūtra*.[34] In the passage from the *Treatise* above, the meaning of the elephant and the horse is clear. In the *Ocean Sūtra*, on the other hand, the Buddha does not mention that his organ is like the organs of these magically created animals, and so he appears to be merely playing with his power.[35] Only by referring to the *Treatise*, can we understand the significance of these animals. Considering the generally close affinity between the *Treatise* and the *Ocean Sūtra*, I believe it likely that the authors of the *Ocean Sūtra* referred to Kumārajīva's Chinese text of the *Treatise*.[36]

The Corpse Sticking to the Body

In the third story of the *Ocean Sūtra*, the corpse of the emanation man sticks to the prostitute's body, decays there, and drives the prostitute crazy.

This appears to be another Shaivite motif. Śiva cuts off Brahmā's fifth head, which sticks to Śiva's hand and eventually turns into a skull.[37] Perhaps even the sexual union for twelve consecutive days may have been inspired by the story of Śiva and Pārvatī's thousand-year copulation.[38]

If we look at the story of the *Ocean Sūtra* a little more carefully, we notice one peculiar point. In the story, the Buddha creates three boys, but only one boy plays a role in the subsequent portions, so the creation of the "three boys" does not make much sense in the context of the *Ocean Sūtra*.

In this regard, we should refer to a story in the *Aśokāvadāna*. There, Upagupta gives teaching to a huge audience, but on each occasion a *māra* comes and distracts the audience. As a result, not a single person can realize the truth. In order to subdue the *māra*, Upagupta creates three types of dead bodies: a snake, a dog, and a person. He magically creates a wreath from the three bodies and gives it to the *māra*. The *māra* gladly accepts it, so Upagupta ties the three dead bodies around his neck. Having realized what they are, the *māra* tries to remove them, but to no avail. Finally, the *māra* attains faith in Buddhism, and Upagupta releases him from the dead bodies.[39]

In this text, in contrast to the above story in the *Ocean Sūtra*, the "three" bodies make good sense. Thus, it would not be too far-fetched to suspect that the story of the *Ocean Sūtra* was partly inspired by Upagupta's story in the *Aśokāvadāna*. If we look at the portions of the *Aśokāvadāna* just before and after the summarized part, we find a story of a lustful prostitute at Mathurā and the motif of magical reproduction of the Buddha's physical form.[40] They further strengthen our suspicion. It would not be surprising if this portion of the *Aśokāvadāna* came to the minds of the authors of the *Ocean Sūtra* when they were composing a visualization text filled with narrative elements.

The Śrāvastī Miracle

In the second story, the Buddha goes to a "debate hall" to confront the prostitutes (*fo yi shichang hua zhu yinnü* [*Ocean Sūtra*, p. 684a22]), and all debaters assemble at the debate hall. This is a little strange. The Buddha is trying to dissuade prostitutes from doing evil; he is not having a doctrinal debate with non-Buddhist masters in this story. Why need he confront the prostitutes in a debate hall, and why should all debaters be there? After all, all the participants other than the prostitutes are dismissed before the climax. It would be natural to suspect that some elements from a story about a debate may have crept into the motif of confrontation with prostitutes.

In this regard, we should note the story of the "Śrāvastī Miracle," in which the Buddha subjugates six heterodox teachers by performing a series of miracles. This is a very famous story that appears in a large number of texts.[41] For our present purpose, we should probably note the version in the *Xianyu jing* (Sūtra on the Wise and Foolish, hereafter *Wise and Foolish*, story No. 14, T. no. 202, vol. 4, 360c14–366a10), which is a collection of Jātaka/Avadāna types of stories and is one of the texts that are closely related to the *Ocean Sūtra*. In this regard, we should also compare another distinct but similar story in the *Wise and Foolish* (story No. 48, pp. 418b12–421b17), in which Śāriputra confronts Raudrākṣa representing the six heterodox teachers. Hereafter, I refer to the former as "Miracle story" and the latter as "Raudrākṣa story."[42]

In the *Ocean Sūtra*, three sons of the rich merchant frequented the brothel and used up the gold of one storehouse (*yizang jinjin*, p. 683c27). In the Miracle story of the *Wise and Foolish*, a younger brother of King Bimbisāra supported the six heterodox teachers and used up the money of the household (*jie jiazhi huo*, p. 360c22).

In the *Ocean Sūtra*, King Prasenajit (Bosiniwang) of Śrāvastī (Sheweiguo) asks the Buddha to subdue the prostitutes, and the Buddha responds to the King, saying: "In seven days, the Buddha will know this by himself" (*que houqiri fo zizhi zhi*, p. 684a19).

In the Miracle story of the *Wise and Foolish*, first the six teachers ask King Bimbisāra of Rājagṛha to arrange a debate hall in seven days (*qi houqiri, yuan wang pingzhi jiangshi zhi chang*, p. 361b20). Then the King asks the Buddha to subdue them, but the Buddha simply says: "I know the time by myself" (*wo zizhi shi*, p. 361b24) and leaves Rājagṛha. In this way, the Buddha keeps moving from one state to another for six days. Finally, when the Buddha comes to Śrāvastī (Shewei), King Prasenajit (Bosiniwang) again asks him to subdue the six teachers, but the Buddha gives the same answer ("I know the time by myself," p. 362b6).

In the Raudrākṣa story, the six heterodox teachers declare that in seven days (*que houqiri*, p. 420a20) they will compete with Buddhist monks.

In the *Ocean Sūtra*, on the day of the contest, King Prasenajit beats a golden drum (*jin'gu*) and assembles all debaters from various states (p. 684a25). According to the Raudrākṣa story of the *Wise and Foolish*, the law of Śrāvastī stipulates that a copper drum (*tonggu*) is to summon eight hundred million people; a silver drum (*yin'gu*), one billion four hundred million people; and a golden drum (*jin'gu*), all the people. In this case, they beat a golden drum, and thus all the people are assembled (p. 420a22–25).

In the *Ocean Sūtra*, the Buddha goes to the debate hall (*shichang*[43]) of King Prasenajit to confront the prostitutes (p. 684a22). In the Miracle story of the *Wise and Foolish*, too, the Buddha goes to a debate hall (*shichang*) arranged by King Prasenajit to confront the six teachers (p. 362b8).[44]

Furthermore, it is perhaps also noteworthy that, in the Miracle story of the *Wise and Foolish*, we can find the motif of seeing an invisible bodily mark of the Buddha (in this case, the wheel on the soles of the Buddha) as follows (p. 363c2–5):

> Then King Bimbisāra knelt down and said to the Buddha: "The marvelous marks of the Blessed One are altogether thirty-two. We have already seen the marks on the body and hands, but we have not seen the mark of wheels on the soles of the Tathāgata. Please show them to the assembly. All will view them with respect." The Buddha then extended his legs and showed the mark of the wheels on his soles to the entire assembly.

On the one hand, this passage reminds us of the story of the *Brahmāyusutta* (n. 34). At the same time, perhaps it should also be compared with the following lines found just before the stories about the Buddha's organ in the *Ocean Sūtra* (p. 683a3–5):

> At that time, Ānanda revealed his right shoulder, put his palms together, knelt down, and said to the Buddha: "The Blessed One has said that there is another mark among his thirty-two marks. Why does the Tathāgata not explain it?"

I think it very likely that many elements of the "hidden organ" stories were taken from the "Śrāvastī Miracle" and other "debate" stories. As I said in the beginning of this section, the "Śrāvastī Miracle" is a common topic among Buddhist texts, so it may be difficult to specify the particular text on which the authors of the *Ocean Sūtra* relied. Nevertheless, considering the fact that the *Wise and Foolish* shares some characteristic expressions with the *Ocean Sūtra*, I think the possibility is high that the *Ocean Sūtra* was closely linked to the *Wise and Foolish*.[45]

One point to note here is the chronology. Traditionally, the date of compilation of the *Wise and Foolish* has been considered to be 445 based on its preface preserved in the *Chu sanzang jiji*.[46] If the *Ocean Sūtra* was based on the *Wise and Foolish*, the compilation date of 445 probably suggests that the *Ocean Sūtra* was composed in the latter half of the fifth century. Since the association of this sūtra with Buddhabhadra is unreliable,[47] the latter half of the fifth century might not be an entirely impossible date. Nevertheless, considering that the *Ocean Sūtra* seems to be presupposed by some other visualization sūtras, the first half of the fifth century appears to be a more plausible date for the *Ocean Sūtra*. The traditional date of 445 for the *Wise and Foolish* makes the reliance of the *Ocean Sūtra* on the *Wise and Foolish* difficult. However, Liu Yongzeng argues that the *Wise and Foolish* was actually compiled in Turfan before 435.[48] This makes my argument somewhat easier. The possible relationship between the *Ocean Sūtra* and the *Wise and Foolish*, I believe, merits further investigation.

Sumāgadhāvadana

In the second story, major disciples of the Buddha magically create their vehicles (a cave, nāgas, a jewel tree, etc.), and riding them they fly to the debate hall. A similar scene also appears in another chapter of the *Ocean Sūtra*, "The visualization of the four types of deportment [of the Buddha]" (Chapter 6, Guan siweiyi pin, p. 679c2–27). In the latter case at least, this scene was most probably inspired by the *Sumāgadhāvadāna*, as I have discussed elsewhere.[49]

In the *Sumāgadhāvadāna*, a beautiful daughter of Anāthapiṇḍada (a.k.a. Anāthapiṇḍika) married Vṛṣabhadatta, a son of a rich merchant, who lived in a distant city Puṇḍravardhana. Since the family of Vṛṣabhadatta followed Jainism, in order to show the greatness of the Buddha and his disciples, she invited them to Puṇḍravardhana. Since, however, it was very far from Śrāvastī where they were staying, they magically created various vehicles, and riding them, they flew to Puṇḍravardhana. This is a very popular story that comes down to us in many different versions.[50]

We should consider that this story was well known in Central Asia, judging from the scene of flying monks depicted in mural paintings at Qizil (Caves 178, 198, 205, 224),[51] Toyok (Cave 20),[52] and Dunhuang (Mogao Cave 257; fifth–sixth century).[53] Thus it would not be surprising if this well-known motif came to the mind(s) of the authors of the *Ocean Sūtra* when they were looking for some "spice" to make their own story more dramatic.

As is clear by now, many of the stories of the *Ocean Sūtra* are very unusual and as a whole cannot be traced back to any prior sources. Nevertheless, people usually do not create stories out of a vacuum. Even if the story told seems entirely unparalleled, there must have been something that prompted the authors to form a particular mental image. In this case, it must have been one scene in the popular story of Sumāgadhā.

Concluding Remarks

After considering these possible sources, we can see what was perhaps happening during the process of composition. Probably, the anonymous Chinese authors of this text did not rely on any single source. In the case of the stories we have discussed in this chapter, the very basic motif of the display of the Buddha's hidden organ came from traditional Buddhist sources. Also, the imagery of the magnificent cosmic organ probably came from Indian Shaivite traditions. The authors of the *Ocean Sūtra* seem to have mixed up these elements freely to compose their own version of the stories. Concerning this type of syncretism between Buddhism and other Indian religious traditions, the following observation by Chhaya Haesner is suggestive:

> At Balawaste, situated on the southern Silk Route [near Khotan], Buddhism, Śaivism and Hindu Tantrism are amalgamated in a manner, as if Buddhism and Hinduism were combined to form one religion of Central Asia. Here the Buddhists have freely adopted many of the important and popular Vaiṣṇavite and Śaivite deities.[54]

Haesner observes similar phenomena in other areas of Central Asia as well and concludes that "syncretism seems to be the keynote of all Central Asian art."[55] This syncretistic atmosphere in Central Asia, I believe, was behind the composition of such a hybrid text as the *Ocean Sūtra*.

However, we should further note that information about the Shaivite phallicism was probably not available through Chinese texts. The authors must have had direct contact with people from western regions who were followers of Shaivite traditions. At the same time, they seem to have relied heavily on Chinese Buddhist texts. In doing so, the authors let their imagination roam freely from one text to another. Thus the final outcome seems entirely different from their sources. In other words, the very basic motifs are Indian, but the authors freely put together elements taken from Chinese Buddhist texts and invent their own stories. Perhaps we might be allowed to say that the *Ocean Sūtra* is "Indian wine put in a Chinese bag."

PART II

India in Chinese Imaginings of the Past

Chapter 5

From Bodily Relic to Dharma Relic Stūpa: Chinese Materialization of the Aśoka Legend in the Wuyue Period

Shi Zhiru

> The Wuyue king Qian Chu was naturally disposed to have faith in Buddhism. Admiring Aśoka's building of the stūpas, he [commissioned craftsmen] to manufacture eighty-four thousand [miniature] stūpas using gilt copper and fine iron; inside [each] was deposited the *baoqieyin xinzhou jing* (Sūtra on the Heart Mantra of the Precious Chest Mudrā). [The stūpas] were widely disseminated throughout [the kingdom]. It all took ten years to complete.

Appearing in a thirteenth-century Buddhist anthology, *Fozu tongji* (The Complete Records of the Buddhas and Patriarchs), this passage describes the reenactment of King Aśoka's (r. ca. 273–232 BCE) legendary building of the eighty-four thousand stūpas in the tenth century by Qian (Hong)chu (928–988; r. 947–978), the last king of Wuyue Kingdom (907–978).[1] This historic event is well documented in an array of literary sources, and modern scholars now refer to the artifact as "Gilt Stūpa" (*jintu ta*), or "Stūpa of the Precious Chest Mudrā" (*baoqieyin ta*), or even "Aśoka Stūpa" (*Ayuwang ta*).[2] In the twentieth century, excavations in Southeast China, particularly in Zhejiang province, have yielded miniature stūpas across different sites, some of which bore inscriptional confirmation of belonging to Qian Chu's production.

This chapter studies Qian Chu's production of the eighty-four thousand miniature stūpas through a close analysis of both literary sources and archaeological artifacts. I analyze the paradigmatic changes in material and religious expressions, particularly highlighting the shift from bodily relic (*shensheli*) to dharma relic (*fasheli*) in stūpa veneration. I also study this Chinese re-materialization of the Aśoka myth as evidence of continuing cross-cultural exchanges in Buddhist Asia long after the first transmission of Buddhism into China around the turn of the Common Era. However, explicating the Wuyue production of reliquary stūpas solely in terms of Buddhist antecedents from India or Central Asia cannot fully render the complex array of embedded cultural, political, and religious dynamics, which critically shaped this tenth-century imagining of Indian kingship. My paper further shows that the Indian legend of Buddhist kingship was publicly reenacted using the new wealth, trade, and technology in southeast China, so as to establish a Buddhist state in this region following the relocation of political and economic powers to this part of China in the tenth century.

Before beginning the analysis, it is necessary to clarify my use of the terms "pagoda" and "stūpa." In India, stūpa was originally the funerary mound of the *cakravartin* king, which the Buddhists appropriated to house the remains of the Buddha after cremation. So successful was the appropriation that the stūpa came to be defined as a Buddhist funerary monument containing the Buddha's relics, or those of other Buddhist saints. The Chinese word *ta* is used to translate stūpa, and refers both to architectural imaginings of the Indian stūpa in China, as well as miniature stūpas for enshrining relics or other Buddhist treasures. Hence, to reflect this distinction, I use pagoda for the monument-type architecture and stūpa for the miniature artifact when discussing the Chinese developments.

The Legend of Aśoka's Eighty-Four Thousand Stūpas

The story of King Aśoka building eighty-four thousand stūpas is related in the *Aśokāvadāna*, which was translated into Chinese twice, once in the fourth century and once in the sixth.[3] The text opens with Aśoka's past life as the little boy Jaya who spontaneously presented a handful of dirt as a gift to the Buddha. Thereupon the Buddha predicted the boy, having become a universal monarch (*cakravartin*) in a future life, would one day build a spectacular number of stūpas to venerate the Buddha. This boy was born as Aśoka, one of King Bindusāra's sons, who successfully wrestled the throne from his stepbrother, the legitimate heir. He then embarked on the merciless path of a conqueror bent on unifying India under the

Mauryan empire (ca. 323–185 BCE). Chancing to meet a monk, he embraced Buddhism. To signal his conversion, Aśoka dispatched representatives to procure seven parts of the Buddha's relics, which were redistributed and re-enshrined throughout his kingdom.[4]

The *Aśokāvadāna* describes this legendary act in the following manner:

> Then Aśoka had eighty-four thousand boxes made of gold, silver, cat's eye, and crystal, and in them were placed the relics. Also, eighty-four thousand urns and eighty-four thousand inscribed plates were prepared. All of this was given to the yakṣas for distribution in the [eighty-four thousand] dharmarājikās he ordered built throughout the earth as far as the surrounding ocean, in the small, great, and middle-sized towns, wherever there was a [population of] one-thousand [persons].[5]

The description suggests that Aśoka had reliquary urns fabricated for depositing the relics and then had them installed in larger monuments called dharmarājikās or stūpas.

Stories of Aśoka's kingship were widely circulated throughout Buddhist Asia where his actions were repeatedly invoked and exalted as the paradigm of Buddhist kingship *par excellence*. Aśoka evidently deployed the Buddha's relics and stūpas as material and visual emblems that constituted common, unifying threads across the diverse territories under his rule. Aśoka is said to have redistributed the Buddha's relics into equal shares to every city of one hundred thousand people throughout his continent.[6] John Strong concludes, "We are left with an image that the relics—the body of the Buddha—must be spread evenly throughout the whole of Jambudvīpa."[7] The king thus constitutes a mediating agency who enabled his subjects to *encounter* and *experience* the Buddha's form through gathering, redistributing, and re-enshrining the Buddha's relics.

Wuyue Enactment of the Aśoka Legend: Literary Accounts and Archaeological Artifacts

Temporally and geographically moving away from third-century India to the Chinese landscape, one prominent re-enactment of the Aśoka legend took place in southeastern China during the Wuyue rule (907–978), long after Aśoka's golden era had passed in India. With its capital in Qiantang (Hangzhou), the Wuyue kingdom at its height covered present-day Zhejiang, Shanghai, southern Jiangsu, and even some part of northern Fujian following the fall of the Min kingdom in 945.[8] The Wuyue kings were generous patrons of Buddhism who unstintingly commissioned large-scale production and repair of Buddhist architecture and art, leaving behind a staggering legacy of cave-temples, libraries, monasteries, stūpas, sculptures, and other devotional objects.[9] Under state sponsorship, Buddhism flourished so greatly that Hangzhou monasteries and academies emerged as major centers of culture, learning, religion, and trade. Artists, craftsmen, literati, merchants, and monastics flocked from other regions to this new cultural and economic center. Famous monks like the syncretic thinker Yongming Yanshou (904–975) and the court administrator-historian Zanning (919–1001) served the Wuyue state. Foreigners from far away lands, notably Japan and Korea, also arrived on the shores of this coastal region, often for purposes of trading, but also in pursuit of culture, religion, learning, or merely adventure.

Like his forbears, Qian Chu provided state patronage of Buddhism. But his reenactment of Aśoka's building of stūpas distinguished him in the history of Wuyue Buddhism—an event documented in several literary works, from which one can piece together the circumstances and motivations underlying his sponsorship of miniature stūpas. One Japanese pilgrim, the monk Dōki (ca. 965), records that shortly after successfully quelling the Yellow Turban Rebellion in 954, Qian Chu suffered from a chronic fever:

> Hongchu, who had committed the crime of slaughtering the innocent quite a few times, became gravely ill for several months. He often raved madly: "Knives and swords are piercing my chest; a raging fever clings on to my body!" He tossed and turned in his sleep, and raised his hands to confess his crimes. One of his beloved monks said: "You [should] aspire to build stūpas and copy the *Sūtra on the Precious Chest Mudrā* (*Baoqieyin jing*) to deposit in [the stūpas], and to venerate with incense and flowers." Hongchu gulped out this aspiration, placing his palms together to pay homage in gratitude two or three times. He instantly attained the bodhicitta. He joyfully and poignantly said: "The strength of aspiration is boundless [so that] abruptly, some change [has taken place] in my grave ailment." At that time, thinking of King Aśoka's past deed, Hongchu had eighty four thousand stūpas engraved and [copies of] this sūtra folded and deposited into each stūpa.[10]

King Qian Chu evidently took the monk's counsel to heart and in 955 decreed a project to manufacture eighty-four thousand miniature stūpas as an act of repentance and emulation of Aśoka's celebrated act.[11] This enterprise lasted ten years, according to the *Fozu tongji*.[12]

An illustration of the Gilt Stūpa is found in the *Qianshi jiasheng* (Family History of the Qian Clan), compiled by Qian Wen (b. 1874), the thirty-second descendant in Qian Liu's family lineage.[13] In this diagram, the stūpa can be divided into the base, body, and summit. The squarish body has a hollow interior (for depositing relic, text, or other treasure), while the summit has banana-leaf ornaments (*shanhua jiaoye*) at the four corners and a pole threaded with disks in the center (see Figure 16). Qing-dynasty (1644–1911) works contained descriptions of the miniature stūpas which Qian Chu commissioned. For instance, the epigraphical gazetteer of the Two Zhe region (*Liang Zhe jinshi zhi*), in an entry on the "Gilt Stūpas" (*jintu ta*) commissioned by Qian Chu, elaborated their height (6.3 inches) and weight (36 taels), as well as their design and inscription.[14] According to this record, the stūpa's body has jātaka scenes engraved on its four sides, such as Prince Mahāsattva giving his body to the hungry tigress, and King Śibi cutting off a slab of flesh to save a dove from a raptor.[15] From archaeological artifacts, one knows that the other two sides typically portray the jātaka stories of the Quick-eyed prince (Kuaimu wang) giving away his eyes, and Prince Moonlight (Yueguang, or Candraprabha) severing his head as a gift to a brahmin.[16]

The travel records of Chinese pilgrims indicate that these four jātaka scenes represented on Wuyue miniature stūpas provided the mythology for certain sites in India (an ancient place called Suvastu, as well as Gandhāra, Takṣaśilā in present-day Northwestern Pakistan, and an unnamed site east of Takṣaśilā) which were commemorated as the sacred geography where the Buddha Śākyamuni had carried out heroic bodily sacrifices in his past lives. Since the fifth-century pilgrim monk Faxian hailed these places collectively as "Four Great Stūpas" where "kings, ministers, and the people of the four countries vied with one another in making offerings," and "the practices of scattering flowers and lighting lamps at the stūpa never ceased," scholars believe that the four great stūpas were most likely key destinations on an important pilgrimage circuit for devotees venerating relics in Northwestern India.[17] As Reiko Ohnuma explains, because Northwest India could not be clearly associated with the final life of the Buddha, it made sense to "localize and acclimatize Buddhism in this region by identifying various northwestern sites as the locales of some of his previous lives, as recorded in the Buddhist jātakas."[18] The art historian Alexander Soper suggests that placing the four scenes together as a set might perhaps be traced to devotional and artistic trends flourishing in northwest India. The pilgrimage route of the Four Great Stūpas is evidently memorialized through visual representation of scenes from the

Figure 16. Gilt Stūpa from Qianshi Jiasheng, compiled by Qian Wen (b. 1874).

four jātaka stories on the body of a single miniature stūpa.[19] Engraving the jātaka scenes on the stūpa thus transforms the artifact into a portable microcosm of Buddhist India, some kind of a pilgrimage souvenir which the pilgrim can carry home to venerate. Moreover, through the scenes of bodily sacrifices from the Buddha's past lives, the stūpa in effect becomes the Buddha's body, or more accurately bodies. This material embodiment is paradoxical since in the narrative and visual scenes, the value of the body is negated through the repeated theme of bodily renunciation.

In the 1950s, Chinese archaeologists digging in Zhejiang province, an area that once belonged to the old Wuyue territories, unearthed numerous copper or iron gilt miniature stūpas belonging to the same architectural family. They corresponded stylistically to the Qing descriptions of Qian Chu's stūpas, and a significant portion further possessed collaborating inscriptions. The biggest corpus of miniature stūpas was excavated at the Wanfo ta (Pagoda of Ten Thousand Buddhas) at Jinhua city. This pagoda's crypt yielded eleven bronze gilt stūpas and four iron ones[20] (see Figure 17). Each bronze stūpa typically has nineteen characters inscribed on it: "Recorded in the *yimao* year (955) when the Wuyue King Qian Chu reverently forged eighty-four thousand precious stūpas."[21] The iron stūpas usually have twenty-three characters inscribed: "Recorded in the *yichou* year (965) at the time when the King of Wuyue Kingdom [Qian] Chu reverently forged eighty-four thousand precious stūpas as an eternal offering."[22] The *Liang Zhe jinshi zhi* cites both inscriptions, ascribing the inscription dated to 955 to the bronze stūpas and the inscription dated to 965 to the iron stūpas.[23] Gilt stūpas were also unearthed at other sites in Zhejiang: for example, Xi ta (Western Pagoda) of Chongfu si (Monastery of Exalted Merits) in Chongde county; Tianfeng ta (Pagoda of Tianfeng) in Ningbo city; Nansi ta (Pagoda of Southern Monastery) in Dongyang county; and also in the city of Shaoxing.[24]

Archaeological evidence indicates that these gilt stūpas were disseminated as far north as Hebei, as far south as Fujian, and also in Zhejiang, Jiangsu, Shanghai, Anhui, and Henan.[25] The artifacts, mostly made of copper or iron, clearly belong to the same architectural family in terms of their structural design, but may not always closely resemble one another in choice of images, material, or size.[26] The tallest of the bronze gilt stūpas measures about 30 cm high and the small ones 22 cm, whereas the biggest of the iron gilt stūpas are 20.5 cm tall and the small ones roughly 19 cm tall.[27] The bulk of these stūpas are now kept in the Zhejiang Provincial Museum. More than twenty pieces of these artifacts from this collection were on display in a recent exhibition (January 2009–March 2010) at the Zhongtai Museum at Nantou County in Central Taiwan.[28] Judging from the various

Figure 17. Bronze gilt stūpa discovered at Wanfo ta in Jinhua city, now in the Zhejiang Provincial Museum collection. Photograph courtesy of Cao Jinyan.

archaeological reports, the number of gilt stūpas existing today is probably about twice as many, but no exact count can be located. Moreover, similar artifacts have appeared outside of China, particularly in Japan, Paris, Taipei, and United States.[29]

The "Aśoka Stūpa" Legacy in Wuyue Kingdom

The Wuyue construction of gilt stūpas should be contextualized within broader Chinese imaginings of King Aśoka's distribution of the Buddha's relics and stūpa construction—a phenomenon that particularly flourished in southeastern China, especially the region encircling present-day Zhejiang, which roughly corresponds to the Wuyue state.[30] The two renowned Tang Buddhist historians Daoxuan (596–667) and Daoshi (d. 683) enumerated lists of so-called "Aśoka stūpas" (*ayuwangta*) in their encyclopedic works and elaborated on their origins, miracles, and histories.[31] Daoxuan's *Ji shenzhou sanbao gantong lu* (Collected Records of the Miracles of the Three Jewels in Shenzhou; dated to 664) recorded twenty examples from the Aśokan legacy, while Daoshi's *Fayuan zhulin* (Forest of Gems in the Grove of Dharma) enumerated twenty-one. Other Chinese accounts speak of nineteen of the eighty-four thousand stūpas in the Aśokan legacy that made their way to China. Early Chinese Buddhists apparently understood the legend quite literally and embarked on the undertaking of what is comparable to modern archaeological travel and digging to locate the miraculous artifacts associated with Aśoka.[32]

The Aśoka stūpa most directly relevant to the Wuyue gilt stūpas is the Mao county stūpa connected to the layman Liu Sahe, who is credited with discovering the earliest known Aśoka relic stūpas and images. Since previous scholarship has explored Liu Sahe's role in the Aśoka legacy rather extensively, suffice it here to briefly summarize the story.[33] Sahe lived in the county of Lishi in Xihe during the Eastern Jin period (317–420). In a "return-from-death" experience, Sahe saw Avalokiteśvara, who explained that if Sahe wished to avert rebirth in hell, he should repent past misdeeds before the stūpas Aśoka built. Sahe was urged to search out Aśoka stūpas (Ayuwang ta) in Luoyang (Henan), Linzi (Shandong), Jianye (present-day Nanjing), Maoyin (Kuaiji), and Chengdu (Sichuan). When he revived from death, Sahe became ordained as the monk Huida. While the earliest rendition dating from fifth century concluded the tale at this point, subsequent records, especially the Tang accounts, highlighted his travels to the South in search of Aśokan artifacts at Jiankang and Maoyin county (Kuaiji province) respectively.[34] In these treatments, Huida emerged as a pivotal figure in disseminating the cult of Aśokan relics and stūpas in the South. While pre-Tang records noted that Huida found in Mao county an "overgrown stūpa" (that is, the base of a large pagoda) from Aśoka's legacy, the Tang records focused their description on a stūpa reliquary.[35] It is this stūpa reliquary which played an instrumental role in Wuyue imaginings of Aśoka's stūpas.

In the *Ji shenzhou sanbao gantong lu*, Daoxuan describes how Huida, arriving at the predicted site in Mao county, heard the tinkling of bells resounding from underground. Tracing the source of the sound, he located the precious stūpa believed to be from Aśoka's time:

> The numinous stūpa (*ling ta*) has a color resembling green stone even though it is not of stone. It is one foot and four inches in height and seven inches in width. It has five tiers of "dew-dish." It resembles [those] from Khotan in the Western Regions. The faces open into windows, and celestial bells surround the four sides. A bronze chime is suspended within; whenever there is the tinkling of the bell, one suspects it to be from the chime. All around the stūpa's body are images of various Buddhas, bodhisattvas, Vajra bearers, holy monks, and other miscellaneous figures. Their appearances are exceedingly exquisite and detailed [so that] in the twinkle of an eye, there manifest hundreds and thousands of images replete with faces, eyes, hands, and feet! It can certainly be called a miraculous product of divine traces that is impossible for human knowledge to attain. Today it is housed inside a large wooden pagoda.[36]

The measurements of this stūpa, as well as the fact that it was housed in a large wooden pagoda, all confirm that it was a stūpa reliquary. Apparently, the fame of the Mao county Aśoka stūpa was established by the seventh century, as Daoxuan placed it at the head of his enumeration. In his *Fayuan zhulin*, Daoshi echoes almost verbatim Daoxuan's description of the stūpa. Daoshi further records that in the third year of the Datong era (537), Emperor Wu (r. 502–549) of the Liang Dynasty had built a wooden pagoda at the site as well as temple quarters nearby, which he named Ayuwang si (Aśoka Monastery). The fame of the Mao county stūpa must have spread widely, judging from the eminent figures who arrived at Ayuwang si to perform veneration to it.[37]

Another noteworthy account of the Mao county stūpa appears in the *Tōdai wajō tōseiden*, a record of the travels of the missionary monk Jianzhen (688–763), or Ganjin in Japanese, which was composed in 779 by his disciple Mabito Genkai (722–785).[38] During the eighth century, Ganjin and his travel companions boarded a ship to sail to Japan. Stormy weather forced them to disembark temporarily at the southeastern port in Siming (present-day Ningbo). They were brought to the King Aśoka Monastery for temporary lodging. Since this was the site where the Mao county stūpa was kept at that time, Ganjin personally paid veneration to this Buddhist treasure. Genkai described the stūpa as follows:

> This temple [Ayuwang si] possesses a King Aśoka stūpa (Ayuwang ta). Previously, Minzhou was a county of Yuezhou. During the twenty-first year of the *kaiyuan* reign [733], Mao county of the Yue state came under the rule of King [Qian] Chu who separated one county out to specifically establish the Minzhou and further founded three counties, thereby creating one state (*zhou*) and four counties. The remaining counties are now called Yao prefecture. This Aśoka stūpa is one of the eighty-four thousand stūpas which the Iron Wheel king named Aśoka deployed spirits and deities to build about a hundred years after the Buddha's nirvāṇa. This stūpa is not of gold, nor of jade, nor of stone, nor of earth; it is neither of bronze, nor of iron; it is purplish-black in color, and its engravings are most extraordinary. On one side is the transformation story of Prince Sattva; on the second is that of giving the eyes as alms; on the third, that of the disposal of the biran; on the fourth, that of the ransom of the dove. The top does not have "dew-dishes" and inside is a suspended bell.[39]

In Genkai's description, narrative scenes were sculpted on the four sides of the stūpa body corresponding exactly with the Jātaka stories typically engraved on the tenth-century Wuyue artifacts unearthed in Zhejiang. Art historians explain the curious discrepancy between the Tang records and Genkai's account as the result of Chinese monks, who lacked familiarity with Jātaka art, failing to recognize the narrative art scenes. Instead, they presumed the engravings to be generic Mahāyāna assemblies.[40] However, this explanation is hardly satisfactory given that the engravings often depict animals or birds, at times in the act of predation—motifs that make little sense under the classification of Mahāyāna entourage. Both Daoxuan and Daoshi lived during the seventh century, whereas Ganjin's travel and Genkai's record took place in the eighth century. Had the original stūpa been replaced or redesigned over time? There is no conclusive explanation for the discrepancy in the description. From the evidence, it appears that when Tang Buddhists wrote about the Mao county Aśoka stūpa, they typically meant the stūpa reliquary, which by that time was a famous cultic locus that attracted travelers from afar like the Japanese monk Genkai who came to perform homage to it. As the next section shows, the Mao county stūpa evidently functioned as a constitutive element in the cultic imagination in Wuyue, particularly in connection with Chinese imagining of Indian Buddhist kingship in the person of Aśoka.

The Mao County Stūpa and Political Legitimation in the Wuyue Kingdom

The tenth century seems to have been a watershed in the history of the Mao county stūpa, as it emerged as a major cultus in the religio-political evironment of Wuyue rule. Several sources record that in 916, King Qian Liu dispatched court envoys to transport the Buddha Śākyamuni's relic from its long residence at Ayuwang si in Mingzhou to his immediate seat of political power, the Wuyue capital in Hangzhou.[41] On scrutiny, the transfer of the relic stūpa to the Wuyue capital is really a symbolic act intended to foreground Qian Liu's changing role from military leadership to state sovereign, which unfolded at the beginning of the tenth century.

Beginning in 887, the Qian family rose among those military clan powers based in South China who provided the Tang court with combat leadership and army resources. Qian Liu emerged as the natural leader of the Qian clan, following a chain of military successes in quelling uprisings against Tang rule. In 902, the Tang court designated him as Lord of Yue (*Yue wang*).[42] Qian Liu's mounting political ambition is evidenced in his appeal to Zhaozong (r. 888–904) in 904 to be made "Lord of Wuyue" (*Wuyue wang*), which the Tang court rejected.[43] But later in the same year, after the Tang emperor fled from Chang'an to Luoyang, the newly formed power, the Later Liang (*Hou Liang*), pronounced Qian Liu Lord of Wu.[44] In 907, the Liang court further recognized him as Lord of Wuyue (*Wuyue wang*).[45] When the Tang rule gave way to the Later Liang dynasty (907–923) in 908, Qian Liu instituted a new era called *tianbao* (heavenly treasure), thus inaugurating a new reign without formalizing the founding of his kingdom. It was only in 923, toward the close of its rule, that the Later Liang court conferred on Qian Liu the formal designation, "King of Wuyue kingdom" (*Wuyue guowang*). Coronation rites were performed, and the Wuyue kingdom was formally established, that is, long after Qian Liu's ascent to rule. As the king of Wuyue kingdom, Qian Liu held court and power of governance parallel to the emperor's, but the imperial designation ("Heavenly Son") was never explicitly adopted.[46] When the Later Tang (*Hou Tang*) dynasty ascended to power in the North, the ruler of this Shatuo Turk group, Zhuangzong (r. 923–926), accepted Qian Liu's status as King of Wuyue kingdom.[47] In 924 (the second year of the *tongguang* era), Qian Liu presented an array of lavish gifts to the Later Tang emperor, and solicited the court to grant him the gold seal (*jin yin*) and jade tablet (*yuce*), which were the tokens of kingship in Chinese politics. The Later Tang did authorize his sovereignty the next year (925), conferring on him the prized jade tablet and golden seal, in addition to other gifts.[48] Qian Liu also received several honors including the appellation First Commander of the Metropolitan Army and Horses of Under Heaven (*tianxia bingma tu yuanshuai*).[49] However, the neighboring Wu kingdom refused to accept Qian Liu's title of kingship, suspecting that his use of their state's ancient name for the first character of his kingdom's name revealed his political design on their land. Moreover, Qian Liu's ranks and authority were briefly revoked and then reinstated by the second Later Tang ruler, Mingzong (926–933).

The tribulations Qian Liu encountered in securing the formalization of his rule and newly founded kingdom basically indexed the political tensions typical of that age. In the first half of the tenth century, North China was ruled by consecutive powers referred to as the Five Dynasties (Wudai), whereas the South was increasingly split into the Ten Kingdoms (Shiguo), often led by military governors (*jiedushi*), among which was Wuyue. The sociopolitical environment was fraught with instability, rivalry, and tension brought on by the incessant warfare and rapidly shifting fortunes. Smaller states were particularly vulnerable to the designs of larger kingdoms, which often looked to expand themselves by absorbing weaker neighbors. A military chieftain-turned-ruler of a new small kingdom in Southeastern China, Qian Liu looked toward powerful patrons, especially in the North, to authorize his newly founded kingdom and reign. Competition among larger powers to patronize smaller states was always part of the broader political negotiations. Even after Qian Liu received the yearned for insignias of political authority, he cautiously never declared himself "emperor," exemplifying the political constraints and strategizing small kingdoms must exercise in dealings with regional powers.

Against this political background, Qian Liu's transfer of the Mao county stūpa to his immediate domain, the Wuyue capital, was a particularly symbolic act, all the more so since this religious object had been enshrined for several centuries in Mingzhou at a place bearing its namesake, the Ayuwang si. Associated with King Aśoka, the Mao county stūpa not only partook of the Buddha's power but also hearkened to Aśoka's religio-political authority as *the* Buddhist *cakravartin*, whose legends and reign were famous in China by the tenth century. In the face of thwarted efforts to receive political legitimation from the imperial court in the

North, Qian Liu might have deliberately opted for a political vision centered on Buddhism, which would be ideologically distanced from the concept of "Heavenly Son" and its symbols of religio-political authority. In other words, the Mao county stūpa offered an alternate source of religio-political authority for Qian Liu's reign and his newly founded kingdom.

An extended description of the transfer of the relic stūpa from Ayuwang shan to Qiantang at the Wuyue capital appears in an essay composed in 1355.[50] Authored by the Puji Chan monk Wuguang (1292–1357), the essay is titled "Shijia rulai zhenshen sheli baota zhuan" (The Biography of the Precious Stūpa of the Tathāgata Śākyamuni's True Body Relic).

> Qian Wusu [the posthumous name of Qian Liu] commanded his brother Hua, the monk Qingwai, and others to welcome the stūpa by ship with incense and flowers. The ship returned to dock at the bank of Xiling [Western Mound] on the night of the following year. An auspicious light lit up the Jiang river as if it was day. King Wusu personally supported and raised it [from the ship] amidst cheers, and in rows of procession proceeded to the Luohan si [Arhats Monastery], where vast arrays of offerings were presented. One monk carried [the stūpa] on his head and, grasping one corner with one hand, lowered it to the ground. He used his hand to set it down, and it was naturally still like the mountain peak. He prayed devotedly into the night; when fire sparks scattered at its corners, he knew it was cast by divine power. In the year 917, a wooden nine-story relic pagoda was founded by state decree, and [the miniature stūpa] was placed inside a seven-jeweled niche [in the larger nine-story pagoda]. For numberless years there were large gatherings, and many came to view its resplendence.[51]

Since this vivid description of the procession to welcome the stūpa is an elaborated reconstruction from the fourteenth century, it therefore does not necessarily represent the historical circumstances. However, the event is briefly mentioned in the thirteenth-century *Fozu tongji*, which in turn was based on an earlier record by the Wuyue official monk Zanning (919–1001). Some kind of official reception of the Mao county stūpa to its new abode in Hangzhou evidently took place, and it was recorded that the stūpa emitted radiance at night that illuminated Zhejiang like it was daylight.[52] Moreover, public display and veneration of relics were already practiced in earlier periods, notably the court-sponsored parade of the Buddha's finger relic in Chang'an which caused the Confucian literatus Han Yu

(768–824) to protest against the Tang court.[53] So it is quite feasible that Qian Liu would have modeled his reception of the relic stūpa after Tang court practices. Although Wuguang's description may contain retrospective exaggeration, it is quite likely that the state did host some ceremonial reception to mark the auspicious event. As Wuguang's record reveals, the Buddha's relic stūpa was accorded the highest respect by the king himself. It seems likely the relic procession was a public spectacle.[54]

The political symbolism of relics and stūpa must also be understood against indigenous Chinese myths and symbols of kingship. An enduring Chinese symbol of political authority is the nine oversized bronze cauldrons (*jiuding*), believed to be cast by the mythical king, the Sage Yu, an eminent exemplar of Chinese paradigmatic kingship. Possession of the cauldrons would automatically imbue the owner with the right and power to rule all "under heaven" (*tianxia*). In short, the nine cauldrons became the material token for the mandate of heaven, a concept central to Chinese articulation of political authority and legitimacy.[55] Relics and stūpa were introduced to China with the coming of Buddhism; these practices had origins in Indian funerary rites associated with the notion of *cakravartin* king (*zhuanlun shengwang*), which Buddhists had appropriated as death observances for their saints. This implicit royal connection rendered relic worship and stūpa building particularly appealing to Chinese rulers eager to sponsor any machinery or tool of political legitimation to their own advantage. Buddhist leaders probably worked cooperatively with rulers in their quest for religious sanction of political authority and legitimacy, especially since the clerics would have desired to divert attention from the controversial practice of cremating the dead which violated Confucian ethical norms. Tracing relic worship and stūpa building to King Aśoka would only have enhanced the attraction of these practices to a ruler. Confirmation for the success in Buddhist solicitation of state patronage occurs in the Sui Dynasty (589–618) when Emperor Wen (r. 581–604) decreed redistribution of Buddhist relics all over the country in imitation of King Aśoka's famous act on the heels of the success of the "Renshou" relic campaigns led by the court monk Tanqian (542–607).[56] Record has it that one hundred and one stūpas were built in this fashion. Access to the Buddha's relics was deemed to empower the ruler with the Buddha's authority, so that possession of relics was as important for court legitimation as for devotional functions. In this way, stūpas and relics came to be accepted as tokens of sacred investment in the power to rule, that is, endowed with the same authority as the nine cauldrons.

By acquiring the Buddha relic stūpa of Aśoka, Qian Liu had found another source of legitimation for his rule as King of Wuyue to replace the jade tablet and gold seal which eluded his possession in his early reign.[57] The Aśoka stūpa, a Buddhist devotional object, permitted Qian Liu to circumvent the political control of larger states and their power to determine the right to state formation and governance. Qian Liu's use of the Mao county stūpa as an iconic symbol for his new state is probably as much a conscious religio-political choice as a statement of religious preference. It is perhaps telling that Qian Liu's search for relics was continued in 929, when he dispatched official envoys on a relic hunt to Shangyu county also in Mingzhou. They obtained a golden vase with two kinds of relics, said to belong to the past Buddha(s) (*gu fo*). Again, a procession welcomed the relics into Hangzhou and another stūpa was built to house the newly recovered relics. A large stūpa was built to the north of the city to pair with the Nansi ta (Southern Monastery Pagoda) housing the Mao county stūpa on the south.[58] In other words, Qian Liu styled himself in the manner of the Indian *cakravartin* Aśoka and the Chinese emperor Wen of the Sui Dynasty, who sent out envoys to track down relics and stūpas. This relic hunt has discernible parallels with the quest for the nine cauldrons which the mythology traces to the sage king Yu the Great (Da Yu). Like Yu who was known best for inventing flood control techniques of channeling excessive water flows, Qian Liu also made major hydraulic contributions that significantly enhanced agricultural production and the economy of the region, so much so that he and other Wuyue rulers were popularly mythologized and venerated as dragon kings. Given the political pressures of his time, it was impossible for Qian Liu to style himself publicly after Yu the Great. So, in lieu of Yu's cauldrons, he sent his envoys to seek out the Buddha's relics and stūpas.

This early religio-political background sheds important light for understanding a bronze gilt stūpa in the Taipei National Museum collection which is epigraphically dated to 905, that is, during Qian Liu's rule. The inscription reads: "On the fifth day of the third month in the second year of the *tianyou* reign [i.e., 905], one relic stūpa was reverently constructed for the happiness of our parents and all living beings alike."[59] The stūpa has the threefold division and design typical of Wuyue gilt stūpas (see Figure 18).[60] Its basic design thus associates it with the gilt stūpas from Qian Chu's production. But since the earliest of the Qian Chu stūpas date to 955, how does one account for the fifty-year gap? While this inscriptional dating might be a false retrospective attribution, the salient disparities in the make and design with other pieces from Qian Chu's collection requires one to rethink the implications of the dating. For example, the metal is considerably thicker, not the thinly spread layer deployed in Qian Chu's time. Moreover, the Jātaka engravings in the niches around the stūpa's body are all open artwork, with openings interlacing the metal layers and looking into an enclosed hollow space for storing a relic or other treasure, which really makes it more comparable to the silver stūpa reliquaries from the Leifeng Pagoda which are used to store Buddha relics, not the *Baoqieyin Sūtra*, as we will see later. The spire and body of the Taipei artifact are conjoined into a single unit that could be separated from its pedestal to reveal a flat surface, on the four borders of which is etched the inscription. Finally, the inscription calls itself a "Śārira Stūpa" or "Relic Stūpa" (*sheli ta*), rather than Baoqieyin or Gilt Stūpa, and makes no reference to the stūpas typically associated with Qian Chu's production.

The political tensions involving Qian Liu before and after 905 may explain the rationale for manufacturing the relic stūpa in 905. When the Tang court thwarted Qian Liu's desire for coronation in 904, he might have channeled his ambition for political legitimation from the imperial court power in the North to the search for religious authorization. The acquisition of the Mao county stūpa and relics and their transfer to Hangzhou was followed by another relic hunt for the past Buddha's relics in Shangyu. It is plausible that Qian Liu might have commissioned the gilt copper stūpa in 905 as a token of his growing political power, as he began to re-align his rule with the Indian king Aśoka and Buddhist authority. Certainly, his patronage of Buddhism began earlier, since there exist several records of his sponsoring Buddhist temple construction and appointing renowned monks to preside over monasteries in Wuyue. Given its intricate metalwork and expensive material, the Taipei reliquary must have been commissioned by a person with considerable affluence and assets, as well as significant social status and political power to mobilize resources—possibly somebody from the powerful Qian clan, or even Qian Liu himself. The Wuyue rulers particularly sought out a pool of diversified talents to serve their court, commissioning architects, craftsmen, literati, masons, sculptors, and technicians to provide the skills for building and embellishing their kingdom.[61] Possibly, Qian Liu's court commissioned the 905 Śārira Stūpa as part of its acquisition of Buddhist treasures and vigorous religious building.[62] Admittedly, the inscription dedicates the stūpa reliquary to the sponsor's parents and to all living beings. But this is hardly unusual, since Qian Liu's grandson Qian Chu, who sponsored the production of Baoqieyin stūpas, also dedicated the building of the Leifeng ta (Thunder Peak Pagoda) to and named it after his deceased wife when in reality as the *in situ* colophon shows, the pagoda was really built to house the Buddha's hair relic. As bronze inscriptions from the Zhou dynasty (1046–246 BCE) reveal, courtiers of the early Chinese court, when they received a promotion in the rank of office, would commission ritual bronzes and hold ceremonies to report to their ancestral dead their achievement and

Figure 18. Bronze gilt stūpa (dated to 905) from the Taiwan Palace Museum collection. Reproduced from *Lidai jintong fo zaoxiang te zhan tulu* (A Special Exhibition of Recently Acquired Gilt-Bronze Buddhist Images) (Taipei: National Palace Museum, 1996), 51.

express gratitude for blessings from their ancestral spirits. It is plausible that Qian Liu commissioned the reliquary stūpa to mark his military success, humbly announcing his assumption of power through the liturgical discourse of Buddhist rites of merit dedication.

This scenario seems even more likely when one considers another bronze gilt stūpa recovered at the city of Chi in Tiantai county of Tai province. Measuring 42.5 centimeters, this stūpa bears an inscriptional declaration that its donor was the second Wuyue king, Qian Yuanguan (r. 932–941). The stūpa's base is elongated and its body section has narrative art engravings; the body is made up of three tiled layers conjoined by two rows of seated figures interspersed with little windows; the finial is made up of five tiers of five discs topped with a flame-shaped jewel.[63] An inscription on the pedestal reads: "The Wuyue king recorded that on the sixth month in the fourth year of the *tianfu* era (939), he again donated [this stūpa] to the Feixia si (Monastery of Flying Mist) as an everlasting offering." The three tiled layers are more reminiscent of Chinese architecture than the design typical of the other Wuyue gilt stūpas. The immediate circumstances prompting the commissioning of this stūpa are uncertain. It is plausible that Qian Yuanguan was continuing his family's practice if indeed the Taipei reliquary was commissioned by somebody from the Qian clan, or Qian Liu himself. Evidently, in early Wuyue history, the gilt stūpa had yet to evolve a standardized, normative design that would appear during Qian Chu's time.

Concerning the Taipei reliquary's design, it is based rather closely on the Tang authors' descriptions of the Mao county stūpa. In the engravings on the stūpa's body, the craftsmen followed Genkai's description of jātaka scenes. Regional craftsmen probably would be more familiar with local oral stories, so it makes sense for them to follow Genkai's record, rather than Daoxuan's or Daoshi's accounts. As the art historian Yoshikawa Isao pointed out, the gilt stūpa's design can be discerned in Tang sculptures, like the eight tiny stūpas interspersed among the thousand buddha engravings on a copper plate, inscriptionally dated to 797, now kept in the Xi'an Museum Stele Forest (*beilin*) collection.[64] This design, Yoshikawa further argues, was already anticipated by the Northern Zhou stone stūpa with four-sided images, dated to 571, now kept in the Osaka National Museum of Art.[65] In short, the Wuyue stūpas were based as much on contemporary stūpa designs as literary descriptions of the Mao county stūpa.

Qian Chu's Production of Eighty-Four Thousand Stūpas: From Relic Stūpas to Dhāraṇi-sūtra Stūpas

As several literary records noted, in Qian Chu's production of eighty-four thousand stūpas, a roll of the *Baoqieyin dhāraṇi-sūtra* was "interred" inside the gilt stūpa. The *Baoqieyin jing* is an abbreviation for the *Yiqie rulai xinmimi quanshensheli baoqieyin tuoluoni jing* (the Dhāraṇī-sūtra on the Precious Chest Mudrā of the Whole Body Relics Concealed in the Minds of All the Tathāgatas).[66]

Inserting a sacred text, instead of the relic, into the stūpa was a practice that apparently flourished among Buddhist communities before the tenth century.[67] Wuyue Buddhists, or even the craftsmen, were probably familiar with at least two antecedents from India and Japan. First, the record of the famous pilgrim monk Xuanzang's (602/603?–664) travels to the Western Regions includes the following anecdote:

> An Indian practice is to make tiny stūpas (*sutubo*) using the powder from grinding incense. Their height is five or six inches, and inside them are deposited copied texts of scriptures. This is called dharma relic (*fasheli*). Over time, large stūpas were erected, and these [tiny stūpas] were congregated and placed inside [the larger stūpa] as an eternal observance of making offering.[68]

The same kind of practice is also introduced in a Chinese Buddhist canonical text titled the *Sūtra on the Merits of Erecting Stūpa* (*Fo shuo zao ta gongde jing*), translated by the Indian monk Divākara (613–687).[69] The text reiterates that the merit of inserting a text in a stūpa is the same as installing a body relic of the Tathāgata. Among the methods of erecting a stūpa, it prescribes writing down and installing a four-line verse on the teaching of dependent origination (*yinyuan fa*) called "The Dharma Body." This is because all who perceive the nature of conditioned origination also see the Tathāgata's True Body.[70]

Apparently, this installation of Buddhist texts inside stūpas was introduced to Japan fairly early, as evidenced in the early examples of woodblock printing, a technique known as *seihanbon*, in an edition known as "Million Dhāraṇī stūpas" (*hyakumantō darani*). From 764 to 770, Empress Kōken, probably heeding the advice of her favorite priest Dōkyō (700–772) in the Nara court, had one million copies of the *dhāraṇī* known as the *Sūtra on the Great Dhāraṇī of Pure Light* (*Wugoujingguang da tuoluoni jing*) printed, and then deposited each individual slip inside a foot-tall three-level wooden stūpa.[71] These cylindrical stūpas were then distributed to temples all over Japan to be venerated to secure protection and peace in each locality. An early eighth-century copy of the *Great Dhāraṇī of Pure Light* has been excavated in Korea, but there is no conclusive evidence of the mass production of the text, or its installation and distribution through miniature stūpas.[72]

Qian Chu's enterprise of creating eighty-four thousand stūpas had conspicuous parallels with Empress Kōken's production of the *hyakumantā darani*, although there exist salient divergences in design and material between the Nara and Wuyue stūpas. Invented in North China during the Tang period, block printing was incorporated by the Wuyue kingdom in the South into their array of technologies. In fact, the Wuyue kingdom has produced an impressive body of printed literature and illustrations, among which the *Baoqieyin Sūtra* was evidently a popular text. Evidence indicates that at least three editions of this dhāraṇī text were printed separately in 956, 965, and 975. Several copies of the earliest edition of 956 exist; they typically open with the following dedication: "Qian Hongchu, King of Wuyue Kingdom and First General of the World Metropolis, printed eighty-four thousand scrolls of the *Baoqieyin Sūtra*, which are deposited inside the precious stūpas for veneration; recorded in the third year of *xiande*, the *bingchen* year."[73] This dedication is typically followed by an illustration of paying respects to the Buddha, then the title, and finally, the text itself. One gilt bronze stūpa unearthed in 1971 during construction in Shaoxing city in Zhejiang province has these lines inscribed on its bottom: "Recorded in the *yichou* year (965) at the time when the king of Wuyue kingdom [Qian] Chu reverently forged eighty-four thousand precious stūpas as an eternal offering."[74] Inside the body of the same stūpa lies a little wooden cylinder containing a roll of the *Baoqieyin Sūtra*, wound around a wooden stick. The text opens with this dedication: "Recorded in the *yichou* year (965) at the time when the king of Wuyue kingdom Qian Chu reverently printed eighty-four thousand rolls of *Sūtra on the Precious Chest Mudrā* as an eternal offering."[75] This is really the only surviving sample of a Baoqieyin stūpa with its text intact, a phenomenon registered in several writings. The inscriptions confirm that the mass printing of the *Baoqieyin Sūtra* was indeed connected to the large-scale production of stūpas, both initiated by Qian Chu. In fact, the timing of the 956 and 965 editions correspond well to the stūpa production in 955 and 965.

Several copies of the third edition of the printed *Baoqieyin Sūtra*, dated to 975, were recovered among numerous cultural artifacts and treasures from the magnificent Leifeng Pagoda on the southern bank of the West Lake built from 972 to 976. When this famous stūpa collapsed in 1924, some of the bricks from its top section broke and rolls of the *Baoqieyin Sūtra* were found inserted inside through cylindrical openings, which were drilled into the bricks.[76] Copies of the text were also buried together with other printed materials under the stūpa. While the 975 edition had rather crude print types, with ink smudges, the 965 edition evinced sophisticated printing technology in their small, fine, and elegant print types, even ink-spread, and the capacity to produce block illustrations. The expertise required to produce the Baoqieyin sūtras and stūpas, as well as the craftsmanship needed for designing and drilling the bricks to hold and seal the texts inside, all eloquently testified to the advanced technologies possessed by the Wuyue kingdom. Indeed, the splendor of Leifeng Pagoda and its entombed treasures are excellent barometers of the resources, skills, technology, and wealth this kingdom had at its disposal.

Inserting the *dhāraṇī-sūtra* in place of the Buddha's relics seems to have been Qian Chu's signature contribution in the making of reliquary stūpas. It implied a shift in the cultic focus from the physical body relic (*rūpakaya śārira*, or *shensheli*) to the *dharmakāya* relic (*dharmakāya śārira*, or *fasheli*). An early Indian Mahāyāna text, the *Lotus Sūtra* (*Saddharmapuṇḍarika Sūtra*, or *Fahua jing*) authorizes the use of the book (scripture) to replace the physical relic as a cultus locus:

> Where the scripture roll is placed, all should erect a seven-gem stūpa, and make it to be exceedingly tall, wide, and ornate. There is no need to install relics again. Why so? The Tathāgata's whole body is already inside it. This stūpa should be venerated, respected, esteemed, and exalted with fragrant incense, jeweled necklaces, colored banners, music, songs, and gāthas.[77]

As indicated in its full title, the *Baoqieyin dhāraṇī* or mantra should be understood as the whole body relic (*quanshen sheli*) of all the Tathāgatas. The *Baoqieyin sūtra* lauds its own efficacies as follows:

> Again, the Buddha said to Vajra: "Should a living being copy this sūtra and place it inside a stūpa, this stūpa will then be the Adamantine Treasury Stūpa of all the Tathāgatas. Also it will be a Stūpa consecrated by the *dhāraṇī* and mind mysteries of all the Tathāgatas. It will also be the Stūpa of ninety-nine hundred thousand koṭis of Tathāgatas, and also the Stūpa of the Buddha's crown (*foding*) and Buddha's eyes (*foyan*) of all the Tathāgatas. [The person] will then receive protection from the numinous power of all the Tathāgatas. If this sūtra is installed inside a Buddha image, or a

stūpa, this image should be fabricated from seven gems, or this stūpa should have a canopy of seven gems.[78]

The religious appeal of this text is transparent: it promises benefits not just from a single religious power but is able to stimulate the aggregated powers of all the Buddhas. Given this symbolism and the many benefits the text holds out, it is understandable that, in lieu of the historical Buddha's relics in Aśoka's time, Qian Chu had printed copies of this efficacious *dhāraṇī-sūtra* installed inside the miniature stūpas he commissioned.

But not all the gilt stūpas Qian Chu commissioned were necessarily "Baoqieyin stūpas." Notable exceptions are two silver reliquaries unearthed at Leifeng Pagoda: one fragmented stūpa originally located in the pagoda's summit, and an exquisite silver gilt stūpa which was protected by layers of encasing and buried in the underground cache. The fragmented stūpa evidently contained a pure gold vase bottling eleven grains of relics. The other finely preserved silver stūpa measures about 35.6 cm high, and 9.5 to 12.6 cm in breadth. Peeping into the hollow within, via the openings between the intricate metallic engravings on the four-sided body, one catches gold glimmerings emitting from a tiny coffin. Chinese archaeologists suspect the tiny coffin enshrines a lock of the Buddha's hair, based on the dedicatory prefaces by Qian Chu, which are inscribed on a clay tile in the Leifeng Pagoda.[79] In other words, both the silver artifacts are *śārira* or relic stūpas, rather than Baoqieyin or dharma relic stūpas. In short, Qian Chu venerated and sponsored both relic stūpas as well as the *Baoqieyin dhāraṇī-sūtra* stūpa, or both objects of the relic and book cults. The latter, as I argue in the next section, allows a configuration that expedites multiplication and dissemination, and thus provides an accessible and portable iconic symbol of the Wuyue kingdom.

Indian Buddhist Kingship Through Chinese Eyes

As previously indicated, literary accounts usually present Qian Chu's production of the eighty-four thousand stūpas in terms of his profound emulation of Aśoka's religious piety and repentance of past evil doings. In other words, literary works, especially Buddhist records, typically explain Qian Chu's action in relation to the *Indian* paradigm of Buddhist kingship Aśoka embodied. However, Qian Chu's imitation of Aśoka's actions really unfolded within Chinese religious, social, and political landscapes, which critically reconfigured the material and conceptual expressions of Buddhist kingship.

It was thus hardly coincidence that Qian Chu pronounced in 955 the enterprise to copy Aśoka's building of eighty-four thousand stūpas, that is, the same year that the Latter Zhou emperor Shizong (954–59) in the North decreed prohibitive state policies that legally reduced the number of Buddhist institutions to only monasteries owning imperial plates.[80] Consequent to the prohibitive measure, Buddhism not only suffered the downsizing of clerical communities and damages to monasteries, but also incurred tremendous losses to their textual corpora. It was right on the heels of this devastating blow to Buddhism that Qian Chu declared his ambition to create eighty-four thousand stūpas. Within the broader environment of the Buddhist crisis in the North, it is all the more symbolic for Qian Chu to emulate Aśoka and to publicly "enact" state patronage of the religion. Shizong evidently ordered a statistical count of monasteries, to which Qian Chu responded by reporting a total of 480 monasteries or temples just in Hangzhou, the capital of his city, which constituted 17 percent of the total count of 2,694 monasteries in the entire country at that time.[81] Wuyue Buddhism apparently was unscathed by the change in state policy, since there is no record of closing down Buddhist institutions. Judging from this anecdote, Qian Chu apparently had sufficient political autonomy to continue rendering his support of Buddhism despite the imperial court's legislature. Although Buddhist records ascribe his commissioning of stūpas to heartfelt repentance for his errant past, it is probably equally true that he was "coached" by his monk consultants to simulate Aśoka's role as protector of Buddhism. Besides manufacturing eighty-four thousand stūpas, Qian Chu dispatched ambassadors to recover lost Buddhist texts from overseas, and generously patronized Buddhist art, building, printing, and rituals in his kingdom.[82] Certain records also portray Shizong ruling against fervent pious behavior often associated with relic veneration, like self-immolation and bodily mutilation. It would seem that the Buddhist persecution in the North expedited the relocation of stūpa production and veneration from the North to the Wuyue kingdom in the South.

As evident from Qian Liu's usage, the Mao county stūpa was deemed to have religio-political symbolism authorizing the ruler with the Buddha's charisma. This relic stūpa continued to have a salient role in Qian Chu's time. Historical documents record that Qian Chu first restored in 964 the stūpa to the south of the city (where the Mao county relics were deposited) and then repaired in 965 the stūpa to the north (where the Shangyu relics were stored). Most likely, both were damaged during a raging fire in 958, which burned through the south city into the inner quarters. Qian Chu also installed portraits of the first three kings of Wuyue at the newly restored stūpa monastery to the south of the city. In 966, a ceremonial reception took place to welcome the Aśoka relic back to its original abode, the stūpa monastery in the south city.[83] All these events relating to the Mao county stūpa helped foreground Qian Chu's place within a lineage of rulers who drew their political sovereignty from the spiritual authority of the Buddha's relics in King Aśoka's legacy. If the Mao county relic stūpa was the iconic symbol par excellence for religio-political authority in the Wuyue kingdom, then the Baoqieyin stūpas were its portable emanations, which facilitated travel across space beyond the territorial confines of its homeland. State-of-the-art technologies enabled the mass production of these portable replicas so that they could be dispersed far and wide, even crossing the ocean to Japan and Korea. Printing in particular was indispensable in rendering possible speedy replication of the *Baoqieyin sūtra* as a substitute for rare, hard-to-come-by bodily relics. The Buddhist kingdom of Wuyue, *icon-ized* in the Aśoka stūpa from Mao county, was then replicated incessantly in the form of Baoqieyin stūpas, in a manner reminiscent of the emanations of the Buddha's body to different parts of the universe. The basic disparity between the original and the replicas is striking: that is, physical relic contraposed to dharma relic. Mimi Yiengpruksawan's interpretation of the *hyakumantā darani* comes to mind here: the dissemination of these dhāraṇī stūpas all over Japan, she argued, likened them to the emanations of Buddha Vairocana (Daibutsu, or Great Buddha) in Nara; they reconfirmed the presence of the Buddha and also, by extension, the centralized power of the ruler in the Nara court.[84] Similarly, the Baoqieyin stūpas, traveling far from their origins, also point back to the Buddha's relics centralized in Wuyue. Literary sources record Qian Chu sending out envoys on sea voyages bearing the gilt stūpas among other tributary gifts to rulers and courts of distant lands, notably Japan and Korea.[85] Ultimately, the Buddha's presence in Wuyue via his bodily and dharma relics endorsed a body politic epitomized in its popular epithet, "Southeast Buddhist Kingdom" (*dongnan foguo*). Presiding over this Southeast Buddhist kingdom, the Wuyue king became likened to the Buddha and partook of this spiritual authority. Hence, although Qian Chu never acquired imperial status for himself and his court, through the Buddhist religio-political *imaginaire*, he came to preside as a centrifugal authority, and his kingdom emerged as the center of the Buddhist universe. In historical reality, however, Wuyue always remained a small state in tutelary subordination to the imperial power in the North.

In addition to having unfolded within a broader sinitic environment, Qian Chu's enactment of Indian kingship also drew heavily from East Asian conceptions of kingship. If the production of stūpas was an imitation of Aśoka's piety, it also borrowed from religio-political practices in East Asia, notably Empress

Kōken's *hyakumantā darani* and Emperor Wen's distribution of relics in Sui China. Particularly, the Japanese antecedent most probably wielded some influence. Although no record mentions Kōken as an inspiration for Qian Chu's enterprise, the maritime trade relations between Wuyue and Japan stimulated a steady stream of cultural and religious exchange, so that the Wuyue court would have been familiar with the Japanese precedent. However, as previously indicated, the design of the Baoqieyin stūpa was drawn from antecedents in Chinese sculptures.

Finally, Qian Chu's materialization of Buddhist kingship also evinced elements that are best explained in terms of indigenous expressions of kingship. My previous analysis of Qian Liu's use of the Mao county stūpa already pointed to embedded references to the sage king Yu and his nine cauldrons. The classic paradigm of kingship highlights a quasi-shamanistic tradition of legendary sage kings like Yao, Shun, and Yu who lived in a prehistoric golden age. These shaman kings are idealized as mythical sages and cultural heroes responsible for civilizing inventions like writing and building dams. Furthermore, in the historic model of the Shang shaman king (1600–1046 BCE), the king was really the head shaman of his clan, who deployed the technological inventions and economic resources he commanded (like bronze casting and writing) to conduct rituals or for the purpose of political legitimization.[86] Similarly, in tenth-century Southeast China, Qian Chu materialized Aśoka's building of stūpas through the use of new wealth and technologies, which in turn were the fruits of successful commerce and agriculture in the region.

On the one hand, printing, the most recent invention in written communication, was deployed in this context to create sacred texts to be inserted in stūpas. After all, temporally and spatially remote from the Buddha's time, it would have been difficult, if not impossible, for Qian Chu to acquire enormous collections of the Buddha's relics for his reenactment of Aśoka's building of eighty-four thousand stūpas. The new technology, block printing, thus enabled Wuyue craftsmen to mass produce the enormous quantity of Buddhist writings required for an undertaking of this magnitude. On the other hand, the arts of metal making and sculpting were used to manufacture the gilt stūpas. It is thus noteworthy that the material chosen to forge the stūpa (at least during the Wuyue period) was typically copper or iron, thus aligning it with the accepted index of economic and political power of ritual bronzes in early Chinese imaginings of kingship. Particularly, the silver relic stūpas excavated from Leifeng Pagoda epitomized the ostensive wealth and fine craftsmanship Qian Chu had at his disposal. The Wuyue kingdom evidently possessed rare, highly skilled masters of metalwork and sculpting.

As final evidence for how the relic stūpa was employed as a religio-political symbol, one can look at the final chapter of Wuyue history when Qian Chu renounced his kingship to the powerful Song court. Although the Song court acknowledged Qian Chu as king of Wuyue kingdom in 968, political circumstances swiftly evolved in ways that forced Qian Chu to abdicate his kingship in 978 and turn over his kingdom to the Song court. Accompanying Qian Chu on this mission was Zanning, the monk controller at the Wuyue court, who reportedly carried the Mao county stūpa to present to the Song emperor during the political negotiation between the two powers.[87] The symbolism is evident: the stūpa functioned as an insignia of Wuyue kingship so that its transfer from the Wuyue capital Hangzhou to the Northern Song court in Kaifeng materialized the transaction of political rights from the regional Wuyue power to the Song imperial court.[88]

In a sense the Wuyue kings have transferred their political ambition to the religious realm. Given that theirs was a relatively small kingdom, even with its wealth and power, it would have been disastrous for the Wuyue kings to rival the powers of the north, so that they opted, instead, for a Buddhist kingdom in Southeastern China where they could enact their vision of kingship, albeit over a delimited territory. But, as we saw, these territorial boundaries were broken in the imagination of the Wuyue rulers, who sent envoys and missionaries to far away lands. This was particularly the case for Qian Chu, who, by reenacting Aśoka's deeds, was able to stretch his power, wealth, and kingship into regions well out of his actual dominion. Buddhism was deployed as one means to attract new talents to his state and to promote cultural exchanges with faraway lands, which in turn enabled the Wuyue kings to rapidly develop the culture of their kingdom. Ironically precisely because he was so successful in building the peaceful, prosperous Buddhist kingdom in southeastern China, Qian Chu was a threat to the Northern Song Emperor and his court, where he was detained until his death in 988.

Chapter 6

"Ancestral Transmission" in Chinese Buddhist Monasteries: The Example of the Shaolin Temple

Ye Derong

The expansion of Indian civilization into East Asia is doubtless among the momentous events of human history. Indian culture was brought to China by the medium of the Buddhist faith, which left an indelible mark on China, even as it was deeply influenced by it. In this chapter I am concerned with the Chinese transformation of Buddhist monasticism. In order to survive in its new environment, Buddhism had been forced to adapt to the Chinese family system. The structure and the operation of the Chinese sangha had been fashioned after those of the Chinese clan, with "ancestor worship" becoming an integral part of monastic rituals.

Under the leadership of Song-period Confucianism, the ritualized structure of the clan had spread throughout Chinese society. In the wake of this societal evolution, the organization of the Buddhist monastic communities had become practically indistinguishable from the laity's. This chapter seeks to illustrate the kingship-modeled structure of Chinese monasticism by an examination of two related terms that had figured simultaneously throughout its history: "ancestral transmission" (*zong tong*) and "Dharma transmission" (*fa tong*). Investigating the interplay of these concepts in the history of the renowned Shaolin Temple demonstrates the underlying identity of the monastic institution and the ritually structured family. The interplay of "ancestral transmission" and "Dharma transmission" might serve as a prism for the investigation of the Chinese transformation of Buddhism.

The term "ancestral transmission" designates the relation between a monk and the abbot who had ordained him, that is under whom he had been tonsured. This relation is similar to the vertical blood ties connecting a person to his father. The term "Dharma transmission" describes the intellectual and spiritual indebtedness of a monk to the master who had bestowed the teachings upon him. It might be likened to the relation of a university student to his professor. On the surface, the two types of transmission are similar, for they are governed by the same rules of ceremony (*li*). However, their functions are entirely different. The "ancestral transmission" defines the social group to which a monk belongs, whereas the "Dharma transmission" identifies his spiritual affiliation.

In general, every monk receives upon his tonsure a group identity, namely a position within a given line of "ancestral transmission." By contrast, the "Dharma transmission" is much harder to obtain. In order to be bestowed a position within a line of "Dharma Transmission" one has to spend years of arduous study under a master who had himself been awarded it. Furthermore, the transmission of the teachings is attested by the bestowal of a "Dharma symbol" (*fa wu*), such as a cassock or a bowl. Thus, only a tiny fraction of the total number of monks are ever awarded a link within a given line of "Dharma transmission."

The distinction between "Dharma transmission" and "ancestral transmission" is crucial because of the latter's connection to monastic property. The "ancestral transmission" determines the rights of management and exploitation of monastic resources. In order to administer the temple's finances it is essential to keep a detailed genealogy of the "ancestral transmission," including all its branches. The historical records leave no doubt that, by the Yuan period at the latest, Shaolin property rights were determined by "ancestral transmission." Managerial and financial authorities were never delegated in the line of "Dharma transmission." By the time of Abbot Xueting Fuyu (1203–1275), the Shaolin inheritance system of "ancestral transmission" had been firmly established.

Whereas administrative posts have been invariably determined by "ancestral transmission," the abbot as a spiritual leader could sometimes be chosen by "Dharma transmission." By virtue of their spiritual or religious reputations, eminent monks from temples other than Shaolin were occasionally offered its leadership. However, invited from the outside, such abbots held no authority over the temple's finances. Even as they occupied the monastery's highest religious position, they remained outsiders to its community. The temple's administrators, including its "manager" (*zhishi*), were chosen from within the Shaolin family only.

Our investigation of the Shaolin "ancestral transmission" is facilitated by the monastery's epigraphic resources. Epigraphy relating to Shaolin is among the most extensive of any monastery in China. According to a recent count, it possesses over 550 inscriptions, some of which are on steles and others on the burial stūpas of eminent monks. These epigraphic materials provide detailed information on the changing composition of the Shaolin monastic community: numbers, names, and ecclesiastic posts. Thus, Shaolin epigraphy might serve as a prism for the investigation of the Chinese monastic community.[1]

The Size of the Monastic Community

The changing scope of the Shaolin monastic community is reflected in its epigraphic sources. The temple possesses several engraved steles that list all its monks, one by one. These inscriptions provide a reliable measure of the changing number of monks, as Table 1 demonstrates. The number of 428 monks suggested by the 1314 stele dedicated to Shaolin Abbot Xueting Fuyu (1203–1275) should doubtless be revised downward. This is because the stele was erected some forty years after the abbot's death, and it likely listed monks from two successive generations. The 1318 engraved biography of abbot Guyan Pujiu (held office

Table 1. Number of Shaolin Monks Beginning in the Yuan Period

Year	*Total number of monks*	*Monastic office holders*	*Other monks*	*Epigraphic source*
1314	428	85	343	Xueting Fuyu (Yugong) Stele
1513	190+			Gushan Xiangong Stele
1568	310	51	259	Biandun Stele
1578	403	50	353	Huanxiu Ru Chanshi Stele
1599	440	45	395	Wuyan Dao Chanshi Stele
1609	402	46	356	Daogong Chanshi Stele
1630	129+			Hanhui Xigong Chanshi Stele
1677	134			Ningran Gaigong Stupa Commemoration Stele
1756	255			Ningran Gaigong Stupa Inscription
1781	214			Stele of the Ancestral Temple for Xueting Fuyu (Yugong) and Ningran Gaigong

between 1313 to 1318) records "two-thousand fingers at the monastery." It is likely that the Shaolin community of the early fourteenth century numbered approximately 200 ordained monks.

Permanent Abbey and Branch Convents

The spatial organization the Shaolin Temple is comprised of a central "permanent abbey" (*changzhu yuan*) which is surrounded by numerous "branch convents" (*mentou*; or, less formally, *fangtou*). The relationship between the "abbey" and the "convents" has its counterpart in lay society. It might be likened to that of a clan's ancestral hall with the surrounding residences of the extended families of which it is made. Functionally, the "permanent abbey" serves as the site of the monastic community's religious activities, whereas the monks reside and work at the "branch convents." Within the "branch convents" the monks are engaged in labor and various daily activities that are not necessarily different from those of lay people. Therefore, the "branch convents" are closer than the "permanent abbey" to lay society.

The emergence of the "branch convents" depends on the size of the parent temple. When the monastic community is sufficiently large, the temple splits into numerous convents. It is possible to trace the emergence of the Shaolin "branch convents" by the appearance—within the same generation—of monks sharing the same clerical name. Only when the monks are divided between various houses could two monks—belonging to two different convents—be given the same Buddhist name. As long as the monks are living within the same ancestral monastery they would never be identically named. A survey of the names on the Shaolin steles permits us to conclude that the temple was divided into "branch convents" by 1314 at the latest.

By the mid-eighteenth century the Shaolin Monastery featured no fewer than twenty-five "branch convents," as attested by an exchange between the governor-general of Henan and Shandong, Wang Shijun (?–1756), and the Yongzheng emperor (reigned 1723–1735). The governor had submitted to the throne his detailed plans for the temple's renovation, and the emperor's response alluded to its large number of "branch convents." The sovereign's reply reflects the common perception that subsidiary-shrine monks were hard to control. Their residences being spatially removed from the parent temple, the members of the "branch convents" were more likely to disregard monastic regulations. The emperor would have preferred that they be relocated to the "permanent abbey":

> We have inspected the drawings and noticed that there are twenty-five "branch convents" (*mentou*), which are located at some distance from the monastery proper. Like stars scattered far apart, none is situated within the temple. Throughout our empire, it has always been the case that most "branch-convent" (*fangtou*) monks do not observe monastic regulations. Doing evil and creating disturbances, they are Buddhism's inferior sort. Today, as the Shaolin Monastery is undergoing renovation, and it is becoming one temple, these subsidiary-shrine monks should not be allowed to stay outside of it, where they are hard to supervise and control. The current buildings of the "branch convents" should all be destroyed. These monks should be provided instead with small houses to the left and the right of the main temple's walls.[2]

The twenty-five "branch convents" described in the emperor's edict were scattered among various shrines and courtyards in the temple's vicinity. It is likely, for example, that they had been located in the First Patriarch's Hermitage (Chuzu an) and in the Second Patriarch's Hermitage (Erzu an), (which were dedicated to Bodhidharma and Huike respectively), as well as in the South Garden (Nanyuan). (It is a great pity that the latter has been torn down during the recent relocation of the villagers from the temple's vicinity.)

The number of "branch convents" varies in accordance with the size of the central "permanent abbey." A small monastery is likely to have no more than one or two branches, whereas a big one might have many. We may well compare each of these "branch convents" to individual households within a same-surname village. In lay society the term household (*jiating*) usually designates blood-related relatives who are residing together with a living ancestor (most commonly several brothers who, together with their wives and children, occupy the same residential compound with their father). A same-surname village is made of many such households, all of which are descendants of a common (deceased) patrilineal ancestor. Similarly the monkish inhabitants of a "branch convent" have all been ordained by the same living master, who is residing with them. For his part, the master—like his colleagues in the other Shaolin "branch convents"—is an heir to the temple's "ancestral transmission."

The Branch Convents

The similarity of the monastic organization and the Chinese family structure is evinced by identical vocabulary. Shaolin epigraphic sources apply the lay terminology of the clan (*zu*) and the household (*jia*) to the description of their monastic community. The term household describes an individual branch convent (*mentou*), whereas the term clan is reserved for a higher level organization that is made of several branch convents. During the late imperial period, the Shaolin community was already large enough, and sufficiently complex, to include several clans, each divided into numerous households. Consider, for example, the 1851 "Stele Inscription on the Tenfold Division of the Shaolin Temple Consecrated Estate" ("Shaolin chansi xianghuo tiandi fenwei shifen bei"), which describes the division of the temple's landed-property between ten "households" ("branch convents"):

> The Chan Shaolin Temple of the Central Peak (Mt. Song) had been established by an imperial decree. Such were its origins. In the beginning all of its monks resided together. From morning till night they offered incense and recited the sūtras, venerating the Buddha. In the course of time, the temple's several dozen monks split into over ten households (*jia*). Offering incense and reciting the sūtras, they continued to venerate the Buddha. Thus, its present conditions do not differ from its origins.
>
> Our ancestors divided the temple's lands into ten parts, so that each [household] could cultivate its food-supplies. For the benefit of future generations, we hereby engrave in stone the exact boundaries of each of the Shaolin Temple's ten divisions of landed property, lest there be among our descendants a lawless monk who would contrive to sell consecrated property for his private profit. If anyone disobeys, his fellow convent, and clan, monks, shall file a complaint with the state authorities, having him punished in accordance with the law:
>
> First parcel: From the General Shrine's concave, eastward to the stone road, westward to the road, southward to the permanent abbey, northward to Zhenyou's [convent lands].
>
> Second parcel: From the cave-bend in the lower river, eastward and westward to Jiyuan's [convent lands], southwards to the end of the small road, northwards to the permanent abbey.
>
> . . .
>
> Stele erected by: The abbots of the Ciyun Hermitage (Ciyun an) Jijin

> and Jiqi, together with their household's (*hejia*) grand-disciple (*sun*) Zhenlan, and great-grand-disciples (*chongsun*) Suting and Suting; their clansmen Qilin, Qichao, Ruhong, and Haishui; their lay (*su*) grand-disciple Liu Tianxu, lay great-grand disciple Liu Yulin, and lay nephew-disciple Wei Zhenzhong.

The structure and size of the individual convents may be gauged from the inscriptions that were engraved on their principals' burial stūpas. The epitaph of each principal (or, as he is sometimes titled, abbot [*zhuchi*]) usually lists all of the monks in his household (*hejia*). Thus, for example, the 1597 stūpa inscription of Jungong Yun'an names thirty-two disciples in his convent (see Figure 19). It is noteworthy that the inscription employs the Confucian vocabulary of filial piety:

> Filial disciples: Guangwei, Guangying, Guangmei.
> Filial grand-disciples: Zongyi, Zongju, Zongjian, Zongjing, Zongyan, Zonghan, Zongyao, Zong'guang.
> Great-grand-disciples: Daoran, Daoxin, Daopu, Daoquan, Daode, Daozhang, Daozhan, Daochu, Daoyi, Daojing, Daocun, Daoyuan;
> Qingwu, Qinghui, Qingtong, Qingyuan,Qingshe, Qingzan, Qingshan, Qingyu
> Great-great-grand-disciple: Tongxi.

Some inscriptions employ other family terms such as "brother" and "nephew," which most likely denoted monks outside of the household. The brother of a household principal would have been ordained by the latter's master, but would have most likely gone off to head another Shaolin household. A nephew would be someone studying under such a brother. Recall that the 1851 inscription on the division of the Shaolin lands was erected by members of the same household, as well as members of the same clan (i.e., belonging to different households). Furthermore, the inscription alludes to lay disciples, disclosing the fuzzy lines separating the Shaolin community from the surrounding lay society. Operating in close proximity to the laity, the branch convents were closely related to it.

We have mentioned the Yongzheng emperor's edict of 1735, in which he decreed the relocation of the Shaolin Temple's twenty-five branch convents. It should be noted that even if the decree influenced the location of the households, it likely impacted neither their number nor their internal organization. This is

Figure 19. 1597 Jungong Yunan inscription listing the disciples in his convent. Photo courtesy the Shaolin Monastery.

evinced by the 1784 stele commemorating the renovation of the Abbot Gaigong Ancestral Shrine. The back side of the stele is engraved with a list of 214 Shaolin monks, underneath which were inscribed the locations of their household estates, as well as the names of at least six household principals. Note that Zhenyou and Jiyuan (who are mentioned in the above quoted 1851 stele on the division of the Shaolin estate) were likely household principals as well.

After the fashion of lay society, the twenty-odd Shaolin households (i.e., branch convents) were grouped into several clans, each with its venerated ancestor. It is difficult to assess with accuracy the number of the Shaolin clans (some of which were considered sub-clans of others). Further research into the internal divisions of the temple's burial grounds—made primarily of the Stūpa Forest (Talin)—might shed light on this question. Yet another indication might be provided by an investigation of the Shaolin ancestral shrines, which have been dedicated to the monastic progenitors of its clans. A 1932 inscription mentions five ancestral temples, in honor of monks Gaigong, Daogong, Wengong, Kuigong, and Qin'gong respectively. Judging by it, the Shaolin community included approximately half-a-dozen clans.

Ancestral Shrines, Household Genealogies, and Clerical Names

Beginning in the Ming period (1368–1644) and continuing to the present, the most important Shaolin ancestral temple has been dedicated to Xueting Fuyu (1203–1275) and his descendant Ningran Liaogai (1335–1421). In their combined temple the two have been worshiped under the titles Yugong and Gaigong respectively.

A 1781 inscription commemorating the shrine's renovation opens with the following statement:

> Ever since the ancient kings of old had founded the state it has been thus:In order to build a palace, an ancestral temple had to be established first. Verily, if there be water, there needs be a source. The further the source, the longer the stream. A tree must have roots. When the roots are deep, its branches naturally flourish. Thus, those who build shrines and venerate their ancestors are not merely tending the spring and the roots [but the stream and the branches as well].

The stele goes on to describe the late Ming destruction of the Yugong and Gaigong ancestral temple, which necessitated its Qing-period reconstruction.

It is hard to ascertain the exact date—within the Ming period—in which the Xueting Fuyu shrine was established. However, it appears likely that his worship was closely related to the rise of the Ningran Liaogai clan. These were likely the latter's disciples who sought to elevate his name by associating him with the venerable Fuyu. In other words, the genealogy linking the two masters, as well as their combined ancestral temple, were likely created by Liaogai's descendants in an attempt to bolster their position within the Shaolin community. Some evidence for this hypothesis is provided by a small Ming-period shrine, in the shape of an elongated stone tablet, which is situated to this day within the Fuyu temple. The stone shrine bears an uncanny resemblance to a 1455 stele that Liaogai's disciples had erected in honor of their master.[3] It would seem, therefore, that the combined ancestral cult of Fuyu and Liaogai was initiated—in the mid-fifteenth century—by the latter's disciples. We may note, further, that the eighteenth-century reconstruction of the temple might have been due to the growing prominence of the Liaogai clan. This is suggested not only by the renovated shrine itself, but also by two Qing steles that Liaogai's descendants had erected in honor of their long-deceased ancestor.

The similarities between the lay and the monastic ancestral cults are attested by identical vocabularies. The titles Shaolin monks bestowed upon their venerable founders had been borrowed from the surrounding village cults. As in any other clan temple—including the emperor's—the three principal Shaolin ancestral divinities were named Primordial Ancestor (Shizu), Great Ancestor (Taizu), and Elevated Ancestor (Gaozu). In the Fuyu shrine they were Xueting Fuyu, Songyuan Juexun, and Ningran Liaogai, respectively.

The compilation of family genealogies has been an important aspect of the Chinese clan. Even though we do not possess paper copies of Shaolin family trees, such documents have been engraved in stone. In 1802 the temple entertained a visit by members of a sub-clan that had emigrated outside of it. The returning monks were descendants of the Shaolin clan that had occupied the First Patriarch's Hermitage. Celebrating their clan reunion, they erected a stele carved with its detailed genealogy. "We have gathered all, young and old, at our ancestor's shrine," opens the inscription, which traces the clan's evolution over one hundred thirty years. All in all, the family tree—which has been engraved on the stele's back side—lists 219 monks belonging to that one Shaolin clan (see Figure 20). It should be noted that the 1781 stele of the Yugong and Gaigong ancestral shrine had been similarly engraved with a family tree. In terms of content and style alike, these monastic genealogies are identical to the laity's. The engraved Shaolin genealogies leave no doubt that the concept of the clan tree had been firmly embraced by the Chinese sangha.

Naming individual members according to their generation has been a common practice of the Chinese clan. Those born into the same layer on the family tree share one character of the two that make up their given names (Kezheng, Keding, Keying, etc.). The common character is usually taken from a memorable poem, the wording of which would determine the successive appellations of the entire clan. The custom has several advantages: It facilitates clan-mates recognizing each other; and it enables them to place each other in a correct hierarchical relation (so that they address each other properly). The generational appellations are also useful for the subsequent ordering of names on the clan's ancestral tablets.

That Buddhist monks have been named in accordance with their generation is one indication of the adaptation of Buddhism to Chinese society. Shaolin monks have been sharing a class appellation since the thirteenth century at the latest. Beginning with Abbot Xueting Fuyu (1203–1275), their clerical names have been determined by a seventy-syllable-long poem, which opens with the characters *Fu hui zhi zi jue, liao ben yuan ke wu* ("Blessings and wisdom are the seeds of

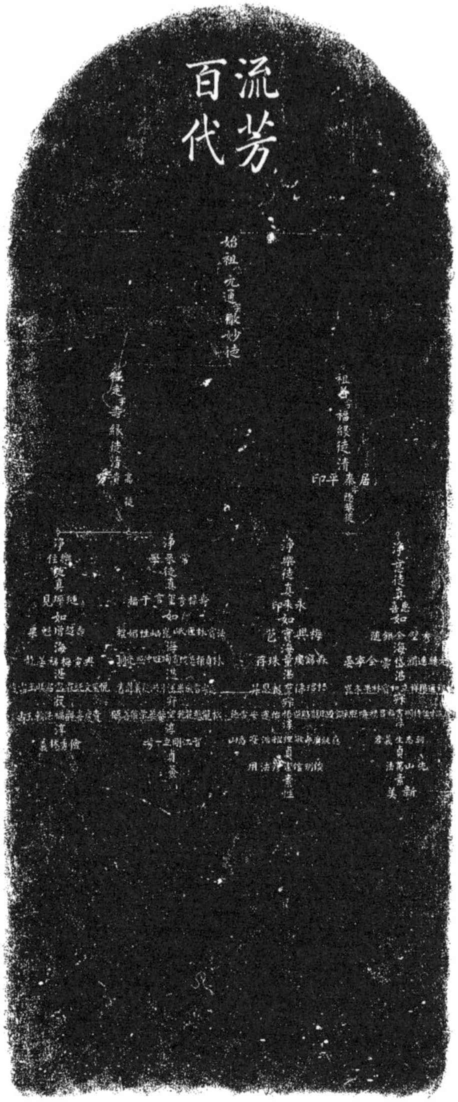

Figure 20. Engraved 1802 family tree of the first patriarch's hermitage clan. Photo courtesy the Shaolin Monastery.

awareness; Enlightenment is attained by the investigation of the roots"). Over thirty generations later, contemporary Shaolin monks are given names from the poem's fourth stanza: *De xing yong yan heng, miao ti chang jian gu* ("Practicing virtue forever continuously, the Buddhist body is eternally solidified"). The current abbot Yongxin (b. 1965) belongs to the *yong* generation.[4]

Local tradition attributes the Shaolin generational poem to Xueting Fuyu. However, it is doubtful that the venerable master composed it in its entirety. Stanzas in honor of the Shaolin ancestor were probably added by his descendants. The verse *Xueting wei daoshi, yin ru gui xuan lu* ("Xueting is [our] guiding master, leading you to the Buddhist path") is unlikely to have been written *by* the master. I would suggest that the Shaolin generational verse was authored in two stages. The opening twenty characters were selected by Xueting Fuyu, whereas the remaining fifty characters were supplemented by the temple's seventeenth-century abbot Bi'an Haikuan (1596–1666). This hypothesis can be supported by several pieces of evidence: First, the complete seventy-character naming verse was recorded for the first time in the "The Complete Lineages of the Buddhist Names of the Ancestral Shaolin Temple's Five Sects," which was engraved on a Shaolin stele in 1802;[5] second, Bi'an Haikuan is known to have supplemented another Buddhist genealogical poem, that of the Ciyun Monastery;[6] third, the Qing Dynasty rose to power during Bi'an Haikuan's tenure, for which likely reason he chose *qing* as the opening character of the fifty he had supplemented.

"Ancestral Transmission" and the Layout of the Stūpa Forest

Ever since the Tang period, the cremated remains of eminent Shaolin monks have been interred at the Stūpa Forest (Talin). Abbots and monastic office holders (such as managers and household principals) have been honored there with elegant stone pagodas. All in all, the Stūpa Forest contains 232 pagodas: 2 from the Tang period (618–907); 3 from the Northern Song (960–1127); 16 from the Jin (1115–1234); 51 from the Yuan (1279–1368); 146 from the Ming (1368–1644); 10 from the Qing (1644–1911); and 4 from modern times.

The Stūpa Forest is situated west of the "permanent abbey," on the southern slopes of a small mountain. Its central north-south axis has been reserved for the stūpas of the abbots, whereas lesser monastic officials have been interred to the east and to the west. Broadly, the burial ground has evolved from the north to the south, so that recent pagodas are located on its southern edges. Each stūpa is engraved with an epitaph, commonly listing the deceased's teachers, classmates, and disciples. An investigation of these inscriptions enables us to determine the relation between the various stūpas, as well as the layout of the entire cemetery. In particular, it is possible to examine whether the arrangement of the stūpas follows the "Dharma transmission" or the "ancestral transmission." My analysis of the epitaphs suggests that the Stūpa Forest could be broadly divided into eight burial grounds: (1) The central axis reserved for the abbots, followed by the stūpas of (2) the Kejing branch of the Liaogai Clan; (3) the Kezheng branch of the Liaogai Clan; (4) the Keding branch of the Liaogai Clan; (5) the Keying branch of the Liaogai Clan; (6) the Juejinbranch of the Zining Clan; (7) the Jueyu branch of the Zining Clan; and (8) the Wuayan Clan.

The internal layouts of seven burial grounds have been clearly determined by the "ancestral transmission," whereas one only, the abbots' central axis, could be said to reflect the "Dharma transmission" (even though the correlation between the abbots' Dharma-lineages and the spatial layout of their pagodas is fuzzy at best). In the seven burial grounds that have been reserved for the lesser monastic officials, the location of individual stūpas have been unmistakably decided by their family affiliation, so much so that it is possible to demarcate with precision the boundaries of the household plots. This is especially true of the pagodas that have been erected beginning in the Ming Jiajing period (1522–1566). Prior to the sixteenth century, the exact location of the stūpas within a given family parcel were chosen at random. By contrast, beginning in the 1520s, monastic office holders were regularly interred at the nearest available spot south of the household principal's stūpa. Thus, in the cemetery's southwest, where most Ming monks have been enshrined, the divisions between the household plots are easily discernible.

"Ancestral transmission" and Ordination

Established by Xueting Fuyu, the Shaolin "ancestral transmission" has flourished uninterrupted from the Yuan period to this day. It has played a key role in ordering the monastic community, its importance growing in direct correlation to the rising significance of the clan in Chinese society. The evolution of the monastery's ordination system might illustrate the growing significance of the "ancestral transmission" as the guiding principle of the Shaolin community.

In the early Chinese tradition, the abbot alone was qualified to ordain new monks. Daocheng's *Buddhist Essentials* (preface 1020) explicitly states: "All ordinations are conducted by the abbot alone. Other monks are all forbidden to ordain novices."[7] Even though Yuan-period Shaolin abbots have attempted to follow this tradition, by the late fourteenth century their monopoly over the ordinations broke down. A survey of the Stūpa Forest epitaphs reveals that by the late Yuan some ordinations were conducted by the temple's manager (*zhishi*), who would often concurrently function as a household principal. It was perhaps in this fashion that the ordination prerogative gradually slipped from the central abbey to the branch convents, so much so that by the late imperial period most ordinations were conducted by the household principals rather than by the abbot.

The centrality of the clan to the ordination process might be illustrated by the fate of those monks who had been ordained by abbots from outside the Shaolin family. We have noted earlier that some Shaolin spiritual leaders had been invited from other monasteries, rather than being members of its clan. Beginning in the Ming Jiajing period (1522–1566), such abbots could no longer ordain monks into the Shaolin community. The novices they tonsured were listed instead in their own—pre-Shaolin—lines of "ancestral transmission." A monk who had been ordained by a non-Shaolin abbot—even if the ordination took place at the temple—would not be accepted into its clan. The distinction between "ancestral transmission" and "Dharma transmission" could not have been more carefully kept.

The evidence of the Shaolin ordination system, no less than that of the Stūpa Forest, suggests that the Ming Jiajing period was a turning point in the emerging consciousness of the Shaolin clan. The growing attention to the spatial boundaries of the Shaolin sub-clans coincided with the emergence of strict rules of ordination by "ancestral transmission." These sixteenth-century developments likely reflected the government policies that had facilitated the consolidation of clans throughout Chinese society. All through the fifteenth century, the state had attempted to curb the emergence of large clans, prohibiting commoners from worshiping ancestors beyond (usually) the fourth generation. The restrictions were significantly eased during the Jiajing reign, permitting commoners to venerate the ancestor who had established the family line in their locality (no matter how many generations removed). The result was a flourishing of clan-related activities, from the establishment of ancestral temples to the publication of family genealogies. Thus, the structure of the Buddhist sangha was influenced by government policies that were meant to shape society at large.

Conclusion

We have surveyed six aspects of the Shaolin community, suggesting that the concept of the clan has played a major role in it. In order to adapt to Chinese society, the Buddhist sangha has been fashioned after the Chinese family. As the clan became dominant in Chinese society, its significance grew in monastic circles as well. During the late imperial period, the "ancestral transmission" had superseded "Dharma transmission" in determining the structure and the management of Buddhist temples.

Far from being unique to Shaolin, the "ancestral transmission" (*zong tong*) has been common in many Chinese monasteries. In his "Complete lineages of the Buddhist names of the ancestral Shaolin Temple's five sects," the seventeenth-century Shaolin Abbot Bi'an Haikuan listed 101 Buddhist lines of "ancestral transmission": 24 belonging to the Caodong School, 11 to the Yunmen School, 12 to the Fayan School, 17 to the Linji School, 3 to the Weiyang School, and 34 others.[8]

Chapter 7

The Hagiography of Bodhidharma: Reconstructing the Point of Origin of Chinese Chan Buddhism

John R. McRae

The Historical Relationship Between Chinese Chan and Pan-Asian Buddhism

What is the historical relationship between Chinese Chan and Buddhism in the rest of the first-millennium world? No one could deny that there is a deep connection over the long term, since no matter how quintessentially "Chinese" Chan may have been, it arose only as part of the massive historical event that was the propagation of Buddhism across Asia. Previous scholarship has focused on long-range connections between Indian Buddhism and Chan, suggesting continuities from Buddhist meditation practice or the doctrinal impact of the perfection of wisdom and Mādhyamika philosophy. Are such analyses sound, and are there other such continuities that we should consider?

Then again, if the longue durée relationship between pan-Asian Buddhism and Chinese Chan were not difficult enough to evaluate, what about short-term or roughly contemporaneous connections? Since Chan arose within the complex religious and cultural context of sixth- through eighth-century China, it might also be possible to identify particular aspects of pan-Asian Buddhism as secondary factors in its emergence. Given the exertions of missionary monks and the multiple routes of communication throughout Asia during the early centuries of the common era, is it possible that Chinese Chan emerged somehow in dialogue with religious developments in South Asia, Central Asia, and/or Southeast Asia?

One of the problems that has hampered treatment of these issues in the past has been a fixation on images of the mature Chan school from the Song dynasty (960–1279) and later. If in contrast we limit our focus to the emergence of Chan in the sixth to eighth centuries, how might that event have been related to developments outside China from the fifth century or so onward?

As far as I am aware, the questions just posed have not been given rigorous consideration by any scholar in any relevant academic language (i.e., Chinese, English, French, German, or Japanese). Perhaps this neglect should not be surprising. No doubt the issues are simply too vast and unwieldy, requiring too much background information in too many areas of study. Specialists in the study of Chinese Chan, Korean Sŏn, Japanese Zen, and Vietnamese Thiền Buddhism have focused on the texts of their own chosen traditions, while scholars with broader interests in East Asian Buddhism and other religions have found those very texts highly resistant to integrated analysis. In addition to these very real factors of overall complexity and individual scholarly inclination, though, I suspect the topic has gone unconsidered due to a number of other factors, including distaste for the teleological rhetoric of earlier comprehensive histories of Zen, a postmodern disinfatuation with historical narrative in general, and the assumption that Chan was an intrinsically Chinese phenomenon properly explained in terms of purely Chinese factors. To cite one very important case that will constitute the major focus of the present paper, readers have been dissuaded from considering the possibility of any contemporaneous relationship between pan-Asian Buddhism and Chinese Chan because of the biographical obscurity of Bodhidharma (d. ca. 530), the hallowed forefather of Chan and the most likely nexus of any early relationship.

This chapter represents the second part of a larger endeavor. In the initial stage of this project, being published in a volume edited by Tansen Sen and based on a conference on "Buddhism Across Asia: Networks of Material, Intellectual, and Cultural Exchange" hosted by the Institute of Southeast Asian Studies, National University of Singapore on February 16–18, 2009, I sketch the intellectual background to the issues just described, focusing on the foundation of Chan scholarship at the beginning of the twentieth century. There I concentrate on the first volume of a comprehensive history of Chan/Zen in India and China, *History of the Thought of Zen Training* (*Zengaku shisōshi*), published in 1923 by Nukariya Kaiten (1867–1934).[1] Nukariya was a gifted thinker, a versatile scholar, and a productive writer, altogether an impressive example of the religious leadership of the Meiji (1868–1912) and Taishō (1912–26) periods. His magnum opus of 1923 was ultimately concerned with a unique type of religious training that distinguished the Chan/Zen tradition from earlier approaches based on meditative contemplation and, indeed, from the rest of Buddhism entirely. In particular, Nukariya's marking off of the period from Bodhidharma to Huineng (638–713) as a period of "pure Zen" (*junzen no yo*), which transcended the yogic craftsmanship of earlier Buddhism but lacked the demonstrative defects of later times, was the foundation on which Hu Shi (1891–1962) argued that the sudden teaching (*dunwu*) of Huineng and Shenhui (684–758) was a revolutionary teaching, in his famous formula a "Ch'an that was no *ch'an* at all."

In this chapter I turn from a review of the earliest modern scholarship on Chan and its interpretation of the earliest historical phase of the Chinese tradition, to the philological and historical analysis of the earliest extant primary source for the putative founder of Chan Buddhism. That is, I consider the first written description of Bodhidharma and its implications for the role of Indian or pan-Asian elements in the formation of Chinese Chan ideology. This topic is logically warranted by the considerations introduced above, that is, that the school's non-Chinese progenitor Bodhidharma represents the earliest possible nexus of interaction between Chinese Chan and Buddhism in the rest of first-millennium Asia. In addition, below I will show that a rereading of the earliest source for Bodhidharma's biography leads to important new conclusions about his historical identity and the articulation of his teachings.

Our first step in this undertaking is actually to *de-familiarize* ourselves with the images of Bodhidharma that are widely known both in premodern East Asian history and throughout contemporary world culture. For example, in Chinese art and literature Bodhidharma is now invariably depicted as a large and powerful individual, with full beard and long hair—resembling nothing so much as a traditional martial deity, albeit without the weaponry and armor that a sage of his caliber would find unnecessary. This energetic figure is capable of all sorts of martial arts moves, such as those depicted in the Hong Kong and mainland Chinese movies, or as enacted by the troop of Shaolin gymnasts that perform such exotic dance routines in Bodhidharma's name. Although the image of Bodhidharma as *gongfu* practitioner derives from only the Qing dynasty (1644–1911) and later, as Meir Shahar has amply demonstrated in his wonderful book on Shaolin, the red-robed, bearded, and earringed image of the Indian sage goes back at least to the Yuan dynasty (1280–1368). The earliest extant graphic images of Bodhidharma, which date from the Song but seem to retain an earlier stage of iconographic development, show him as a skinny dark-skinned Indian wearing little more than a *dhoṭi*. Although this may have been how Bodhidharma was imagined several centuries before, we can only look to the earliest written texts for guidance.

The problem with the textual evidence concerning the image of Bodhidharma is that it underwent a long process of hagiographical evolution, a historical process that was of great religious significance but profoundly transformed the identity of the sage as time went on.[2] Our purpose here is to attend to the very beginnings of this hagiographical process, so we need to avoid being distracted by demonstrably later innovations. We must therefore ignore any suggestion that Bodhidharma was accomplished in martial arts, a very late if important fiction. We may also put aside the famous depictions of Bodhidharma with a beard, an earring, and very often an intemperate scowl. The skinny dark-skinned figure in the *dhoṭi* may be closer to the truth, but as we will see there is a strong likelihood that Bodhidharma was from Central Asia rather than India proper. Hence it would be better to wipe all visual images away completely, were that possible.

Moving to the contents of Bodhidharma's hagiography, we can dispense with the most famous motifs like peeling away the layers of an onion, or the leaves of a plaintain tree. The first to go is the famous account in which Emperor Wu of the Liang dynasty (r. 502–49) is supposed to have described his efforts at building monasteries and casting images of the Buddhas, which Bodhidharma discounted as having no religious merit. This encounter is clearly anachronistic, given other evidence to be introduced below placing Bodhidharma in north China from the closing years of the fifth century. More to the point, it only appears in the written record in a text associated with Shenhui and dating from perhaps as late as 758 or so, but certainly no earlier than 730—some two centuries after Bodhidharma's death.

The next widely known anecdote to be set aside is that in which Huike (ca. 485–ca. 555 or after 574) severs his own hand or forearm (the character *bi* refers to the arm below the elbow) in order to hear the teachings of Buddhism, after which he and Bodhidharma engage in the famous "pacification of the mind dialogue" (*anxin wenda*), the gist of which is Huike's realization that he has no "mind" that could be pacified. Here we need to take the two parts of this anecdote separately, although in both cases there is clear evidence suggesting how the story developed over time.

The claim that Huike cut off his own hand is recorded for the first time in the Shenhui text alluded to just above. Well before this, though, Daoxuan's (596–667) *Continued Biographies of Eminent Monks* (*Xu gaoseng zhuan*) of 645[3] describes Huike as having his arm cut off by ruffians, using a term *zei* that can refer to either political rebels or common bandits. Although this account was written so as to show Huike in a favorable light, it engendered resistance in the burgeoning Chan movement. That is, a history of Chan composed around 710–12 states that the story involving ruffians was untrue, and as we have seen the account of Huike's self-amputation appears in writing perhaps as soon as two decades thereafter. Clearly, it did not do for an esteemed sage to suffer such a fate at the hands of others.

When we peel these stories away, what is left? Bernard Faure has argued, in effect, that there is *nothing* at the center of the Bodhidharma hagiography.[4] Indeed, Faure argues strongly that the very notion of a historical nucleus to the story of Bodhidharma's life is untenable, and that the very quest for his historical origins is fundamentally misguided. In posing this argument Faure introduced a new form of postmodern structuralist analysis to the study of Chinese Chan Buddhism, and in doing so he enriched the field immeasurably. In spite of this very positive contribution, though, it is unfortunate that no one has chosen to question his line of reasoning until now.[5] Faure's argument is based on an unquestioning faith in the infallibility of modern methodologians, and it was constructed in an a priori fashion, without actually considering the textual evidence involved. By reexamining that textual evidence, in the following pages I show that we can indeed say certain specific things about the historical personage Bodhidharma. Certainly there will be questions remaining and points of ambiguity, but the historical enterprise is by no means untenable as a scholarly method.

The Earliest Depiction of Bodhidharma

The earliest depiction of Bodhidharma is found in the *Record of the Monasteries of Luoyang* (*Luoyang qielan ji*), a nostalgic account of the glories of the former capital of the Northern Wei dynasty (386–534). The author, Yang Xuanzhi, is otherwise unknown, but given his access to documents of the Northern Wei, which disintegrated into eastern and western regimes in 534, he must have been an official of some standing. Yang visited the deserted former capital in 547, the *terminus ante quem* of his book. In it he describes a glorious city with over 1,000 monasteries, the most spectacular of all being the nine-level pagoda of Yongningsi.

This building was supposed to be 1,000 feet tall (another contemporary source gives a still not quite believable height of 500 feet), so tall that it could be seen a hundred *li* (434 km) away from the city. Golden bells suspended from the eaves could be heard from over ten *li* away. When construction was initiated 32 golden Buddha images were found under the ground, which Imperial Consort Ling (Ling taihou), the monastery's patron and the most powerful figure in the

Northern Wei at the time, took to be an indication of the purity of her faith. Expenditures on construction exceeded all bounds, and in addition to the 130 golden bells the many doors of the pagoda were sealed with a total of 5,400 golden nails. Yang wrote, "It was the ultimate in architectural technology, the most wondrous of the creative arts. Its exquisite beauty was beyond this world, and the carving on the pillars and golden fixtures moved to amazement the hearts of all who saw them."[6]

In addition to describing this amazing building in his own words, Yang introduces a well-traveled foreign monk to testify to its magnificence within the larger Buddhist world:

> At the time, there was a monk named Bodhidharma who had come from the western region, a barbarian from the country of Bosi. After a long trip from his faraway country, when he arrived in China and saw the golden plates of the Yongningsi [pagoda] gleaming in the sun with a brilliance that pierced the clouds, and the elaborately created bells echoing to the heavens, he exclaimed in praise, "This is a truly amazing building."
>
> He said he was 150 years old and had traveled throughout all the corners of the world, but that he had never seen anything as beautiful as this monastery. "I have been to the edges of the world, but I have never seen anything like this before." He held his palms together [in *añjali-mudrā*] and recited "Namo" for several days.[7]

If this was the Bodhidharma of Chan-school fame, it would mean that he was in Luoyang during the heyday of the Yongningsi pagoda, which was built in 516, damaged by fire in 526, and occupied by the military in 528. Paul Pelliot (1878–1945) was the first modern scholar to notice this reference to Bodhidharma, which he took as the Chan figure rather than some other individual of the same name, and he gave his article mentioning the point to Hu Shi during the latter scholar's visit to Paris in 1926.[8] Hu was troubled by the apparent difference between this devout traveler and the idiosyncratic patriarch of Chan, but not enough to prevent him from inferring that Bodhidharma had been in northern Luoyang sometime during the years 516–26. Incidentally, although Bodhidharma's country of origin has been mistakenly interpreted as Persia, in this text the name Bosi is clearly identified as a small entity in the Hindu Kush, in an area now under the jurisdiction of Afghanistan and Pakistan.[9] Later sources were to ignore this, placing Bodhidharma's origin in southern India.

One of the problems facing Hu and other early scholars was that they took the mature hagiographical image of Bodhidharma, as found in the *Record of the Transmission of the Lamp [Compiled During the] Jingde [Period]* (*Jingde chuandeng lu*) and other texts of the Song dynasty and later, as their standard of comparison. It was Hu who discovered the Shenhui text in which the Bodhidharma-Emperor Wu story is first found, but as a positivist researcher working on the basis of very new discoveries, he recognized only its historical anachronism, and he was unable to appreciate the religious creativity implied in hagiographical fabrication. Effectively, Hu reduced the evidence found in the *Record of the Monasteries of Luoyang* and the *Continued Biographies of Eminent Monks* to a set of dated events, ignoring nuances he could not understand. Thus Bodhidharma entered China from the south during the Song dynasty (420–479) because the *Continued Lives* mentioned him passing through the region, but he was in the north by 495 or so because of the same text's evidence concerning a disciple of Bodhidharma's, Sengfu (fl. 497–515). And, given the account just introduced above involving the Yongningsi pagoda, Bodhidharma was in the north during the years 516–26. All subsequent scholars have in effect accepted his chronology for Bodhidharma's life.

All scholars, that is, except Faure.

Faure is presumably interested in Bodhidharma for many reasons, but his primary focus is on changing how his hagiography should be understood in postmodern scholarship. Faure thus uses the case of Bodhidharma to explain his new methodological approach, which he identifies as structural criticism.[10] Although Faure makes brief gestures toward the validity of the "historical approach" to the study of Chan, stating that it "is certainly necessary and needs to be encouraged,"[11] his general tendency is to dismiss such attempts as misguided or worse. He depicts historians as lacking in critical self-awareness, because their efforts at compiling evidence from multiple sources resemble those of religious hagiographers in mistakenly treating literary texts as if they were straightforward historical reportage, and because they blindly adopt patently false attributions of authorship so as to fill out the story lines of their subject matter.[12] Faure parodies historically based scholarship using a memorable metaphor:

> Usually, the main task of historians is to try to uncover the facts behind the legend. Hagiographical texts are considered by them to be documents that need interpretation to bring to light their hidden truths. Often enough, after this mortuary washing only a skeleton remains, and it is this skeleton that will enter the museum of history. Often, some missing bones may have to be taken from other skeletons to complete the exhibit. In the case

> of Bodhidharma, there is not even a skeleton—only one sandal left, according to legend, in an empty grave. In most cases the biographical process is characterized by an "essentialist" attitude in that they consider a figure as some kind of individual entity whose essence is reflected in specific biographical or doctrinal texts.[13]

A compelling image, and perhaps earlier generations of historians would have embraced the description of their mission as "to uncover the facts behind the legend"—Hu Shi certainly did, but not anyone writing about Chan history these days. Perhaps we should credit this change in part to Faure's impact. Nevertheless, I also react to the static quality of Faure's metaphor. That is, in my mind the hagiographical identity of Bodhidharma has functioned dynamically within Chinese culture and the Chan tradition. In recent classes and lectures I have introduced Bodhidharma's hagiographical image as an energetic and unpredictable beast, that rampages through subsequent generations like Frankenstein's monster terrorizing the village. While this depiction is no doubt overdrawn, to describe Bodhidharma's hagiographical image as a wired-together collection of bones on display in a glass exhibition case is to emasculate it. Not only does this render it devoid of all interest, the very hagiographic dynamism involved here was an important historical process of the Chinese religious tradition.

In contrast to the stultifying concoction of historical specimens, according to Faure the approach of structural analysis is to imitate Georges Dumézil's research on Indo-European gods by studying Chan masters in relationship with each other, rather than as individual entities.[14] With regard to Bodhidharma, the reliance on written documents implies one should treat his supposed "life" "as a literary piece belonging to the hagiographical genre, a genre characterized by a 'predominance of explanations concerning places over explanations concerning time.'"[15] Faure continues by describing the steps involved in such analysis. First, one is to inquire of the genre of hagiographical writing itself, to determine the "rules by which it is governed." That is, what is the syntagmatic structure of the hagiographical text itself, the set of linkages between its various internal functions? Second, one should examine the text's paradigmatic structure, the virtual relations between similar or dissimilar functions in all the texts of the corpus under consideration.[16] From this, Faure infers a fundamental quality of uncertainty about whether the hagiographical text is ever fixed once and for all. He cites Ferdinand de Saussure to the effect that the various elements of any legend are symbols operating in ever-changing relationships to each other. Elsewhere in his work Faure introduces Jacques Derrida's concept of the "trace" and its implication of the fundamental impossibility of ever following a hagiographical trail back to its absolute origins: "the trace is not only the disappearance of origin, it means . . . that the origin did not even disappear, that it was never constituted except reciprocally by a nonorigin, the trace, which becomes the origin of the origin."[17]

When he turns to the Bodhidharma material himself, Faure attends first to the relationship between him and his contemporaneous meditation teacher, Sengchou (480–560). Introducing Daoxuan's description of the two men's teachings as being like the two wheels of a cart, Faure concludes that here Bodhidharma and Sengchou represent variants of a model provided by Roland Barthes, who suggested that many narratives "set two adversaries in conflict over some stake; the subject is then truly double, not reducible further by substitution; indeed, this is even perhaps a common archaic form, as though narrative, after the fashion of certain languages, had also known a *duel* of persons."[18] Observing that the French *duel* means both a contest between two sides and a category of duality, Faure proceeds to suggest that the Bodhidharma/Sengchou contrast is "structurally analogous to the alleged rivalry between Huineng and Shenxiu, which appears as its sectarian hyperbole." Even though the original basis of this distinction has now been shown to be overdrawn, in that Daoxuan's primary goal was not, as so many Chan scholars have assumed, to compare Bodhidharma and Sengchou,[19] the notion of a "*duel* of persons" has become a useful rubric of analysis. Faure uses this rubric to guide his other ruminations on Bodhidharma, which mostly concern confusions involving him and similarly named Indian figures in slightly later texts and thus are of little interest here.

In the preceding summary I have made a point of showing the extent to which Faure draws on European scholarship, presenting their insights at length and as authoritative dicta. I would go so far as to say that he takes the writings of Barthes, de Certeau, Derrida, Dumézil, Ducrot and Todorov, Saussure, et al. as *canonical*, in the sense that they contain inviolable truths that may be applied to all human culture. To examine the validity of this impression would be beyond the scope of this chapter, so here I will restrict myself to observing how different this attitude is from how he treats the sources for Bodhidharma's biography, which he summarizes in less than a page.[20] Primary sources are of merely incidental interest to Faure, whose primary expertise is the infallible insights of his European intellectual forebears.

At the end of his brief introduction of the early sources for Bodhidharma's life and teachings, Faure presents a description of the relevant passage from the *Record of the Monasteries of Luoyang* in the context of another denigration of historians' past efforts:

> In this text, however, Bodhidharma is presented as an elderly Central Asian monk who spent several days singing the praises of the great *stūpa* in the precincts of Yongning Monastery.[21] After endless discussions, historians have harmonized these conflicting images of Bodhidharma—the devout and somewhat senile monk, the austere practitioner of some esoteric type of meditation, and the transmitter of Buddhist scriptures—to give a coherent account of his personality, but it diverges greatly from that of the legendary figure of the later Chan tradition.[22]

From context it is clear that the image of Bodhidharma as a "devout and somewhat senile monk" is intended as a characterization of his description in the *Record of the Monasteries of Luoyang*. Were this phrase not included in both Faure's "Bodhidharma" (1986) and his *Chan Insights* (1993), I would have concluded it was merely an egregious slip of the keyboard, as it were.

The problem is that Faure has not followed his own instructions to examine his sources as literary texts rather than as historical documents. Indeed, given his interest in critiquing modes of interpretation rather than undertaking textual criticism and historical analysis himself, he has exaggerated beyond repair the manner in which previous scholars have characterized Bodhidharma's historical identity. That is, the description of Bodhidharma in the *Record of the Monasteries of Luoyang* as being 150 years old and deeply moved by the magnificence of the Yongningsi pagoda contains no hint that he was "somewhat senile," and no earlier scholar prior to Faure himself has ever suggested such a thing. Given the great respect for age in the East Asian tradition, the assertion of such an advanced age for Bodhidharma attributed to him great religious authority. He had achieved such a great age because of his religious cultivation, and the matter is recorded in the text so as to give additional weight to his reportage.

What earlier scholars have noticed about the depiction of Bodhidharma in this text is that it is markedly different from the iconographic image of the founder of Chinese Chan found throughout later texts. However, we have already worked to defamiliarize ourselves with this later imagery, and the fact that it "diverges greatly from that of the legendary figure of the later Chan tradition" is now beside the point. Here our first question is, paraphrasing Faure, what is the identity of Bodhidharma within the syntagmatic structure of the *Record of the Monasteries of Luoyang?* And, second, what are the relations between the multiple functions of Bodhidharma in that text and the other texts under consideration here? To rephrase the questions, first, what is the religious identity of Bodhidharma as presented in the *Record of the Monasteries of Luoyang*, and how does his depiction work within the editorial agenda of that text? Second, what inferences may we draw from our literary analysis about Bodhidharma as a historical figure?

The Understanding of Religious Practice in the *Record of the Monasteries of Luoyang*

As it turns out, all we have to do is sit down and actually read the *Record of the Monasteries of Luoyang,* which provides a clear indication of the proper religious endeavors of Buddhist monks. This emerges in the following story involving a recurrent Chinese motif, the individual sent by bureaucratic mistake to the court of King Yama, where the dead are judged, but who returns to the world of the living with precious knowledge of the fate of others:

> Huining, a monk of Chongzhensi, died and regained life after seven days. He had been interrogated by King Yama, who released him because there had been a mistake with his name.
>
> When Huining described what had happened in detail, [he said that] five monks had been questioned along with him. The monk Zhisheng of Baomingsi, because of his [diligence at] seated meditation and asceticism (*zuochan kuxing*), was able to ascend to paradise. Another monk, Daopin of Banruosi, was also able to ascend to paradise because he had recited the forty-volume *Mahāparinirvāṇa Sūtra*.
>
> Another monk said, "I am Tanmozui of Rongjuesi. In lecturing on the *Mahāparinirvāṇa* and *Flower Garland Sūtras*, I had an assembly of a thousand people." King Yama said, "Lecturers on the sūtras are inclined to be discriminatory and arrogantly intimidating. This is the most detestable behavior a monk may pursue. At present I am only inquiring about seated meditation and recitation of the sūtras; I'm not asking about lecturing on the sūtras!" Tanmozui said, "This foolish monk [i.e., "I"] has since ordination only preferred to lecture on sūtras, and I never recited them from memory." Great King Yama then ordered that he be handed over to the appropriate functionaries. Immediately ten persons dressed in blue appeared and took Tanmozui toward a gate in the northwest, where the rooms were all dark. It did not seem to be a good place.
>
> Another monk, who identified himself as Daohong of Chanlinsi, said, "I gave lectures to the four groups (monks, nuns, laymen, and laywomen) of almsgivers, I made copies of the canon, and I created ten life-size

> images [of the Buddha]." Yama said, "The essence of being a monk is to control one's mind and maintain the teaching. One's dedication should be to meditating and chanting (*chan song*). You should not be involved in mundane affairs, nor undertake conditioned [activities]. Although you copied sūtras and made Buddhist images, you wanted to acquire money and things from others. Acquiring what you wanted made you only greedier, and you are not free from the three poisons that cause distress." He too was taken through the black gate in the company of Tanmozui.
>
> Another monk, Baoming of Lingjuesi, said of himself, "Before ordination I was Governor of Longxi before leaving home to become a monk. As Governor I built Lingjuesi, and upon its completion I resigned and became a monk. Although I have neither meditated nor chanted [sūtras], I was never negligent in religious worship." Yama said, "As Governor you impaired justice, twisted the law, and stole the people's property. You might claim to have built the temple, but it was not due to your efforts [alone]. Why bother me with such talk!" [Baoming] was also handed over to the functionaries, and the blue-robed [workers] took him through the black gate.

On hearing of this, the empress dowager had the details of Huining's account thoroughly verified. The story concludes:

> Thereupon, one hundred meditator monks were invited to reside within the palace, where they were supported at public expense. . . . Huining entered White Deer Mountain, where he lived in seclusion and continued to practice Buddhism. After this, monks in the capital all meditated and chanted, and did not subsequently lecture on the sūtras.[23]

What may we infer from this account? No doubt there are many fascinating aspects of this story that might attract our attention, but our sole interest here is the understanding expressed of valid religious cultivation. That is, in the *Record of the Monasteries of Luoyang* lecturing, fundraising, copying scriptures and images, and building monasteries are all rejected as superficial and without karmic benefit for monks. (The author's expectations of laypeople, especially rulers and aristocrats, were quite different.) In contrast, only two activities are promoted as being equally beneficial and having karmic benefit for monks: reciting scriptures and seated meditation, with the latter sometimes referred to as asceticism. In addition, there is a sharp dichotomy posed between the activities of seated meditation and scriptural recitation, on the one hand, and explaining the scriptures in public lectures, on the other. This dichotomy is reminiscent of that occasionally encountered in information about meditators (the best examples concern the meditator Sengchou and the scholiast Jingying Huiyuan[24] [523–92]), but what is unique here is the close identification of seated meditation with scriptural recitation.

We may conclude, therefore, that Yang Xuanzhi's depiction of Bodhidharma holding his hands together in *añjali-mudrā* and chanting *namo* was encoded as the presentation of a legitimate religious practitioner. Rather than a disconnect between the recitation of scriptures and the practice of meditation, as has been assumed in contemporary research, in this text the two were seen as effectively identical.

This argument is buttressed by the figures available to Yang that he did *not* choose to testify to the glories of the Yongningsi pagoda. In his text Yang mentions the translator Bodhiruci, as well as the lecturer Tanmozui from the account above. Bodhiruci is well known in modern scholarship as the translator of the *Sūtra on the Ten Stages* and the *Treatise on the Pure Land* attributed to Vasubandhu, and he performed some of his translation work at the very Yongningsi under consideration here. Tanmozui is not so familiar today, but he was recognized as a very gifted figure in his own times, or at least by the compiler of the *Record of the Monasteries of Luoyang*. Here we read that Bodhiruci was so impressed with Tanmozui's *Discourse on the Mahāyāna* (*Dasheng yizhang*) that he translated it into Sanskrit and submitted it to Buddhist colleagues in the "western region" for their appreciation, and they recognized its value by referring to Tanmozui as a "sage of the east" (*dongfang shengren*).[25] Hence these two figures were certainly more prominent than Bodhidharma at the time, given the prestige accorded the endeavors of translation and exegesis within traditional Chinese Buddhism, and Yang Xuanzhi's decision not to use them in this context was a meaningful editorial choice.

Therefore, although the image of "practitioner" in the *Record of the Monasteries of Luoyang* differs from that of later years, Bodhidharma is clearly depicted in this text as a revered practitioner. Since the practices of scriptural recitation and seated meditation are effectively identified here, there is no reason to differentiate between devotionalism and self-cultivation. Even more, the identification of Bodhidharma as 150 years old is testimony to the fruits of his cultivation, and to suggest that this depiction is one of a "devout and somewhat senile monk" is absurd.

In making this identification of the Bodhidharma of this text with the putative founder of the Chan school, we can only be reassured by the fact that later members of that tradition made the same connection. One indication of this is the adoption of the 150–year age for Bodhidharma in later texts, and another is the creation of a dialogue between Bodhidharma and Yang Xuanzhi found in the *Transmission of Treasure Grove* [*Monastery*] (*Baolin zhuan*) of 801.[26] It is possible, of course, that in the future we will discover some even earlier depiction of Bodhidharma, but at this point it is reasonable to conclude that it represents the oldest known point of origin for his hagiography.

PART III

Chinese Rethinking of Indian Buddhism

Chapter 8

Is Nirvāṇa the Same as Insentience? Chinese Struggles with an Indian Buddhist Ideal

Robert H. Sharf

> Certain forms of perplexity—for example, about freedom, knowledge, and the meaning of life—seem to me to embody more insight than any of the supposed solutions to those problems.
>
> —Thomas Nagel

Preamble

What makes an animate thing animate? How do we know if something is sentient? Is consciousness ultimately material or immaterial? Or is it neither—perhaps an "emergent property" that cannot be reduced to or disaggregated from a physical substrate?

These are big, complex, and conceptually muddy questions about which philosophers, biologists, and ethicists have had much to say over the millennia. Recently, cognitive psychology has gotten into the act as well, producing hundreds of empirical studies on the cognitive foundations of the conceptual distinction we make between the animate and inanimate. Studies show that very young children have markedly different predispositions (or cognitive intuitions) with regard to animate versus inanimate things, intuitions that cannot be explained as the result of language acquisition and socialization alone. Newborn infants, for example, respond to animate objects differently than they do to inanimate ones: animate entities sustain their attention for significantly longer periods of time. And young children have markedly different intuitions about the unseen interiors of objects depending upon whether said objects are registered as animate or inanimate.[1] The growing literature on the subject, representing various disciplinary and methodological perspectives, suggests that the animate/inanimate distinction is innate rather than acquired.[2]

"Animacy" or "agency" is not the only cognitive category that appears to be hardwired, but it certainly has garnered the lion's share of attention to date. This is owing to the role agency-detection is presumed to play in "theory of mind" on the one hand, and in the cross-cultural belief in supernatural agents on the other.

"Theory of mind" refers to the cognitive capacity or insight that allows young children to relate to others as conscious subjects rather than mere objects. The early acquisition of theory of mind is, according to the "theory-of-mind" theory, essential to human empathy and social bonding; a deficiency or impairment in this capacity may be responsible for autism spectrum disorders.[3] It would seem, then, that humans have evolved to distinguish, virtually from birth, animate from inanimate things, and as a species we are neurologically predisposed to regard animate entities as centers of sentient experience—in Nagel's terms, "there is something it is like to *be* that organism."[4]

Evolutionary theory offers a ready explanation for our innate neurological capacity for agency-detection: the ability to instantly register the presence of predators in the wild would have had considerable survival value for our prehistoric ancestors. But this selective advantage is gained only insofar as the agency-detection mechanism errs on the side of caution. *Is that a tiger I see in the bushes?* In such ambiguous situations, those who are biased toward false positives rather than false negatives are more likely to survive. Our agency-detection circuit explains, according to some scholars of religion, the widespread but erroneous belief that the natural world is populated by spirits, ghosts, ancestors, gods, and other supernatural agents. The evolution of a trigger-happy agency-detection neural module has become a popular naturalistic explanation for the emergence and persistence of religious belief.[5]

Does the distinction we make between "animate" and "inanimate" correspond to an objective fact—something "out there" in the natural world? Or is it merely epiphenomenal, a somewhat accidental byproduct of our cognitive evolution? The tendency, I believe, is to assume that our agency-detection circuit affords us a selective advantage precisely because it attunes us to a natural state of affairs. But the relationship between our percepts and what exists in the noumenal world is, as philosophers since the "axial age" have pointed out, a complex one, and there is reason to suspect that our perception of agency may be epiphenomenal in the same sense that our perception of color or taste or sound is epiphenomenal. That is to say, the relationship between the experience of "red" or "bitter" or "euphonious" on the one hand, and the physical and biological conditions that occasion such experiences on the other, is not mimetic in any simple sense; *qualia* such as "red" and "bitter" and "euphonious" do not inhere in the physical, mind-independent world.[6] In the same way, our visceral apprehension of things as animate or inanimate may have survival value for our species, and it may remain essential to our interactions as social animals, but this does not in itself warrant the distinction as an inherent property of the world.

There is, as it turns out, considerable evidence to support the *unnaturalness* or epiphenomenal status of the animate/inanimate distinction. The world is filled with what, borrowing from Bruno Latour, we might call "hybrids," that is, things that don't fall neatly on one side or the other of the animate/inanimate divide.[7] As our understanding of biological processes advances, the lines between mineral, plant, and animal have come to blur: should acellular agents like viruses or prions be considered forms of "life"? Are sponges or fungi or yeasts best classified as "plants" or "animals"? And where along this complex evolutionary spectrum might we draw the line between sentient and insentient? Our evolutionary development, which predisposes us to perceive things as either animate or inanimate, may help us elude predators, but it may be misleading when it comes to understanding the natural world.

The existence of hybrids that threaten taxonomic order is not the only reason to question the naturalness of the animate/inanimate distinction. Introspective reflection quickly reveals the conceptual ambiguity of terms like "mind," "self," "agency," and "consciousness." There is little consensus among psychologists, philosophers, or cognitive scientists as to the ostensive referent(s), if any, of these terms. Social scientists from Durkheim to Marx to Weber to Freud have argued that our sense of ourselves as authors of our thoughts, desires, and goals is, to a significant extent, a fiction. Many anthropologists would claim that our notions of self and identity are in large part culturally and historically determined; at the same time philosophers and neuroscientists have argued that we are not, in any simple sense, unified and self-determining agents.[8]

In working through these issues, philosophers have been drawn to various "thought experiments" (*Gedankenexperimente*). Descartes famously used the image of the "evil demon" to undermine our certainty about the veracity of the sensate world—since we know things only indirectly, through the senses, how do we know that what we perceive is real? Times have changed, and science fiction has come to replace theology as a source for puzzling but productive "intuition pumps." Philosophers now ponder "brains in vats" to evoke many of the same epistemological puzzles that preoccupied Descartes. They discuss "brain transplants" in order to hone their thinking about selfhood, identity, and embodiment. The "Turing test"—a test of a computer's ability to perfectly emulate human behavior—serves as a reference point in debates over behaviorism, determinism, and free will. ("Philosophical zombies"—fictional creatures indistinguishable from humans except that they lack subjective experience—are used to the same effect.) In the fraught debates over *qualia*, Daniel Dennett has considered a "brainstorm machine" that wires the subjective experience of one person into another, while Ned Block discusses an "inverted earth"—a planet exactly like the earth except that colors are reversed.[9] Block has also assayed the "China brain," a thought experiment in which each person in China assumes the role of a distinct neuron such that, connected by walkie-talkies, they collectively simulate the activity of a single brain.[10] (Can this collectivity be said to be "conscious"?) In each case, scholars contrive fantastic, entertaining, but implausible scenarios to help think through conundrums associated with mind-body dualism, self-identity, determinism, and the ontological status of consciousness. One can imagine scholars, some hundreds of years hence, struggling to make sense of earnest tracts on brain transplants, philosophical zombies, and the China brain.

In this chapter I examine some medieval Buddhist doctrines that, at least on the surface, seem similarly strange and implausible. Indeed, some of the Buddhist notions to be examined below were perplexing to audiences in their own day, much as discussions of brain transplants are perplexing to us today. On the Indian side, I will begin with the notion of *nirodha-samāpatti*, a meditative state akin to a vegetative coma in which all consciousness has ceased. I will then turn to a class of beings known as "beings without conception" (*asaṃjñika-sattvāḥ*), denizens of a celestial realm who are devoid of sentience, thought, and consciousness. In both cases, an insentient state seems to be followed by (or gives rise to) a sentient state, which poses serious challenges to the classical Buddhist understanding of karma. On the Chinese side, we will consider the debate over the buddha-nature of insentient objects—can an insentient thing such as a wall or roof tile attain buddhahood and preach the dharma? This doctrine too could be (and was) seen as a threat to the coherence of Buddhist teachings.

Modern scholars tend to approach such doctrines as the products of intelligent but misguided scholastics struggling to make sense of the universe, all the while hobbled by the dictates of tradition, scripture, and a prescientific understanding of the cosmos. They are the proverbial schoolmen calculating how many angels can dance on the head of a pin. But I would suggest another perspective. Such theories, I argue, serve as frames of reference for pondering issues of personal identity, ethical responsibility, sentience, and death. Given that we ourselves are still far from clarity on these issues, and given that we too devise fanciful thought experiments to help gain a conceptual toehold, perhaps it is time to look afresh at what the Buddhists might have been up to.[11]

Nirvāṇa, *Nirodha*, and Insentience

In our earliest surviving Buddhist texts, the notion of *nirvāṇa* seems pretty straightforward: *nirvāṇa*, which means literally "to blow out" or "extinguish," refers to the permanent cessation of the defilements (*kleśa*), and the final end to suffering and rebirth (*saṃsāra*).[12] There are two kinds, or better yet moments, of nirvāṇa: "nirvāṇa with remainder" (*sopadhiśeṣa-nirvāṇa*) and "nirvāṇa without remainder" (*nirupadhiśeṣa-nirvāṇa*).[13] The nirvāṇa attained by Siddhārtha as he sat under the *bodhi* tree is nirvāṇa with remainder, meaning that even though his defilements, and with them all grasping and pain, are forever extinguished, his body continues on its natural course. Nirvāṇa without remainder (sometimes called *parinirvāṇa*) refers to the final death of a buddha or *arhat* from which there is no further birth. With this final nirvāṇa the buddha or *arhat* is finished, annihilated, extinct. Indeed, in early texts this nirvāṇa looks much the same as death looks to a modern atheist who does not believe in an afterlife: it is simple annihilation or, if you will, eternal insentience.[14]

Given the mores of the day, the early Buddhist view of nirvāṇa as cessation would have seemed rather austere, grim, stoic. Despite the protests of the Buddhists, their rivals, many of whom were drawn toward a liberation more akin to eternal bliss, accused the Buddhists of being nihilists. In the *Alagaddūpama-sutta* the Buddha says:

> I have been baselessly, vainly, falsely, and wrongly misrepresented by some recluses and brahmins thus: "The recluse Gotama is one who leads astray; he teaches the annihilation, the destruction, the extermination of an existing being." As I am not, as I do not proclaim, so have I been baselessly, vainly, falsely, and wrongly misrepresented by some recluses and brahmins thus.[15]

Similarly, the *Yamaka-sutta* opens with the Venerable Yamaka musing: "As I understand the Dhamma taught by the Blessed One, a bhikkhu whose taints are destroyed is annihilated and perishes with the breakup of the body and does not exist after death." This time it is Sāriputta's turn to refute the charge. Sāriputta explains that it is not the Tathāgata or *arahant* per se that is annihilated, but rather it is the aggregates—all that is impermanent and suffering—that have "ceased and passed away."[16] Indeed, the notion that the Buddha taught the "middle path"—one of the cornerstones of Buddhism—can be seen in part as a strategy to diffuse the charge of nihilism. Again and again the scriptures insist that the Buddha's middle path rejects both nihilism (*uccheda-vāda*) and eternalism (*śāśvata-vāda*). But in claiming, first, that there is no abiding *ātman* but only a karmically conditioned psycho-physical continuum (*santāna*), and second, that the goal is the final extinction of this karmic continuum, Buddhist apologists were left without much wiggle room.

But wiggle they did. One strategy lay in simply insisting that the Buddha's nirvāṇa does not necessarily entail his eternal absence. Nirvāṇa, it was argued, only looks like cessation to the unenlightened. In truth, it is beyond thought and comprehension. This strategy is put to work in the ten (or fourteen) "undetermined" (*avyākṛta*) questions—questions on which the Buddha refused to take a position. Four of these questions bear on the Tathāgata's existence after death, viz.: Does the Tathāgata exist after death? Or does he not exist after death? Or does he both exist and not exist after death? Or does he neither exist nor not exist after death?[17]

Much has been written about the undetermined questions. Did the Buddha know the answers but refuse to reveal them because they were unnecessary distractions not conducive to liberation? Or was the Buddha incapable of answering? And if incapable, was it because he did not know the answers? Or because the questions themselves were conceptually flawed and thus unanswerable? Or because his benighted audience did not have the wherewithal to comprehend them? Various rationales have been offered, but one of the motives behind the doctrine may well have been apologetic: to defend against the charge that the Buddha was not omniscient. (That the Buddha intentionally remained silent on a number of key cosmological issues did not, in other words, bespeak his ignorance of said issues.) In any case, the Buddha's alleged refusal to comment on the possibility of post-nirvāṇic existence was one response to the charge of nihilism, since it implies that, contrary to appearances, nirvāṇa is *not* simply annihilation.

There were other wiggles as well, the most salient of which involved positing a state that so resembles nirvāṇa that the two are easily confused. This advanced meditative state, called *nirodha-samāpatti* (attainment of cessation) or *nirodha* for short, is insentience pure and simple.

Nirodha, which simply means "cessation," is an old concept that may have been widespread in the *śramaṇic* culture of the Buddha's day. (In the later *Yoga-sūtra*s attributed to Patañjali, *nirodha* refers to the final goal of yogic practice: the eradication of the defilements and the end to the illusion of separation between self and absolute.)[18] As part of his quest for enlightenment, the Buddha is said to have mastered the highest yogic techniques then available under the teachers Ārāḍa Kālāma and Udraka Rāmaputra.[19] Later Buddhist exegetes organized the meditative attainments associated with these masters into a system of eight stages of trance or equipoise, four associated with the material realm (*rūpa-dhyāna*) and four immaterial absorptions or "attainments" (*samāpatti*). Ārāḍa Kālāma is said to have taught Siddhārtha the first seven stages, culminating in the "sphere of no conception" (*ākiṃcanyāyatana*), while Udraka Rāmaputra taught him the eighth, "neither conception nor non-conception" (*naivasaṃjñānāsaṃjñāyatana*). The Buddhist scholastic tradition is generally clear that these rarified states of trance may be useful, particularly for those who aspire to supernormal powers, but they are not essential to the Buddhist path. It seems that one of the motives behind the systematization of these meditative states was to assimilate and subordinate, at one and the same time, the practices and teachings of rival ascetic traditions.[20]

In early Buddhist materials the term *nirodha* is more or less synonymous with nirvāṇa; *nirodha* regularly appears as a shorthand for the third noble truth (*duḥkha-nirodha* "cessation of suffering"), for example.[21] But as the tradition develops, *nirodha* takes on a second, more technical meaning; it now denotes an extraordinary state of meditative absorption, a ninth trance (or fifth *samāpatti*) set above the "sphere of neither conception nor non-conception," in which, according to most accounts, all conscious activity is extinguished. In this state the ongoing continuum of mental factors is not merely inhibited or suppressed but, more radically, ceases altogether, if only temporarily. The only thing that distinguishes this state from death is that the physical body remains alive, sustained by the dharmas of "heat" (*uṣman*) and "vitality" (*āyus*).[22]

Having distinguished *nirodha* from nirvāṇa, scholiasts were free to contrast the two; they could argue that those who see the Buddha as preaching annihilation mistake the state of *nirodha-samāpatti* for nirvāṇa. Apparently, the mistake is easy to make: Buddhaghosa himself seems to consider *nirodha* phenomenologically close to, if not identical with, nirvāṇa. In his *Visuddhimagga*, in response to the question why an advanced practitioner would aspire to *nirodha*, he writes: "Being wearied by the occurrence and dissolution of formations, they attain [*nirodha*], thinking 'Let us dwell in bliss by being without consciousness here and now and reaching the cessation that is nibbana.'"[23]

Much has been written about *nirodha*, notably the fine study by Paul Griffiths (which builds on the work of Lambert Schmithausen).[24] I will, therefore, forgo an extended treatment here, and simply confine myself to some of the conceptual puzzles entailed by this rather peculiar state.

There is no minimizing the philosophical and doctrinal problems that attend the notion of *nirodha*. The central teaching of Buddhism is precisely that all things arise due to causes, and that *saṃsāra* is sustained by—or better, coextensive with—the psycho-physical continuum (*santāna*) of dharmas. Once the continuum of mental events ceases—once the chain is broken—it is difficult to account for its reappearance at a later point in time. (The insentient yogi certainly cannot *will* himself out of *nirodha*.) And what happens if someone dies in *nirodha*? Logically, you cannot be reborn, since there is no final moment of consciousness to impel a future birth. Thus death in *nirodha* should be tantamount to nirvāṇa without remainder. But the tradition is clear that *nirodha* is *not* nirvāṇa, and besides, *śamatha* practices and states such as *nirodha* are not supposed to yield, in and of themselves, final liberation.

Different exegetical traditions responded to these conundrums in different ways. As to how one emerges from *nirodha*, Buddhaghosa states that the yogi, prior to entering *nirodha*, resolves to emerge after a specified period of time, typically seven days. (Buddhaghosa notes that the prudent yogi will take additional vows to emerge earlier should he be needed by the community or summoned by the master, lest he inconvenience anyone by his absence.)[25] But the Theravāda commentaries fail to explain, from the standpoint of karma theory, how the vow works; it would appear that the effective force of the vow is extrinsic to the psycho-physical continuum of the yogi. Meanwhile, some Sarvāstivādin exegetes such as Saṅghabhadra solve the problem through the signature Sarvāstivādin theory that dharmas exist in all three periods of time, a theory that allows for causal continuity across the temporal gap. Since past dharmas continue to exist in the present (and future), and since there are no intervening moments of consciousness during *nirodha*, the last moment of consciousness prior to *nirodha* can be said to be the "contiguous" or "proximate" (*samanantara*) condition for the subsequent arising of mind that marks the end of *nirodha*.[26]

There were other theories as well. The Sautrāntikas, for example, held to the "mutual seeding" of mind and body, meaning that the karmic seeds of mental activity lie dormant in the physical body during *nirodha*. Advocates of the seed theory insist that this is, in principle, no different from the situation of the inhabitants of the formless realms, who eventually will be reborn in one of the lower realms of form or desire. Beings in the formless realms don't have physical bodies, so in order to give rise to one in a subsequent birth the "seeds" of the physical aggregate (*rūpa-skandha*) must have remained dormant in their mental continua during their formless existence. The Yogācāras appear to have built on this seed theory with their notion of the *ālayavijñāna* (store-house consciousness).[27] The unmanifest or noumenal *ālayavijñāna*, which persists during *nirodha*, stores all mental and physical karmic seeds, thus effectively eliminating the problem. Finally, Dārṣṭāntikas such as Vasumitra simply assert that conscious activity is not completely eliminated in *nirodha*; rather, some kind of "subtle thought" (**sūkṣmacitta*) or "unmanifest thinking consciousness" (*aparisphuṭamanovijñāna*) persists throughout the comatose state.[28]

As for the problem of dying while in *nirodha*, various ad hoc solutions were proffered. Buddhaghosa says that before entering *nirodha*, the yogi must use his preternatural powers to determine the time of death, so as to ensure that he emerges before his allotted lifespan is up. Some commentators also hold that *nirodha* renders the body indestructible, and thus it is simply impossible to die while in *nirodha*. (Buddhaghosa cites the story of Mahā Nāga, who sat immobile in cessation while the building around him caught fire and burned to the ground. Mahā Nāga is embarrassed when he emerges several days later and is accused of being a "lazy monk"!)[29] Finally, some traditions, including the Sarvāstivāda, hold that only noble ones (*ārya*) or an elite subset thereof are capable of attaining *nirodha*; spiritually undeserving worldlings (*pṛthagjana*) could not, therefore, use *nirodha* as a shortcut to nirvāṇa.[30]

It is clear that the concept of *nirodha* spawned a number of complex and somewhat exotic theories to account for the return of consciousness following its cessation. But putting such theories aside, I would ask: *why did the Buddhists need such a nirodha in the first place*? Why contrive a state that (1) seems so similar to nirvāṇa as to invite confusion, and at the same time (2) seems to violate, or at least threaten, the Buddhist understanding of cause and effect?

Might the uncanny similarity to nirvāṇa be precisely the point? The Buddhists were, in effect, saddled with a notion of nirvāṇa—extinction—that, however attractive it may have been to an early tradition of forest-dwelling ascetics, appeared to later audiences distressingly like an end to conscious existence. By devising a state that was almost, but not quite, identical to nirvāṇa, the Buddhists could argue that the desire for nirvāṇa was not, despite appearances, a desire for annihilation.

Insentient Beings

In the *Pāṭika-sutta* of the *Dīgha-nikāya*, in a discussion of various theories of creation, we find to following curious passage,

> There are, Bhaggava, some ascetics and Brahmins who declare that the beginning of things was due to chance. I went to them and asked them if this was their view. "Yes," they replied. I asked them how this came about, and when they could not explain, I said: "There are, friends, certain devas called Without Conception. As soon as a perception arises in them, those devas fall from that realm . . . *remembering nothing* they think: 'Now from non-being I have been brought to being.' That, Reverend Sirs, is how it comes about that you teach that the beginning of things was due to chance."[31]

The "devas without conception" (*asaṃjñika-sattvāḥ*, *asāṃjñika-deva*, Pali: *asañña-sattā-nāma-devā*) mentioned here are a class of celestial beings that have no cognition or consciousness or sentience at all; Theravāda commentators consider them "one-aggregate-beings" constituted by the material aggregate alone.[32] These rather odd creatures abide in one of the seven (or eight or nine) heavens of the "fourth *dhyāna* sphere" (*caturtha-dhyāna-bhūmi*), the highest of the four spheres of the realm of form (*rūpa-dhātu*).

Rebirth in the heavens of the fourth *dhyāna* sphere comes about through mastery of the fourth *dhyāna*. While there are varying enumerations of the heavens of the fourth sphere, one common scheme places the Heaven of the Gods Without Conception together with (or as a subdivision of) the Heaven of Extensive Rewards (Bṛhatphalāḥ) in the lower strata.[33] These two abodes are available to *pṛthagjana*s (ordinary persons who have not yet attained the stage of *ārya* or noble ones) who may or may not have been followers of the Buddha-dharma. The remaining five heavens—Avṛhā, Atapā, Sudṛsā, Sudarśanā, and Akaniṣṭhā—are collectively known as the Pure Abodes (*śuddhāvāsa*) since, unlike the lower two, they are reserved for Buddhist non-returners (*anāgāmin*). The beings of the lower two heavens live for five hundred eons (*kalpa*), while those in the higher heavens live for anywhere from one thousand eons to, in the case of the gods of the Akaniṣṭha Heaven, sixteen thousand eons.[34]

The notion of an entire heaven consisting exclusively of mindless zombies, all of whom had previously mastered the absorption of non-consciousness (*asaṃjñi-samāpatti*), raised similar issues to those that dogged the idea of *nirodha*: once the continuum of consciousness has been severed, how does it get going again? And how is rebirth out of such an existence possible? Thus it is not surprising to find these states discussed together in the major compendia of the Sarvāstivāda and Yogācāra schools, including the *Abhidharmakośabhāṣya*, *Mahāvibhāṣāśāstra*, *Nyāyānusāra*, and *Cheng weishi lun*.

Such texts contain, for example, extended exchanges about whether the gods without conception are devoid of consciousness altogether, or whether, as some claim of *nirodha*, there is some residual or subliminal consciousness that persists some or all of the time. This issue constitutes one of the controversies addressed in the *Kathāvatthu* (3.11), where the Andhakas claim that some consciousness must exist, if only for a short time, at the beginning and end of one's existence in the Heaven of the Gods Without Conception.[35] In fact, most commentators agree that it is the eventual reappearance of consciousness in a mindless god that triggers, almost but not quite immediately, rebirth back into the realm of form (*kāma-dhātu*). The alternative scenario, namely, that of a god dying while still mindless and being reborn as a sentient being, would have engendered the same conundrum as death while in *nirodha*. The *Abhidharmakośabhāṣya*, for example, explains,

> Question: Are the Non-Conscious Ones called this because they are always non-conscious, or are they sometimes conscious? Answer: They are conscious at birth and at death; they are called non-conscious because their consciousness is suspended for a very long time. When, after this long time, they produce a consciousness again, they die. As it says in the *sūtra*, "When they produce consciousness again, they die, like a person awakening after sleep." Dying in the non-conscious heaven, they are necessarily reborn in the realm of form and nowhere else. In fact, the force of *asaṃjñi-samāpatti*, by which these beings are born among the Non-Conscious Ones, is exhausted; they have not been in a position to practice *asaṃjñi-samāpatti*: hence they die, as arrows fall to the ground when their impetus is spent.[36]

This image of the arrow falling back to earth after its inertia is spent is also found in Buddhaghosa's analysis of the mindless gods in his commentary to the *Dīgha-nikāya*.[37] This analogy may have been widely employed in attempts to escape the karmic conundrum, but it does not address the underlying problem, namely, in the absence of the conscious stream—in the absence of any aggregate other than that of form (*rūpa-skandha*)—what sustains or transmits this inertial mental energy?

That others insisted on alternative mechanisms, such as the persistence of some subtle consciousness while still in a mindless state, is evidence the problem is not ours alone.

While there was some agreement among Sarvāstivādin exegetes that there must be some moments, however brief, of consciousness at the beginning and end of one's sojourn in this realm, the precise duration of these moments became a topic of some debate.[38] But the Sarvāstivādins had another problem as well, namely, how to account for a state that is characterized primarily by an absence. The Sarvāstivādins held that *all* phenomena result from the interactions of discrete and irreducible dharmas that persist through time, and thus if the existence of gods without conception is characterized by "mindlessness," this mindlessness must, they reasoned, be the defining property of a unique dharma. So they were obliged to posit one.

> Among the beings who take birth among the Non-Conscious Ones, i.e., the non-conscious gods, there is a dharma that arrests the mind and its mental states, and which is called "Non-consciousness." By this dharma, the mind and future dharmas are, for a certain time, hindered from being produced and do not have the power to arise. This dharma is similar to what arrests the water of a river, that is, to a dike. This dharma is exclusively the retribution of non-conscious absorption (*asaṃjñi-samāpatti*).[39]

Such a mechanism or dharma was required to account for (1) the state of "non-conception" (*āsaṃjñika*) of the mindless devas, (2) the "absorption of non-conception" (*acittaka-samāpatti*, *asaṃjñi-samāpatti*) that gave rise to it, as well as (3) the attainment of *nirodha*. All three phenomena are characterized by mindlessness, and all are grouped together by Sarvāstivādins in the category of "conditioned factors dissociated from thought" (*cittaviprayukta-saṃskāra*).[40] In each case, the Sarvāstivādins (or at least the Sarvāstivāda-Vaibhāṣikas) associated the absence of cognition or mindlessness with an irreducible ontic entity; as Saṅghabhadra writes, "apart from the moment of thought just prior [to cessation], there definitely exists a discrete dharma that is capable of obstructing mind."[41]

While these three states would seem to be identical with respect to their content, namely mindlessness, they are each associated with their *own* individual dharma. Collett Cox explains,

> These factors all do the same thing—they obstruct thought—but they are "distinguished by their location, the practitioner who produces them, their

> intended purpose, and so on . . ." For the Sarvāstivāda-Vaibhāṣikas, this activity entails the obstruction of both the single thought factor (*citta*) that demarcates each moment of the mental stream and the simultaneous and associated thought concomitants (*caitta*) that represent the various mental events operating in each moment."[42]

Logically, these rather unusual dharmas belong neither to the domain of mind nor to the domain of form, which is why they end up placed among the aforementioned "conditioned factors dissociated from thought."

Many Buddhist scholiasts found this an unwarranted reification. Mindlessness could be explained adequately, they felt, by reference to what happens immediately preceding such a state—there was simply no need to associate the ensuing *absence* of conception with a discrete dharma. Thus Vasubandhu regarded all three states of mindlessness as simply "provisional designations that describe the condition of the non-operation of thought (*apravṛttimātra*); they do not exist as real entities."[43]

Putting aside, once again, these rather involved debates, we are prompted to ask, *why did the Buddhists need the mindless gods in the first place?* Were there not enough Buddhist heavens already? Why complicate things with a heaven that would further rattle their understanding of karma and rebirth?

As for the origins of the Heaven of the Gods Without Conception, the *Pāṭika-sutta* cited above suggests one theory, according to which the mindless gods are invoked to explain the heterodox belief in *creatio ex nihilo*. As creation from nothing is, according to the Buddhists, *prima facie* irrational ("I asked them how this came about, and . . . they could not explain"), the notion must persist due to the testimony of those who, in their previous life, were mindless gods and thus cannot recollect their previous state: "'There are, friends, certain devas called Unconscious. As soon as a perception arises in them, those devas fall from that realm . . . *remembering nothing* they think: 'Now from non-being I have been brought to being.' That, Reverend Sirs, is how it comes about that you teach that the beginning of things was due to chance." This ingenious if fanciful explanation for the heretical belief in creatio ex nihilo suggests an early association, at least in the minds of scholiasts, between mindlessness on the one hand, and simple inexistence (*nihilum*) on the other. I will return to this below.

Whatever the origins of this cosmological oddity, the exegetical tradition was drawn to the mindless gods not because of their role in perpetuating a spurious creation myth, but rather by the question of how they lost their minds in the first place. As mentioned above, the denizens of the fourth *dhyāna* sphere were all previously masters of the fourth *dhyāna*. But the fourth *dhyāna* sphere is comprised of multiple heavens; why are some born in one heaven and some in another?

The answer lies in the differences in the *manner* of their yogic attainment—the use of different meditation objects or techniques, for example, or differences in the practitioners' intentions or motivations (*chanda*). We have seen that only *pṛthagjana*—yogis who have not yet attained the stage of the noble ones—are reborn among the mindless gods, while the higher heavens are reserved for Buddhist *ārya*. But there is another thing the mindless gods have in common: they were all motivated to attain *dhyāna* by an aversion to sentient experience, and hence they intentionally cultivated the "absorption of non-conception" (*asaṃjñi-samāpatti*). Due to their erroneous belief that conception is itself the cause of all suffering, and that the ultimate goal of yogic practice is a state in which there is no cognition, they engaged in practices designed to arrest all conscious activity and experience.

This explanation is found in works associated with virtually all of the major scholastic traditions. Buddhaghosa's commentary to the *Dīgha-nikāya*, for example, explains rebirth among the mindless gods as follows:

> Someone who has gone forth in a non-Buddhist school does the preparatory work [for *jhāna*], achieves the fourth *jhāna*, emerges and sees the fault in consciousness; he thinks, "When there is consciousness there is the pain of hands being cut off and all sorts of fears; enough of consciousness, only the unconscious state is peaceful." Once he has seen the fault of consciousness in this way, if he dies without having lost the *jhāna* he is reborn among the unconscious beings. With the cessation of the death-consciousness his mind disappears from this world and only the physical aggregate appears there [in the world of unconscious beings].[44]

The *Abhidharmakośabhāṣya* provides much the same account:

> The ascetic falsely imagines that non-conception (*āsaṃjñika*), the non-conception that constitutes the result of the absorption of non-conception, is true deliverance. . . . This absorption is cultivated only by *pṛthagjanas*, not by *āryas*. The *āryas* consider this absorption as a precipice, a calamity, and do not value entering it. On the contrary, *pṛthagjanas* identify non-consciousness with true deliverance; they have no idea of "going out" with respect to it; hence they cultivate the absorption that leads to it.[45]

The *Cheng weishi lun* concurs:

> As for the unconscious gods, they are born into that heaven through the power of their aversion to profane thought that attends their cultivation of the absorption [of non-conception]. Since the principle is the obstruction of the mental factors that are not perpetually active [i.e., all conscious activity except that of the *ālayavijñāna* and the *manas*] as well as the cessation of all conscious thought, they are called unconscious gods. Therefore, all six consciousnesses have been eliminated in them. . . .
>
> The absorption of non-conception belongs to ordinary people (*pṛthagjana*) who have subdued the craving of the Śubhakṛtsna [Realm—the highest heaven of the third *dhyāna*], but who have not yet subdued the defilements of the higher [realms]. Since their primary motivation is liberation from conception, this causes the cessation of the mental factors that are not perpetually active as well as the objects of mind. Since the cessation of conception is foremost, it is called "without conception," and since it renders the body serene and harmonious, it is also called "absorption."[46]

This gets to the crux of the difference between the absorption of cessation (*nirodha-samāpatti*) on the one hand, and the absorption of non-conception (*asaṃjñi-samāpatti*) and the beings without conception (*asaṃjñikasattvāḥ*) on the other. *Nirodha* is reserved for noble ones (*ārya*) who, while free of aversion to consciousness, nevertheless seek a temporary respite from it. Although *nirodha* is not inimical to the Buddhist path, it is not essential either. In contrast, the mindlessness of the mindless gods comes about through a profound error: ignorantly believing that insentience is the goal, their meditation practice was directed toward the cessation of consciousness rather than the cessation of *saṃsāra*.[47]

In short, Buddhist scholiasts needed not just one kind of mindlessness to contrast with nirvāṇa, but two: one (*nirodha-samāpatti*) which is acceptable if not laudable, and another (*asaṃjñi-samāpatti*) which is baneful.[48] In both cases, a clear distinction was drawn between non-conception or insentience on the one hand, and true liberation on the other. But in conjuring states that look like nirvāṇa but are not, the tradition gerrymandered the soteriological landscape. The gerrymandering is evident in the topographical confusion that resulted. Note, for example, that *asaṃjñi-samāpatti*—the fourth-*dhyāna* absorption of non-conception that leads to birth as a mindless god—is, for all intents and purposes, phenomenologically identical with *nirodha*; both entail the cessation of all conscious activity. As we have seen, the similarities were appreciated by the exegetical tradition. But this created a problem, namely, where to locate *asaṃjñi-samāpatti* among the hierarchy of dhyānic states, and where to locate the heaven of mindless gods in the hierarchal cosmology of the three realms.

There is a natural progression among the *rūpa-dhyāna*s, with each successive absorption marked by the elimination of certain factors present in the previous stage. Thus in the first *dhyāna* the factors of investigation (*vitarka*), observation (*vicāra*), joy (*prīti*), happiness (*sukha*) and concentration (*samādhi*) are all active. The second *dhyāna* is characterized by the elimination of investigation and observation, leaving only joy, happiness, and concentration. In the third, joy drops away, leaving happiness and concentration, and in the fourth concentration alone remains. These *rūpa-dhyāna*s are succeeded, in turn, by the *arūpa-dhyāna*s, which continue the progression toward increasingly rarefied states until we reach a point when consciousness itself ceases completely:

1: the abode of limitless space (*akāśa-anantya-āyatana*)
2: the abode of limitless consciousness (*vijñāna-anantya-āyatana*)
3: the abode of nothingness (*akiñcanya-āyatana*)
4: the abode of neither conception nor non-conception (*naivasaṃjñāna-asaṃjña-āyatana*)
5: *nirodha*

Given the internal logic of the sequence, one would expect to find *asaṃjñi-samāpatti*—the attainment of non-conception—located among the formless *dhyāna*s, abutting *nirodha* perhaps. After all, in terms of content (or lack thereof), *asaṃjñi-samāpatti* appears to be identical with *nirodha*. But this would create an insoluble problem: with the noted exception of *nirodha*, each of the *dhyāna*s has a corresponding heaven. Were *asaṃjñi-samāpatti* placed in the formless sphere, masters of this absorption would be born into a realm in which they lacked not only minds but bodies as well. And even the most adroit Buddhist exegete would have had a difficult time explaining that! So *asaṃjñi-samāpatti* had to find a place among the *rūpa-dhyāna*s, and the mindless gods a corresponding heaven in the realm of form. *Asaṃjñi-samāpatti* is accordingly situated among the highest of the *rūpa-dhyāna*s, but even then there is confusion, as the tradition could not agree on its precise geographical location; some texts situate it within the Heaven of Extensive Rewards (Bṛhatphalāḥ), while others see the two realms as distinct.

What are we to make of this? The tacit assumption among scholars seems to be that the architectonic systems associated with Buddhist scholasticism are the products of obsessive literalists unable or unwilling to step beyond the confines of scriptural orthodoxy. But perhaps the architects of the system were not as slavish to tradition as some might assume. Perhaps the proliferation of bodies without minds and minds without bodies are better viewed as thought experiments bearing on existential conundrums of inarguable import to the tradition: conundrums relating to insentience, death, nothingness, and nirvāṇa. Contemplating variant versions of mindlessness allowed them to refine their understanding of the path and the goal, and to rebut the charge of nihilism—the allegation that Buddhists preach mindlessness and that nirvāṇa is a mystification of insentience.

And this brings us to China and to Chan.

Terminological Confusions

The notions of non-conceptualization, cessation, and nirvāṇa are all inextricably tied to the seminal Buddhist doctrine of "non-self" (*anātman*). It is precisely because there is no permanent, unchanging, ontologically extant self or soul that the temporary cessation of consciousness in *nirodha*, and the permanent cessation of the aggregates in nirvāṇa, can be construed in positive terms. Buddhist practice, as depicted in the early textual tradition, is directed not toward the realization of some true self or transcendent other, but rather to the end of delusion. The notions of non-self (*anātman*), non-conception (*asaṃjñā*), cessation (*nirodha*), and nirvāṇa are all intertwined in complex and sometimes contentious ways.

The Buddhist tradition employed a host of terms in their technical analyses of self, consciousness, and personhood. *Vijñāna*, *citta*, *saṃjña*, and *manas* are among the Sanskrit terms commonly used for what we might call mind, consciousness, cognition, or conception, for example, and "self" can be rendered, depending on context and ethical valence, as *ātman*, *pudgala*, or *sattva*. The distinctions among these terms are not always easy to parse, and there are inconsistencies in usage across our sources.

As we move to China, the terminological complexity is exacerbated by the problem of translation and the profusion of alternative Sinitic renderings of key Indic terms. Some equivalences became somewhat standardized in mature Chinese translations of South Asian sources: *wuwo* for *anātman*; *miejinding* for *nirodha-samāpatti*; *wuxiang* for *asaṃjñā*; and so on. But at the same time we find *vijñāna*, *citta*, *saṃjña*, and *manas* all rendered, in different contexts, as *xin*, for example, and *xin*, *xiang*, and even *shi* are not consistently or clearly distinguished in commentarial materials.

The terminological confusion slips into havoc as we turn to indigenous Chinese Buddhist exegesis on a term such as *wuxin* or "no mind"—a multivocalic term with roots in both Buddhist and non-Buddhist Chinese traditions. Much has already been written on the term, but given its relevance to the issues at hand a few words are in order.

One of the earliest appearances of *wuxin* is in *Laozi* 49, where it appears as a textual variant: "The sage is always mindless (*wuxin*); he considers the minds of the common people to be his own mind."[49] But the pre-Buddhist use of the concept is more commonly associated with *Zhuangzi*, notably a passage in chapter 12, "Heaven and Earth":

> Those who shepherded the world in ancient times were without desire and the world was satisfied, without action and the ten thousand things were transformed. They were deep and silent and the hundred clans were at rest. The Record says: "Stick to the One and the ten thousand tasks will be accomplished; achieve mindlessness (*wuxin*) and the gods and spirits will bow down."[50]

Like the *Laozi* passage, *Zhuangzi* could here be understood as claiming that the sage has no desire, volition, or intentionality of his own; rather, he responds spontaneously to the needs of others. This is in keeping with the image of the sage emperors of old, who did not act (*wuwei*) yet ruled well; they did nothing, but nothing was left undone.[51] "No mind" in such passages may simply refer to the absence of intention or desire or egotism, and there is little reason to equate it with insentience or unconsciousness.

However, in chapter 22 of the *Zhuangzi* there is a more intriguing passage, a song by Piyi:

> Body like a withered corpse,
> mind like dead ashes,
> true in the realness of knowledge,
> not one to go searching for reasons,
> dim dim, dark dark,
> mindless, you cannot consult with him:
> what kind of man is this![52]

The notion of a mind "like dead ashes" comes closer to the notion of insentience proper, and, as we will see below, this caught the attention of later Buddhist commentators.

Turning to Buddhist understandings of *wuxin*, scholars often cite Sengzhao (374–414) as an influential early source on the subject. Unfortunately, although the term appears some fifteen times in his *Collected Essays* (*Zhaolun*), it is difficult to pin Sengzhao down on his understanding of the term; as is often the case with this author, the passages in question are susceptible to multiple, sometimes contradictory, readings. The following passage, from the essay *Prajñā Has No Knowing* (*Banruo wuzhi lun*), is typical:

> Objection: Though the mind of the sage is without knowing, it does not err in its path of responding to situations. Therefore, it responds to what should be responded to, and leaves alone what should not be responded to. Consequently, the mind of the sage sometimes arises and sometimes ceases. How can this be?
>
> Reply: "Arising and ceasing" is the arising and ceasing of mind. As the sage has no mind, how can arising and ceasing occur therein? Thus it is not that there is no mind, but only that his mind is without mind. Also, it is not that he does not respond, but only that his response is without response.[53]

Sengzhao may be echoing the ideal referenced in *Laozi* and *Zhuangzi* above, namely, that the sage has no intentions (or even agency) of his own; the sage responds spontaneously in accord with cosmic necessity. While Sengzhao's writings are not always clear, here too there is little evidence that *wuxin* was understood as unconsciousness or insentience.

With the emergence of early Chan, however, the notion of *wuxin* is brought to the fore, along with a number of related and equally complex notions such as *jueguan* (severing discernment), *linian* (transcending thought), and *wunian* (no thought). While there is little consensus in our sources on the use and application of these terms—early Chan writers often champion one term as denoting correct practice while disparaging others—all these terms appear in discussions concerning the relationship of means and ends in Buddhist *dhyāna* practice.[54] And repeatedly, the controversies bear on the relationship between Buddhist practice on the one hand, and the simple insentience (*wuqing*) of the physical world on the other. This, I will suggest, gave rise to the Chinese Buddhist thought experiment *par excellence*: the notion that insentient objects possess buddha-nature, become enlightened, and preach the dharma.

The Buddha-Nature of Insentient Objects

The medieval Chinese controversy concerning the buddha-nature of insentient objects (*wuqing foxing*) extended over several centuries and involved leading clerics from every major Chinese Buddhist tradition. The source materials are, accordingly, vast and complex. As I have written on the topic elsewhere, I will limit the discussion below to an overview of the key players, texts, and issues bearing on the debate.[55]

The roots of the doctrine are usually traced to the monk Daosheng (360–434), who may have been the first in China to insist that all living beings, including *icchantika* (*yichanti*), possess buddha-nature. This was an odd if not oxymoronic claim. *Icchantika* is a technical term for beings who lack the potential for buddhahood; they are, by definition, bereft of "buddha-nature." Nevertheless, Daosheng's controversial pronouncement was vindicated with the appearance of a new recension of the *Nirvāṇa-sūtra* in 421, which stated that all beings—including *icchantika*—possess buddha-nature and will eventually attain enlightenment. While this "northern-recension" of the *Nirvāṇa-sūtra* is celebrated as the earliest canonical sanction for the universality of buddha-nature, it clearly restricts buddha-nature to the sentient. In the oft-repeated words of the scripture, "'Non-buddha-nature' refers to insentient things such as walls and fences, tiles and stones. Everything apart from insentient things such as these is called 'buddha-nature.'"[56]

More than a century later the monk Jingying Huiyuan (523–592) revisited the *Nirvāṇa-sūtra*'s position in the context of the relationship between "buddha-nature" and "originally pure mind." Huiyuan approached the topic by distinguishing between buddha-nature as a mode of cognition ("the buddha-nature that knows") and buddha-nature as the metaphysical ground that makes such cognition possible ("the buddha-nature that is known"). The former, which is capable of awakening through the elimination of ignorance, is restricted to living beings; this, according to Huiyuan, is the referent of the *Nirvāṇa-sūtra* passage. The latter—the "nature that is known"—is the dharma-realm itself, and thus it logically encompasses all things, both animate and inanimate.[57]

A similar strategy is found in the writings of the Sanlun exegete Jizang (549–623). Following a Mādhyamika line of reasoning, Jizang argues that the distinction between sentient and insentient cannot pertain at the level of ultimate truth.[58] As such, if you deny buddha-nature to something,

> then not only are grass and trees devoid of buddha-nature, but living beings are also devoid of buddha-nature. But if you hold to the existence of buddha-nature, then it is not only living beings that have buddha-nature, but grass and trees must also have buddha-nature. . . . If we understand that all dharmas are equal and do not view the two marks of the contingent and the absolute, then in reality there are no marks of attainment or non-attainment. Since there is no non-attainment, we provisionally speak of attaining buddhahood. Thus at the moment when sentient beings attain buddhahood, all grass and trees also attain buddhahood.[59]

Jizang is quick, however, to concede that this represents the perspective of "pervasiveness" (*tongmen*, i.e., absolute truth). From the perspective of "difference" (*biemen*, i.e., conventional truth), it makes little sense to speak of grass and trees actually attaining enlightenment.

> Because sentient beings have mental delusions, they can attain awakening. Grass and trees have no mind, and thus they have no delusion. What would it mean for them to obtain awakening? It is like waking from a dream: if you are not dreaming, then you cannot wake up from it. Therefore it is said [in the *Nirvāṇa-sūtra*] that since sentient beings possess buddha-nature they can attain buddhahood, but since grass and trees are devoid of buddha-nature they cannot attain buddhahood.[60]

This "two-truth" hermeneutic allowed scholiasts to affirm the universality of buddha-nature while upholding (from a provisional perspective) the teachings of the *Nirvāṇa-sūtra*. Several other writers, including the Huayan patriarch Fazang (643–712) and the Tiantai patriarch Zhanran (711–782), adopted a similar tactic to defend the buddha-nature of the insentient. Zhanran, to pick but one example, writes, "The individual of the perfect [teaching] knows, from beginning to end, that the absolute principle is non-dual, and that there are no objects apart from mind. Who then is sentient? What then is insentient? Within the Assembly of the Lotus there are no differences."[61]

While the treatment of the buddha-nature controversy by renowned monks such as Huiyuan, Jizang, Fazang, and Zhanran has been studied in some detail, less attention has been paid to the controversy as it appears in early Chan materials.

As it turns out, the buddha-nature-of-the-insentient doctrine surfaces in a surprising number of Dunhuang manuscripts, and it was evidently the focus of a passionate (if not rancorous) debate among leading Tang Dynasty Chan prelates. This debate bore directly on the relationship between Buddhist practice, enlightenment, ethics, insentience, and death.

The earliest reference to the topic in a Chan lineage text is found in the *Record of the Masters and Disciples of the Laṅkāvatāra* (*Lengqie shizi ji*) attributed to Jingjue (683–ca. 750).[62] Here both the fourth patriarch Daoxin (580–651) and the fifth patriarch Hongren (601–674) are depicted defending the notion that insentient objects not only possess buddha-nature but also "preach the dharma." Hongren, for example, says, "At the moment when you are in the temple sitting in meditation, is your body not also sitting in meditation beneath the trees of the mountain forests? Are earth, trees, tiles, and stones not also able to sit in meditation? Are earth, trees, tiles, and stones not also able to see forms and hear sounds, wear a robe and carry a bowl? When the *Laṅkāvatāra-sūtra* speaks of the dharma-body of the realm of objects, it [refers to] precisely this."[63] For both Daoxin and Hongren, the non-duality of the subjective and objective realms, as well as the *Laṅkāvatāra* doctrine that "all is mind," lead directly to the inference that even the inanimate objects of our perception can be said to preach the dharma.

A more developed discussion of the doctrine can be found in a slightly later text, the *Treatise on Severing Discernment* (*Jueguan lun*), also found at Dunhuang,[64]

> [The student] asks, "Is the Way found only in embodied spiritual entities, or does it reside in grass and trees as well?" [The master] replied, "There is no place the Way does not pervade." Question: "If the Way is pervasive, why is it a crime to kill a person, whereas it is not a crime to kill grass and trees?" Answer: "Talk of whether it is a crime or not is a matter related to sentience and is thus not the true Way. It is only because worldly people have not attained the Way and falsely believe in a personal self, that their murder entails mental [intent]. This intent bears karmic fruit, and thus we speak of it as a crime. Grass and trees have no sentience and thus originally are in accord with the Way. As they are free of a self, there is no calculation involved in killing them, and thus we do not argue over whether it is a crime or not.
>
> "Now one who is free of a self and is in accord with the Way looks at his own body as he would at grass or at trees. He treats the cutting of his own body as do trees in a forest. . . ."

> Question: "If grass and trees have long been in accord with the Way, why do the scriptures not record the buddhahood of grass or trees, but only of persons?" Answer: "They do not only record [the buddhahood] of persons, but of grass and trees as well. A scripture says, 'A single mote of dust contains all dharmas.' Another says, 'All dharmas are suchness; all sentient beings are also suchness.'[65] Suchness is devoid of any duality or discrimination."[66]

This argument is a significant departure from the Mādhyamika-style arguments associated with the Sanlun, Tiantai, and Huayan writers mentioned earlier. Rather than insisting that, from the perspective of ultimate truth, there is no distinction between insentient and sentient, the *Treatise on Severing Discernment* argues that grass and trees have buddha-nature *precisely because* they are insentient. Being insentient they have no mind (*wuxin*) and thus no thought of "me" or "mine" and no fear of death. Insentient things are not only "in accord with the way" but they are de facto buddhas!

This innovative position seems to have been favored by masters associated with the so-called Northern and the Ox-Head lineages of Chan, masters who playfully proclaim that insentient objects "cultivate realization" and "become buddhas."[67] It may thus be significant that one of the most strident *critiques* of the doctrine is found in the record of Heze Shenhui (684–758)—the de facto founder of the Southern school of Chan. In his *Recorded Sayings* he debates an Ox-Head master on precisely this point:

> Chan Master Yuan of Ox-Head Mountain asked: "[You say that] buddha-nature permeates all sentient things and does not permeate all insentient things. I heard a venerable elder say:
>
> Lush groves of emerald bamboos,
> Are wholly the dharma-body.
> Luxuriant clusters of chrysanthemums,
> Nothing is not *prajñā* (wisdom).[68]
>
> Now why do you say that [buddha-nature] only permeates sentient things and does not permeate insentient things?" [Shenhui] answered: "Surely you do not mean that the merit of groves of emerald bamboos equals that of the dharma-body, or that the wisdom of clusters of chrysanthemums is the same as *prajñā*? If the groves of bamboos and chrysanthemums are

> equal to the dharma-body and to *prajñā*, then in which sūtra does the Tathāgata predict that an emerald bamboo or a chrysanthemum will attain *bodhi*? The notion that emerald bamboos and chrysanthemums are the same as the dharma-body and *prajñā* is a heterodox doctrine. Why so? Because the *Nirvāṇa-sūtra* says: 'That which lacks buddha-nature is deemed an insentient thing.'"[69]

Shenhui is believed to have been instrumental in shaping the biography of the Sixth Patriarch and the *Platform Scripture of the Sixth Patriarch* (*Liuzu tanjing*). As such, it is not surprising to find that surviving versions of the *Platform Scripture* also come out in opposition to the buddha-nature-of-the-insentient doctrine. This is clear from the "transmission verse" attributed to the fifth patriarch Hongren, found near the end of the Dunhuang version of the text:

> Sentient beings come and lay down seeds,
> And insentient flowers grow.
> Without sentiency and without seeds,
> The ground of mind produces nothing.[70]

Recall that, according to the *Masters and Disciples of the Laṅkāvatāra*, Hongren was a champion, rather than a critic, of the buddha-nature-of-the-insentient doctrine. But that did not stop the compilers of later versions of the *Platform Scripture* from altering the wording of the verse to make Hongren's opposition to the doctrine even more explicit:

> Sentient beings come and lay down seeds,
> From the earth fruit is produced.
> Without sentiency and without seeds,
> There is no [buddha-]nature and nothing is produced.[71]

This position is endorsed by a number of figures associated with the early "Southern Chan" lineage. The second fascicle of Dazhu Huihai's (dates unknown) *Essential Gateway for Entering the Way of Sudden Enlightenment* (*Dunwu rudao yaomen*), for example, contains a number of exchanges on the topic,[72] of which the following is typical:

> Deluded people do not know that the dharma-body has no appearance, but manifests form in response to things. Thus they say that, "Lush groves of

emerald bamboos are wholly the dharma-body; luxuriant clusters of chrysanthemums, nothing is not *prajñā*." But if chrysanthemums were *prajñā*, *prajñā* would be the same as the insentient, and if emerald bamboos were the dharma-body, then the dharma-body would be the same as grass and trees. Then when people munch on bamboo shoots, they must be munching on the dharma-body. . . .

A master who lectured on the Huayan scripture asked: "Does the Chan Master believe that insentient things are the buddha or not?" The Master said: "I don't believe it. For if insentient things were the buddha, then living people would be inferior to the dead. Even dead donkeys and dead dogs would be superior to a living person. A scripture says: 'The buddha-body is precisely the dharma-body; it is born of the precepts, meditation, and wisdom; it is born from the three wisdoms and the six supernormal powers; it is born from all the excellent dharmas.' If you claim that insentient things are the buddha, then were you, venerable one, to die right now, you would be a buddha."[73]

Huangbo Xiyun (d. ca. 850) is yet another famous master who considered the notion that insentient objects have buddha-nature simply absurd. Huangbo is best known for his teaching that buddha and mind are one, and thus his opposition to the buddha-nature of the insentient logically follows: one can only ascribe buddhahood to things that have minds.[74]

The position taken by these early Chan opponents of the buddha-nature of the insentient is straightforward. According to the classical Buddhist understanding of karma, only a sentient being can produce the kind of activity—the karmic seeds—that will germinate into *bodhi*. But this ignores the problem that sits at the very center of Buddhist soteriology, namely: How can any conditioned cause (karmic activity) ever give rise to an unconditioned effect (nirvāṇa)? And this, I believe, is what was driving the debate.

One Chan "solution," already hinted at in the *Masters and Disciples of the Laṅkāvatāra* and developed in the *Treatise on Severing Discernment*, is to adopt a Yogācāra perspective, a "phenomenological" point of view that collapses the distinction between the knowing subject and the object that is known. At the same time, and again following Yogācāra precedents, one affirms the universality of buddha nature, such that the phenomenological realm is but an expression of the absolute. Here the identification of buddha-nature and mind, rather than supporting the distinction between the sentient and insentient, actually undermines it, since mind now subsumes the material realm. (In other words, "matter" is reinscribed as a series of perceptual events.) This seems to be the approach taken by the figure who, in the later tradition, is most closely associated with the buddha-nature-of-the-insentient theory, Nanyang Huizhong (675–775):

> A student asked: "Within the teachings of the scriptures one only sees sentient beings receiving the prophecy of future perfect enlightenment and then, at some future time, becoming a buddha named so-and-so. One never sees an insentient being receiving the prophecy of future perfect enlightenment and becoming a buddha. Among the thousand buddhas of the current *bhadrakalpa*, if there is a single case of an insentient object becoming buddha, please show it to me." The Master said: "I now ask you, imagine a prince at the time of his coronation as king. Does the person of the prince receive the kingship [all at once], or must every territory in the kingdom be individually bestowed upon him?" [The student] replied: "When the prince is crowned king, everything in the kingdom becomes his. What need is there for him to receive anything else?" The Master said: "The present case is just the same: at the moment when sentient beings receive the prophecy of their future buddhahood, all the lands of the three-thousand great-thousand worlds are completely subsumed within the body of Vairocana Buddha. Beyond the body of the buddha, could there still be some insentient object to receive the prophecy?"[75] . . .
>
> [The student] asked: "A venerable elder has said:
>
> Lush groves of emerald bamboos,
> Are wholly suchness.
> Luxuriant clusters of chrysanthemums,
> Nothing is not *prajñā*.
>
> Some people do not accept this teaching while others believe in it. The words are inconceivable, and I do not know what to make of it." The Master said: "This pertains to the realms of great beings such as Samantabhadra and Mañjuśrī; it is not something that lesser men are able to believe and accept. This teaching is fully in accord with the intent of the superlative scriptures of the Mahāyāna. Thus the *Huayan Sūtra* says: 'The buddha-body fills the dharma-realm and manifests itself before all beings. It responds in accord with conditions, extending everywhere, yet it remains constantly ensconced on the seat of *bodhi*.'[76] As emerald bamboos

> do not lie beyond the dharma-realm, are they not the dharma-body? Moreover, the *Mahāprajñāpāramitā-sūtra* says: 'Since matter is boundless, *prajñā* is also boundless.'[77] As chrysanthemums are but matter, are they not *prajñā*?"[78]

Huizong cites the *Huayan Sūtra* notion that the phenomenal universe itself is the body of Vairocana Buddha in support of his claim that all things, including the insentient, embody buddha-nature and "preach the dharma." This position would eventually win the day: in later *gong'an* materials, the inert silence of a staff or tree, rather than bespeaking the inconceivable absence that is insentience and death, is rendered the perfect expression of the selfless quiescence of no-mind.[79] "A monk asked Zhaozhou, 'What is the meaning of the patriarch [Bodhidharma] coming from the west?' Zhaozhou replied, 'The cypress tree in front of the garden.'"[80]

Chinese Mindlessness

It may seem curious that the Chinese did not reference the rich Indian Buddhist discourse on *nirodha*, *asaṃjñi-samāpatti*, and the mindless gods as they pondered the buddha-nature of the insentient. But it should not be surprising: that the term *mie* was commonly used as a Chinese translation (rather than transliteration) for both *nirodha* and nirvāṇa blurred the distinction between the two. Discussion of *nirodha-samāpatti* in Chinese Buddhist treatises is uncommon, and when such a state is mentioned it typically appears in the context of supernatural attainments and powers. Note, for example, Xuanzang's *Great Tang Record of Western Regions* (*Datang xiyu ji*), where he reports coming across two *arhat*s, each ensconced in a cave, who had remained in *nirodha-samāpatti* (*miejinding*) for more than seven hundred years. As the hair and beards on their immobile bodies continued to grow, monks regularly shaved them and changed their clothing.[81]

So while the Chinese showed little overt interest in the scholastic controversies surrounding *nirodha* or *asaṃjñi-samāpatti*, they were, I am suggesting, just as invested as the Indians in the problem of nirvāṇa and its puzzling affinity to insentience. Indeed, the linguistic and cultural differences that made it difficult for the Chinese to negotiate the Indian scholastic terrain made it even more difficult for them to appreciate the underlying existential issues that galvanized the Indian debates. And so they had to come up with thought experiments—"intuition pumps"—of their own.

In other words, the philosophical dilemmas that animated Indian theories of *nirodha* and the mindless gods—confusions about sentience, agency, death, and nirvāṇa—were the same dilemmas that energized the buddha-nature-of-the-insentient debates in China. That there were so many approaches to the issues, and so little consensus, underscores the experimental character of this discourse. Note how many of our Chinese authors, including Shenhui and Huizong, honed their positions in response to the single adage: "Lush groves of emerald bamboos are wholly suchness; luxuriant clusters of chrysanthemums; nothing is not *prajñā*." Reference to this aphorism functions much like reference to a brain transplant or a Turing test in modern philosophical discourse: it is a point of common reference, encapsulating a complex set of epistemological issues and arguments, that serves as a springboard for analyses and debate. The probative and even playful nature of the debate is evident in the *Treatise on Severing Discernment*, to pick a single example, which argues that it is precisely because insentient things *do not* have mind that they can be considered buddhas. The *Treatise on No Mind* (*Wuxin lun*), another Dunhuang text that appeared around the same time as the *Treatise on Severing Discernment*, takes a similarly innovative position:

> Question: "The Reverend has already said that everything without exception is without mind, and thus trees and rocks are also without mind. But surely it cannot be the same for trees and rocks?"
>
> Answer: "My mind that is without mind is not identical with trees or rocks. Why so? It is like a celestial drum which, although it also lacks a mind, spontaneously emits various marvelous teachings that instruct sentient beings. Or it is like the wish-fulfilling gem that, although it also lacks a mind, is able to spontaneously produce various apparitions. My own absence of mind is just like that; although I am without mind, I am perfectly able to apprehend the true form of all dharmas, and, endowed with true *prajñā*, the three bodies have freedom and responsive functioning without constraint. Therefore the *Ratnakūṭa-sūtra* says: 'In the absence of mental intention it is still manifestly active.' How could this be the same as trees and rocks? Indeed, the absence of mind is precisely true mind. And true mind is precisely the absence of mind."[82]

Here the *Treatise on No Mind* argues that "no-mind" does indeed refer to a kind of insentience—the absence of intention, mind, and consciousness. But this is not, according to the text, of a piece with the insentience of trees and rocks, since trees and rocks are manifestly incapable of doing the sorts of things that animate things do. Rather, the text would have us consider the insentience of "supernatural" objects like celestial drums and wish-fulling gems; insentient things that have no mind or intention but are still capable (like us) of autonomous activity. In other words, the *Treatise on No Mind* is positing a medieval Chinese version of a "hybrid"—a category of things that conflates or confutes the sentient/insentient distinction.

This is not to suggest that Indian and Chinese Buddhist conceptions of "mindlessness" *never* came into direct contact and dialogue. There is, to my knowledge, one documented instance, associated with the "Samyé debate" that supposedly took place between the Indian master Kamalaśīla and the Northern Chan master Moheyan in mid-eighth-century Tibet. In this exchange, as recorded in a Dunhuang manuscript, Kamalaśīla critiques what he takes to be the Chan position, namely, that Buddhist practice is directed toward the elimination of thought and cognition. Kamalaśīla makes his point by polemically likening the goal of Chan to the mindlessness of the mindless gods:

> [Kamalaśīla] further asked, "There are divine beings who [in their former life] suppressed all deluded conception, and as a result of their suppression of deluded conception attained rebirth in the Heaven of [Gods] Without Conception. [But we know that] such beings don't attain the way of the Buddha, and thus it is clear that the elimination of conception is not the way to buddhahood."
>
> [Moheyan] respectfully replied, "Those divine beings posit the existence of both meditative discernments and paths of rebirth, and they grasp at the absorption of non-conception. It is precisely because of such deluded conceptualization that they are born into that heaven. If they could free themselves from [attachment to] the meditative absorption into non-conception, then there would be no deluded thought nor rebirth into that heaven. The *Vajracchedikā-sūtra* says, 'To be free of all marks, this is called [the way of] the buddhas.' In what scripture is it said that freedom from deluded conception is *not* the way to buddhahood?"[83]

Kamalaśīla's point is that to strive for no-thought, no mind, no conceptualization, is to be no better than the mindless denizens of the Heaven of Gods Without Conception—beings who ignorantly mistake insentience for the goal of spiritual practice. Moheyan responds that it is precisely such ideas—ideas like a state of non-conceptualization, or a heaven wherein there are beings without sentience—that keep people bound to *saṃsāra*.[84] The goal of practice is to let go of attachment to any and all discursive formations, to abandon conceptualization altogether, to reach a state of no mind. Is this tantamount to insentience, as Kamalaśīla believed? The Chan tradition—the tradition that rose to dominate Buddhism in China—was weaned on precisely this struggle.

Chapter 9

Karma and the Bonds of Kinship in Medieval Daoism: Reconciling the Irreconcilable

Christine Mollier

The confrontation of Daoism with Mahāyāna Buddhism, during the first centuries of the common era, led the "indigenous" religion to an identity crisis which was manifest in a pattern of simultaneous rejection and appropriation of the foreign tradition. Among the results were Daoism's ever-increasing production of "sūtras," the creation of its first canonical corpuses, and the development of its liturgy. Erik Zürcher, in his pioneering article "Buddhist Influence on Early Taoism," showed through a systematic examination of Daoist sources how this influence remained, as a whole, rather superficial, since it was essentially a matter of formal and stylistic elements.[1] However, there is one broad domain in which the impact of Buddhism considerably affected the medieval Daoist outlook, namely, eschatology and morality. Challenged by the overwhelming Mahāyāna doctrinal apparatus, Daoism saw itself obliged to revisit the conceptual gray zones of the Chinese tradition of which it considered itself the representative. Although little inclined to theoretical speculation, it nonetheless found it necessary to elaborate its visions of the world and the self, whether by explicit or tacit reformulation, or by simply abandoning them in order to adopt the conceptions of its Buddhist rival. Thus, during the period of the Six Dynasties, a geography of hell takes shape, and previously unanticipated perspectives on the afterlife, such as the theory of rebirth in the Six Realms, are revealed. The postmortem world comes to be seen as a huge court of justice, as well as a place of punishment and torture, as impartial as it is pitiless. In the *imaginaire* of death, the "underground jails" (*diyu*, Skt. *naraka*) progressively replace the traditional "yellow springs" hidden within the obscure world (*you*) which the deceased must traverse.[2] As a compensation for these terrifying prospects, rituals for the salvation of the living and the dead develop. One has, by all means, to "gain merits" (*jian gongde*) and to actively participate in cultivating universal compassion, lest the gates of salvation close before one's eyes. In this way, the new horizons opened by Buddhism on the questions of death and the apocalypse, predestination and the world beyond started to transform and to shape the Chinese *imaginaire* for ever after.

The eschatological system imported by Buddhism rests on the notion of karmic causality and its correlates, retribution and rebirth. "The karmic machine," as the late Michel Strickmann put it, "functions not only as a supple explanation of all that happens in the course of everyday life, but above all as an instrument of psychological pressure in relation to the destiny of the living and of their ancestors in the next world."[3] However, considering the existential and moral interrogations that it involves, the idea of karma inevitably leads to contradictions, even within one and the same religious tradition. When introduced into the framework of Chinese society, these contradictions became all the more acute. Thus, for instance, given a strict construction of the notion of karmic causality, only the individual's own acts play a role in determining his or her fate, in this world and the next. One of the foremost obstacles, therefore, that this concept raised for Chinese ways of thought was the problem of reconciling its egocentric implications with traditional views that stressed the preeminence of genealogy and familial solidarity in matters of human existence and the afterlife.

The transfer of merits was in some respects familiar to Chinese sensibilities, even if some aspects of karma and samsara appeared antagonistic to common belief. In effect, in traditional China, the question of the ancestor, and above all the male forebear, one's patrilineal link, weighed most heavily in psychological, social and cultural terms. Ascendants and descendants are forever joined, for better or for worse, across the generations, by the ties of blood and of name. This intergenerational responsibility operating even beyond the grave among the members of a common clan is explained by an almost supersensible quality attributed to heredity. It treats each human individual as a passing embodiment in the continuity of a lineage whose maintenance is assured by the cult of the ancestors, the pillar of the social, political, and religious life of the Chinese. The sociological implications of this hieratic vision of familial lineage are well known. It is clear, for example, that the Chinese penal system provided that sentences could be applied, in certain cases, to family members no less than to the guilty party, so that the former consequently might also be subject to punishment and dishonor. Such conceptions were equally at the center of the religious ethic, serving as a virtual Chinese theodicy.

The introduction of the concept of karma in medieval society thus poses a crucial problem: is retribution the result of personal acts and choices or rather is it conditioned by the interrelations among the generations? How can one reconcile the idea of karmic causality with the sacrosanct principle of filial piety, or, at the very least, that of genealogical solidarity? How to reconcile the irreconcilable?

We need not enter here into the details of sinicized Buddhism. One should note simply that it had to face the foregoing dilemma and adjust itself appropriately. During the early period of its implantation, as Stephen Teiser notes, Buddhism was still "consigned to a position in Chinese society outside the continuum of descent that constituted the family."[4] Thus, Zhi Qian, in the mid-third century, in his well-known compilation, the *Taizi ruiying benqi jing*, emphasizes strictly personal responsibility in treating of karmic retribution.[5] It is only after it had been fully assimilated, by the fourth or fifth century, that "Buddhism as a social institution had been woven—albeit ambiguously, as a differently colored strand—into the rope of descent."[6]

For its part, the answers that Daoism tried to provide to these fundamental questions were far from unanimous. As we shall see, they diverged considerably in relation to the theological orientations adopted by different traditions and, certainly, their varied affinities with Buddhism. The subject is a colossal one, both in terms of the quantity of sources and its doctrinal complexity. I will therefore attempt only to indicate how two major tendencies were opposed throughout the medieval period in regard to the laws of retribution. One, defined by the Way of the Celestial Master, made no concession to Buddhism and insisted upon a traditional approach to human destiny. The alternative was that of the Lingbao tradition. By promoting a Mahāyāna (*dasheng*) form of Daoism, Lingbao deliberately adopted the notion of karma and greatly contributed to inscribing this important aspect of Indian thought in the Chinese collective imagination. It will be seen that, besides these two opposing trends, other medieval Daoist currents managed, mainly by means of ambiguous terminology, to amalgamate the two systems without any attempt to solve the doctrinal contradictions this brought forth.

Divine Retribution and Morality in the Early Way of the Celestial Master

During the first century of the Common Era, the renowned Han dynasty philosopher Wang Chong (27–97) had already affirmed that: "Hidden virtue is recompensed by Heaven with preservation from death. Crimes are punished by Heaven just as they are punished by the human sovereign."[7]

In accord with this traditional Chinese conviction, the flock of the first Daoist organization, that of the Way of the Celestial Master (Tianshi dao), considered that human destiny is for the most part subject to the divine, and that Heaven is in constant interaction with the human world, upon which it exercises punitive or favorable effects. One of the most ancient surviving works issued from the early Celestial Master movement, the *Xiang'er* commentary on *Laozi*, dating to the end of the second or beginning of the third century CE, seems, in this respect, to echo Wang Chong's statement. As the *Xiang'er* puts it: "Those who are sincere by themselves will naturally be rewarded by Heaven, and those who are not will naturally be punished by Heaven. Heaven's scrutiny is even more thoroughgoing than that of human beings. It knows fully who reveres the Dao and fears Heaven."[8]

For the adepts of the Celestial Master, the effects of this implacable, divine justice are perfectly discernible because they inexorably affect health and lifespan. Illnesses and physical or mental deficiencies are, in effect, provoked by the penetration of the body by demonic entities, which are themselves the products of the moral lapses and transgressions of which the individual is guilty. The Way of the Celestial Master's doctrinal rigor entailed that illness was the most convincing sign of sin, and could only be cured by ritual, notably the confession of faults. Thus, a human being's physical condition reflects the degree of his or her virtue and affinity with the Dao, in other terms, his or her aptitude for salvation. This idea of a correlation between physical and moral perfection served also the interests of the elitist, even eugenic, convictions of the movement, notably in its determination to create perfect beings, the chosen or "seed-people" (*zhongmin*).[9]

To be irreproachable in one's moral and religious conduct is thus one of the conditions sine qua non for salvation. It leads the virtuous adept to be inscribed in the life-registers that are scrupulously maintained by the celestial bureaucracy. Evil deeds are, by contrast, consigned to the registers of death and punished by deductions from one's life-capital, the lifespan that one is alloted at birth. Control and accountability are the masterwords of the divine justice that the Celestial Masters sought to represent. As the mirror of the empire, "Heaven" is a colossal administration, hierarchic and repressive, and composed of myriad functionaries, judges, accountants, and censors in the service of the Dao. Charged with assuring the management of the world, they exercise an omniscient oversight, recording the slightest acts and gestures of each, rigorously taking account of good and of bad, and rendering impartial verdicts.[10] For these administrators of morality are also judges endowed with the full power to reward or to punish. Written requests, prayers, and petitions are the tools thanks to which the clerics of the Celestial Masters movement come to intercede, on behalf of the faithful, before the celestial bureaucracy.

From its beginnings, the organization of the Celestial Masters thus endeavored to enact regulations and interdictions in order to establish its adepts within an ethical and communal framework. According to the tradition, the first regulations reached back to the legendary origins of the sect, that is to say, the investiture of the first Celestial Master, Zhang Daoling, by Lord Lao (Laojun), in the year 142: "Zhang was to stabilize and correct the Three Heavens, eradicating the frivolous and returning the people to simplicity and truth. [For this purpose] he received the true scriptures of the Most High and established regulations and ordinances."[11]

The *Xiang'er* provides an initial idea of the nature of the rules of this new orthodoxy. The work proposes "Nine Practices" to be adopted by the faithful, practices that, for the most part, deal with psycho-physiological instructions aiming to extend life. These recommendations are founded on the ethico-philosophical values of *Laozi*: non-action, quietude, and harmony.[12] Besides this, one finds twenty-seven additional rules, set down in the text of the *Xiang'er*, advocating general principles of behavior to be observed (such as rectitude, respect for the divinities of the body, and repression of desires), as well as several interdictions, in particular those forbidding the killing of living creatures, the consumption of meat, and the worship of spirits of heterodox cults.[13] However, it is significant that these recommendations remain general. No more than in the other great manual of conduct, the famous *Taiping jing* which introduces the theory of *chengfu* (inherited burden) and presents numerous moral prescriptions and prohibitions, is there an attempt here at systematic codification of morality and retribution. In fact, the principles governing retribution are basically the same for both the *Xiang'er* and the *Taiping jing*. They make no appeal to Buddhist notions of karma and rebirth, and remain constant in the teachings of the Way of the Celestial Masters.

As a general rule, their system of morality takes as its point of departure the principle that no act will be without retribution, though justice may function on several levels. It operates in three temporal periods: the past (one's ancestral inheritance), the present (one's individual condition), and the future (postmortem salvation and transmission to one's descendants). Retribution is in effect the consequence, positive or negative, not just of the individual's acts, but also of those of one's familial lineage. Stated otherwise, there is a direct, immediate retribution that applies to individuals and their close relations, as well as a deferred retribution that reaches to descendants, often for several generations (one speaks most often of seven).

Destined to guide the daily lives of adepts, the ancient codes of conduct of the Celestial Master movement, of which the earliest examples reach back to the third or fourth centuries of our era (and which are preserved in later versions in the *Daozang*), were alike in advocating, to various degrees, "ancestral predestination."[14] The *Code of Nüqing for [Controlling] Demons* (*Nüqing guilü*), for example, sets forth a preliminary sketch of the arithmetics of retribution. The text promulgates a group of twenty-two commandments which aim, in essence, to restrain such behavior as is universally reproached in Chinese society, to establish astro-hemerological prescriptions, and to proscribe heterodox cults as well as certain sexual practices.[15] In case of the infringement of these commandments, a period of time (*suan*) in proportion to the gravity of the offence is subtracted from the life-capital of the guilty party. Unfortunately, the work does not specify the quantitative value of the units thus subtracted. Faults of medium weight, it explains simply, are punished by the withdrawal of several hundred units, while the gravest transgressions such as the failure to respect ritual practices, lack of filial piety, or the conception of children outside of ritual prescription[16] are punished by the elimination of 30,000 units. One notes that these basic principles of retribution are practically identical to those articulated during the same epoch by Ge Hong (283–343). In the sixth chapter of his renowned *Master Who Embraces Simplicity* (*Baopuzi*), he sets forth a list of evil actions (moral as well as environmental), indicating, as well, that they belong to two categories: those of great and minor faults.[17]

> In heaven as on earth, there are divinities charged with the assessment of faults who subtract [a period of time] from the life-account (*suan*) of culpable individuals in proportion to the gravity of the transgressions they have committed. As their life-account diminishes, people fall into poverty and illness, and they become frequently prone to afflictions and misfortune. When their *suan* is finally exhausted, they die. The causes of the *suan*'s being cut back are so numerous that it is impossible to expose them all. . . . Grave faults are punished by the deduction of one *ji*, equivalent to 300 days. Minimal faults count a *suan,* which is to say, three days.[18]

Besides this, Ge Hong accentuates the fact that retribution does not function uniquely in a direct manner, but may be deferred, which permits one to explain the fundamental inequalities characterizing human existence: "Wise men do not necessarily live long, and fools do not necessarily die young. There is neither immediate reward for good, nor immediate punishment for evil."[19]

This perspective is largely shared by the *Code of Nüqing*, which furnishes more substantial explanations of this system of twin-speed retribution. The penalties do not apply necessarily to the guilty party alone, but, in the majority of cases, they may rebound on a person's lineage. Such is the case, for example, with punishments incurred owing to sexual misconduct: these may be transmitted to the descendants of those guilty for as long as seven generations.[20] The inheritance of faults within the family means that humans risk contaminating their relations through their own transgressions. Faults that have not been repaid by the sinner personally, or that are too heavy, are added to the moral account of children and grandchildren. In this way, the moral patrimony of a family conditions the destiny of its members before their birth and after their death.

In the course of time, the organization of the Celestial Masters endeavored to rationalize this system. For the *Petition Almanac of Master Red Pine* (*Chisong zi zhangli*, Dz. 615) one of the major scriptures of the movement,[21] ancestral predestination allows, somewhat in the manner of karma, for an explanation of the inequities of the human condition, notably with regard to longevity, a theme particularly cherished by the Daoists:

> If those who have never committed faults die in the flower of youth, the reason is that they have inherited the excess faults (*yuguo*) of their ancestors. [Similarly,] it is due to the surplus of felicity (*yufu*) their ancestors have transmitted to them that those who perpetuate evil and disorder nevertheless reach the full term of life without disease or misfortune.[22]

The *Petition Almanac of Master Red Pine* proposes, in addition, an accounting of divine retribution. The work expounds the "interdictions and admonitions" (*jinlü*) which are supposed to restrict the behavior of the faithful. Violations of the rules are evaluated according to diverse scales. Each type of transgression corresponds to a penalty and a sanction administered by the divine censors charged with cosmic justice. The more serious the faults, and the more the penalties accumulated, the more will the compensatory damages be multiplied. Punishments may be realized in terms of simple material problems, diseases, infirmities and pains of all sorts, or, even worse, a fatal affliction following the commission of 720 faults (ch. 2.30a–31a). The *Almanac of Master Red Pine* insists also on the fact that the infringements of one person might also have all kinds of disastrous consequences for his family: "The [consequences] of minor faults only apply to the one responsible for them. Grave faults [however] are transmitted to his children and grandchildren."

Among the problems afflicting the descendants of the guilty, the *Almanac* mentions physical or mental defects which are transmitted through several generations, repeated internal family conflicts, successive generations of troublemakers or outcasts, the family's loss of moral reputation, and so on. The ultimate threat, even more fearsome than death, is to be without descendants (which occurs when 1,200 faults are accumulated), and above all, the extinction of one's line. The definitive breaking of the family chain is considered to be the most horrible of condemnations.

Later on, the seventh century *Penal Code of the Mysterious Capital* (*Xuandu lüwen*) will endeavor to impart greater specificity to this system.[23] This important manual of regulations of the religious life further insists that it is the spiritual and moral legacy of the ancestors that conditions the lives of their descendants. A respectable provision of good deeds acquired by one's forebears will benefit all their descendants, who will rejoice in their fortune, longevity, and virtue. Genetically transmitted moral debts and faults produce bad destinies for their families through the generations. Two standards of good and bad actions are set up by this Code on a scale from one to a thousand. A quota of a few good actions is simply recompensed by positive effects on health (a good action, for example, confers heartfelt serenity and bodily calm, while twenty good deeds permit one to escape all illness). The benefactor who performs forty to fifty good actions also enjoys material comfort, and his prosperity will be eventually transmitted to his children and grandchildren. Rare, evidently, are those who succeed in reaching the maximum record of a thousand good deeds, which confers supreme grace, that is to say, celestial immortality for oneself and all one's descendants. As for the negative scale, the *Penal Code of the Mysterious Capital* adopts a strict standard: four hundred faults are sufficient to provoke the death of the guilty party, together with those of his children and grandchildren. For the Daoists of the Way of the Celestial Master, divine retribution is thus definitely a family affair. The moral patrimony may be transmitted from one generation to the next. The positive or negative effects of merits and faults that the person accumulates ineluctably rebound on the members of his line.

Before turning our attention to the radically different position defended by Lingbao Daoism, I would like to mention how other contemporaneous Daoist movements attempted to merge this traditional idea of genealogical retribution with the notion of karma. The best example is furnished by the major early fifth-century Daoist apocalypse, the *Scripture of Divine Incantations* (*Dongyuan shen zhou jing*, Dz. 335). For the *Shen zhou jing,* the coexistence of familial responsibility with karmic retribution is made possible thanks to ambiguous terminology. The expressions *xianshen* or *xianshi*, which can be understood either as "previous lives" or as "prior generations" thus conveniently lend themselves to a double use:

> Fortunate persons are those who, in their past lives (or whose ancestors), have studied the Dao, have an affinity with immortality, and acquired numerous merits. Daoist adepts who are poor are those who, in their past lives (or whose ancestors), studied the Dao, but did not instruct others. Those among the six domestic animals or slaves are those who, in their past lives (or whose ancestors), have committed grave sins, did not obtain merit, and did not respect the Dao.[24]

The result, for the *Shen zhou jing*, is thus a sort of hybrid notion which might be translated as "ancestral karma."

The Karmic Tribulations of the Immortal Ge Xuan

The position adopted by Lingbao Daoism is, in itself, completely clear: retribution is subject to the iron law of karmic determination. Among the early scriptures of the Lingbao canon that have survived, one finds several didactic texts which convincingly preach a Mahāyānist Daoism. They offer an apology for the bodhisattva-saint, and for an altruistic salvation rather than a strictly personal one. One finds there substantial developments relative to the laws of samsara and karmic retribution, with ardent appeals for individual responsibility in the conduct of human destiny. Genealogical dependence is relegated to second rank. A few scriptures in particular deserve to be mentioned here. One is the *Precepts of the Three Primordials* (*Sanyuan pinjie*) which offers a long statement of the dilemma dividing individual karma from collective retribution.[25] The text insists that karma is a strictly individual affair and that our biological parents are not our "real" parents: "The self's birthing father and mother are not the father and mother that originally gave birth to the self."

Another ancient Lingbao scripture, relevantly entitled *Scripture of the Wheel of the Law*, proclaims itself to have been revealed to Ge Xuan, the Daoist patriarch and "master of esoterica" who is said to have lived during the end of the second and the first half of the third century.[26] This scripture advocates practicing the teachings of the Great Vehicle (*dasheng*). It claims to possess the power to enable all beings to leave the cycle of transmigration, reach *samādhi*, and enter nirvāṇa (*miedu*). But it also envisions the attainment of Delivery from the Corpse (*shijie*) and immortality.[27] One sees here a blending of Daoist and Buddhist ideals.

In the Lingbao *Scripture of the Karmic Factors of Causation and Deeds in Previous Existences* (*Taishang dongxuan lingbao benxing yinyuan jing*; Dz. 1115), the same Ge Xuan relates, in the style of the Buddhist *avadāna* stories, his own former existences to a group of Immortals. They have arrived to interrogate him as to why it is that after six hundred years of Daoist practice, they have not gotten beyond the stage of terrestrial immortals. Ge Xuan explains to them that their Daoist practice belongs exclusively to the Lesser Vehicle (*xiaosheng*), because they are only concerned with their own salvation and not that of others. For this reason, they have not acquired more than slight merits and so have remained at the modest level they have attained. Even the illustrious, legendary immortal Peng Zu was similarly constrained to dwell here in the world below and could never raise himself to heaven, explains Ge Xuan! Having thus underscored the limits of the hermitic life and extolled religious proselytism and the bodhisattva-saint, Ge Xuan relates the adventures of his own past lives, and the diverse conditions that he experienced. He was noble and rich, enslaved and miserable; he was subjected to the hells and repeated rebirths in animal forms. It was only after many existences devoted to the Great Vehicle that he became a transcendent Immortal.

In *The Questions of Sir Immortal* (*Xiangong qingwen jing*), belonging also to the Lingbao corpus, Ge Xuan is informed that one must observe the Ten Injunctions (*shijie*) in order to improve one's karmic condition, and that one should absolutely avoid the Ten Evils (*shi'e*). For, as it has been proclaimed, everything is subject to the inevitable laws of retribution:

> If there are people in this world who do evil and suffer no consequence for it, it is because they have not exhausted the merits of their past lives. When merits are exhausted, sorrow will arrive. As for those who do good actions but are not rewarded, it's [also the case] that they are not done with the faults [accumulated] in their past lives. When their sins will be expiated, happiness will arrive.[28]

Several other Lingbao texts of later provenance, concerning karmic retribution, deserve to be mentioned here as well. I am thinking for example of the Sui or early Tang *Scripture on Transmigration in the Five Paths [according to] the Karma of Previous Life* (*Taishang shuo zhuanlun wudao suming yinyuan jing*, Dz. 647) which is modeled on the Buddhist *Shan'e yinguo jing* (T. no. 2881, vol. 85). Dating also to the end of the sixth or the beginning of the seventh century, the *Scripture of Karmic Retribution* (*Yebao yinyuan jing*, Dz 336) seems the ultimate Lingbao synthesis concerning the questions of karma and transmigration.[29] In this case, it is not to Ge Xuan that this divine scripture is revealed, but to the Zhenren of Universal Salvation (Puji zhenren). This voluminous work amounting to ten *juan* seems likely to have been inspired by the *Karmavibhaṅga*, a well-known sūtra studied by Sylvain Lévi (1932).[30] The text seeks to present all the data possible concerning the gears of the karmic machine and of samsara. It provides, in the third chapter, numerous lists of all kinds: of virtuous persons and of sinners, of interdictions, of good and bad deeds, of condemnable ways of killing animals, of the good conditions of reincarnation, together with enumerations of evil conditions including those of all the beasts under heaven from mammals down to the most disgusting insects and worms, as well as endless lists of infirmities, ugliness and defects afflicting sinners, and more.

The *Lingbao Scripture of Karmic Retribution* demonstrates that by the period of its composition, the principles of karma and samsara were fully assimilated within the cadre of the Lingbao. The accent is now placed on their concrete roles in the lives of the faithful, and accordingly it is to instruct the latter in their mechanisms that Lingbao promotes their taxonomies and classifications.

During the same period, that is the beginning of the Tang, the mania for the classification and enumeration of retributions seems to have equally struck the Zhengyi clerics of the new Way of the Celestial Masters. Nevertheless, they remained resistant to Buddhist theories and continued to defend their traditional positions in respect to retribution and destiny. In the seventh century *Code of the Mysterious Capital*, mentioned above, it is clear that the Celestial Masters also sought to use lists and quotas, perhaps as a response to their Lingbao competitors, in order to render their system more compelling and to lend it an air of credibility.

Chapter 10

This Foreign Religion of Ours: Lingbao Views of Buddhist Translation

Stephen R. Bokenkamp

When I was asked to participate in the discussion that has resulted in this volume, I planned to contribute a continuation of Erik Zürcher's influential "Buddhist Influence on Early Taoism."[1] I wanted to rehearse, and hopefully improve on, Zürcher's findings concerning what the Daoist Lingbao scriptures might tell us about Chinese reception of Buddhist cosmology, morality, narrative styles, and the like. The early Lingbao scriptures, composed around 400 CE in the environs of present-day Nanjing, contained, Zürcher found, the "lion's share of Buddhist loans."[2] The uses to which Lingbao Daoists put this material show the oscillation between the poles of attraction and repulsion that greets a powerful "other" in matters of religious and cultural identity.[3] Used judiciously, these scriptures might, I had hoped to show, reveal one strand of the multifarious early medieval Chinese views of India and its most widely exported religion.

While that project might have worked out well, I was soon sidetracked. As I searched through the texts, I found myself having first to confront the ways each of these reconfigured Buddhist elements was always explicitly or implicitly tied to the idea of kalpa cycles. The Lingbao scriptures, like earlier Daoist texts, claim to be translations of celestial originals. Unlike earlier Daoist texts, though, the Lingbao scriptures present examples of the original celestial script together with their translation into humanly accessible writing. Further, the authors of the Lingbao texts accept the Buddhist idea of kalpa cycles. Thus, in their original form, the scriptures appeared first in world systems like our own, but many, many years in the past. Borrowings from other scriptural traditions, even outright plagiary, are justified in the Lingbao texts with the claim that all "later" scriptures were in fact copies of Lingbao "celestial script" originals. For instance, one Lingbao scripture contains the Buddhas and Bodhisattvas of the ten directions and the names of their lands copied directly from Zhi Qian's (fl. 220–250) *Pusa benye jing*. This list is followed by the explicit claim that "the Buddhas of the Ten Directions all find their source in Lingbao."[4]

But references to the marvelous celestial writing claimed as the basis for the Lingbao scriptures were not limited to assertions of scriptural superiority and priority. In other passages, characterizations of celestial text are worked quite naturally into the scriptural presentation. For example, I had originally planned to write a bit about how Daoist accounts of heaven were stimulated by Buddhist models, to include the roles of Indic notions of cosmic time and of political organization. One of the most compelling Lingbao accounts of Buddhist-style chiliocosms appears in the *Book of Salvation in the Numinous Writing of the Various Heavens*.[5] The opening pages of this text take the form of a dialogue between the highest deity of the Lingbao scriptures, the Celestial Worthy of Primordial Origins (Yuanshi tianzun), and the lords of heavenly kingdoms in the five directions. In each case the Celestial Worthy questions why there is no suffering or death in the kingdom. The answers vary, but uniformly trace the tranquility of the kingdom and the longevity of its inhabitants to the appearance of the Lingbao scriptures. Take the description of the paradise lands of the south:

> This kingdom has a Hall of Penetrating Yang in which there is a pool of refining fire. The citizens visit this pool three times a year to refine themselves with the flaming essences and thereby render their bodies decorous and lustrous. In this way, there are [residents] who never age. . . . The origins of this pool of refining fire of the Hall of Penetrating Yang goes back to the first appearance of the *Perfected Script of Lingbao*. Together with the Lofty and Great Sage, the Jade Thearch, I refined the yet illegible graphs of the *Perfected Script* in the fire [of this pool] so that the graphs' shapes shone forth.[6]

In short, what is said in this scripture about marvelous buildings, parks, groves of seven-treasure trees, and even the health of each locale's celestial inhabitants is always explicitly caused by the wondrousness of the scriptures.

Surveying such accounts, I came to a striking conclusion. Arguably, the mere fact that Buddhism arrived in China clothed in the trappings of a complex and subtle written language that, when translated, strained the descriptive powers of Chinese, made a powerful and important impression on literate Chinese.[7]

Confronted with another written language, the Chinese were at first able to dismiss it as the horizontal writing of ghosts.[8] But as more and more elaborate scriptures were translated into Chinese, the potentialities of the foreign writing system started to become apparent. New worlds, striking new divinities, new postmortem possibilities, new spiritual threats and ritual solutions, new moral imperatives, new modes of religious organization—all were contained, for the first time in their experience, in a *written* language that could be translated into Chinese script.

In this chapter, I intend to explore further the results of this specific encounter as evidenced in the Lingbao scriptures of Daoism. As has already been revealed in several studies, the Lingbao texts attempt to tap into the perceived potency of Buddhism as translated from foreign scripts by presenting their own translations, not from Sanskrit or any human language, but from the language of heaven revealed in prior world systems. Attention to this response to Buddhism will reveal certain aspects of the foreign religion's image among those who first sought to compete with it for the hearts and minds of the Chinese populace.

There are two distinct examples of celestial script presented in the original Lingbao scriptures. Both are described as products of prior kalpa eras, appearing miraculously in the heavens, and spontaneously formed of primal *qi*, the basic creative stuff of the universe. Modern scholars have not yet answered the question as to why two scripts were thought necessary. The first, the Perfected Script in Five Parts, is responsible for creation at the beginning of each of the world-eras, while the second, the Hidden Language of the Great Brahmā, recounts the salvific actions of the scriptures in the first era and is apparently to be understood as the language of the celestial denizens of that era. Whether composed later by the same author or the product of a new sect in the burgeoning Lingbao movement of the early fifth century, the Hidden Language is certainly part of the same movement and it was so accepted by the earliest collator of the texts, Lu Xiujing (406–77).[9] We will therefore deal most closely with the Hidden Language, as explicated in the *Inner Sounds of the Several Heavens* (hereafter *Inner Sounds*), since this text cleaves most closely to Buddhist models.[10]

The *Inner Sounds* explicitly foregrounds the translation of the Hidden Language in ways that are described as comparable to the translation of Buddhist scripture. First, it depicts a translation "team" similar to those formed to translate Buddhist scripture. The primary translator is a deity known by title only, the Resplendent Heavenly Perfected, Tianzhen huangren.[11] Within Daoism, this deity was held to be responsible for earlier revelations and is particularly chosen by the highest deity of the Lingbao scriptures, the Celestial Worthy of Primordial Origins, to provide glosses on the celestial language for humans. Yet, the Heavenly

Perfected is not the only deity who participates in the dramatic scene of translation into human script, depicted as follows:

> Thereafter, the Numinous Consort wielded the brush, the Grand Perfected straightened the mat, Jade Maidens held hand cloths, Gold Lads wafted incense, those of the lunar palaces scattered flowers, solar sprites poured out liquids, the Five Ancient [Lords] oversaw and checked [the transcription], and the Perfected Guards of the Three Realms divided [the text] according to its divisions.[12]

While some of these actions—wafting incense, scattering flowers—are ceremonial, the provision of a calligrapher, a writing mat, and hand towels all relate to the transcription process.[13] And, as in the translation of Buddhist text, the resulting copy is checked for accuracy, in this case by the Five Ancient Lords, prominent deities in the scriptures.[14]

Second, the Hidden Language's 256 graphs, resembling ancient seal script, are divided into four stanzas. Each stanza is composed of eight lines of eight graphs each. Each one of these lines stands for one of the thirty-two heavens, a construct that imitates the thirty-three heavens that ring Mt. Sumeru (Skt. *trayastrimsās*) of Buddhist cosmography.

Third, the eight graphs of each heaven are glossed by placing them each in a line of poetry, where they form further words. These "words" of one to four graphs in length, resemble Chinese transcriptions of Buddhist terms, use a number of transcription characters, and, in some cases, actually contain bits of recognizable Buddhist translation or transcription. Among Zürcher's examples are "*dan lou a hui wu he guan yin* *dhar(ma)ruyabhāmova GUANYIN" and "*na yu yu fu mo luo fa lun* *naśokayubhuktimāra FALUN."[15]

Despite the scripture's emphasis on *translation*, including elements that we will explore more fully below, modern scholars have portrayed the Hidden Language of the Great Brahmā as less a reflection of Chinese awareness of the languages of India than as an attempt to subsume Buddhist translation under traditional ideas of celestial script, especially as expressed in the production and use of talismans by Daoists and other wonder-workers.[16] It is quite true that the Hidden script, like talismanic "writing," builds on the mythical origins of the Chinese writing system as patterns inherent in nature that both encode messages from the mythic past and provide access for the sagely into the very workings of the cosmos. Scholarly description of the appearance and function of talismans would also seem to include the Hidden Language. For example, James Robson calls talismans "script," and "writing" and gives the following definition: "Talismans were sacred images that mirrored the forms of the primordial energies at the inception of the world and were therefore imbued with a spiritual power drawn from an ability to share in the essence of the thing it names or represents."[17] And, in fact, Daoists did consider the written languages of Buddhism the detritus of celestial language on a par with their own talismans. In an oft-cited passage, a goddess explains to the Daoist medium Yang Xi (330–386?) the origins and development of written language in terms of devolution. The primal unity devolved into two scripts which were further simplified into "dragon-phoenix emblems," *longfeng zhi zhang*, and "Brahmā writing tracing the forms [of things]," *shunxing fanshu*. These devolve further into the "sixty-four kinds" of script currently employed. Interestingly, it is "Brahmā writing" that is the source of talismans and, presumably, of Sanskrit, one of the "sixty-four" debased human scripts.[18]

While there are many similarities in both form and use with talismans, and while the Hidden Language draws equally on traditional Chinese ideas of script, it is not possible to trace a teleological development from early talismans to the Hidden Language. This is first of all because the Lingbao celestial scripts differ from talismans in that they are provided with translation and interpretation. This simple difference has a number of implications. The Hidden Language is not simply a "celestial script," but one that has been translated for human use. It is modeled closely on the translation of scriptural texts from the languages of Buddhism and depends on that stimulus for its development, features, and function. I would also, for the same reasons, argue against the idea that the Hidden Language is a type of "hierolalia," which I understand to mean glossolalia, or automatic speech, understood to be holy language.[19] If I am correct in divining what scholars mean by the term, I would object that hierolalia is situational and ecstatic, while the Hidden Language is stable and scholarly.[20] The Hidden Language is meant to be translated, dissected and discussed; while hierolalia serves other purposes. These prominent features—stability, translation, annotation—distinguish the Hidden Language as a constructed mimicry of Buddhist translation and, for subsequent Daoists, mandated its inclusion in the "basic texts" (*benwen*) section of the twelve-part generic division of the Daoist canon rather than in the "divine talismans" (*shen fu*) section.[21]

Contemporary Buddhists soon became aware of this attempt to steal one source of their religious prestige. Without rehearsing again the early history of Buddho-Daoist debate and controversy, we might look briefly at three explicit mentions of the Hidden Language in Zhen Luan's (fl. 538–581) *Treatise Deriding the Dao* (*Xiao dao lun*).[22] The first of these cites the *Inner Sounds* explanation of the eight graphs corresponding to the second heaven of the south to criticize the scripture's reference to the Buddhist deity Guanyin, one translation of the Sanskrit name Avalokiteśvara.[23] The name Guanyin does not appear in the received, canonical version of this scripture, and we do not have a Dunhuang or other early manuscript version that confirms the passage that seems to have prompted Zhen Luan's criticism. It is thus likely that this passage was at some point revised to remove the offensive term.[24] The third passage objects to the very name of the Hidden Language, pointing out that Brahmā is a Buddhist term. The second passage requires fuller discussion. Here is a translation that shows clearly the ellipses in Zhen Luan's citation of the text:[25]

> The third [*juan*?] of the *Inner Sounds of the Various Heavens* eight graphs of the Zongpiao Heaven are *ze luo jue pu tai yuan da qian*.[26] The Resplendent Heavenly Perfected explains them by saying: "*Ze* is the name of a mountain in this heaven. [. . . This is where] the various dragons have their lairs. [. . .] *Luojue* is the [. . .] Lord of the Dao's inner name. [. . .] *Putai*[27] is the secret name of the [. . .] Perfected. [. . .] The Jade Tower [*tai*] is on the south side of Mount *Ze*. Thirty thousand suns and moons illuminate it from all around. *Luohan*[28] is the Lady of the Moon. [. . .][29] When it comes to the juncture of the grand kalpa cycles, all the suns and moons of the various heavens join below[30] the Jade Tower. At this division of the great chiliocosm [*daqian shijie zhi fen*], heaven and earth[31] will be transformed and the great chiliocosms will rush together."[32]

Zhen Luan is interested here in the Lingbao use, and, from his perspective, abuse, of the Buddhist term that I have translated "great chiliocosm." According to standard Buddhist explanations, the term *daqian shijie* "translates" *mahā-sahasra-loka-dhātu,* which is most easily explained in "Russian doll" fashion. A world system consists of Mount Sumeru, the seven continents and eight seas surrounding it, and the wall of iron mountains enclosing them. One thousand of these are a small chiliocosm, one thousand small chiliocosms are a medium chiliocosm, and one thousand medium chiliocosms are a great chiliocosm. Zhen Luan explains the term in precisely the same way and then wonders why Daoists might think that one thousand to the third power might equal "only thirty thousand suns."

Now it is easy enough to point out that Zhen Luan is, perhaps willfully, misconstruing his source, since the thirty thousand suns and moons that normally illumine the mountain in this heaven are, according to the passage he cites, not necessarily the same number that will congregate at the juncture of the two great kalpa cycles. But it is more important to try and understand what has excited Zhen Luan's indignation. In each case, Buddhist terms are used in unusual ways, stretched beyond their canonical significances. *Guanyin* is taken to be a manifestation of the Celestial Worthy of Primordial Origins; Brahmā is shown to be a swirling primal *qi* that forms graphs; and the importance of the great chiliocosm is that it collapses into a generative concretion at the end of a kalpa cycle. And, as Zhen Luan's criticisms make clear, from the perspective of standard Buddhist doctrine these "explanations" are incorrect. Nowhere does Zhen Luan attack the central notion of the Hidden Script, that there is a written language descending from earlier kalpas and other world systems that might be translated. Instead, the way he sets up his critiques implies that he accepts this much. Elsewhere, Zhen Luan does question Daoist access to divine knowledge, yet here he does not.[33] Instead, he carefully lists the words of the Hidden language that are glossed and the central points of the Resplendent Heavenly Perfected's explanations, even in cases where he might have simply cited the offending passage. His reticence to declare the whole matter of translation bogus is, I think, telling. Because Buddhist scripture was likewise subject to translation and explication in order to be understood, Zhen Luan must have felt the need for caution. As he explains it, then, Daoist interpretations were at fault, not the procedure itself.

There was a good reason for Zhen Luan's reticence. Daoist imitation in this case was close in style, terminology, and presentation to what Buddhist preachers and translators had to say about the sources of their knowledge. Take, for instance the description of the process, likely by Zhi Qian, found in his introduction to a translation of the *Dhammapada*:[34]

> The Buddha is difficult to encounter; his scriptures difficult to hear about. Furthermore, the Buddhas all reside in India and the language of India has a different sound from that of the Han [people, i.e. Chinese]. It is said that the writing is a celestial writing and that the language is a celestial language. The names they give to things are different and transmitting the real substance is not easy.[35]

This passage shows that, whether their views were based on a faint knowledge of the Indian myths surrounding *devanāgarī* and the god Brahmā's creation of language or simply on the fact that India became known in China as "Heavenly *Zhu*," contemporary Chinese held that the written texts of the western regions were in a "celestial writing." Zhi Qian, the likely author of this passage, goes on to discuss how he received an original copy of the scripture from Weiqinan (= Vighna?) sometime after the latter's arrival in Wuchang in 224. Zhi Qian then asked another monk, Zhu Jiangyanto, to translate them. This brings up another discussion of translation issues.

> Although Jiangyan was skilled in the languages of India [*Tianzhu yu*], he did not yet fully understand Han [language]. In the words transmitted by him, he either retained the Central Asian [pronunciations], or he spoke out the general meaning in close to an unadorned, direct fashion. At first I was displeased with the fact that his expressions lacked elegance. Weiqinan said: "As for the words of Buddha, rely on their meaning—there is no need for adornment! Take their doctrine without embellishment! Those who transmit the scriptural texts should ensure that they are easily understood. When their true meaning is not lost, that is skilful." The seated gathering unanimously said: "Laozi said that beautiful words are not reliable, and that reliable words are not beautiful.[36] Confucius also said: Writing does not exhaust the meaning of words, and words cannot fully express ideas.[37] It is clear that the ideas of the Saint [= the Buddha] are profound without limit." Now, when transmitting the meaning of the Indian language, one really ought to go to the heart of the matter. Therefore, after having received the gāthās from the mouth of the translator, one must follow their fundamental purport, without adding embellishment. What the translation does not convey, remains wanting and untransmitted. There are thus omissions, and many things remain unrevealed. But [in this case], though the expressions are coarse, their bearing is profound; though the text is abbreviated, its meaning is vast.[38]

This passage provides a further glimpse of what we learn from other sources, that the discussions of Buddhism in salons and translation circles were collective affairs and that they often centered on traditional Chinese ideas of language and its ability to fully express ineffable truths.[39] The discussion begins with Zhi Qian's desire to see greater "elegance" in the translations of Jiangyan. The issue of literary embellishment and its ability at once to entice and deceive had been a topic of Chinese discussions of literature for hundreds of years.[40] The assembled auditors are thus not without resources to contribute to the discussion. Zhi Qian summarizes their statements to the effect that, according to both philosophical Daoist and Confucian sources of authority, words cannot express, but only hide, ultimate truth. In an interesting turn, they deduce that the ideas of the Buddha must indeed be profound, in that they are so difficult to express. It is inevitable though, that "things remain unrevealed," but there is the implied hope that interpretation can still deduce from what is conveyed something of the underlying profundity. In the end, as we will see more fully below, Zhi Qian concludes, as Daoists would also conclude, that even the imperfect meaning that can be rescued through the process of translation is too valuable to abandon faith in the process altogether.

In previous studies of celestial writing and the Daoist appropriation of the translation trope, we have not given much consideration to this recognition of the limitations of translation and language. As I hope to show, though, Lingbao accounts of the Hidden Language actually exploit this feature, both to reveal Buddhist truth as provisional and to privilege their own interpretations of celestial writing.

Traditional Chinese views of language acknowledged that, despite its supposed holy origin in the inherent patterns of the cosmos and the genius of the ancient sages who were first able to "read" these patterns and abstract them as human script, the writing employed now in the mundane world remains humanly fashioned. It is thus, as one Daoist account puts it "subject to the vicissitudes of the world."[41] This is the implied point of Daoist stories on the origin of script, each of which traces a process of devolution by which script is gradually alienated from its divine origins and extricated from its inherence within nature to become an imperfect medium available for the use and instruction of humans.[42]

The continued insistence on the divine nature of script and its priority over speech contributed further to anxieties concerning the truth value of text. The Chinese, like other cultures, distinguished in their language the true from the false (in the sense of "borrowed, not proper to the thing itself," *jia*), the "constructed," *zuo*, or the "humanly made," *wei*. How could the humanly constructed embody the hidden truth of things, as writing was held to do? Generally, the answer to this question involved various iterations of what we might style "inspiration." Rather than an intrusion of divine breath from outside, however, Chinese images concerning a writer's entrance into an "inspired" mental state more often feature the externalization of the spiritual components of the person. Witness, for instance, the description of inspiration found in the opening sections of Lu Ji's (261–303) "Rhapsody on Literature" (*Wen fu*):

> As for its beginnings: the complete retraction of vision, the inward turn
> of hearing,
> [Allows] absorptive thought to seek widely:
> My essences gallop to the eight limits [of horizontal space];
> My mind roams ten thousand spans [of vertical space].[43]

Here the author's creativity begins with a withdrawal from quotidian sights and sounds in a way that might be compared with Daoist "maintaining [psycho-physical] unity" *shou yi*. The material to be expressed is then gathered by the mystical roving of the author's essences *jing* and heart/mind *xin*, entities that were often depicted as spirits [*shenming*], even in nonreligious texts.[44] What is important here is that the authors of such explanations designed them to counter the sorts of concerns raised by Zhi Qian through contending that humanly fashioned language might indeed point to something beyond sight and hearing.

We noticed at the beginning of this chapter that, again and again in the Lingbao scriptures, the author's attention is drawn back to the centrality of the script in his representations of the fantastic celestial locales, characters, and scenes he describes.[45] There is a certain circularity in such representations. The central role of scripture in delineating the fantastic is written into scriptures so constructed as to highlight this role. It is almost as if the author knows subconsciously that the hyperbolically vast expanses, the fantastic flora and fauna, and the impossible celestial beings are literary constructions and cannot help but return to probe the ache of this realization through descriptions of how writing "makes" the fantastic. In fact, beyond descriptions of how celestial writing literally "makes" the world, the Lingbao scriptures contain several explicit statements on questions of the fantastic and authorship. Importantly for our current project, these passages do contain oblique references to Buddhist sūtra literature.[46]

Take, for instance, the following passage concerning Zhuangzi and his fantastical book:

> The Most High Lord of the Dao said: Zhuang Zhou is the Transcendent of Western Efflorescence. Formerly, when he was studying the Dao, he made an oath, saying: "When I achieve Transcendence and the Dao, and my abilities and knowledge are unlimited, I will come into the world to save people." . . . Later, his wish was fulfilled and he authored a book which entirely expresses the intentions of the Dao. Those in the world do not know that he is an elevated person of transcendent or perfected status and take all the creations of the *Zhuangzi* to be parables. The great Peng-bird, the Grand Cedrela, the Mingling Tree—these are all veritably recorded, not creations. It is just that large places give birth to large things, so that the Lang-garden, Mount Kunlun, and Penglai Isle in the midst of the northern sea all contain such [immense] spiritual things. And small places give birth to smaller things. If you believe only what you see and doubt the existence of what you do not then there are many things under heaven that you will

> deny. [For example], the metaphorical passages of scriptures of the Dao speak of the vast time span of the kalpa as follows: If there was a stone like Mount Kunlun, with a mustard seed [buried] forty *li* within it, and a celestial being in gauze robes passed by it once every hundred years, then the time it would take [for the celestial being's robes] to brush through this stone so that she could take this mustard seed, that would be like the length of a kalpa. A length of time like this—who would believe it?!?[47]

This particular Lingbao scripture, I have hypothesized, was written to convince prospective Celestial Master adherents to abandon some of the more regrettable practices of that movement and to adopt Lingbao salvific ritual.[48] It is likely that the specific Celestial Master adherents targeted were members of the gentry class, those who read the *Zhuangzi* and the *Daode jing*, included Buddhist ideas in their store of knowledge, and practiced a Celestial Master Daoism at least partly tempered by the Shangqing scriptures. The claim that the length of a kalpa might not be believable would have struck this audience as wrong-headed and only possible for lesser intellects.

Similar polemical defenses of the truth of Lingbao pronouncements appear fairly frequently in the scriptures, but few name specific beliefs as does this passage. The last item in this defense, we note, seems to conflate two separate metaphors concerning the length of a kalpa, one that portrays it as the time it will take for the gossamer silk robes of a celestial being to wear away a massive stone and another that portrays it as the length of time that it would take to empty a huge walled city filled with sesame seeds if only one seed were taken out every hundred years.[49] It is noteworthy, I think, that what began as defense of Zhuangzi's hyperbole as factual information leads the author to think of Buddhist ideas of cosmic time and of the metaphors that express them.

Even in passages exploring the miraculous appearance of the Hidden Language of the Great Brahmā and its careful celestial exegesis there are signs that one should not expect total comprehension; that, as Zhi Qian wrote, "though the expressions are coarse, their bearing is profound; though the text is abbreviated, its meaning is vast." This can be seen most clearly in a passage in which the Resplendent Heavenly Perfected, the deity responsible for explaining the Hidden Language of the Grand Brahmā [*Dafan yinyu*] expresses his own struggles with celestial place names and other metaphors.

> Although having passed through billions of kalpas of previous lives, I have traveled to the origins of the heavens and, following the law through

> life and death, have always been born together with the Perfected Script, still I have not mastered its mysterious transformations nor penetrated to its origins. I am mindful of my own shortcomings, yet seek to express this self-generated script and explain its elusive graphs, thus striking the green-gem chimes and knocking harmonies from the red-gem stones. Though I do not fully comprehend the significance or the graphic forms, I [know] enough to rehearse the origins of heaven and earth. The affairs of the various heavens, their breadth, cycles, climates, transformations, suns, moons, constellations, palaces, natural features, Perfected beings, cities, towers, demon-kings, ghosts and spirits, and the sources of their coordination—such things are deep mysteries and cannot be entirely explained. Moreover, questions concerning karma have already been addressed in older chapters and so it would be troublesome and repetitious to discuss them separately here. Now I have roughly explained the meanings of the Celestial Script. The Dao revealed is sufficient to save the people of Heaven and to pluck out the roots of suffering [= karmic debt].[50]

The difficulty of making plain the meaning of these "elusive" graphic forms is further symbolized in the opening scene of the scripture.[51] When the Celestial Worthy assembles the hordes of gods, saints, and perfected beings in a fantastic garden, they are suddenly plunged into total darkness for three days and nights and the celestial beings quail in fright. Queried as to the reason for this, the Celestial Worthy assures them that they are about to witness a miracle of salvation. The assembled celestials close their eyes and bow when suddenly, in a simulacrum of the cosmogenesis, the forms of Hidden Script in graphs one hundred feet square appear to illumine the scene. This miracle is followed by a rhymed *gatha* that, like those appearing in Buddhist scripture, reiterates in verse form the preceding actions.

It is at this point that the Celestial Worthy summons the Resplendent Heavenly Perfected, who proclaims his lack of worthiness in words similar to those cited above. And again, when he writes his "translation," the transition from the darkness of incomprehension to the light of dawning understanding is reiterated in words that might express the meditative state of the original human author of the Hidden Script:

> The graphs were fluid and mysterious. It was not that the celestial writing was formless, but it had truly hidden its complete perfection in order [to show] the worth of its marvelous imaging. In wondrous response to its

> charts, its Way was set in motion. And the Celestial Worthy did not regard my abilities [to express these truths] as incoherent, but ordered me to explain [the graphs'] meaning and to express their jade sounds. The mystic ordinances commanded it, how could I disobey? On the day that I began to write, my form and *hun* immediately departed and guided that which I observed, so that I could more or less annotate these graphs. As to the true and false [of what I write] I have been extremely thoughtful and careful. And, since the illustrious Way has thus been clarified, all of the heavens announced their felicitations.[52]

In the face of the mysterious and hidden, the Resplendent Heavenly Perfected responds in precisely the same fashion as Lu Ji's human author. The spiritual constituents depart from his body and guide him to an apprehension of the true significance of the Hidden Graphs. And, despite his efforts, the result is but an approximation. While this is so, the passage implies that we should trust the results of the Heavenly Perfected's translation efforts. The phrase I have clumsily rendered "the Celestial Worthy did not regard my abilities [to express these truths] as incoherent [*na*]" contains a reference to the *Laozi*'s forty-sixth section: "Great skill seems but awkwardness; great eloquence seems but stammering [na^2]."[53] Despite this, and his status as a celestial, the best the Heavenly Perfected can claim is that "Though I do not fully comprehend the significance or the graphic forms [of the Hidden Script], I [know] enough to rehearse the origins of heaven and earth . . . sufficient to save the people."

It is significant, I believe, that the Daoist author of the Lingbao scriptures here endorses, at least implicitly, the faulty syllogism presented by Zhi Qian. We have seen that Zhi Qian's audience, recalling passages attributed to Laozi and Confucius on the inability of words to express the unseen, concluded that the words of the Buddha must be profound. Their reasoning seems to be: (1) Truly profound ideas cannot be expressed in language. (2) The truths of Buddhism cannot be fully expressed in our language. (3) Thus, the truths of Buddhism are profound. The Lingbao author, too, highlights the difficulty of translation in ways that accord higher value to his composition. Further, in reinforcing the difficulty of translation, he seems to cast doubt on one Buddhist claim to prestige—that its texts were translated from, as Zhi Qian puts it, "a celestial script." The success of this Lingbao strategy, it seems to me, is what makes Zhen Luan loathe to attack the notion of the Hidden Language directly and to instead criticize items of terminology that he can reveal as appropriated and incorrectly glossed.

Judging by the prominent role celestial script plays in the Lingbao scriptures, it thus seems to me that what made the most profound impression that Buddhism made upon Daoist writers was not the sorts of "influences," whether formal, conceptual, or complex, studied by Erik Zürcher. Instead it was the very fact of Buddhist scripture itself, with all of the problems and perplexities attendant upon its translation into Chinese graphs. While it is certainly true that ancient Chinese writers were very sophisticated about language (witness the passages from the *Zhuangzi* discussed earlier), Buddhism and its scripts presented them with a new challenge: philosophically dense texts that had not just to be "translated and retranslated" from a foreign tongue, but painstakingly worked out, often by committee, from a foreign *writing system*. This brought with it the realization that what once had passed for *tianshu*, the writing of heaven, did not in fact broach all things in heaven and earth. And this realization, in turn, presented new opportunities for creativity, but also awoke old perplexities concerning the truth value of linguistic expression.

Appendix

Below, I append a translation of the first eight graphs of the Hidden Language of the Great Brahmā as interpreted by the Resplendent Heavenly Perfected.[54] These eight graphs are associated with the Taihuang huangzeng heaven, the first of the eight heavens of the east. The explanation for each heaven is laid out in the same way and can be divided into three parts. First is the general introduction of the eight graphs. Following this introduction is the verse that includes the eight graphs. The eight graphs appear in each verse in a regular pattern. The first graph appears as the third character of the first line. Each subsequent character figures as the first graph of succeeding lines. These verses introduce even more pseudo-transcriptions and my translation is thus especially tentative at this point. Finally, we get the glosses proper. Here the Resplendent Heavenly Perfected explains the terms of the eight graphs and of the further terms introduced in the verses. In each of these appearances of the eight graphs, I highlight their transcription or translation by marking them in bold.

> Within the Taihuang huangzeng heaven are eight self-generated graphs. They are pronounced **dan lou e hui yuan**[55] **he guan yin**. The Resplendent Heavenly Perfected said: "These eight graphs are self-generated writing that flies in the darkness. Each graph is ten feet by ten feet. They are patterned and multicolor, flashing brightly and penetrating with their beams

the eight directions of space. The [Celestial Worthy] of Primordial Origins sent down instructions that I write out these graphs and explain their pronunciations. Together, they form the limitless sounds of the Hidden Language of the Great Brahmā of the Huangzeng heaven. They were given to the Lord of the Dao with the instructions that he teach them to those who have transcendent rank [through the merit of] former lives and to save those who are to achieve the Dao in the Huangzeng heaven.

> The Huangzeng heaven **ends** with the primal strands.
> **Lou**du borders the upper metropolis.
> Within **A**na, the shaken jade-slips sound—
> How long and winding [the road to] **Hui**xiu.
> Within **primal** nothingness Perfected are born,
> Through **He**da the bright bridge extends.
> **Guan**jue brightens the stygian realms in the four directions.
> The **rhymes** by themselves form strophes.

The Resplendent Heavenly Perfected said: This stanza is formed of the joined flying mysterious *qi* of the five directions in the Huangzeng heaven in order to harmonize the self-actualized tones of the eight graphs. It is called the "limitless cavern strophe." The Huangzeng heaven is 900,900,000 *qi* distant from the Taiming yuwan heaven [the second heaven of the east]. "Primal strands" [describes] the extremities of the netting covering the eight directions. ***Loudu*** is the name of a tall tower in the middle of the heaven. Above it joins with the Palace of Great Mystery, which is on Jade Capitoline Mountain.[56] ***Ana*** is the overseer of *Loudu*, in charge of the regulation of the Six Brahmā [*qi*].[57] When the numbers indicate the conjunction, the drums of *Loudu* sound and the Perfected all assemble in audience. ***Huixiu*** is the Thearchical Lord's loft building for roaming. ***Heda*** is the gate of the sun and moon. The Perfected ride golden chariots to open the stygian blackness; the Jade Maidens carry floriated banners to unloose the bonds [confining the dead to the underworld]. ***Guanjue*** is responsible for the registers of [those in the postmortem halls] of eternal night. In the tenebrous regions of the four directions, he plucks forth [the dead] from the nine stygian halls. Those who are able to practice Retreats on the days of the eight nodes and chant the cavern strophe in order to pacify their cloudsouls will find that their seven generations of ancestors will receive illumination and their desiccated frames will return home. Those who wear at their waists the eight graphs in red writing and who clearly understand their limitless tones will ride cloud carts to reach and travel aimlessly in the seven treasure groves.[58] Transcendent youths and Jade Maidens will attend and guard them there.

According to another passage in this scripture, the eight graphs of the Hidden Language are divided into "words" as follows: *danlou'e huiyuan heguanyin*. Thus, while *guanyin* seems, as Zürcher noticed, to be a recognizable bit of Sanskrit transcription, it is not in fact presented here as an independent word. As we saw earlier, the other mention of Guanyin in the scripture is also suspect.

It is important to note that each of the words are said to be inscribed on the specific spots in the heavens that are found in the passage translated above. *Danlou'e* is found on the tall tower of the Mystic Metropolis, presumably the tower *Loudu*. The word is said to "regulate the movements of heaven and earth and to summon the Perfected and Great Gods of the ten directions." *Huiyuan* appears on the southern balustrade of the Thearchical Lord's loft building for roaming (*Huixiu*) and "spontaneously gives birth to the spirits and Perfected in the air above." *Heguanyin* is written on the gate of sun and moon (*Heda*), and is responsible for the salvific beams of light that "penetrate the nine stygian regions and the bureaus of eternal night."

The ritual uses of each of the words correspond to these locations in the heavens.[59]

First, each of the words might be written in red on paper and ingested. The first word, *danlou'e*, is to be swallowed on the ten Retreat days of the month to summon the deities. The second word, *huiyuan*, is used on the fifteenth and the thirtieth of the month for a period of twenty-four years to ensure that one might visit the loft building of the Thearchical Lord. The third word, *heguanyin*, should be ingested on the days of the full and the new moon. After only eight years, one's body will glow internally and one will be assured a physical refinement in the offices of the sun and moon.[60]

Second, the graphs should be written out and worn on the body. When this is done, "the three offices will no longer keep records of evil recompense [toward you] and your name will be inscribed in the Huangzeng heaven, where you will be reborn endlessly, kalpa after kalpa, along with the cycles [of time]."[61]

Glossary

A

Ana 阿那
Annen 安然
Anxin wenda 安心問答
Api damo da piposha lun 阿毘達磨大毘婆沙論
Ayuwang jing 阿育王經
Ayuwang ta 阿育王塔
Ayuwang zhuan 阿育王傳

B

Banruo wuzhi lun 般若無知論
Baojuan 寶卷
Baoming of Lingjuesi 靈覺寺寶明
Baopuzi 抱朴子
baoqieyin ta 寶篋印塔
Baoqieyin xinzhou jing 寶篋印心咒經
Beilin 碑林
Benwen 本文
Bi 臂
Bian 變
Bi'an Haikuan 彼岸海寬
Bianhua 變化 (nirmāṇa)
Bianwen 變文
Biemen 別門
Biyan lu 碧巖錄
Bodhidharma 菩提達摩
Bosi 波斯國

Bosiniwang 波斯匿王
Bukong 不空

C

Caodong 曹洞
Cao Jinyan 曹錦炎
Chang ahan jing 長阿含經
Changzhu yuan 常住院
Chan song 禪誦
Chengdu 成都
Chengfu 承負
Chengjiu xian 成就仙
Cheng weishi lun 成唯識論
Chen Jingyuan 陳景原
Chi 赤
Chisong zi zhangli 赤松子章曆
Chongde 崇德
Chongfu si 崇福寺
Chongsun 重孫
Chongzhensi 崇真寺
Chuanqi 傳奇
Chūjin 忠尋
Chu sanzang jiji 出三藏記集
Chuzu an 出祖庵
Ciyun 慈雲
Ciyun an 慈雲庵

D

Da banniepan jing 大般涅槃經
Da bannihuan jing 大般泥洹經
Da fang guang fo huayan jing 大方廣佛華嚴經
Dafan yinyu 大梵隱語
Daibutsu 大仏
Dakiniten 荼吉尼天
Da loutan jing 大樓炭經
Danlou'a 亶婁阿

Danlou'a hui wu he guan yin 亶婁阿薈無惒觀音
Danlou'a huiyuan heguanyin 亶婁阿薈元惒觀音
Danuo 大儺
Daocheng 道誠
Dao de jing 道德經
Daogong 道公
Daohong of Chanlinsi 禪林寺道弘
Daojiao yishu 道教義樞
Daolü jinji 道律禁忌
Daopin of Banruosi 般若寺道品
Daosheng 道生
Daoshi 道世
Daoxin 道信
Daoxuan 道宣
Daqian dongran 大千洞然
Daqian shijie 大千世界
Daqian shijie zhi fen 大千世界之分
Daqian tongyi er cun yan 大千同一而存焉
Dasheng 大乘
Dasheng yizhang 大乘義章
Da Tang Sanzang qu jing shihua 大唐三藏取經詩話
Datang xiyu ji 大唐西域記
Datong 大同
Datong 大統
Da yaocha jiang 大藥叉將
Da Yu 大禹
Da zhidu lun 大智度論
Dazhu Huihai 大珠慧海
Dechajia 得(德)叉迦 (Takṣaka)
De xing yong yan heng, miao ti chang jian gu 德行永延恒，妙体常坚固
Ding 定
Diyu 地獄
Dizang pusa 地藏菩薩
Dōgen 道元
Dōki 道喜
Dōkyō 道鏡
Dongfang shengren 東方聖人
Dongnan foguo 東南佛國

Dongshan Liangjie 洞山良价
Dongyang 東陽
Dunwu 頓悟
Dunwu rudao yaomen 頓悟入道要門
Duowen Tian 多聞天
Duren miaojing sizhu 度人妙經四注

E

Enchin 圓珍
Erzu an 二祖庵

F

Fahua jing 法華經
Fan 梵
Fangtou 房頭
Fanmo jing 梵摩經
Fanmoyu jing 梵摩渝經
Fanxing liuqi 梵行六氣
Fasheli 法舍利
Fa tong 法統
Fa wu 法物
Faxian 法顯
Fayan 法眼
Fayuan zhulin 法苑珠林
Fazang 法藏
Feixia si 飛霞寺
Fengdao kejie yingshi 奉道科戒營始
Fengtan 風壇
Fengshen yanyi 封神演義
Fennu 忿怒
Fennu Nazha 忿怒那吒
Foding 佛頂
Fo shuo zao ta gongde jing 佛說造塔功德經
Fotucheng 佛圖澄
Fotuo batuoluo 佛陀跋陀羅
Foyan 佛眼

Foying ku 佛影窟
Fo yi shichang hua zhu yinnü 佛詣試場化諸婬女
Fozu tongji 佛祖統紀
Fu hui zhi zi jue, liao ben yuan ke wu 福慧智子觉,了本圆可悟
Fukuoka 福岡

G

Gaigong 改公
Gan Bao 干寶
Gaoseng zhuan 高僧傳
Gaozu 高祖
Geboluo 葛波羅
Ge Hong 葛洪
Ge Xuan 葛玄
Geyi 格義
Gongfu 工夫
Guanfo sanmei hai jing 觀佛三昧海經
Guanjue 觀覺
Guan mawangzang pin 觀馬王藏品
Guan siweiyi pin 觀四威儀品
Guan wuliangshoufo jing 觀無量壽佛經
Guanyin 觀音
Gu fo 古佛

H

Han Yu 韓愈
Heda 曷答
Heguanyin 曷觀音
Heilongtan 黑龍潭
Hejia 合家
Henan Songshan zuting Shaolin chansi di ershiwu dai zhuchi Ningran gong chan shi daoxing bei 河南嵩山祖庭少林禅寺第二十五代住持凝然改公禅师道行碑
Hetian 和田
Hexi 河西
Heze Shenhui 荷澤神會

Hōkyōin kyōki 寶篋印經記
Hongren 弘忍
Hou Liang 後梁
Hou Tang 後唐
Hua 鏵
Huachu 化出
Hua hu jing 化胡經
Huangbo Xiyun 黃檗希運
Huangfeita 皇妃塔
Huangzeng heaven 皇曾天
Huayan 華嚴
Huainan 淮南
Huijiao 慧皎
Huike 慧可
Huineng 慧能
Huixiu 薈秀
Huiyuan 薈元
Hun 魂
Hu Shi 胡適
Hyakumantō darani 百万塔陀羅尼

J

Ji 紀
Jia 假
Jia 家
Jian gongde 建功德
Jiangshi zhi chang 講試之場
Jiangliang yeshe 疆良耶舍
Jianye 建業
Jianzhen 鑑真
Jiating 家庭
Jiedushi 節度使
Jie jiazhi huo 竭家之貨
Jigudu zhangzhenü dedu yinyuan jing 給孤独長者女得度因縁經
Jing 精
Jin gang bei 金剛鉀
Jingjue 淨覺

Jinshiqie 金石契
Jingu 金鼓
Jingying Huiyuan 淨影慧遠
Jinhua 金華
Jinlü 禁律
Jinshi 謹識
Jin tu ta 金塗塔
Jin yin 金印
Ji shenzhou sanbao ganying lu 集神州三寶感應錄
Jiuding 九鼎
Jizang 吉藏
Juan 卷
Jueguan 絕觀
Jueguan lun 絕觀論
Juejin 覺金
Jueyu 覺玉
Jungong Yun'an 均公芸庵
Junzen no yo 純禅の代
Jusheng shen 俱生神

K

Kai 開
Kaibao si 開寶寺
Kaifeng 開封
Kaiming 開冥
Kaiyuan 開元
Kangwang zhi gao 康王之誥
Keai 可愛
Keding 可定
Kejing 可敬
Keying 可瑛
Kezheng 可政
Kokuya-shin 黑夜神
Kongōji 金剛寺
Kontaiji 金胎寺
Kuaiji 會稽
Kuaimu wang 快目王

Kuigong 魁公
Kūkai 空海
Kunlun 崑崙

L

Lang Garden 閬苑
Languages of India, see Tianzhu yu 天竺語
Laojun 老君
Leifeng 雷峰
Leifeng ta 雷峰塔
Lengqie shizi ji 楞伽師資記
Li 禮
Li 里
Liang dynasty 梁
Liangshu 梁書
Liang Zhe jinshi zhi 兩浙金石志
Liaogai 了改
Lidai fabao ji 歷代法寶記
Li Jing 李靖
Lingbao 靈寶
Lingbao jing shumu 靈寶經書目
Ling ta 靈塔
Ling taihou 靈太后
Linian 離念
Linji 臨濟
Linzi 臨淄
Li Shaowei 李少微
Lishi 離石
Liu Sahe 劉薩荷
Liu Songnian劉松年
Liuzu tanjing 六祖壇經
Long 龍
Longfeng zhi zhang 龍鳳之章
Loudu 婁都
Lu Ji 陸機
Luocha 羅刹
Luohan 羅漢

Luohan si 羅漢寺
Luo jue 落覺
Lu Xiujing 陸修靜
Lu Xun 魯迅
Luoyang 洛陽
Luoyang qielan ji 洛陽伽藍記
Luoye 絡腋
Luoying 羅映

M

Mabito Genkai 真人元开
Maoyin 鄮鄞
Mentou 門頭
Miaoyi 妙意
Mie 滅
Miedu 滅度
Miejinding 滅盡定
Mijiao 密教
Ming 名
Ming 命
Mingling 冥靈
Ming xiang ji 冥祥記
Mingzong 明宗
Minjian ta 民間塔
Minzhou 閩州
Mu jing 木經
Mulian 目蓮

N

Na 吶
Na 訥
Na 拏 (transliterating the Sanskrit ṇa)
Nai 乃
Naixin 乃心
Naluojiupoluo 那羅鳩婆羅
Naluojubaluo 捺羅俱跋羅

Naluoyan 那羅延
Naṇa 那拏
Nansi ta 南寺塔
Nantuo 難陀
Nanyang Huizhong 南陽慧忠
Nanyuan 南園
Na yu yu fu mo luo fa lun 那育郁馥摩羅法輪
Nazha 那吒
Nazha Cheng 那吒城
Nazhajuboluo qiu chengjiu jing 那吒俱鉢囉求成就經
Nazhajuwaluo 那吒矩韈囉
Nazha Taizi qiu chengjiu tuoluoni jing 那吒太子求成就陀羅尼經
Nezha 哪吒
Nichiren 日蓮
Nihuanseng 泥洹僧
Ningbo 寧波
Ningran Liaogai 凝然了改
Niu 紐
Niutou zong 牛頭宗
Nukariya Kaiten 忽滑谷快天
Nüqing guilü 女青鬼律

P

Peng 鵬
Penglai 蓬萊
Peng Zu 彭祖
Pi 披
Pingdeng wang 平等王
Piniu 披紐
Piniu guanjue 披紐觀覺
Pishamen 毗沙門
Pishezuo 毘舍左
Puji 普濟
Puji zhenren 普及真人
Pusa benye jing 菩薩本業經
Putai 菩臺
Puyao jing 普耀經

Q

Qi 氣 or 炁
Qian Chu 錢俶
Qian (Hong) chu 錢(弘)俶
Qian Liu 錢鏐
Qianshi jiasheng 錢氏家乘
Qiantang 錢塘
Qian Wen 錢文
Qian Wusu 錢武肅
Qian Yuanguan 錢元瓘
Qi houqiri, yuan wang pingzhi jiangshi zhi chang 期後七日，願王平治講試之場
Qilisena 訖哩瑟拏
Qimutian 七母天
Qing 清
Qingong 欽公
Qingwai 清外
Qishi'er bian (hua) 七十二變(化)
Quanzhen 全真
Que houqiri 却後七日
Que houqiri fo zizhi zhi 却後七日佛自知之

R

Renshou 仁壽
Rulüda 如閭達
Ryōgen 良源

S

Saichō 最澄
Sanjiao yuanliu soushen daquan 三教源流搜神大全
Sanlun 三論
Sanmojie jing 三摩竭經
Sanyuan pinjie 三元品誡
Seiganji 誓願寺
Seihanbon 整版本

Sengchou 僧稠
Sengfu 僧副
Sengyou 僧祐
Sengzhao 僧肇
Shamonda 遮文荼
Shangqing 上清
Shangyu 上虞
Shanhua jiaoye 山花蕉葉
Shanzhao 善昭
Shaolin chansi xianghuo tiandi fenwei shifen bei 少林禪寺香火田地分為十份碑
Shaoxing 紹興
Shenfu 神符
Shenhui 神會
Shenkeng 深坑
Shenming 神明
Shensha shen 深沙神
Shensheli 身舍利
Shenshi 神識
Shentong 神通
Shenxiu 神秀
Shewei 舍衛
Sheweiguo 舍衛國
Shi 識
Shichang 試場
Shi'e 十惡
Shiguo 十國
Shiguo chunqiu 十國春秋
Shihu 施護
Shiji Niangniang 石磯娘娘
Shijia rulai zhenshen sheli baota zhuan 釋迦如來真身舍利寶塔傳
Shijie 尸解
Shijie 十誡
Shimen zhengtong 釋門正統
Shisanjing zhushu 十三經注疏
Shizong 世宗
Shizu 始祖
Shōten 聖天
Shou 受

Shouyi 守一
Shuangwang 雙王
Shujing 書經
Shun 舜
Shunxing fanshu 順形梵書
Sifen lü 四分律
Silu 司禄
Siming 司命
Siming 四明
Song dynasty 宋朝
Songyuan Juexun 松源覺訓
Sou shen ji 搜神記
Su 俗
Suan 算
Sui Wendi 隋文帝
Sun 孫
Sun Wukong 孫悟空
Sutubo 窣土波

T

Ta 塔
Tai 台
Taiji zuoxian gong 太極左仙公
Taiping jing 太平經
Taihuang huangzeng Heaven 太黃皇曾天
Taishan Fujun 泰山府君
Taishang lingbao zhutian neiyin ziran yuzi 太上靈寶諸天內音自然玉字
Taishang zhenren fu lingbao zhaijie weiyi zhujing yaojue 太上真人敷靈寶齋戒威儀諸經要訣
Taishang zhutian lingshu duming miao jing 太上諸天靈書度命妙經
Taishō shinshū daizōkyō 大正新修大藏經
Taiyi 太乙
Taizang jie 胎藏界
Taizu 太祖
Takakusa Junjirō 高楠順次郎
Talin 塔林
Tanmozui of Rongjuesi 融覺寺曇謨最

Tianbao 天寶
Tiandi 天地
Tianfeng ta 天封塔
Tianfu 天福
Tianshi dao 天師道
Tianshu 天書
Tiantai 天台
Tianxia 天下
Tianxia bingma du yuanshuai 天下兵馬都元帥
Tianxizai 天息災
Tianzhen huangren 天真皇人
Tianzhu 天竺
Tianzhu yu 天竺語
Tōdai wajō tōseiden 唐大和上東征傳
Tonggu 銅鼓
Tongguang 同光
Tongmen 通門
Tongming 同名
Tongsheng shen 同生神
Tuoluoni 陀羅尼

W

Wai jingang bu 外金剛部
Wanfo ta 萬佛塔
Wang Chong 王充
Wang Shijun 王士俊
Wang Xuance 王玄策
Wang Yan 王琰
Wei 偽
Wei dynasty 北魏
Wei Huacun 魏華存
Weinu 威怒
Weiqinan 維祇難
Weiyang 溈仰
Wen fu 文賦
Wengong 文公
Wen xuan 文選

Wo zizhi shi 我自知時
Wu 無 or 无
Wu 吳
Wudai 五代
Wudao dashen 五道大神
Wudao Jiangjun 五道将軍
Wugoujingguang da tuoluoni jing 無垢浄光大陀羅尼經
Wuguang 悟光
Wu Keji 吳克己
Wulin 武林
Wunian 無念
Wupian zhenwen五篇真文
Wuponantuo 烏波難陀
Wuqing 無情
Wuqing foxing 無情佛性
Wushi 五時
Wuwei 無為
Wuwei zhongxue 無為中學
Wuwo 無我
Wuxiang 無想
Wuxin 無心
Wuxin lun 無心論
Wuyan 無言
Wuyue 吳越
Wuyue guowang 吳越國王
Wuyue Kingdom 吳越國
Wuyue wang 吳越王

X

Xian 現
Xianchun Lin'an zhi 咸淳臨安志
Xiang 想
Xiang'er 想爾
Xiang mo bianwen 降魔變文
Xianshen 先身
Xianshi 先世
Xianyu jing 賢愚經

Xiao 孝
Xiaodao lun 笑道論
Xiaosheng 小乘
Xiaoshuo 小說
Xiao Tong 蕭統
Xihe 西河
Xiling 西陵
Xin 心
Xi ta 西塔
Xiwei 西魏
Xiyou ji 西遊記
Xuda qi jingshe 須達起精舍
Xumotinü jing 須摩提女經
Xuanzang 玄奘
Xueting Fuyu 雪庭福裕
Xueting wei daoshi, yin ru gui xuan lu 雪庭為導師, 引汝皈鉉路

Y

Yang Xi 楊羲
Yang Xuanzhi 楊衒之
Yao 堯
Yaocha 藥叉
Yao prefecture 姚郡
Yecha 夜叉
Yichanti 一闡提
Yijing 易淨
Yijing 義淨
Yiqie rulai xinmimi quanshensheli baoqieyin tuoluoni jing 一切如來心秘密全身舍利寶篋印陀羅尼經
Yixing 一行
Yizang jinjin 一藏金盡
Yongming Yanshou 永明延壽
Yongningsi 永寧寺
Yongxin 永信
You 幽
You lou 有漏
Yuanjia 元嘉

Yuanshi tianzun 元始天尊
Yuanshi wuliang duren shangpin miaojing sizhu 元始無量度人上品妙經四注
Yuce 玉冊
Yueguang 月光
Yue wang 越王
Yuezhou 越州
Yufu 餘福
Yugong 裕公
Yuguo 餘過
Yu Hao 喻皓
Yulanpen hui 盂蘭盆會
Yushi 於是
Yushi 餘史
Yunji qiqian 雲笈七籤
Yunmen 雲門

Z

Zanning 贊寧
Ze 澤
Ze luo jue pu tai yuan da qian 澤落覺菩臺緣大千
Zei 賊
Zengyi ahan jing 增壱阿含經
Zhang Daoling 張道陵
Zhang Daoling qi shi Zhao Sheng 張道陵七試趙昇
Zhang Xiaolian 張孝廉
Zhanran 湛然
Zhaolun 肇論
Zhaozong 昭宗
Zhen'gao 真誥
Zheng Qiao 鄭樵
Zhengyi 正一
Zhen Luan 甄鸞
Zhenren 真人
Zhi 至
Zhiguai 志怪
Zhi Qian 支謙
Zhisheng of Baomingsi 寶明寺智聖

Zhishi 知事
Zhiyi 智顗
Zhong ahan jing 中阿含經
Zhongguo 中國
Zhong Kui 鍾馗
Zhongmin 種民
Zhongtai 中台
Zhongtan yuanshuai 中壇元帥
Zhuangzi 莊子
Zhuangzong 莊宗
Zhuanlun shengwang 轉輪聖王
Zhuchi 住持
Zhu Jiangyan 竺將焰
Zining 子寧
Zongjing lu 宗鏡錄
Zongpiao 宗飄
Zong tong 宗統
Zu 族
Zuo 作
Zuochan kuxing 坐禪苦行

Notes

Introduction

1. It would be impossible to cover here the vast literature on the Indian-Chinese cultural exchange. Some noteworthy examples include Erik Zürcher, *The Buddhist Conquest of China* (Leiden: Brill, 1959); Kenneth Ch'en, *The Chinese Transformation of Buddhism* (Princeton, N.J.: Princeton University Press, 1973); Stephen Teiser, *The Scripture of the Ten Kings and the Making of Purgatory in Medieval Chinese Buddhism* (Honolulu: University of Hawai'i Press, 1994); John Kieschnick, *The Impact of Buddhism on Chinese Material Culture* (Princeton, N.J.: Princeton University Press, 2003); Victor Mair, *Painting and Performance: Chinese Picture Recitation and Its Indian Genesis* (Honolulu: University of Hawai'i Press, 1988); Victor Mair, *T'ang Transformation Texts* (Cambridge, Mass.: Council on East Asian Studies, 1989); Xu Dishan, "Fanju tili jiqi zai Hanjushang de diandian didi," in *Zhongguo xiju qiyuan*, ed. Xia Xieshi et al. (Shanghai: Zhishi chubanshe, 1990), 86–118; Victor Mair and Tsu-lin Mei, "The Sanskrit Origins of Recent Style Prosody," *Harvard Journal of Asiatic Studies* 51, 2 (December 1991): 375–470; Richard Mather, "Chinese and Indian Perceptions of Each Other between the First and Seventh Centuries," *Journal of the American Oriental Society* 112, 1 (1992): 1–8; Wang Bangwei, "Buddhist Nikāyas Through Ancient Chinese Eyes," in *Untersuchungen zur buddhistischen Literatur*, Sanskrit-Wörterbuch der buddhistischen Texte aus den Turfan-Funden, Beiheft 5 (Göttingen: Vandenhoeck & Ruprecht, 1994), 166–203; and Victor Mair, "Xie He's 'Six Laws' of Painting and Their Indian Parallels," in *Chinese Aesthetics: The Ordering of Literature, the Arts, and the Universe in the Six Dynasties*, ed. Zong-qi Cai (Honolulu: University of Hawai'i Press, 2004), 81–122.

2. The first military conflict between India and China took place in 648, when, according to Chinese sources, a Chinese embassy led by Wang Xuance was attacked by the Indian king Aruṇāśa. Wang survived the attack and retreated to Tibet, where he recruited twelve hundred mercenaries and seven hundred Nepali cavalry. These troops returned and conquered Aruṇāśa and his men. The circumstances of this conflict are obscure and are not attested in Indian sources. Significantly for the argument below, even according to Chinese sources Chinese troops did not play a major role in the attack; as in the case of trade and religious exchange, this first Chinese-Indian military encounter took place between

surrogates. See Tansen Sen, *Buddhism, Diplomacy, and Trade: The Realignment of Sino-Indian Relations, 600–1400* (Honolulu: University of Hawai'i Press, 2003), 22–25.

3. On Indian-Chinese trade, see Xinru Liu, *Ancient India and Ancient China: Trade and Religious Exchange AD 1–600* (Oxford: Oxford University Press, 1988) and Sen, *Buddhism, Diplomacy, and Trade.*

4. For evidence of Indian merchants in China, see Sen, *Buddhism, Diplomacy, and Trade*, 162–64.

5. See Li Rongxi's translation of Xuanzang's travelogue, *The Great Tang Dynasty Record of the Western Regions*, BDK English Tripitaka 79 (Berkeley, Calif.: Numata Center, 1996); and Junjiro Takakusu's translation of Yijing (I-Tsing), *A Record of the Buddhist Religion as Practiced in India and the Malay Archipelago (A.D. 671–695)* (Oxford: Clarendon, 1896). See also Timothy H. Barrett, "Did I-Ching Go to India? Problems in Using I-Ching as a Source on South Asian Buddhism," *Buddhist Studies Review* 15, 2 (1998): 142–56; Wang Bangwei, *Nanhai jigui neifa zhuan jiaozhu* (Beijing: Zhonghua shuju, 2000); Sen, *Buddhism, Diplomacy, and Trade*, 17–19; and Max Deeg, *Das Gaoseng-Faxian-Zhuan als religionsgeschichtliche Quelle: Der älteste Bericht eines chinesischen buddhistischen Pilgermönchs über seine Reise nach Indien mit Übersetzung des Textes* (Wiesbaden: Harrassowitz, 2005).

6. As Robert Sharf puts it: "The Chinese 'encounter' or 'dialogue' with Buddhism took place almost exclusively among the Chinese themselves, on Chinese soil, in the Chinese language." See his *Coming to Terms with Chinese Buddhism* (Honolulu: University of Hawai'i Press, 2002), 2. The Chinese translation of Sanskrit and Prakrit Buddhist scriptures is a discipline unto itself; see among recent studies Jan Nattier, *A Guide to the Earliest Chinese Buddhist Translations* (Tokyo: International Research Institute for Advanced Buddhology, Soka University, 2008); Daniel Boucher, "Gāndhārī and the Early Chinese Buddhist Translations Reconsidered: The Case of the *Saddharmapuṇḍarīkasūtra*," *Journal of the American Oriental Society* 118, 4 (1998): 471–506; Stefano Zacchetti, *In Praise of Light: A Critical Synoptic Edition with an Annotated Translation of Chapters 1–3 Dharmarakṣa's* Guang zan jing (Tokyo: International Research Institute for Advanced Buddhology, Soka University, 2005); and the twelve essays edited by Max Deeg in the special edition devoted to early Chinese Buddhist translations in *Journal of the International Association of Buddhist Studies* 31, 1–2 (2008). It is not impossible that in some instances Chinese Buddhist texts were back-translated into Sanskrit, providing for Chinese influence on the evolution of Indian Buddhism; see Jan Nattier, "The *Heart Sūtra*: A Chinese Apocryphal Text?" *Journal of the International Association of Buddhist Studies* 15, 2 (1992): 153–223.

7. Zheng Qiao (1104–1162) is a possible example; see Victor Mair, "Cheng Ch'iao's Understanding of Sanskrit: The Concept of Spelling in China," in *A Festschrift in Honour of Professor Jao Tsung-I on the Occasion of His Seventy-Fifth Anniversary* (Hong Kong: Chinese University of Hong Kong Press, 1993), 331–41; and Sen, *Buddhism, Diplomacy, and Trade*, 229–30. Some Chinese *monks* did contemplate of course the linguistic differences between Sanskrit and their native tongue; see Daniel Boucher, "Buddhism and

Language in Early-Medieval China," in *A Reader of Traditional Chinese Culture*, ed. Victor H. Mair, Paul R. Goldin, and Nancy Steinhardt (Honolulu: University of Hawai'i Press, 2005), 265–69.

8. Xuanzang was reluctant to take on this project, and it is unclear whether it was accomplished. Paul Pelliot believes it was, whereas Tansen Sen has argued that it likely was not; compare Pelliot, "Autour d'une traduction sanscrite du Tao Tö King," *T'oung Pao* 13, 3 (1912): 351–430; and Sen, *Buddhism, Diplomacy, and Trade*, 45–46, 263 n131.

9. On the legend of Aśoka, see John Strong, *The Legend of King Aśoka* (Princeton, N.J.: Princeton University Press, 1983). For Chinese claims to have discovered relics distributed by Aśoka, see Kieschnick, *Impact of Buddhism on Chinese Material Culture*, 33–34; Sen, *Buddhism, Diplomacy, and Trade*, 59–63.

10. See Chen Jinhua, *Monks and Monarchs, Kinship and Kingship* (Kyoto: Italian School of East Asian Studies, 2002), and his "Sarira and Scepter: Empress Wu's Political Use of Buddhist Relics," *Journal of the International Association of Buddhist Studies* 25, 1–2 (2002): 33–150.

11. For a study of several biographies from India and their reception in China, see Stuart H. Young, "Conceiving the Indian Buddhist Patriarchs in China," Ph.D. dissertation, Princeton University, 2008.

12. The seventh-century monk Daoxuan, for instance, recorded in great detail his vision of a monastery in India. See Zhihui Tan, "Daoxuan's Vision of Jetavana: Imagining a Utopian Monastery in Early Tang," Ph.D. dissertation, University of Arizona, 2002. In addition to providing a complete translation of Daoxuan's text, Zhihui's work includes analysis of the Chinese conception of Indian Buddhism more generally.

13. It was the eighth-century Chan monk Shenhui who referred to Indians as spiritually accomplished and "guileless" in contrast to the Chinese who he said were prone to deceit. See Hu Shi, *Shenhui heshang yiji* (Taibei: Hu Shi jinian guan, 1982), 296. For examples of Daoist criticisms of Indians (though of course rival Chinese Buddhists were the real target), see passages translated in Zürcher in which Indians are referred to as "cruel" and "obstinate," and as "primitive savages." Zürcher, *Buddhist Conquest of China*, 298, 304.

14. Examples include Richard Cronin, *Imagining India* (London: Macmillan, 1989); Ralph J. Crane, *Inventing India: A History of India in English-Language Fiction* (London: Macmillan, 1992); and Ronald B. Inden, *Imagining India* (Oxford: Blackwell, 1990).

15. See especially his *Golden Peaches of Samarkand* (Berkeley: University of California Press, 1963) and *The Vermilion Bird* (Berkeley: University of California Press, 1967).

16. The representative expression of the view of Buddhism as basically counter to Chinese tastes and values is Hu Shih, "The Indianization of China: A Case Study in Cultural Borrowing," in *Independence, Convergence, and Borrowing in Institutions, Thought, and Art* (Cambridge, Mass.: Harvard University Press, 1937), 219–47. For a representative work of the view that Chinese Buddhism embodies Chinese values, see Ch'en, *The Chinese Transformation of Buddhism*.

17. For discussion of the theoretical issues involved in use of the term "Sinification" (or "Sinicization"), see Robert M. Gimello, "Random Reflections on the 'Sinicization' of

Buddhism," *Society for the Study of Chinese Religions Bulletin* 5 (1978): 52–89; Sharf, *Coming to Terms with Chinese Buddhism*; and John R. McRae, "State Formation, Indigenization, and Buddhism in East Asian History: The Theoretical Foundation," *Indo tetsugaku bukkyōgaku kenkyū* 13 (2006): 45–72.

18. For a discussion of the diverse definitions and terminologies that have been applied to Tantric (i.e., Esoteric) Buddhism, see Charles D. Orzech, Henrik H. Sørensen, and Richard K. Payne, eds., *Esoteric Buddhism and the Tantras in East Asia* (Leiden: Brill, 2011), 3–13. Shahar and Faure largely follow Michel Strickmann's usage of the term in his *Mantras et mandarins: Le bouddhisme tantrique en Chine* (Paris: Gallimard, 1996), and *Chinese Magical Medicine*, ed. Bernard Faure, Asian Religions and Cultures (Stanford, Calif.: Stanford University Press, 2002).

Chapter 1. Transformation as Imagination in Medieval Popular Buddhist Literature

I wish to thank Jidong Yang and Josh Capitanio for helping me with computer searches and Anthony C. Yu for providing precise information about *Journey to the West*.

1. For a magisterial treatment of all the main facets of the historiographical tradition in China, see Endymion Wilkinson, *Chinese History: A Manual*, Harvard-Yenching Institute Monograph Series 52 (Cambridge, Mass.: Harvard University Asia Center, 2000).

2. This is Průšek's "segmented progress" of Chinese narrative. See Jaroslav Průšek, *Chinese History and Literature: Collection of Studies* (Prague: Academia, 1970).

3. Andrew Jones, "The Poetics of Uncertainty in Early Chinese Literature," *Sino-Platonic Papers* 4 (February 1987): 17.

4. Victor H. Mair, "The Contributions of T'ang and Five Dynasties Transformation Texts (*pien-wen*) to Later Chinese Popular Literature," *Sino-Platonic Papers* 12 (August, 1989): 22–23.

5. Karl S. Y. Kao, ed., *Classical Chinese Tales of the Supernatural and the Fantastic: Selections from the Third to the Tenth Century* (Bloomington: Indiana University Press, 1985), 2.

6. Lu Hsun, *A Brief History of Chinese Fiction* (Peking: Foreign Languages Press, 1976), 1.

7. *Hanyu da cidian*, 2.1635ab.

8. See Mair, "Contributions of T'ang and Five Dynasties Transformation Texts," especially the chart on 41, for evidence and discussion of the relationship between the oral storytelling tradition and the history of fiction and drama.

9. Patrick Hanan, "The Making of *The Pearl-Sewn Shirt* and *The Courtesan's Jewel Box*," *Harvard Journal of Asiatic Studies* 33 (1973): 124–53.

10. E.g., Patrick Hanan, "The Early Chinese Short Story: A Critical Theory in Outline," *Harvard Journal of Asiatic Studies* 27 (1967): 171.

11. Patrick Hanan, "The Nature of Ling Meng-ch'u's Fiction," in *Chinese Narrative: Critical and Theoretical Essays*, ed. Andrew Plaks (Princeton, N.J.: Princeton University Press, 1977), 87, emphasis added.

12. Henry Zhao, *The Uneasy Narrator: Chinese Fiction from the Traditional to the Modern* (Oxford: Oxford University Press, 1995).

13. Victor Mair, "The Narrative Revolution in Chinese Literature: Ontological Presuppositions," *Chinese Literature: Essays, Articles, Reviews* 5, 1 (July 1983; actually published July 1985): 1–27 (lead article of a symposium on the origin of Chinese fiction). This article has been translated at least twice into Chinese, first as classified material for internal circulation only (*neibu cankao ziliao*) and then by Yang Yi as "Zhongguo wenxue xushiti de biange: bentilun de jiading," *Wenxue yanjiu cankao* 6 (1986): 13–19; 7 (1986): 27–33, 26.

14. In his monograph on *zhiguai*, Robert Campany in *Strange Writing: Anomaly Accounts in Early Medieval China* (Albany: State University of New York Press, 1996), 250ff., discusses many different types of "Anomaly by Transformation," but it is crucial to note that all these belong to the modality of one thing changing into something else.

15. Damien Keown, *A Dictionary of Buddhism* (Oxford: Oxford University Press, 2003), 194, 308.

16. For a detailed summary of the story and a description of the manuscripts, see Victor Mair, *T'ang Transformation Texts: A Study of the Buddhist Contribution to the Rise of Vernacular Fiction and Drama in China*, Harvard-Yenching Institute Monograph Series 28 (Cambridge, Mass.: Harvard University Council on East Asian Studies, 1989), 8–19. A complete, annotated translation of the text may be found in Victor Mair, *Tun-huang Popular Narratives* (Cambridge: Cambridge University Press, 1983), 31–84, 174–223 (notes). The Buddha's most noted disciples in China were Śāriputra (for his wisdom) and Maudgalyāyana (for his magical abilities and filial piety). This is in contrast to India, where Ānanda was the clear favorite because of his extensive experience. Moreover, in the folk Buddhist traditions of China, Maudgalyāyana was even more popular than Śāriputra, while the latter was himself often (as in "Transformation Text on the Subduing of Demons") depicted as something of a conjurer (Mair, *T'ang Transformation Texts*, 58).

17. Victor Mair, "Śāriputra Defeats the Six Heterodox Masters: Oral-Visual Aspects of an Illustrated Transformation Scroll (P4524)," *Asia Major* 3rd ser. 8, 2 (1995): 3–4.

18. Mair, "Śāriputra Defeats the Six Heterodox Masters."

19. Victor Mair, *Painting and Performance: Chinese Picture Recitation and Its Indian Genesis* (Honolulu: University of Hawai'i Press, 1988).

20. Victor Mair, "A Medieval, Central Asian Buddhist Theme in a Late Ming Taoist Tale by Feng Meng-lung," *Sino-Platonic Papers* 95 (May 1999): 1–27, 1–5.

21. This is the so-called "Demon of Havoc."

22. Wu Cheng'en (c. 1500–c. 1582), *Xiyou ji* (Record of a Journey to the West) (Beijing: Zuojia chubanshe, 1954), vol. 1, chap. 2, 22; Arthur Waley, trans., *Monkey* (New York: John Day, 1943; New York: Grove, 1958), 30; Anthony C. Yu, *The Journey to the West* (Chicago: University of Chicago Press, 1977–1983), vol. 1, 97. Cf. also Wu, *Xiyou ji*, vol. 1, chap. 4, 43, and chap. 7, 71; Waley, *Monkey*, 49, 73; Yu, *Journey to the West*, vol. 1, 128, 169.

23. Victor Mair, "The North(west)ern Peoples and the Recurrent Origins of the

'Chinese' State," in *The Teleology of the Modern Nation-State: Japan and China*, ed. Joshua A. Fogel (Philadelphia: University of Pennsylvania Press, 2005), 70–72; *Hanyu da cidian* 1.148b.

24. See the complete translation by Charles J. Wivell in Victor Mair, *The Columbia Anthology of Traditional Chinese Literature* (New York: Columbia University Press, 1994), 1187, 1189.

25. Daniel Overmyer, *Precious Volumes: An Introduction to Chinese Sectarian Scriptures from the Sixteenth and Seventeenth Centuries* (Cambridge, Mass.: Harvard University Asia Center, 1999), 111, 122, 149, 155, 162, 165, 186, 196–97, 260–61; Rostislav Berezkin, "Tang Dynasty Transformation Texts (*bianwen*) and Ming-Qing Precious Scrolls (*baojuan*): Legacy of Tang Narratives in Chinese Popular Literature" (manuscript, 2006), 12–13.

26. For extensive discussions of pre-Buddhist and post-Buddhist conceptions of change, evolution, and transformation in China, see Mair, *T'ang Transformation Texts*, 44–72; *Tun-huang Popular Narratives*, 3; *Painting and Performance*, passim; plus the notes cited in these three works.

Chapter 2. Indian Mythology and the Chinese Imagination: Nezha, Nalakūbara, and Kṛṣṇa

I am indebted to Alex Cherniak for his generous help with the Sanskrit and the Tibetan. My research was supported by the Israel Science Foundation (grant no. 586/07).

1. *Honglou meng* (Dream of the Red Chamber), by Cao Xueqin and Gao E (Beijing: Zuojia, 1957), 7.75.

2. Liu Cunren [Liu Ts'un-yan] initiated the study of Nezha with his "Pishamen tianwang fuzi yu Zhongguo xiaoshuo zhiguanxi," in his *Hefengtang wenji* (Shanghai: Shanghai guji, 1991), 2: 1045–94, followed by his English monograph: *Buddhist and Taoist Influences on Chinese Novels* (Wiesbaden: Kommissionsverlag, 1962), 217–42. His study has been superseded by Chen Xiaoyi, "Nezha renwu ji gushi zhi yanjiu" (Ph.D. dissertation, Fengjia University, 1994), and by a recent collection of essays, *Diyijie Nezha xueshu yantaohui lunwenji*, ed. Guoli Zhongshan daxue qingdai xueshu yanjiu zhongxin (Gaoxiong: Zhongshan daxue, 2003). Note in particular Xiao Dengfu, "Nezha suyuan," in *Diyijie Nezha xueshu yantaohui lunwenji*, 1–66. Chen Xuelin [Hok-Lam Chan] has studied the Beijing lore of the child-god in his *Liu Bowen Nezha cheng: Beijing jiancheng de chuanshuo* (Taipei: Sanmin, 1996), followed by his English monograph *Legends of the Building of Old Peking* (Hong Kong: Chinese University Press, 2008); see also NikaidoYoshihirō, "Natataishikō," in *Dōkyō no rekishi to bunka*, ed. Yamada Toshiaki and Tanaka Fumio (Tokyo: Yūzankaku, 1998), 176–96.

3. Taiwanese Nezha temples are listed in Qiu Dezai, *Taiwan miao shen zhuan* (Douliu: Xintong, 1985), 361–70; on his cult in the island see Zeng Guodong, "Xinying Taizigong de lishi yanjiu," in *Diyijie Nezha xueshu yantaohui lunwenji*, 117–45; on the child-god in spirit-medium cults see, among others, David Jordan, *Gods, Ghosts and Ancestors: The*

Folk Religion of a Taiwanese Village (Berkeley: University of California Press, 1972), 71–73; Alan Elliott, *Chinese Spirit-Medium Cults in Singapore* (1955; London: Athlone, 1990), 76–77; Charles Stafford, *The Roads of Chinese Childhood: Learning and Identification in Angang* (Cambridge: Cambridge University Press, 1995), 131–43; and Hong Shuling, "Nezha xinyang yu nüxing shenmei yanjiu," in *Diyijie Nezha xueshu yantaohui lunwenji*, 215–40; on his Daoist title see Li Fengmao, "Wuying xinyang yu Zhongtan yuanshuai: qi yuanshi ji yanbian," in *Diyijie Nezha xueshu yantaohui lunwenji*, 549–94.

4. See *Fengshen yanyi* (Investiture of the Gods), author given as Xu Zhonglin, edited by Li Guoqing (Beijing: Beijing tushuguan, 2001), 12.101–14.128; compare also the translations by Stephen Owen, "Romance of the Gods," in his *An Anthology of Chinese Literature: Beginnings to 1911* (New York: Norton, 1996), 771–806; Gary Seaman and Victor H. Mair, "Romance of the Investiture of the Gods," in *Hawai'i Reader in Traditional Chinese Culture*, ed. Victor H. Mair et al. (Honolulu: University of Hawai'i Press, 2005), 467–89; and Gu Zhizong, *Creation of the Gods* (Beijing: New World Press, 1992), 1: 131–67. Liu Cunren [Liu Ts'un-yan] has suggested that the novel dates from as early as the sixteenth century, but the bulk of the evidence suggests a seventeenth-century time frame. Zhang Peiheng has convincingly argued for a 1620s date of composition; see his preface to *Fengshen yanyi: Xin zhengli ben* (Nanjing: Jiangsu guji, 1991), 1–13.

5. See Ho Kin-Chung, "Nezha: Figure de l'enfant rebelle," *Études Chinoises* 7, 2 (Autumn, 1988), 7–26; Fan Sheng, "Yidipasi yu Nezha" ("Oedipus and Nezha"), *Taiwan Yijie* 39, 12 (1996): 57–61; and Steven Sangren, *Chinese Sociologies: An Anthropological Account of the Role of Alienation in Social Reproduction* (London: Athlone, 2000), 186–223.

6. See *Sanjiao yuanliu shengdi fozu sou shen daquan*, Ming edition, photographic reprint in vol. 3 of *Zhongguo minjian xinyang ziliao huibian*, ed. Wang Qiugui and Li Fengmao (Taibei: Xueshengshuju, 1988), 326–27; and *Xiyouji, by Wu Cheng'en* (Beijing: Zuojiachubanshe, 1954), 83.948.

7. *Sanjiao yuanliu shengdi fozu sou shen daquan*, 326–27; on the collection's possible Yuan origins see Glen Dudbridge, *Legend of Miaoshan* (Oxford: Oxford University Press, 2004), 67–69.

8. See Li Qiao, *Zhongguo hangye shen chongbai* (Beijing: ZhongguoHuaqiao, 1990), 199–200, and Chan, *Legends*, 30.

9. See Chan, *Legends*, 63–85.

10. See Edwin O. Reischauer, *Ennin's Diary: The Record of a Pilgrimage to China in Search of the Law* (New York: Ronald Press, 1955), 303; compare *Kai Tian chuanxin ji*, Siku quanshu edition, 13a–b; and Zan'ning (919–1001), *Song gaoseng zhuan*, T. no. 2061, vol. 50, 791a; see also Xiao Dengfu,"Nezha suyuan," 20–23.

11. The exception is Amoghavajra's (705–74) *Beifang Pishamen Tianwang sui jun hufa yigui* (The Tantric rituals of the northern Heavenly King Vaiśravaṇa, who follows the army, protecting the Dharma), T. no. 1247, vol. 21, 224c–225a.

12. In his translation of Aśvaghoṣa's (first century) *Buddhacarita* (The Acts of the Buddha), Dharmakṣema (385–433) has for Nalakūbara: Naluojiupo; compare Asvaghosha,

The Buddha-Karita or Life of the Buddha, ed. and trans. Edward B. Cowell (1894; photographic reprint 1977), English text, 1.16; Sanskrit, 1.11; and *Fo suo xing zan jing*, T. no. 192, vol. 4, 3c.

13. For information on this text, see respectively *Kongque wang zhou jing*, T. no. 984, vol. 19, 451b; *Foshuo da kongque zhou wang jing*, T. no. 985, vol. 19, 466b; and *Fomu da kongque mingwang jing*, T. no. 982, vol. 19, 425b; compare the Sanskrit original in Takubo Shūyo, ed., *Ārya-Mahā-Māyūrī Vidyā-rājñī* (Tokyo: Sankibo, 1972), 23, and Sylvain M. Lévi, "Catalogue géographique des yakṣa dans la Mahāmāyūrī," *Journal Asiatique* 5 (1915), 55; see also Henrik H. Sørensen, "The Spell of the Great, Golden Peacock Queen: The Origin, Practices, and Lore of an Early Esoteric Buddhist Tradition in China," *Pacific World* 3rd ser., 8 (Fall 2006): 89–123; and Mochizuki Shinkō, ed., *Bukkyō daijiten*, vol. 4, 3994–95.

14. *Beifang Pishamen Tianwang sui jun hufa yigui*, T. no. 1247, vol. 21, 224c–225c.

15. Diverse *Mahāmāyūrī* manuscripts have Nalakūvara, Nalakūvala,or Narakuvera; see respectively Sylvain Lévi, "Catalogue géographique," 55; the *Taishō* editors' gloss in T. no. 982, vol. 19, 425b; and Takubo Shūyo, *Ārya-Mahā-Māyūrī Vidyā-rājñī*, 23. The *Buddhacarita* manuscripts consulted by Cowell have Nalakūvara; see Asvaghosha, *The Buddha-Karita*, English 1.16, Sanskrit, 1.11. The Pali *Kākātī-Jātaka* has Naṭakuvera; see Edward Cowell, ed., *The Jātaka or Stories of the Buddha's Former Births* (1895; New Delhi: Munshiram Manoharlal, 1990), vol. 3, trans. H. T. Francis and R. A. Neil, 60–62.

16. *Mahā yakṣa senāpati nartakapara kalpa*, (*Gnodsbyin gyi sdedpon chen po gar mkhanmchoggibrtag pa*), Tôh. no. 766. *DergéKanjur*, vol. WA, folios 69r.7–81v.7, tr. by Dānagupta and Rabzhi Lo tsā ba; and *Gnod sbyin gar mkhan mchog gi rgyud*, Tôh. no. 767, *DergéKanjur*, vol. WA, folios 81v.7–88v.7, tr. by Dānagupta and Rab zhi Lo tsā ba.

17. On Vaiśravaṇa (Kubera) in Hinduism see Ananda K. Coomaraswamy, *Yakṣas: Essays in the Water Cosmology*, ed. Paul Schroeder (Delhi: Indira Gandhi National Center for the Arts and Oxford University Press, 1993), 35–44. On Vaiśravaṇa's Chinese and Japanese cult see Phyllis Granoff, "Tobatsu Bishamon," *East and West*n.s. 20, 1–2 (1970): 144–68; and Valerie Hansen, "Gods on Walls: A Case of Indian Influence on Chinese Lay Religion?," in *Religion and Society in T'ang and Sung China*, ed. Patricia Buckley Ebrey and Peter N. Gregory (Honolulu: University of Hawai'i Press, 1993), 75–113. On his iconography, see Alice Getty, *The Gods of Northern Buddhism* (1928; New Delhi: Munshiram Manoharlal, 1978), 156–60, 164–68; and Louis Frédéric, *Les Dieux du bouddhisme* (Paris: Flammarion, 2006), 242–46.

18. The dating of the process requires further investigation. In the Ming compendium *Sanjiao yuanliu shengdi fozu sou shen daquan*, 326, Nezha's father is already identified as the Heavenly King Li Jing, (as noted above, the compendium likely derives from a Yuan source). Liu Cunren [Liu Ts'un-yan] suggests storytellers were ignorant of Pishamen being the transcription of Sanskrit Vaiśravaṇa. Therefore they mistook Pisha to be the name of a gate (*men*), in which Li Jing was supposed to have kept guard; see Liu Cunren, "Pishamen tianwang fuzi," 1048, 1092 n. 2, and Liu Ts'un-yan, *Buddhist and Taoist Influences*, 219.

19. On Chinese Tantric Buddhism see, among others, Chou Yi-liang, "Tantrism in China," *Harvard Journal of Asiatic Studies* 8, 3/4 (March 1945): 241–332; Osabe Kazuo, *Tō Sō Mikkyōshi ronkō* (Kyoto, 1982); Michel Strickmann, *Mantras et Mandarins: Le Bouddhism Tantrique en Chine* (Paris: Gallimard, 1996); Charles Orzech, *Politics and Transcendent Wisdom: The Scripture of the Humane Kings in the Creation of Chinese Buddhism* (University Park: Pennsylvania State University Press, 1998); and Yan Yaozhong, *Han chuan mijiao* (Shanghai: Xuelin, 1999). Archeological discoveries (of *dhāraṇī* pillars for instance) are shedding new light on the school's prevalence in medieval China; see Liu Shufen, *Miezui yu duwang: Foding zunsheng tuoluoni jing chuang zhi yanjiu* (Shanghai: Shanghai guji, 2008).

20. Li Xiaorong has noted the significance of esoteric Buddhism to Nezha's history; see his "Nazha gushi qiyuan bukao," *Ming Qing xiaoshuo yanjiu* 65 (2002.3): 139–49; on the Horse-Headed Avalokiteśvara, see Robert Hans van Gulik, *Hayagrīva: The Mantrayānic Aspect of the Horse-Cult in China and Japan* (Leiden: Brill, 1935); on Śiva and Gaṇeśa in Chinese Tantric literature, see Strickmann, *Mantras et Mandarins*, 243–90; on the esoteric aspect of the Chinese Kṣitigarbha cult, see Zhiru Ng, *The Making of a Savior Bodhisattva: Dizang in Medieval China* (Honolulu: University of Hawai'i Press, 2007), 97–101; on the Wutong sexual vampires' indebtedness to Tantric Buddhism, see Yan Yaozhong, *Han chuanmijiao*, 270–87; on the Tantric Garuḍa bird and the Daoist Sire Thunder (Leigong), see Mark R. E. Meulenbeld, "Civilized Demons: Ming Thunder Gods from Ritual to Literature" (Ph.D. dissertation, Princeton University, 2007), 74–90. Paul Katz has suggested that the Tantric demon turned demon-queller Āṭavaka contributed to the emergence of the Chinese plague god Marshal Wen; see his *Demon Hordes and Burning Boats: The Cult of Marshal Wen in Late Imperial Chekiang* (Albany: State University of New York Press, 1995), 79–80. The Tantric aspect of the late Ming novel *Fengshen yanyi* is discussed by Liu Ts'un-yan, *Buddhist and Taoist Influences*, 181–86. The Tantric Spirit of the Deep Sands (Shensha shen) penetrated Chinese popular culture, becoming one of the principal protagonists of the *Journey to the West*; see Glen Dudbridge, *The Hsi-yu chi: A Study of Antecedents to the Sixteenth-Century Chinese Novel* (Cambridge: Cambridge University Press, 1970), 18–21, and Michel Strickmann, *Chinese Magical Medicine*, ed. Bernard Faure, Asian Religions and Cultures (Stanford, Calif.: Stanford University Press, 2002), 312–13, n. 47.

21. See the Sanskrit text of the Peacock-Queen spell edited by Takubo Shūyo, *Ārya-Mahā-Māyūrī Vidyā-rājñī*, 24, and Amoghavajra's translation *Fomu da kongque mingwang jing*, T. no. 982, vol. 19, 426a; see also *Bukong juansuo shenbian zhenyan jing*), translated by Bodhiruci (?–727), T. no. 1092, vol. 20, 286a (Bodhiruci has for Nalakūbara: Nazhajiuboluo).

22. *Yiqie jing yinyi*, by Huilin, T. no. 2128, vol. 54, 549c., and *Byakuhō kushō*, by Ryōson, recording the sayings of his teacher Ryōzen (1258–1341), TZ.3119, vol. 7, 136c, 137a; on Nalakūbara the *yakṣa* general see also Chen Xiaoyi, "Nezha renwu ji gushi zhi yanjiu," 19–23.

23. *Gnod sbyin gar mkhan mchog gi rgyud*, Tôh. no. 767, *DergéKanjur*, vol. WA, folios 81v.7–88v.7, tr. by Dānagupta and Rab zhi Lo tsā ba; and *Mahā yakṣa senāpati*

nartakapara kalpa, (*Gnodsbyin gyi sdedpon chen po gar mkhanmchoggibrtag pa*), Tôh. no. 766, *DergéKanjur*, vol. WA, folios 69r.7–81v.7, tr. by Dānagupta and Rabzhi Lo tsā ba.

24. *Maṇibhadra-nāma-dhāraṇī*, (*'Phags pa nor bu bzangpo'igzungs*), Tôh. no. 764. *DergéKanjur*, vol. WA, folios 56r.1–56v.2, tr. by Vidyākarasiṃha and Klu'i dbang po; and *Maṇibhadra yakṣa sena kalpa* (*Gnodsbyin nor bu bzangpo'irtog pa*), Tôh. no. 765, *DergéKanjur*, vol. WA, folios 56v.2–69r.6, tr. by Mañjuśrī and Ba ri.

25. Even though at that early stage their names differed; see Ananda Coomaraswamy, *Yakṣas*, 35.

26. On the Sanskrit fragments of the Maṇibhadra *dhāraṇīs* refer to the three following detailed publications by Rudolf Hoernle, "Three Further Collections of Ancient Manuscripts from Central Asia," *Journal of the Asiatic Society of Bengal* 66 (1897): 242–43; his "The Weber Manuscripts," *Journal of the Asiatic Society of Bengal* 62 (1893): 1–40; and his "A Note on the British Collection of Central Asian Antiquities," *Actes du XIIme Congrès international des orientalistes* (Rome, 1899), vol. 1, 151–85. The Chinese Maṇibhadra sūtra is *Foshuo Baoxian tuoluoni jing*, translated by Devaśantika (Tianxizai) (?–1000), T. no. 1285, vol. 21, 353c–354b. Independently of his father (and brother), Maṇibhadra (Maṇibhadda) figures, for example, in the Pali *Samyutta-Nikāya*; see Caroline A. F. Rhys Davids, trans., *The Book of the Kindred Sayings* (1917; Oxford: Pali Text Society, 1993), vol. 1, 266.

27. Strickmann, *Chinese Magical Medicine*, 229; see also Chou Yi-liang, "Tantrism in China," 284–307.

28. This is Hok-Lam Chan's translation (*Legends of the Building of Old Peking*, 69); the original is *Pishamen Tianwang sui jun hufa yigui*, T. no. 1247, vol. 21, 1247c–1248a. The instructions for drawing Nazha's image are in the same work, vol. 21, 1248a.

29. *Fengshen yanyi*, 12, 104; Owen, *Romance of the Gods*, 776–77; Gary Seaman and Victor Mair, "Romance of the Investiture of the Gods," 472; and Gu Zhizong, *Creation of the Gods*, 1: 135; see also *Xiyouji*, 10, 104; and Pu Songling's (1640–1715) story "*Yakṣa* Kingdom" (Yecha Guo), in *Liaozhai zhiyi huijiao huizhu huiping ben*, ed. Zhang Youhe (Shanghai: Shanghai guji, 1986), vol. 3, 348–54.

30. See Meir Shahar, *The Shaolin Monastery: History, Religion, and the Chinese Martial Arts* (Honolulu: University of Hawai'i Press, 2008), 59.

31. The proper manifestation is the *zhengfalun* ("wheel of the orthodox Dharma"), and the terrifying apparition is the *jiaolinglun* ("wheel of chastisement"); see Amoghavajra's *Renwang huguo banruoboluomiduo jing tuoluoni niansong yigui* ("The Tantric rituals of the recitation of the *dhāraṇī*of the Benevolent-King Buddha protecting the state supreme-wisdom sūtra"), T. no. 994, vol. 19, 514a; see also Chen Xiaoyi,"Nezha renwu ji gushi zhi yanjiu," 33–35, and *Foguang da cidian*, 680, 4599.

32. On the three-headed six-armed *asura* iconography see Louis Frédéric, *Les Dieux du bouddhisme* (Paris: Flammarion, 2006), 281.

33. *Fenyang Wude Chanshi yulu* (The Recorded Sayings of the Chan Master Fenyang Wude [Shanzhao]), T. no. 1992, vol. 47, 598a.

34. *Biyan lu*, compiled by Xuetou Chongxian (980–1052) and Yuanwu Keqin (1063–1135), T. no. 2003, vol. 48, 212a.

35. The two figures are engraved on the lower level of the eastern pagoda (of which Quanzhou has two). Paul Demiéville has suggested that the three-headed and six-armed figure is an *asura* demon. He notes that according to the local tradition the other figure is the dragon king Sāgara (Shajieluo). However, he has been unable to account for its bow and belt attributes; see G. Ecke and P. Demiéville. *The Twin Pagodas of Zayton: A Study of Later Buddhist Sculpture in China*, Harvard-Yenching Monograph Series 2 (Cambridge, Mass.: Harvard University Press, 1935), 68, and plate 45.

36. See Chen Xuelin [Hok-Lam Chan], *Liu Bowen Nezhacheng*, and his *Legends of the Building of Old Peking*.

37. See the collected essays in Alf Hiltebeitel, ed., *Criminal Gods and Demon Devotees: Essays on the Guardians of Popular Hinduism* (Albany: State University of New York Press, 1989).

38. *Rāmāyaṇa*, *Uttarakāṇḍa*, chapter 26.

39. Cowell, *Jātaka*, 61.

40. Ganesh Vasudeo Tagare, trans., *The Bhāgavata-Purāṇa* (Delhi: Motilal Banarsidass, 1976–1978), x.10, (1308–1315).

41. See Piṅgaḷi Sūranna, *The Sound of the Kiss, or The Story That Must Never Be Told*, trans. Velcheru Narayana Rao and David Shulman (New York: Columbia University Press, 2002).

42. As I discovered during fieldwork in Taiwan in September 2008; see also Hong Shuling, "Nezha xinyang yu nüxing shenmei yanjiu,"*Diyijie Nezha xueshu yantaohui lunwenji*, 231.

43. See, among others, Friedhelm Hardy, *Viraha-Bhakti: The Early History of Kṛṣṇa Devotion in South India* (Delhi: Oxford University Press, 1983); John Stratton Hawley, *Krishna, the Butter Thief* (Princeton, N.J.: Princeton University Press, 1983); and W. G. Archer, *The Loves of Krishna in Indian Painting and Poetry* (London: Allen and Unwin, 1957); Edwin F. Bryant, *Krishna: A Sourcebook* (Oxford: Oxford University Press, 2007); on Kṛṣṇa and Viṣṇu see also J. Gonda, *Aspects of Early Viṣṇuism* (1954; Delhi: Motilal Banarsidass, 1969), 154–63.

44. This is the *Bhāgavata Purāṇa* episode as translated by Wendy Doniger O'Flaherty, *Hindu Myths: A Sourcebook Translated from the Sanskrit* (Middlesex: Penguin, 1976), 220.

45. R. P. Goldman, "Fathers, Sons and Gurus: Oedipal Conflict in the Sanskrit Epics," *Journal of Indian Philosophy* 6, 3 (November 1978), 350 (and 364); see also J. L. Masson, "The Childhood of Kṛṣṇa: Some Psychoanalytic Observations." *Journal of the American Oriental Society* 49, 4 (Oct.–Dec., 1974), 454–59; on the Indian Oedipal pattern see also A. K. Ramanujan, "The Indian 'Oedipus,'" in *Indian Literature: Proceedings of a Seminar*, ed. Arabinda Poddar (Simla: Indian Institute of Advanced Study, 1972), 127–37, and Jonathan Silk, *Riven by Lust: Incest and Schism in Indian Buddhist Legend and Historiography* (Honolulu: University of Hawai'i Press, 2009), 164–70.

46. On Kṛṣṇa and Kāliya see John Stratton Hawley, "Krishna's Cosmic Victories," *Journal of the American Academy of Religion* 47, 2 (June 1979): 201–21; and Freda Matchett, "The Taming of Kāliya: A Comparison of the Harivaṃśa, Viṣṇu-Purāṇa and Bhāgavata-Purāṇa Versions," *Religion* 16 (1986): 115–33.

47. Compare *Harivaṃśa* 52.1 and *Viṣṇu Purāṇa*, v.6.35 (quoted in Matchett, "Taming of Kāliya," 116) with *Fengshen yanyi*, 12.103; admittedly Nezha is merely five *days* old when he performs the same feat in the Ming compendium *Sanjiao yuanliu shengdi fozu sou shen daquan*, 326.

48. Compare *Bhāgavata-Purāṇa*, x.16.6; and *Fengshen yanyi*, 103–5.

49. This is Ganesh Vasudeo Tagare's translation, *The Bhāgavata-Purāṇa*, vol. 4, 1360.

50. O'Flaherty, *Hindu Myths*, 221; On Viṣṇu's dragon see also Arvind Sharma, "The Significance of Viṣṇu Reclining on the Serpent," *Religion* 16 (1986): 101–14.

51. See the *Harivaṃśa,* 71.37–54, trans. Manmatha Nath Dutt, *A Prose English Translation of the Harivamsha* (Calcutta: H.C. Dass, 1897), 350–51; and *Bhāgavata Purāṇa*x, 42.15–21, trans. Ganesh Vasudeo Tagare, vol. 4, 1511–12.

52. Robert Goldman, trans., *The Rāmāyaṇa of Vālmīki* (Princeton, N.J.: Princeton University Press, 1984), vol. 1, 248–52.

53. See Yang Qinzhang, "Quanzhou yindujiao diaoke yuanyuan kao" (Research into the Origins of the Quanzhou Hindu Stone-Carvings), *Shijie zongjiao yanjiu* (1982.2): 87–94; John Guy, "The Lost Temples of Nagapattinam and Quanzhou: A Study in Sino-Indian Relations," *Silk Road Art and Archeology* 3 (1993–94): 292–310; his "Tamil Merchant Guilds and the Quanzhou Trade," in *The Emporium of the World: Maritime Quanzhou, 1000–1400*, ed. Angela Schottenhammer (Leiden: Brill, 2001), 283–308; and Tansen Sen, *Buddhism, Diplomacy and Trade: The Realignment of Sino-Indian Relations 600–1400* (Honolulu: Association for Asian Studies and University of Hawai'i Press, 2003), 227–31.

54. See Wu Wenliang, *Quanzhou zongjiao shike*, revised and enlarged by Wu Youxiong (Beijing: Kexue, 2005), 453–60; and Yang Qinzhang, "Quanzhou yindujiao pishinu shen xingxiang shike" (The Quanzhou stone images of the Hindu god Viṣṇu), *Shijie zongjiao yanjiu* (1988.1): 96–105.

55. On Devaśāntika see Sen, *Buddhism, Diplomacy, and Trade*, 120–32; on his translations of the *Rituals of the God Vināyaka* (T. 1272) and *Rituals of the Bodhisattva Mañjuśrī* (T. 1191) see, respectively, Michel Strickmann, *Mantras et Mandarins*, 261–66, and Osabe Kazuo, *Tō Sō Mikkyōshi ronkō*, 298–326; on Song-period Tantric Buddhism see also Yan Yaozhong, *Han chuan mijiao*, 37–51, and Charles Willemen, *The Chinese Hevajratantra*, Orientalia Gandensia 8 (Leuven: Peeters, 1983).

56. The character *na* usually transcribes the Sanskrit retroflex *ṇa*, or less commonly *ḍa*. Kṛṣṇa is commonly transcribed Qilisena, sometimes with the phonetic instruction to combine the consonants (*erhe*).

57. *Luoye* was the Chinese name for the garment Indian men tied under the armpit, leaving their right shoulder bare; see Xuanzang, *Da Tang Xiyuji*, T. no. 2087, vol. 51, 876b, and Li Rongxi's translation, *The Great Tang Dynasty Record of the Western Regions*

(Berkeley, Calif.: Numata Center, 1996), 53; compare also Samuel Beal, *Si-yu-ki: Buddhist Records of the Western World* (1884; Delhi: Motilal Banarsidas, 2004), 75.

58. Nanda, Upananda, and Takṣaka frequently appear in various Buddhist lists of the eight dragon kings; see *Foguang da cidian*, general editor Ci Yi (Gaoxiong: Foguang, 1988), 6378, 6405.

59. The *rākṣasas* and the *piśācas* are two types of Hindu ogres whom Buddhist demonology incorporated. Both types of gruesome demons common in Buddhist literature feed on human flesh; see respectively *Foguang da cidian*, 6673–74, and 3851; Monier-Williams, 871, and 628; see also Strickmann's survey of Buddhist demonology in his *Chinese Magical Medicine*, 62–68.

60. The term *geboluo* (Sanskrit: Kapāla) figures prominently in the contemporaneous Chinese translation of the *Hevajra Tantra* (*Foshuo dabei kongzhi jin gong dajiaowang yigui jing*), T. no. 892, vol. 18, 587–601; see also Willemen, *Chinese Hevajratantra*, 172.

61. *Zuishang mimi Nana tianjing*, T. no. 1288, vol. 21, 358b–c.

62. Mochizuki Shinkō (*Bukkyō daijiten*, vol. 4, 3994–95) was the first to associate the *Zuishang mimi Nana tianjing* with Nezha. Xiao Dengfu ("Nezhasuyuan," 19, n. 10) has disputed the connection because of Naṇa's elevated position; see also Hok-Lam Chan, *Legends of the Building of Old Peking*, 72–73.

63. On the identification of the originally distinct god Nārāyaṇa with Viṣṇu see Freda Matchett, *Kṛṣṇa: Lord or Avatāra? The Relationship Between Kṛṣṇa and Viṣṇu* (Richmond: Curzon, 2001), 4–8; Admittedly, the epithet Naluoyan (Nārāyaṇa) is applied in some Chinese texts to another powerful divinity, Vajrapāṇi; see Shahar, *Shaolin Monastery*, 40; also "Naluoyantian" in *Foguang da cidian*, 3029–30.

Chapter 3. Indic Influences on Chinese Mythology: King Yama and His Acolytes as Gods of Destiny

1. However, as Victor Mair has recently shown, the traditional interpretation of Buddhist-Daoist interaction as a process of "matching meanings" (such as the misleading translation for *geyi*) needs to be abandoned. See Victor H. Mair, "What Is Geyi After All?" in *Philosophy and Religion in Early Medieval China*, ed. Alan Chan and Y. K. Lo (Albany: State University of New York Press, 2010).

2. See Rolf A. Stein, "The Guardian of the Gate: An Example of Buddhist Mythology, from India to Japan," in *Asian Mythologies*, ed. Yves Bonnefoy and Wendy Doniger (Chicago: University of Chicago Press, 1991), 119–21; and Michel Strickmann, *Mantras et mandarins: Le bouddhisme tantrique en Chine* (Paris: Gallimard, 1996).

3. See Strickmann, *Mantras et mandarins*, 16–58, 369–411.

4. See for instance the *Yuqie jiyao jiu anan tuoluoni yankou guiyi jing*, T. no. 21, 1318 T. no. 1318, vol. 21and the *Yuqie jiyao yan shishi qijiao anantuo an yuanyou*, T. no. 1319, vol. 21, compiled by Amoghavajra.

5. See Stephen F. Teiser, *The Ghost Festival in Medieval China* (Princeton, N.J.: Princeton University Press, 1996).

6. See the *Yaoshi rulai benyuan jing*, T. no. 449, vol. 14, 403c.

7. See for instance the *Śatapatha-brāhmana* XIV, 1, 3, 4, quoted in Charles Malamoud, *Le jumeau solaire* (Paris: Seuil, 2002), 15.

8. See Bruce Lincoln, *Death, War, and Sacrifice: Studies in Ideology and Practice* (Chicago: University of Chicago Press, 1991), 32–33.

9. Yama's name is said to mean "twin," but in the Brāhmanas it is also said to derive from the root *yam*, "to restrain," "to curb," "to subdue." Yama appears as one of a pair of twins born to Vivasvant (the Sun-god) and Saraṇyū (the daughter of Tvaṣṭṛ, the divine artisan). The *Rg-Veda* mentions an interesting episode, Yamī's attempt to seduce her twin brother, but the latter resists successfully this incestuous relationship. This "expurgated" version, however, seems to point to the existence of an earlier version in which the incest does take place. Indeed, in the Iranian version of the tale, Yamī argues that she and her brother already had intercourse while in the womb. See Malamoud, *Le jumeau solaire*, 16–17; and Bulcsu Siklós, "The Evolution of the Buddhist Yama," in *The Buddhist Forum*, vol. 4, *Seminar Papers 1994–1996*, ed. Tadeusz Skorupski (London: SOAS, 1996), 168.

10. A bath in the Yamunā was said to prevent rebirth in Yama's realm; see Siklós, "The Evolution of the Buddhist Yama," 173. Yamunā is linked with another river-goddess, Sarasvatī. The latter, indeed, appears as Yama's sister in the translation of the *Golden Light Sūtra* by Yijing (635–713), and this is why she is sometimes listed among his retinue. In this scripture, Sarasvatī is also called Narayanī (a name that points to her role as sister or consort of Narāyaṇa, i.e., Viṣṇu), and she becomes a kind of transcendent mother-goddess.

11. See for instance the *Shimen zhengtong* (1237), quoted in Stephen F. Teiser, *The Scripture on the Ten Kings and the Making of Purgatory in Medieval Chinese Buddhism* (Honolulu: University of Hawai'i Press, 1994), 64. See also *Asabashō*, in TZ. no. 3190, vol. 9, 496.

12. See for instance *Śatapatha brāhmana* XIV, 1, 3, 4, quoted in Malamoud, *Le jumeau solaire*, 17–18.

13. See Siklós, "The Evolution of the Buddhist Yama," 165–89.

14. In Northern and Central India, for instance, the demonic hairstyle (*ūrdhvakeśa*, hair standing on end) has been mostly chosen for Yama, in order to emphasize his fierce nature. See Corinna Wessels-Mevissen, *The Gods of the Directions in Ancient India: Origins and Early Development in Art and Literature*, Monographien zur indischen Archäologie, Kunst und Philologie 14 (Berlin: Dietrich Reimer, 2001), 98.

15. See Teiser, *Scripture on the Ten Kings*.

16. On Dizang, see Zhiru, *The Making of a Savior Bodhisattva: Dizang in Medieval China* (Honolulu: University of Hawai'i Press, 2007); Françoise Wang-Toutain, *Le bodhisattva Kṣitigarbha en Chine du Ve au XIIIe siècle* (Paris: École Française d'Extrême-Orient, 1998); Michel Soymié, "Notes d'iconographie chinoise: les acolytes de Ti-tsang (1)," *Arts Asiatiques* 14 (1966): 45–73; and Soymié, "Les dix jours de jeûne de Kṣitigarbha," in *Contributions aux études sur Touen-houang*, ed. Michel Soymié (Geneva: Droz, 1979), 135–59.

17. See Lourens P. Van den Bosch, "Yam—The God on the Black Buffalo," in *Visible Religion*, ed. H. G. Kippenberg, L. P. van den Bosch, and L. Leertouwer (Leiden: Brill, 1982), vol. 1; and Alex Wayman, "Studies in Yama and Māra," *Indo-Iranian Journal* 3, 1 (1959): 44–73.

18. On Yama as directional deity, see Wessels-Mevissen, *Gods of the Directions*, 6–8, 98; see also *Yanluo wang gongxingfa cidi*, T. no. 1290, vol. 21, 374c.

19. See *Taittirīta-Brāhmana* V, 2, 3, 1, quoted in Malamoud, *Le jumeau solaire*, 26.

20. Quoted in Adrian Snodgrass, *The Matrix and Diamond World Mandalas in Shingon Buddhism*, 2 vols. (New Delhi: Aditya Prakashan, 1988), 481.

21. *Usuzōshi kuketsu*, T. no. 2535, vol. 79, 282c.

22. See *Da Piluzhena chengfo jing shu*, T. no. 1796, vol. 39, 684b.

23. Ibid.

24. See *Da Piluzhena chengfo shenbian jiachi jing*, T. no. 848, vol. 18, 35a; and Yixing's *Commentary* (*Da Piluzhena chengfo shenbian jing shu*), 744a.

25. See *Da Piluzhena chengfo shenbian jiachi jing*, T. no. 848, vol. 18, 35a; and Yixing's *Commentary*, 744a}.

26. See Snodgrass, *Matrix and Diamond World Mandalas*, vol. 1, 641.

27. See *Asabashō*, TZ. no. 3190, vol. 9, 497c; and Snodgrass, *Matrix and Diamond World Mandalas*, 484.

28. See for instance *Betsugyō*, T. no. 2476, vol. 78, 178c; *Yōson hō*, T. no. 2478, vol. 78, 209a; *Shoson yōshō*, T. no. 2484, vol. 78, 319c, 329a; *Hizō konpōshō*, T. no. 2485, vol. 78, 365c; *Hishō*, T. no. 2489, vol. 78, 572a; *Usuzōshi*, T. no. 2495, vol. 78, 646a; and *Kakuzenshō*, in *Dai Nihon bukkyō zensho*, vol. 50, 306.

29. See Nakamura Teiri, *Kitsune no Nihon shi: Kodai chūsei-hen* (Tokyo: Nihon editā sukūru shuppanbu, 2001), 75–76.

30. On Kālarātrī, see Yixing's *Commentary*: "On the west of Yama-deva, draw Yama's Consort and the consort Death, who is also Yama's consort. On the east, draw the goddess Dark Night (kokuya-shin) and the Seven Mothers," T. no. 1796, vol. 39, 634b, quoted in Mochizuki Shinkō, ed., *Bukkyō daijiten* (Tokyo: Sekai seiten kankō kyōkai, 1936), vol. 2, 1133–34. In Hinduism, she is especially invoked to protect people from dangers peculiar to the night, and from the darkness of ignorance. Occasionally, however, she is associated with the very creatures or dangers of the night from whom she is elsewhere asked to protect people. Rātrī, then, is not only the guardian of the night, who protects people during the dark hours of their rest, but the night itself and those things, both benign and hostile, which inhabit the night. See David Kinsley, *Hindu Goddesses: Visions of the Divine Feminine in the Hindu Religious Tradition* (Berkeley: University of California Press, 1986), 14.

31. On this tradition, see Iyanaga Nobumi, "Dākinī et l'Empereur: Mystique bouddhique de la royauté dans le Japon médiéval," *Versus: Quaderni di Studi Semiotici* 83/84 (1999): 41–111.

32. T. no. 1796, vol. 39, 684b.

33. In the Womb Realm mandala, they are described as black demonesses, and also placed in the Western section; see *Ishiyama shichishū*, TZ. no. 1, 181a.

34. According to Ariane MacDonald, "the group of the Seven Mothers, ambivalent deities, benevolent or ogresses, seems distinct from that of the mātṛkā or grahī, which is not well fixed." See Ariane MacDonald, ed., *Le Maṇḍala du Mañjuśrīmūlakalpa* (Paris: Maisonneuve, 1962), 84.

35. See Yuvraj Krishan, *Gaṇeśa: Unravelling an Enigma* (Delhi: Motilal Banarsidass, 1999), 134.

36. See "Shamonda," in Mochizuki, *Bukkyō daijiten*, vol. 3, 2182c–2183a; and Snodgrass, *Matrix and Diamond World Mandalas*, 499–50.

37. See Stein, "Guardian of the Gate"; Strickmann, *Mantras et mandarins*; Robert Duquenne, "Gaṇapati Rituals in Chinese," *Bulletin de l'Ecole Française d'Extrême-Orient* 77, 1 (1988): 321–54; Alexander Kabanoff, "The Kangi-ten (Gaṇapati) Cult in Medieval Japanese Mikkyō," in *Esoteric Buddhism in Japan*, ed. Ian Astley (Copenhagen: Seminar for Buddhist Studies, 1994), 99–126; and Bernard Faure, "The Elephant in the Room: The Cult of Secrecy in Japanese Tantrism," in *The Culture of Secrecy in Japanese Religion*, ed. Bernhard Scheid and Mark Teeuwen (London: Routledge, 2006), 255–68.

38. On the Twelve Mothers, see the *Luofunu shuo jiuliao xiaoer jibing jing*, trans. Dharmabhadra, T. no. 1330, vol. 21, 491c–494a; and Jean Filliozat, *Étude de démonologie indienne: Le Kumāratantra de Rāvaṇa et les textes parallèles indiens, tibétains, chinois, cambodgien et arabe* (Paris: Imprimerie Nationale, 1937). On the Seven Mothers and Cāmuṇḍa in medieval Japan, see *Kakuzenshō*, in *Dai Nihon bukkyō zensho*, vol. 50, 308.

39. See *Dai Nihon zokuzōkyō*, ed. Nakano Tatsue (Kyoto: Zōkyō shoin, 1905–12), 2b, 23, 4 (new ed., vol. 150: 381). On Citragupta, see Malamoud, *Le jumeau solaire*, 318.

40. T. no. 1796, vol. 39, 643c.

41. The identity between Taishan Fujun and Citragupta (or the takeover of the latter by the former) is suggested by the fact that both have the same mantra. See *Asabashō*, TZ. no. 3190, vol. 9, 498.

42. T. no. 185, vol. 3, 475c. The name of this god, translated by Dudbridge as "Great Knowledge" is also used in the *Asabashō*, TZ. no. 3190, vol. 9, 498b. It might also refer to the Storehouse-consciousness (*ālaya-vijñāna*). See Glen Dudbridge, "The General of the Five Paths in Tang and Pre-Tang China," *Cahiers d'Extrême-Asie* 9 (1996–97): 89.

43. See Sawada Mizuho, *Jigoku-hen: Chūgoku no meikai setsu* (Kyoto: Hōzōkan, 1968), 90–91; and Dudbridge, "The General of the Five Paths," 91.

44. See Dudbridge, "The General of the Five Paths," 92.

45. See Danielle Eliasberg, "Quelques aspects du grand exorcisme No à Touen-houang," in *Contributions aux études de Touen-houang: Volume III*, ed. Michel Soymié (Paris: École Française d'Extrême-Orient, 1984), 237–40.

46. On Siming and Silu, see Michel Soymié, "Notes d'iconographie chinoise," 45–73.

47. On the daṇḍa-staff, see Anna Seidel, "Danda," in *Hōbōgirin: Dictionnaire encyclopédique du bouddhisme d'après les sources chinoises et japonaises*, vol. 8 (Paris: Adrien Maisonneuve, 2003), 1113–22.

48. See ibid., 1121a.

49. See *Dafangguangfo huayan jing*, T. no. 278, vol. 9, 680b–c. Note that in Chinese, *ming*[2] (name) is homophonous with *ming*[4] (life).

50. See *Yaoshi rulai benyuan jing*, T. no. 449, vol. 14, 403c.

51. See *Yaoshi liuliguang rulai benyuan gongde jing* (translated by Xuanzang in 650), T. no. 450, vol. 14, 407b. A Sanskrit original, almost identical in content with Xuanzang's translation, was discovered in 1931 in Northern India. It mentions "deities that are born at the same time as that person and that accompany him (*tasya puruṣaya sahājanubaddhā devatā*). See Gregory Schopen, "The Bhaiśajyagurusūtra and the Buddhism of Gilgit," Ph.D. dissertation, Australian National University, 1978, 61.

52. See T. no. 450, vol. 14, 407b; and Raoul Birnbaum, *The Healing Buddha* (Boulder, Colo.: Shambhala, 1979), 165 (slightly modified).

53. The term "spiritual consciousness" (*shenshi*) designates the sixth vijñāna; it is a kind of dream-state.

54. It is in China that the companion deities came to be identified with the pair of spirits mentioned in the *Avataṃsaka-sūtra*, and commentators on the *Sūtra of the Healing Buddha* have somewhat anachronistically read that identity into that scripture.

55. On this question, see Nagao Kayoko, "Kan'yaku butten ni okeru 'kushōjin' no kaishaku," *Pāri-gaku bukkyō bunkagaku* 13 (1999): 55–66; and Nagao, "Kushōjin no tenkai," *Bukkyō bunka* 10 (2000): 43–70.

56. T. no. 1911, vol. 46, 110a; see also Zhanran's commentary, the *Zhiguan fuxing chuan hongjue*, T. no. 1912, vol. 46, 401a.

57. See *Wuliangshou jing yishu*, T. no. 1746, vol. 37, 124b.

58. See *Jizō bosatsu hosshin innen jūō kyō* in *Dai Nihon zokuzōkyō* 2b, 23, 4.

59. Donald Harper, personal communication.

60. See Iyanaga, "Ḍākinī et l'Empereur"; and Faure, "The Elephant in the Room."

Chapter 4. Indian Myth Transformed in a Chinese Apocryphal Text: Two Stories on the Buddha's Hidden Organ

I thank Professor Meir Shahar for his kind invitation to this project and Professor John Kieschnick for his patient editorial assistance. Several others gave me very helpful suggestions during the discussion after my presentation at the conference. I regret that due to time constraints, I could not fully incorporate their valuable suggestions to this chapter. My thanks are also due to Professor Robert Kritzer for kindly checking the English. The research for this paper has been supported by JSPS Kakenhi (24320014).

1. T. no. 643, vol. 15, 645c–697a.

2. There is a fragmentary Sogdian version, which is regarded as a translation from "Buddhabhadra's" Chinese version. Friedrich Weller, "Bemerkungen zum soghdischen Dhyāna-texte," pt. 1, *Monumenta Serica* 2 (1936–37): 342. See also Émile Benveniste and Paul Demiéville, "Notes sur le fragment sogdien du *Buddhadhyānasamādhisāgara-sūtra*,"-*Journal Asiatique* 223, 2 (1933): 193–248.

3. T. no. 365, vol. 12, 340c–346b.

4. Nobuyoshi Yamabe, "The Sūtra on the Ocean-Like Samādhi of the Visualization of the Buddha: The Interfusion of the Chinese and Indian Cultures in Central Asia as Reflected in a Fifth Century Apocryphal Sūtra," Ph.D. dissertation, Yale University, 1999.

5. Briefly, the basic line of my argument is as follows. As has already been pointed out by Tsukinowa Kenryū in *Butten no hihanteki kenkyū* (Kyoto: Hyakkaen, 1971), 59–86, there are many questionable expressions in the *Ocean Sūtra* that do not seem to be restorable to Sanskrit. In addition, many passages of this sūtra appear to have been taken from earlier Chinese Buddhist texts, not from an Indian original. These points strongly suggest that the *Ocean Sūtra* was not a translation of an Indian text but rather an apocryphal text composed in Chinese by some Chinese authors. In this connection, we should further consider the detailed story about the origin of the "Buddha Image Cave" (Foying ku) in this text. The "Buddha Image Cave" was a mysterious cave in Nagarahāra (near present-day Jelālābād, Afghanistan), where a resplendent image of the Buddha appeared. This was a famous pilgrimage spot, and well-known Chinese pilgrims, like Faxian and Xuanzang, visited there. However, the description of this cave in the *Ocean Sūtra* contradicts those given by Chinese pilgrims in important details. Since Buddhabhadra seems to have been from Nagarahāra, he must have been quite familiar with the site. Therefore, if he was indeed involved in the translation of this sūtra, such disagreements are difficult to understand. Thus, I strongly suspect that the relevant portion of the *Ocean Sūtra* was written by somebody who did not know the actual site and relied on hearsay. Accordingly, I believe the association of this sūtra with Buddhabhadra should be disregarded (for a diverging view of this point, see Marilyn Martin Rhie, *Early Buddhist Art of China and Central Asia*, vol. 3, *The Western Ch'in in Kansu in the Sixteen Kingdoms Period and Inter-Relationships with the Buddhist Art of Gandhāra* [Leiden: Brill, 2010], 82, n. 45). On the other hand, it should be noted that the people who composed this sūtra were familiar with Indian (or Central Asian) traditions that would not have been accessible to most Chinese people. For example, an Indian sūtra translated into Chinese in 541 (later than the *Ocean Sūtra*), the *Maitreyamahāsiṃhanāda-sūtra* (Pek. no. 760[23]; T. no. 310 [23]), describes a method of visualization that significantly resembles the methods found in the *Ocean Sūtra*. Furthermore, the *Ocean Sūtra* describes several mystical visions very similar to those found in a Sanskrit meditation manual, the so-called *Yogalehrbuch,* manuscripts of which were found in Qizil and Shorchuq. See Dieter Schlingloff, *Ein buddhistisches Yogalehrbuch,* Textband, Sanskrit texte aus den Turfanfunden, vol. 7 (Berlin: Akademie-Verlag, 1964); *Ein buddhistisches Yogalehrbuch,* Tafelband, Sanskrit texte aus den Turfanfunden, vol. 7a (Berlin: Akademie-Verlag, 1966); *Ein buddhistisches Yogalehrbuch*, repr. [2 pts. in 1], with editions of the subsequently identified manuscripts, ed. Jens-Uwe Hartmann and Hermann-Josef Röllicke (Munich: Iudicium, 2006). Since this text has not been translated into Chinese, it must not have been accessible to most Chinese people; see Nobuyoshi Yamabe, "The Significance of the *'Yogalehrbuch'* for the Investigation into the Origin of Chinese Meditation Texts," *Bukkyō bunka* 9 (1999): 1–74. These points are understandable only if we suppose the Chinese authors of the *Ocean Sūtra* had direct access to the religious traditions of western areas.

We should further note that there are several mural paintings in the Turfan area suggesting that the types of visualization described in the *Ocean Sūtra* and the *Amitāyus Visualization Sūtra* were indeed practiced in this area. See also Yamabe, "An Examination of the Mural Paintings of Toyok Cave 20 in Conjunction with the Origin of the *Amitayus Visualization Sutra*," *Orientations* 30, 4 (1999): 38–44; "Practice of Visualization and the *Visualization Sūtra*: An Examination of Mural Paintings at Toyok, Turfan," *Pacific World: Journal of the Institute of Buddhist Studies* 3rd ser., 4 (2002): 123–52; and "An Examination of the Mural Paintings of Visualizing Monks in Toyok Cave 42: In Conjunction with the Origin of Some Chinese Texts on Meditation," in *Turfan Revisited: The First Century of Research into the Arts and Cultures of the Silk Road*, ed. Desmond Durkin-Meisterernst et al. (Berlin: Dietrich Reimer, 2004).

6. Ono Genmyō, *Kendara no Bukkyō bijutsu* (Tokyo: Heigo Shuppansha, 1923), 77–114; Alexander Soper, "Aspects of Light Symbolism in Gandhāran Sculpture," *Artibus Asiae* 12 (1949): 279.

7. Guan mawangzang pin, pp. 683b–687a.

8. What exactly this means is a bit problematical. In Pāli texts, this bodily mark is usually expressed as *kosohita-vatthaguyha*, which seems to mean "the male organ (*vatthaguyha*) hidden (*ohita*) in the foreskin (*kosa*)." This means that the organ was covered up with the foreskin but not that the organ itself was retracted in the body. We should further note that the male organ of a horse, to which the Buddha's organ is often compared, is covered with a foreskin but not retracted in the body. I thank Professor Stanley Insler for drawing my attention to these points. On the other hand, in Buddhist Sanskrit texts we find *kośopagatavastiguhya* or similar forms, which seem to be a wrong Sanskritization of *kosohita-vatthaguyha* (or some similar Middle-Indic form). Thus, the Buddha's male organ came to be interpreted as *vastiguhya*, "(something) to be hidden in the lower belly." The *Ocean Sūtra* follows this interpretation of Buddhist Sanskrit. For more details, see Yamabe, "Sūtra on the Ocean-Like Samādhi," 377, n. 1.

9. See, for example, the *Brahmāyusutta* quoted in n. 34 of the *Treatise*.

10. "The *Ocean Sūtra* as a Cross-Cultural Product: An Analysis of Some Stories on the Buddha's 'Hidden Organ,'" in *"The Way of Buddha" 2003: The 100th Anniversary of the Otani Mission and the 50th of the Research Society for Central Asian Cultures*, ed. Irisawa Takashi (Kyoto: Ryukoku University, 2010).

11. I cannot think of a plausible Sanskrit reconstruction for this name. A search for this word in the SAT database yields only three hits, all in the *Ocean Sūtra*. I think we should treat this name as another indication of the apocryphal nature of the text.

12. This refers to those who show off their male organs in the fourth story. See Yamabe, "The *Ocean Sūtra* as a Cross-Cultural Product," 258.

13. *Ocean Sūtra*, pp. 683c4–685b24, in summary. Underlined parts are those that have comparable elements in the relevant texts discussed later. Similarly below.

14. *Ocean Sūtra*, pp. 685b24–686a25, in summary.

15. See *Treatise* passage in note 32.

16. Soper, "Aspects of Light Symbolism in Gandhāran Sculpture: Continuation,"

Artibus Asiae 12 (1949): 326. This is even more likely because, as Soper points out, the *Ocean Sūtra* itself mentions the male organ of Īśvara, i.e., Śiva, in the fourth story, not discussed here ("My bodily organ is as powerful as that of Maheśvara," p. 686b2).

17. The fourth story, not discussed here, says that the flowers surrounding the organ reach the world of Brahmā (*Ocean Sūtra*, pp. 686c12–14).

18. *The Kūrma Purāṇa (with English Translation)*, ed. Anand Swarup Gupta, trans. Sri Ahibhushan Bhattacharya et al. (1972), verses 1.25.67–92. Another English translation in Cornelia Dimmitt and J. A. B. van Buitenen, eds. and trans, *Classical Hindu Mythology: A Reader in the Sanskrit Purāṇas* (Philadelphia: Temple University Press, 1978), 205–6. Variant versions of the story appear also in the *Śiva-Mahāpurāṇa*, trans. Shanti Lal Nagar (Delhi: Primal Publications, 2007), 1: 51–62 [Vidyeśvara Saṃhitā verses 6.1–9.46]; 3: 599–607 [Vāyavīya Saṃhitā, Uttarabhāga verses 34.17–35.85]).

19. See also Stella Kramrisch, *Manifestations of Shiva* (Philadelphia: Philadelphia Museum of Art, 1981), 10; Tachikawa Musasi, Ishiguro Atsushi, Hishida Kunio, and Shima Iwao, *Hindū no kamigami* (Tokyo: Serika Shobō, 1980), plates 66–67 (eighth century).

20. Ananda K. Coomaraswamy, *Elements of Buddhist Iconography*, 3rd ed. (New Delhi: Munshiram Manoharlal, 1935, 1979), plate II, figure 6 shows an example from Amarāvatī (ca. 200 CE).

21. For the fiery pillar, see ibid., 10.

22. Iyanaga Nobumi, "Daijizaiten," in *Hōbōgirin: Dictionnaire encyclopédique du bouddhisme d'après les sources chinoises et japonaises*, vol. 6 (Paris: Maisonneuve, 1983), 713–75. Moreover, the few texts besides the *Ocean Sūtra* listed by Iyanaga (ibid., 731) that do mention the Shaivite phallicism are all later than the *Ocean Sūtra*.

23. I do not know if the *Ocean Sūtra* was composed by a single author or a group. Considering the disorganized nature of the text, it seems more likely that more than one person was involved in the composition. So, in what follows I simply say "authors." It should be noted, however, that I have no definite reason to deny that the *Ocean Sūtra* was composed by a single author.

24. Albert Grünwedel, *Alt-Kutscha: archäologische und religionsgeschichtliche Forschungen an Tempera-Gemälden aus Buddhistischen Höhlen der ersten acht Jahrhunderte nach Christi Geburt* (Berlin: Elsner, 1920), plates 26–27, figure 4 [MIK III 8725]. See Sasaki Ritsuko, "Tonkō Bakkōkutsu dai 285 kutsu seiheki naiyō kaishaku shiron" (Interpretation of the West Wall of Tun-huang Ma-kao Cave No. 285), *Bijutsushi* (Journal of the Japan Art History Society) 142 (1997): 128–29. According to Zhao Li, "Verification of the Original Locations of the Murals from Caves in Kizil Kept in the Museum für Indische Kunst, Berlin," in *Turfan Revisited: The First Century of Research into the Arts and Cultures of the Silk Road*, ed. Desmond Durkin-Meisterernst et al. (Berlin: Dietrich Reimer, 2004), 418, this painting was taken from Qizil Cave 178. See also Simone Gaulier, Robert Jera-Bezard, and Monique Maillard, *Buddhism in Afghanistan and Central Asia*, Iconography of Religions, sec. 13, fasc. 14, pt. 2 (Leiden: Brill, 1976), 39.

25. See Joanna Williams, "The Iconography of Khotanese Painting," *East and West* n.s. 23, 1–2 (1973): 142.

26. Williams ("Iconography," 109–10) dates these types of Khotanese paintings to the eighth century, but more recently, Roderick Whitfield, *The Art of Central Asia*, trans. into Japanese by Ueno Aki as *Saiiki bijutsu: Daiei Hakubutsukan Stain korekushon*, vol. 3, *Someori, Chōso, Hekiga* (Tokyo: Kōdansha, 1984), 315, dates them to the sixth century.

27. See the bull's head to the left of the figure.

28. See Sasaki, "Tonkō Bakkōkutsu," 128.

29. The fourth and the fifth year of the Datong era (538–39) of Western Wei (Xiwei). See *Chūgoku sekkutsu Tonkō Bakkōkutsu* (Chinese Caves, Dunhuang Mogao Caves), ed. Tonkō Bunbutsu Kenkyūjo, vol. 1 (Tokyo: Heibonsha, 1980), 244.

30. *Chūgoku sekkutsu Unkō sekkutsu*, vol. 1, ed. Unkō Sekkutsu Bunbutsu Hokanjo, 180–84.

31. For example, the three faces, two upper hands holding the sun and moon, a bull.

32. T. no. 1509, vol. 25, 90b17–22; French translation in Étienne Lamotte, *Le traité de la grande vertu de sagesse de Nāgārjuna* (*Mahāprajñāpāramitāśāstra*), vol. 1 (Louvain-la-neuve: Institut Orientaliste, Université de Louvain, [1944] 1981), 274–75. See also the following passage from the *Treatise*:

> Next, Satyaka Nirgranthīputra [i.e., Jina] wore a copper plate around his belly and swore to himself: "When I refute somebody, there is nobody who does not sweat or is not defeated. . . ." Having spoken thus, he came to debate with the Buddha, but he could not answer any of the Buddha's questions. Sweat flowed [down] and covered the ground, as if his whole body were soaked in it. The Buddha said to Nirgranthīputra: ". . . Now your sweat covers the ground. Try and see if the Buddha has sweat." The Buddha then removed his upper garment (*uttarāsaṅga*), showed [his body] and said: "Where is there sweat?" . . .
>
> There are people who doubt two marks of the Buddha. They, who would otherwise attain awakening, cannot attain it due to their doubt. For this reason, [the Buddha] reveals his two marks. He extends his tongue and covers his face. Though [his tongue] is large, it can return into the mouth without hindrances. . . .
>
> There are people who doubt the mark of the Buddha's hidden male organ, which is invisible. At this time, the Buddha magically creates an elephant-treasure and a horse-treasure and, pointing to them, says that the mark of the hidden male organ is invisible like them.
>
> Some people say: the Buddha reveals the mark of his hidden male organ only to one person to remove the doubt of that person.

Treatise, p. 251c10–29; French trans. in Lamotte, *Le traité de la grande vertu de sagesse de Nāgārjuna*, vol. 3 (1970), 1665–67. This is an interpretation of an obscure passage found in Āgama/Nikāya sources. Let me quote here from the Pāli *Brahmāyusutta* (*Majjhima-nikāya*, PTS ed., no. 91, vol. 2, 143.15–24):

> Then the Blessed One thought as follows: This Brahman Brahmāyu has seen most of my thirty-two marks of a great person except for the two; he doubts,

> hesitates, does not understand and is unsettled about the two marks of a great person: the concealed male organ and the large tongue. Thus the Blessed One exercised his miraculous power so that the Brahman Brahmāyu could see the concealed male organ of the Blessed One. Then, extending his tongue, the Blessed One touched and pressed the two orifices of his ear, the two nostrils, and covered his entire forehead with his tongue.

This passage corresponds to the *Fanmo jing* of the *Madhyamāgama* (*Zhong ahan jing*), T. no. 26(161), vol. 1, 685c21–29; and the *Fanmoyu jing*, T. no. 76, vol. 1, 883c7–8. In these sūtras, how he "exercised his miraculous power" is not concretely explained, and that is why later scholar-monks debated over its exact meaning, as we have seen above. The same story is also mentioned in the *Xianyu jing* (The Sūtra on the Wise and Foolish, T. no. 202, vol. 4, 433b9–10).

33. See Yamabe, "Sūtra on the Ocean-Like Samādhi," 233–49.

34. In the passage quoted from the *Treatise* in note 32, we find the motif of Jina's challenge and removal of the Buddha's garment immediately followed by the story of revealing the Buddha's hidden organ. In chapter 7 of the *Ocean Sūtra*, Jain ascetics' challenge is found in the fourth story, and the opening of the garment in the first and second stories.

35. Indeed the prostitutes did not understand the meaning at all and burst into laughter.

36. Concerning the passage quoted above from the *Treatise* (p. 90b17–22), we find an almost identical statement in the **Abhidharma-Mahāvibhāṣā* (*Api damo da piposha lun*, T. no. 1545, vol. 27, 888b2–5); quoted in Kawamura Kōshō, *Ubu no Budda ron* (*Sarvāstivāda Theories of the Buddha) (Tokyo: Sankibō Busshorin, 1975), 186. Therefore, as is often the case, here again we can confirm that the *Treatise* was based on the tenets of the Sarvāstivāda traditions (cf. Lamotte, *Le traité*, vol. 3, pp. xiv–xxxii). Accordingly, it is not entirely impossible that the *Ocean Sūtra* was directly based on a Sarvāstivāda text in its Sanskrit original. If we consider the generally close affinity between the *Treatise* and the *Ocean Sūtra* in Chinese expressions, however, it is more likely that the authors of the *Ocean Sūtra* actually referred to Kumārajīva's Chinese text of the *Treatise*.

37. *Vāmana Purāṇa: Sanskrit Text and English Translation with an Exhaustive Introduction, Notes and Index of Verses*, ed. O. N. Bimali and K. L. Joshi (Delhi: Parimal Publications, 2005), 5–13, verses 2.19–3.51. See Dimmitt and van Buitenen, *Classical Hindu Mythology*, 206–9. Variant versions of this story are discussed in Wendy Doniger O'Flaherty, *Śiva: The Erotic Ascetic* (Oxford: Oxford University Press, 1973, 1981), 123–27; and Stella Kramrisch, *The Presence of Śiva* (Princeton, N.J.: Princeton University Press, 1981), 250–65.

38. *Śiva-Mahāpurāṇa: An Exhaustive Introduction, Sanskrit Text, English Translation with Photographs of Archaeological Evidence*, trans. Shanti Lal Naga, 3 vols. (Delhi: Parimal Publications, 2007), 2:1–4 [Rudra Saṃhitā, Kumāra Khaṇḍa 1.1–46]. See Kramrisch, *Manifestations of Shiva*, xviii.

39. *The Aśokāvadana: Sanskrit Text Compared with Chinese Versions*, ed. Sujitkumar

Mukhopadhyaya (Delhi: Sahitya Akademi, 1963), 15.18–24.12; John S. Strong, *The Legend of King Aśoka: A Study and Translation of the "Aśokāvadāna"* (Princeton, N.J.: Princeton University Press, 1983; reprint Delhi: Motilal Banrsidass, 1989), 186–93; *Ayuwang zhuan*, T. no. 2042, vol. 50, 118c15–119c20 (translated into Chinese in 306 CE); *Ayuwang jing*, T. no. 2043, vol. 50, 159a19–160b15 (translated into Chinese in 512 CE). See also Strong, *The Legend and Cult of Upagupta: Sanskrit Buddhism in North India and Southeast Asia* 9 (Princeton, N.J.: Princeton University Press, 1992; reprint Delhi: Motilal Banrsidass, 1994), 93–104.

40. As we have seen, the third story of the *Ocean Sūtra* is a story of a lustful prostitute. We have also seen that in the second story, the ring of prostitutes were originally from Mathurā. In the *Aśokāvadāna* (8.13–14.9; Strong, *Legend of King Aśoka*, 179–84), just before the summarized part, there appears a story of Vāsavadattā, a lustful prostitute of Mathurā. Also, after the *māra* has accepted the teaching, Upagupta expresses a desire to see the Buddha, and the *māra* transforms himself into the shape of the Buddha. So moved, Upagupta forgets that it is indeed a *māra* and worships him (23.10–27.6; Strong, *Legend of King Aśoka*, 192–96, *Legend and Cult of Upagupta*, 109–16). There is no directly comparable story in the *Ocean Sūtra*, but obviously "seeing the Buddha" is a major topic in this sūtra.

41. Various versions of this story are translated by Ju-hyung Rhi, "Gandhāran Images of the 'Śrāvastī Miracle': An Iconographic Reassessment," Ph.D. dissertation, University of California, Berkeley, 1991, 207–315.

42. For the latter story, see Victor H. Mair, "The Linguistic and Textual Antecedents of *The Sūtra of the Wise and the Foolish* (*Hsien-yü ching*): With an Appended Translation of "Sudatta Raises a Monastery," *Sino-Platonic Papers* 38 (1993): 1–95.

43. This seems to be a shortened form of *jiangshi zhi chang* mentioned above.

44. After this, the second story of the *Ocean Sūtra* deviates from those of the *Wise and Foolish*, and we can trace no more parallel story lines. We should note, however, in the fourth story of the *Ocean Sūtra,* not discussed here, we find some more parallelism. For the details, see Yamabe, "Sūtra on the Ocean-Like Samādhi," 416–18.

45. According to the preface to the *Wise and Foolish* included in the *Chu sanzang jiji* (T. no. 2145, vol. 55, 67c9–68a1), eight monks from Hexi went to Khotan and attended lectures and then compiled what they heard there into a single text (subsequently titled the *Wise and Foolish*) at Turfan in the twenty-second year of the Yuanjia era (445 CE). Here the noteworthy point is that the *Wise and Foolish* contains many Chinese-style expressions very similar to the ones in the *Ocean Sūtra* (and in the other related meditation texts) that made Tsukinowa skeptical of their authenticity. For the details, see Yamabe, "Sūtra on the Ocean-Like Samādhi," 419–20, n. 42. The overall contents of the *Wise and Foolish* are standard Jātaka/Avadāna stories, and accordingly the authenticity of this text is not doubted, even by Tsukinowa (*Butten no hihanteki kenkyū*, 77). It is noteworthy that, if it had been compiled by Chinese monks at Turfan, even such a text can contain inconsistent translations/transcriptions, Chinese-style expressions, and some obvious misunderstandings. The close similarity of the expressions seems to indicate that the *Ocean Sūtra* was composed in

a very similar environment. We might also consider that the *Wise and Foolish* was a very popular text in the Dunhuang area, and that there are many pictorial representations of the "Raudrākṣa" story, though they are from later periods. See, for example, Sarah E. Fraser, *Performing the Visual: The Practice of Buddhist Wall Painting in China and Central Asia, 618–960*, Stanford, Calif.: Stanford University Press, 2004, 71ff.

46. The composition of the *Ocean Sūtra* seems to have taken place sometime between 421 and ca. 450. See Yamabe, "Could Turfan Be the Birthplace of Visualization Sutras?" in *Tulufanxue yanjiu: Dierjie Tulufanxue Guoji Xueshu Yantaohui lunwenji*, ed. Xinjiang Tulufan Diqu Wenwuju, Proceedings of the Second International Conference on Turfan Studies, Xinjiang Tulufan Diqu Wenwuju (Shanghai: Shanghai Cishu Chubanshe), 2006, 419–30, 424–26.

47. See note 5.

48. "*Xianyu jing* de jicheng niandai yu Dunhuang Mogaoku di 275 ku de kaizao," *Dunhuang yanjiu* 70 (2001): 70–74.

49. In the sixth chapter of the *Ocean Sūtra*, we can find some traces of the frame story of the *Sumāgadhāvadāna*, though the overall story line is entirely different. See Yamabe, "An Examination of the Mural Paintings," 41–43.

50. The Sanskrit text of this *avadāna* is available in two editions, Tokiwai Gyōyū, *The Sumāgadhāvadāna: A Buddhist Legend, Now First Edited from the Nepalese Ms. in Paris* (Tsu: Ise Shinbunsha, 1918); Iwamoto Yutaka, "The *Sumāgadhāvadāna*: A Buddhist Legend, pt. 1, Revised Sanskrit-Text," *Tōkai Daigaku Bungakubu kiyō* 1 (1959): 1–51 [reprinted in Iwamoto, *Sumāgadā avadāna kenkyū*, *Bukkyō setsuwa kenkyū*, vol. 5, Tokyo: Keimei Shoin, 1979, no pagination]). A Tibetan version has also been edited by Iwamoto (*Sumāgadā avadāna kenkyū*). A versified version is included in the *Bodhisattvāvadānakalpalatā* of Kṣementra, an eleventh-century poet from Kashmir. For this one also, there is an edition in Iwamoto, "The *Sumāgadhāvadāna*" and *Sumāgadā avadāna kenkyū*. Corrections of Iwamoto's edition are found in J. W. de Jong, *Text-Critical Remarks on the Bodhisattvāvadānakalpalatā (Pallavas 42–108)*, Studia Philologica Buddhica Monograph Series 2 (Tokyo: Reiyukai Library, 1979), 230–37. In addition, there are four Chinese versions of the text: *Sanmojie jing* (T. no. 129, vol. 2, 843a–845c); *Xumotinü jing* (T. no. 128, vol. 2, 835c–837c); a part of the *Zengyi ahan jing* (T. no. 125[3], vol. 2, 660a–665b); and *Jigudu zhangzhenü dedu yinyuan jing* (T. no. 130, vol. 2, 845c–854a).

51. See *Chūgoku sekkutsu Kijiru sekkutsu*, vol. 3, ed. Shinkyō Uiguru Jichiku Bunbutsu Kanri Iinkai, and Haijōken Kijiru Senbutsudō Bunbutsu Hokanjo (Tokyo: Heibonsha, 1985), 202; Akira Miyaji, "Turufan, Toyoku sekkutsu no zenkansō hekiga ni tsuite: Jōdozu, jōdo kansōzu, fujō kansōzu" Part 3. *Bukkyō geijutsu* 226 (1996): 42.

52. Xinjiang Weiwu'er Zizhiqu Bowuguan eds., *Xinjiang shiku, Tulufan Bozikelike shiku*, Urumchi: Xinjiang Renmin Chubanshe (Shanghai: Shanghai Renmin Meishu Chubanshe, 1990), plate 170.

53. Tonkō Bunbutsu Kenkyūjo, *Chūgoku sekkutsu Tonkō Bakkōkutsu*, plate 45.

54. Chhaya Haesner, "Some Common Stylistic and Iconographic Features in the

Buddhist Art of India and Central Asia," in *Investigating Indian Art: Proceedings of a Symposium on the Development of Early Buddhist and Hindu Iconography Held at the Museum of Indian Art, Berlin, in May 1986*, ed. Marianne Yaldiz and Wibke Lobo, Veröffentlichungen des Museums für Indische Kunst 8 (Berlin: Museum für Indische Kunst, 1987), 105–20, 117.

55. Ibid., 118.

Chapter 5. From Bodily Relic to Dharma Relic Stūpa: Chinese Materialization of the Aśoka Legend in the Wuyue Period

Special thanks are due to art historian Joo Kyeongmi of Pukyong National University, who has published mostly in Korean on the so-called Baoqieyin stūpas and other aspects of Wuyue visual or material culture. Although I do not read Korean, I have benefited from our conversations and correspondence.

Epigraph: *Fozu tongji*, T. no. 2035, vol. 49, 394c,

1. When the Song dynasty ascended to power in 960, Qian Chu reverentially gave up the middle character "hong" in his name as a sign of deference to the Song emperor whose father's name also had this character.

2. For a survey of these sources, see Zhou Feng, ed., *Wuyue shoufu Hangzhou* (Hangzhou: Zhejiang renmin chubanshe, 1988), 117–18.

3. The *Aśokāvadāna* exists as part of the *Divyāvadāna*, an extensive collection of Sanskrit Buddhist legends; see P. L. Vaidya, ed., *Divyāvadānam*, Buddhist Sanskrit texts no. 20 (Dharbhanga, Bihar: Mithila Institute, 1959), 216–82. For a monograph study of the *Aśokāvadāna*, see John S. Strong, *The Legend of Aśoka: A Study and Translation of the* Aśokāvadāna (Delhi: Molital Banarsidass, 1983). The Chinese translations are the *Ayuwang zhuan* (T. no. 2042) translated around 306 by the Parthian monk Zhu Faqin, and the *Ayuwang jing* (T. no. 2043) translated in 512 CE by Saṅghabhara (Sengjiapoluo, 460–524).

4. According to the *Aśokavandāna*, the eighth and last part he left in the care of the *nāgā*s at the site of Rāmagrāma.

5. Strong, *The Legend of Aśoka*, 219–21.

6. This number is given in the *Ayuwang zhuan*, T. no. 2042, vol. 1, 102a17–29.

7. Strong, *The Legend of Aśoka*, 115.

8. Wuyue's territories roughly corresponded to those of the ancient Yue, but did not include the ancient Wu, two kingdoms that flourished in the Spring and Autumn period from 770 to 476 BCE. The name of Wuyue was a source of conflict for years between Wuyue and Wu kingdoms.

9. On Qian Chu's contributions to Buddhism, see Huang Yi-hsun, "Wuyue zhu wang (893–978) yu fojiao," *Chung-hwa Buddhist Journal* 17 (2004): 123–47.

10. This anecdote was noted in the Japanese monk Dōki's record of his travel through Wuyue territories in an essay titled "Hōkyōin-kyō-ki" (Record of the Sūtra on the Precious Chest Mudrā) composed on the twenty-second day of the seventh month in the year 965.

The original essay is preserved in the Kongō ji in Japan. The essay is cited in Kinomiya Yashuhiko, *Nisshi kōtsushi*, 2 vols. (Tōkyō: Kinshi Hōryūdō, 1926), vol. 1, 373–74; the citation is reproduced in Yin Yuzhen and Zhu Geji, eds, *Wuyue shishi biannian* (Hangzhou: Zhejiang guji chubanshe, 1987), 315.

11. *Wuyue shishi biannian*, 313. Also see Lai Jiancheng, *Wuyue fojiao zhi fazhan* (Taipei: Dongwu chubanshe, 1990), 139.

12. See excerpt cited at the beginning of this chapter.

13. In this diagram, a scene from the Jātaka on feeding the hungry tigress is portrayed on the stūpa's body.

14. *Liang Zhe jinshi zhi*, by Ruan Yuan (Qing dynasty) of Yangzhou; collected in *Shikeshiliao xinbian* (Taibei: Xinwenfeng chubanshe, 1986), vol. 14, 10280.

15. The jātaka of Prince Mahāsattva feeding the starving tigress is recounted in the *Fo shuo pusa toushen taierhu qita yinyuan jing*, translated into Chinese by Fasheng of the Northern Liang period (397–439); see T. no. 2153, vol. 3, 424–28. This story is also collected in *Xianyu jing*, translated by Huijue; see T. no. 202, vol. 4, 352–53. The Śibi story in which the king saves a pigeon from a preying hawk is also narrated in the *Xianyu jing*; see T. no. 202, vol. 4, 351c–352b.

16. These two *jātaka* stories are recounted also in the *Xianyu jing*; see T. no.202, vol. 4, 387b–392c. The story of the Quick-eyed Prince is the Chinese narrative for the version of the King Śibi story where he gives away his eyes.

17. *Gaoseng Faxian zhuan*, T. no. 2085, vol. 51, 858b3–11.

18. See Reiko Ohnuma, *Heads, Eyes, Flesh, and Blood: Giving Away the Body in Buddhist Literature* (New York: Columbia University Press, 2006), 2. Moreover, since the stories are all about the bodhisattva prince making bodily sacrifice of some sort, Ohnuma further argues that a virtual cult of the bodhisattva's bodily sacrifice was active throughout the region.

19. Alexander Coburn Soper, "Contributions to the Study of Sculpture and Architecture III: Japanese Evidence for the History of the Architecture and Iconography of Chinese Buddhism," *Monumenta Serica* 4 (1940): 655.

20. Zhejiang sheng wenwu kaogu yanjiusuo, *Leifeng yi zhen* (Beijing: Wenwu chubanshe, 2002), 97, 99. The Wanfo ta dates to 1062, that is, the Northern Song period. However, since this pagoda is surrounded by monasteries that were built from an earlier period during the Five Dynasties, it is not surprising that many of the artifacts unearthed from this pagoda's underground cache actually date to the Wuyue, and even Tang period. See Wang Shilun, "Jinhua Wanfota taji qingli jianbao," *Wenwu cankao ziliao* 4 (1957): 41–44; Zhejiangsheng wenwu guanli weiyuanhui, *Jinhua Wanfota chutu wenwu* (Beijing: Wenwu chubanshe, 1958).

21. *Jinhua Wanfota chutu wenwu*, 4, 58, plate 51.

22. Ibid., 4, 61, plate 54.

23. *Liang Zhe Jinshizhi*, vol. 3, 34, collected in *Shike shiliao xinbian: diyi ji*, 30 vols. (Taipei: Xinwenfeng, 1982), vol. 14, 10280.

24. For a comprehensive listing of such stūpas recovered during archaeological

excavations, see Wang Li, "'Baoqieyinjing ta' yu Wuyue guo dui ri wenhua jiaoliu," *Zhejiang daxue xuebao* (*Renwen shehui kexue bao*) 32, 5 (2002) [pages have no numbers].

25. Zhejiang sheng wenwu kaogu yanjiu suo, *Leifeng yi zhen*, 100–102.

26. The bulk belongs to Qian Chu's period, although some of them do date later, from the Song and Yuan periods. After the Wuyue period, the gilt stūpas become more diversified in design and material, so that there are examples of brick stūpas.

27. Yoshikawa Isao, *Sekizō hōkyōin-tō no seiritsu* (Tokyo: Daiichi Shobō, 2000), 41.

28. A catalog of this exhibition has been published: Zhongtai shan bowuguan, ed. *Diyong tianbao: Zhejiang sheng bowuguan zhenpin tezhan* (Nantou: Wen xin wenhua shiye gufen youxian gongsi, 2009).

29. The Harvard Sackler Museum also has one of these stūpas in its collection. Today, some stūpas commissioned by Qian Chu in 955 which were evidently transported to Japan have shown up in private and public Japanese collections. They are found in Tokyo National Museum, Nara National Museum, Seiganji in Fukuoka prefecture on the island of Kyūshu, Kongōji in Osaka and Kontaiji in Kyōto (Yoshikawa, *Sekizō hōkyōin-tō no seiritsu*, 148, n. 27). Another bronze gilt stūpa of similar style (which I discuss below), although inscriptionally dated to 905 CE, is now part of the collection at the National Museum of Taiwan. The Musée Guimet in Paris also has a silver gilt stūpa with an inscriptional dating of 986, which places it in the Northern Song period (150, n. 58).

30. On the significance of the Wuyue region for relic veneration, see Gong Zhebing, "Wuyue zhi di de sheli wenhua," in *Wuyue fojiao xueshu yantaohui*, ed. Hangzhou foxueyuan (Beijing: Zhongjiao wenhua chubanshe, 2004), 35–46.

31. *Ji shenzhou sanbaogantong lu*, T. no. 2106, vol. 52, 404a–412c; *Guang hongming ji*, T. no. 2103, vol. 52, 201c–202a; *Fayuan zhulin*, T. no. 2122, vol. 53, 584c–591a.

32. Hubert Durt discussed the possibility of premodern practices of archeology in Korea; see his "The Meaning of Archaeology in Ancient Context: Notes on the Stūpas of Aśoka," *Commemorative Volume Celebrating the Eightieth Year of Dongguk University* (Seoul: Dongguk Press, 1987), 1223–41.

33. For example, Koichi Shinohara, "Two Sources of Chinese Biographies: Stupa Inscriptions and Miracle Stories," in *Monks and Magicians: Religious Biographies in Asia*, ed. Phyllis Granoff and Koichi Shinohara (Oakville, Ont.: Mosaic Press, 1988), 119–228; Marilyn Martin Rhie, *Early Buddhist Art of China and Central Asia II: The Eastern China and Sixteen Kingdoms in China and Tumshuk, Kucha and Karashahr in Central Asia* (Leiden: Brill, 2002), 64–82.

34. The earliest record of Liu Sahe is collected in the *Mingxiang ji*, a text that is no longer extant today except for passages cited in the *Fayuan zhulin*, T. no. 2122, vol. 53, 920a. The *Mingxiang ji* is a non-Buddhist collection of popular narratives compiled by Wang Yan (born ca. 454).

35. The pre-Tang records are found in the *Liang shu* by Yao Silian (557–637) and *Gaoseng zhuan* by Huijiao (479–554). It is uncertain whether this discrepancy in the records implies that Huida found two stūpas in Mao county, a full-size monument and a reliquary, or if the differing accounts reflect a general confusion.

36. *Ji shenzhou sanbao gantong lu*, T. no. 2106, vol. 52, 404b.

37. For example, the famous Tiantai master Zhiyi (539–598) undertook observances of profound piety to this Mao county stūpa and its relics; see Koichi Shinohara, "The Maitreyan Image in Shichen and Guanding's Biography of Zhiyi," in *From Benares to Beijing: Essays on Buddhism and Chinese Religions in Honour of Prof. Jan Yün-Hua* ed. K. Shinohara and G. Schopen (Oakvill, Ont.: Mosaic Press, 1991), 7.

38. *Tōdai wajō tōseiden*, T. no. 2089, vol. 51, 988a–994b. The same text is included as no. 553 in the *Dainihon bukkyō zensho*, 100 vols., Suzuki Research Foundation edition (Tokyo: Kōdansha, 1972).

39. *Tōdai wajō tōseiden*, 989a.

40. Soper, "Contributions to the Study of Sculpture and Architecture III," 638–78.

41. For example, *Wuyue beishi*, *juan* 1, collected in *Biji xiaoshuo daguan*, vol. 25, 1648; *Fozu tongji*, 394c.

42. *Wuyue beishi*, *juan* 1, 1605. Cf. *Shiguo chunqiu*, *juan* 77, by Wu Renchen, Qing dynasty (Beijing: Zhonghua shuju, 1983), vol. 3, 1070.

43. *Wuyue beishi*, *juan* 1, 1612.

44. Ibid., 1660.

45. Ibid., 1623.

46. Ibid., 1660–61.

47. Ibid., 1661.

48. Ibid., 1661–63. The Later Tang Dynasty, one of the Five Dynasties, was a short-lived Turkic dynasty that at its height controlled most of northern China.

49. *Wuyue shishi biannian*, 10.

50. The essay concludes by announcing that it was recorded from memory (*jinshi*) in the fifth month of 1355.

51. The essay is recorded in the Ming dynasty gazetteer dated to 1692 and edited by Guo Zizhang *in zhou Ayuwangshan zi*, *juan* 2, http://buddhistinformatics.ddbc.edu.tw/fosizhi/ui.html?book=g010, 0091–009; also cited in *Wuyue shishi biannian*, 156.

52. *Fozu tongji*, 461a–b.

53. For a translation and discussion of Han Yu's famous memorial, see Edwin O. Reischauer, *Ennin's Travels in Tang China* (New York: Ronald Press, 1955), 263–24.

54. Moreover, tenth-century Chinese would have understood the miraculous lights as otherworldly verification of the political authority for the newly founded Wuyue kingdom.

55. The legendary grand sage ruler Yu, known to have divided the land of ancient China into nine states, was said to have cast nine cauldrons that symbolized the nine states (Jizhou, Yanzhou, Qingzhou, Xuzhou, Yangzhou, Jinzhou, Yuzhou, Liangzhou, and Yongzhou), cast with the renowned mountains, rivers, and rare animal species of the states they represented. These cauldrons were assembled in Yang city, the capital of Xia, the seat of power of Yu the Great, who lorded over the nine states as the Emperor of Xia. Hence, the symbolism of the nine cauldrons as the "Mandate of Heaven." Yu was said to have honored the nine cauldrons as "Treasures Guarding the Country," and when the vassals came to the court, they were to pay respects to the cauldrons. The original reference to this legend

appears in the *Zuo zhuan* (Duke Xuan: 3). Later, in Chinese history, to 'inquire about the cauldrons" meant to aspire to seize imperial power.

56. See Chen Jinhua, *Monks and Monarchs, Kinship and Kingship: Tanqian in Sui Buddhism and Politics* (Kyoto: Scuola Italiana di Studi sull'Asia Orientale, 2002).

57. Furthermore, certain historical documents relate that in 906, the Yang family of Huainan presented Qian Liu with the dragon robe, jade tablet, and other insignia of kingship, in recognition of his tremendous contribution to devising irrigation of the waters in the nearby region. Qian Liu rejected the gift in deference to the Tang court. See the historical sources cited in *Wuyue shishi biannian*, 103.

58. *Wuyue beishi, juan* 1, 1669; cf. *Wuyue shishi biannian*, 195.

59. The inscription is cited in Yoshikawa, *Seki hōkyōin-tō no seiritsu*, 19–22.

60. A catalog description and picture of the artifact also appears on the National Palace Museum of Taiwan, http://antiquities.npm.gov.tw/~textdb2/NPMv1/show4.php?_op=?accessionNo 000140N000000000, accessed January 24, 2012.

61. For instance, one classic anecdote relates that the famous carpenter-cum-architect of the tenth century Yu Hao (ca. 989) was sought out for counsel during the building of Nan ta (Southern Pagoda). This story is narrated in the Song literary work *Mengxi bitan*, by Shen Kuo (1029–93). Yu Hao, a native of Zhejiang, is most famous for building the octagonal wooden stūpa of thirteen stories at Kaibao si, as well as for authoring the *Mu jing* (Classic on Woodwork) of three scrolls, the classic Chinese reference for wooden architecture.

62. In his detailed study, Yoshikawa tells us that he originally believes that the Taipei stūpa was from a later period, but after examining the piece on site, he concludes that the attribution of the artifact to the Tang dynasty (that is, the 905 date in the inscription) is accurate; this opinion, he states, is shared also by the scholar Wang Shilun of Hangzhou, one of the foremost experts on this material in China (Yoshikawa, *Seki hōkyōin-tō no seiritsu*, 19–22). I had the opportunity to see the stūpa for myself during a visit to the National Palace Museum of Taiwan in March 2010.

63. For a photo reproduction and a more detailed description of this stūpa at the Feixia si, see Guojia wenwuju, ed., *Zhongguo wenwu jinghua dacidian: qingtong juan* (Shanghai: Shanghai cishu chubanshe, 1995), 367. The topmost broader layer of the stūpa base has solid, flat surfaces with shallow engravings, akin to line drawings. From the catalog pictures, it is unclear whether the drawings are Buddha assemblies, or jātaka stories. The catalog description refers to them as stories of the Buddha.

64. On the Tang bronze plate, including photo reproductions, see Yoshikawa, *Sekizō hōkyōin-tō no seiritsu*, 13, plates 6, 7, 8.

65. Ibid., 13, plate 9.

66. There are three versions of this text in the Taishō canon. Two are attributed to the famous esoteric teacher of the Tang court, Amoghavajra or Bukong (705–774): T. no. 1022A, vol. 19, 710a–712b; and T. no. 1022B, vol. 19, 712b–715a. The third is attributed to Dānapāla (Shihu, ca. tenth century): T. no. 1023, vol. 19, 715–17. The title in Sanskrit is *Sarvatathāgatādhiṣṭhāna-hṛdaya-guhya-dhātu-karaṇḍa-mudrā-nāma-dhāraṇī sūtra*.

67. Hsueh-Man Shen traces this practice in her analysis of the Buddhist relic deposits in the Liao period (907–1125). See Hsueh-Man Shen, "Realizing the Buddha's 'Dharma' Body During the Mofa Period: A Study of Liao Buddhist Relic Deposits," *Artibus Asiae* 61, 2 (2001): 263–303.

68. *Datang Xiyuji* (Records of the Western Regions of the Great Tang Dynasty), T. no. 2087, vol. 51, 920a.

69. Divākara or Dipoheluo is also known in Chinese as Ri Zhao (The Illuminating Sun). He was born in India but came to China in 676.

70. *Fo shuo zao ta gongde jing*, T. no. 699, vol. 16, 801b12–15.

71. The *Shoku Nihon gi* (Supplement to the Japanese Annals) records the empress sponsoring the production of the *hyakumantō darani* to mark a victory over the rebellion led by Emi no Oshikatsu (d. 764). See Fujiwara Tsugutada (727–96) et al., *Shoku Nihon gi*, collected in *Shin Nihon Koten bungaku taikei* (Tokyo: Iwanami Shoten, 1989–98), *kan* 30, 280–81.

72. The *Great Dhāraṇī of Pure Light* first appeared in China, possibly around the year 701. But the earliest printed copy was excavated from the Sŏkkatap or Śākyamuni Pagoda of the Pulguksa Temple in Kyŏngju, which has led Korean scholars to argue for an early role for Korea in the history of printing in East Asia. Modern Chinese scholarship believes the *Great Dhāraṇī of Pure Light* was transmitted to Korea sometime around 703; see Pan Jixing, "Lun Han'guo faxian de yinben 'Wugoujingguang da tuoluoni jing,'" *Kexue tongbao* 42, 10 (1997): 1009–28. However, since there is no conclusive evidence that this example of a printed *dhāraṇī* is part of a large-scale production of texts sealed in pagodas, we need not factor it into our arguments.

73. The inscription is cited in *Wuyue shoufu Hangzhou*, 80. One scroll of the 956 edition of the *Baoqieyin Sūtra* was discovered in January 1971 at the school campus of Wuwei zhongxue in Anhui, which suggests that copies of this text were disseminated also outside Wuyue territories (*Wuyue shoufu hangzhou*, 81). See also Soren Edgren, "The Printed Dhāraṇī Sūtra of A.D. 956," *Museum of Far Eastern Antiquities* (Ostasiastiska Museet) 44 (1972): 141–46.

74. The inscription is cited in Zhejiangsheng wenwu kaogu yanjiu suo, ed., *Leifengta yi zhi* (Beijing: Wenwu chubanshe, 2005), 259.

75. The inscription is cited in Zhang Xiumin, "Wudai Wuyueguo de yinshua," *Wenwu* 12 (1978): 75. Both the stūpa's inscription and the inscription on the scroll of *Baoqieyin sūtra* inside the stūpa are cited by Yoshikawa, *Seki hōkyōin-tō no seiritsu*, 149, n. 37.

76. Li Jining, *Fojing banben* (Nanjing: Jiangsu guji chubanshe, 2002), 28–30.

77. *Miaofa lianhua jing*, T. no. 262, vol. 9, 31b27–29.

78. *Yiqie rulai xinmimi quanshen sheli baoqieyin tuolonijing*, T. no. 1022A, vol. 19, 711a.

79. While the stated reason for building Leifeng Pagoda is to commemorate his beloved deceased concubine (hence it is also called Huangfei ta, or the Pagoda for the Royal Concubine), it really gave Qian Chu an opportunity to have the precious hair relic installed in the Wuyue capital.

80. The decreed regulation is recorded in *Wudaihuiyao*, *juan* 12, by Wang Fu (922–82) (Shanghai: Shanghai guji chubanshe, 1978), 196.

81. The total number of monasteries is recorded in *Zizhi tongjian*, by Sima Guang (1019–1086), vol. 292; http://www.guoxue.com/shibu/zztj/-content/zztj_292.htm. On the persecution of Buddhism by the Later Zhao Dynasty, see Luo Shixian, "*Tang Wudai zhi fanan yu Zhongguo*," *Pumen Xuebao* 50 (2009): 272–83.

82. Previous scholarship has substantially discussed the Wuyue court-sponsored search for lost Tiantai texts from Japan or Korea; see Benjamin Brose, "Crossing Ten Thousand Li of Waves: The Return of China's Lost Tiantai Texts," *Journal of International Association of Buddhist Studies* 29, 1 (2006/08): 21–62. For studies on Wuyue's cross-cultural relations with Japan, see Wang Xinxi, "Qian shi Wuyueguo yu riben de jiaowang ji qi zai zhongri wenhua jiaoliushi shang de diwei," *Zhongguo wenhua yanjiu* (Fall 2003): 60–67. The authoritative study on broader Sino-Japanese relations is the previously mentioned work by Kinomiya Yashuhiko, *Nisshi kōtsushi*.

83. The *Wuyue beishi* only records the return of Aśoka's relic stūpa, without explaining when or why it was moved out of its former abode. But it is recorded that there was a fire in the year 958 on the south side of the city, so ferocious it raged through the inner city and burned down several buildings. The original Nanta monastery and pagoda were probably damaged during this fire, requiring the rebuilding of the place and the return of the relic stūpa.

84. Mimi Hall Yiengpruksawan, "One Millionth of a Buddha: The *Hyakumantō Darani* in the Scheide Library," *Princeton University Library Chronicle* 48, 3 (1987): 224–38.

85. For example, the *Jingshiqie* records Qian Chu dispatching an envoy to Japan in 955 with five hundred of these miniature stūpas. Cited in *Wuyue shishi biannian*, 313–14. As mentioned previously, gilt stūpas with inscriptions dating them to the Wuyue production still exist in Japan; Cf. Yoshikawa, *Sekizō hōkyōin-tō no seiritsu*, 148, n. 27.

86. See K. C. Chang, *Art, Myth, and Ritual: The Path to Political Authority* (Cambridge, Mass.: Harvard University Press, 1988). The Wuyue rulers received veneration as local cultural heroes associated with feats of taming ocean waters. Especially Qian Liu was honored as the "[Sea] Dragon King" for his successful improvisation of irrigational dikes and canals that made the region a fountainhead of the agricultural economy in China for centuries.

87. The anecdote is mentioned in several places, for example, in *Gujin tushu jicheng*, X. no. 1521, vol. 77, 26c10.

88. The Wuyue gilt stūpa was so powerful a visual and material emblem that it took on its own course of development outside of the royal precincts, so that there evolved another category of gilt stūpas Chinese scholars have called "commoners' stūpas" (*minjian ta*). Literary evidence records the circulation of miniature iron stūpas in the local marketplace. For example, one record mentions one Zhang Xiaolian buying an iron stūpa at the Wulin marketplace (*Liang Zhe Jinshi zhi*, vol. 14, 10280); evidently, these reliquary stūpas were commonplace in those days. However, this set of stūpas should be treated in a separate study.

Chapter 6. "Ancestral Transmission" in Chinese Buddhist Monasteries: The Example of the Shaolin Temple

Translated by Meir Shahar.

1. The inscriptions discussed in this chapter are transcribed in Ye Derong, *Zong tong yu fa tong: Yi Songshan Shaolin si wei zhongxin* (Guangzhou: Guangdong renmin, 2010). On the Shaolin monastery, see Wen Yucheng, *Shaolin fanggu* (Tianjin: Baihua wenyi, 1999); on its martial tradition, see Meir Shahar, *The Shaolin Monastery: History, Religion, and the Chinese Martial Arts* (Honolulu: University of Hawai'i Press, 2008).

2. See the 1748 edition of the *Shaolin si zhi*, compiled by Ye Feng et al., revised by Shi Yizan et al., *chenhan*, 4b–5a.

3. Titled "Henan Songshan zuting Shaolin chansi di ershiwu dai zhuchi Ningran Liaogai chan shi daoxing bei" ("The Attainments of the Henan Mt. Song Ancestral Shaolin Chan Temple's Ttwenty-Ffifth abbot, Chan Master Ningran Liaogai").

4. The poem is transcribed in Ye Derong, *Zong tong yu fa tong*, 18.

5. The complete title is "Chici zuting Shaolin Shishi yuanchong wujia zongpai shipu."

6. See the "Newly-Supplemented Caodong Clan-Lineages Stele" (Xinxu Caodong zongpai bei), which is preserved at the Ciyun Monastery, Gongyi County, Henan.

7. Daocheng, *Shishi yaolan*, T. no. 2127, vol. 54, 302b.

8. The text has been engraved on an 1802 Shaolin stele; see note 5.

Chapter 7. The Hagiography of Bodhidharma: Reconstructing the Point of Origin of Chinese Chan Buddhism

I would like to thank Meir Shahar of Tel Aviv University and Tansen Sen of National Singapore University for allowing me to coordinate presentations made at the two institutions in spring 2009. Part of the philological analysis introduced below was previously presented in Japanese at Komazawa University (January 28, 2008) and in English at Tel Aviv University (April 8, 2008), the University of Virginia (January 30, 2009), and University of the West (February 26, 2009).

1. Nukariya Kaiten, *Zengaku shisōshi*, vol. 1 (Tokyo: Genkōsha, 1923).

2. The transformations of Bodhidharma's hagiography were documented first by Sekiguchi Shindai; for documentation and further analysis see John R. McRae, *Seeing Through Zen: Encounter, Transformation, and Genealogy in Chinese Zen Buddhism* (Berkeley: University of California Press, 2003), 24–28.

3. The *Xu gaoseng zhuan* was clearly edited sometime (perhaps on multiple occasions) after its initial composition in 645, but manuscript evidence shows that all the changes relevant to Bodhidharma and Huike were instituted by 649. See Okimoto Katsumi, *Zoku kōsōden* Kōshōji-bon ni tsuite, published online at http://iriz.hanazono.ac.jp/frame/k_room_f2.html/.

4. Bernard Faure, "Bodhidharma as Textual and Religious Paradigm," *History of Religions* 25, 3, (1986): 123–32; and Faure, *Chan Insights and Oversights: An Epistemological*

Critique of the Chan Tradition (Princeton, N.J.: Princeton University Press, 1993), 126–35.

5. I include myself in this criticism. Faure sent me a prepublication version of his article just as I was preparing my dissertation for publication, and the limited extent of my adjustment to its findings is apparent in John R. McRae, *The Northern School and the Formation of Early Ch'an Buddhism*, Studies in East Asian Buddhism 3 (Honolulu: University of Hawai'i Press, 1986), 18–19.

6. T. no. 2092, vol. 51, 1000a12–13. Cf. the translations in Yi-T'ung Wang, *A Record of Buddhist Monasteries in Lo-yang* (Princeton, N.J.: Princeton University Press, 1984), 16; and Iriya Yoshitaka, *Rakuyō garan ki* (Tokyo: Heibonsha, 1990), 18. For sources describing the pagoda as roughly five hundred feet tall, see Iriya, *Rakuyō garan ki*, 53 n. 18.

7. See T. no. 2092, vol. 51, 1000b, 19–25; Wang, *A Record of Buddhist Monasteries*, 20–21; and Iriya, *Rakuyō garan ki*, 22.

8. See Paul Pelliot, "Notes sur quelques artistes des six dynasties et des T'ang," *T'oung pao* 22 (1923): 215–91. Pelliot discusses Bodhidharma on pp. 252–62; the *Luoyang qielan ji* is mentioned on 259–61. In his diary, *Hu Shi riji quanbian 4: 1923–1927*, ed. Cao Boyan (Hefei: Anhui jiaoyu chubanshe, 2001), Hu mentions receiving this article directly from Pelliot (279; September 4, 1926) and discusses its content, quoting Pelliot's position that Bodhidharma's presence at Yongningsi would have occurred between 516 and 534 (396; October 18, 1926), and concluding that Pelliot's conclusions regarding Bodhidharma here and in the *Continued Biographies of Eminent Monks* were "not bad" (Pelliot, "Notes sur quelques artistes"; Hu, *Hu Shi quanbian*, 397). It is curious that Hu never acknowledges his indebtedness to Pelliot in his published writings; judged by today's standard this would be a glaring omission, but perhaps academic mores were different in the early twentieth century.

9. Wang, *A Record of Buddhist Monasteries*, 152 n. 173, identifies Bosi with the near-homophonous Bozhi "in a hill area between modern Zebak and Chetral." These two modern locations are in the Badakhshan province of Afghanistan (36°32'N 71°21'E) and the Malakand Division of the Northwest Frontier Province of Pakistan (35°53'N 71°48'E) respectively.

10. Faure, "Bodhidharma as Textual and Religious Paradigm," posits the hermeneutical approach as another possible alternative to structural analysis, and indeed this and a "performative" interpretation are discussed in Faure, *Chan Insights and Oversights*, 135–51. Since these two alternatives are explained without significant reference to the example of Bodhidharma, I will not comment on them here.

11. Faure, "Bodhidharma as Texual and Religious Paradigm," 187.

12. Faure, *Chan Insights and Oversights*, 127–29.

13. Ibid., 126; cf. Faure, "Bodhidharma as Textual and Religious Paradigm," 188.

14. Faure draws this description of Dumézil's work from Françoise Desbordes, "Le comparatisme de Dumézil: Une introduction," in *Pour un temps: Georges Dumézil*, ed. Jacques Bonnet (Paris: Centre Georges Pompidou/Pandora, 1981), 52.

15. Faure, *Chan Insights and Oversights*, 129; here quoting Michel de Certeau, *L'écriture de l'histoire* (Paris: Gallimard, 1975), 285.

16. Also Faure, *Chan Insights and Oversights*, 129; here quoting Oswald Ducrot and Tzvetan Todorov, *Dictionnaire encyclopédique des sciences du langage* (Paris: Seuil, 1972), 139–46.

17. Faure, *The Rhetoric of Immediacy: A Cultural Critique of Chan/Zen Buddhism* (Princeton, N.J.: Princeton University Press, 1991), 25, quoting Jacques Derrida, *Of Grammatology*, trans. Gayatri Chakravorty Spivak (Baltimore: Johns Hopkins University Press, 1976), translator's preface, viii.

18. Faure, *Chan Insights and Oversights*, 131, citing Roland Barthes, "Introduction to the Structural Analysis of Narratives," in Roland Barthes, *Selected Writings* (Glasgow: Fontana, 1983), 279.

19. See Eric Greene, "Another Look at Early Chan: Daoxuan, Bodhidharma, and the Three Levels Movement, *T'oung Pao* 94 (2008): 49–114.

20. Faure, "Bodhidharma as Textual and Religious Paradigm," 188–89; Faure, *Chan Insights and Oversights*, 127.

21. Faure refers here to a passage in Yang Xuanzhi, *Luoyang qielan ji*, trans. Yi-t'ung Wang, *A Record of Buddhist Monasteries in Lo-yang* (Princeton, N.J.: Princeton University Press, 1984), 20–21.

22. Faure, *Chan Insights and Oversights*, 127; cf. Faure, "Bodhidharma as Textual and Religious Paradigm," 189.

23. T. no. 2092, vol. 51, 1005b8–c8. This translation is partially indebted to that in Yi-T'ung Wang, *A Record of Buddhist Monasteries in Lo-yang*, 73–76; also see Iriya, *Rakuyō garan ki,* 79–81. The anecdote is repeated, with minor differences, in the *Song gaoseng zhuan*, T. no. 2061, vol. 50, 889a4–b7; editor Zanning adds his explanation for Tanmozui's fate at p. 889b8–11. Oddly, both Wang and Iriya read the last monk's name as Baozhen, where CBETA and SAT use Baoming. In addition, the *Song gaoseng zhuan* cites this passage using the latter name; see Baoming's name at T. no. 2061, vol. 50, 990a21. Incidentally, the commandery of Longxi that this monk supposedly governed is in the Gansu corridor and would have had access to donations from merchants along the so-called Silk Road.

24. See John R. McRae, "The Northern School of Chinese Ch'an Buddhism," Ph.D. dissertation, Yale University, 1983, 42–45; for the original accounts see the *Xu gaoseng zhuan*, T. no. 2060, vol. 50, 554b20ff and 491c3ff respectively.

25. See T. no. 2092, vol. 51, 1017b12–18. It is curious that a few lines above (1017b10) Tanmozui is described as preferring the study/practice of meditation (*shan chanxue*), as well as lecturing on the *Nirvāṅa* and *Flower Garland Sūtras*.

26. See Li Naiyang, ed., *Baolin zhuan-Chuandeng yuying ji* (Kyōto: Chūbun shuppansha, 1983), 135b, or Tanaka Ryōshō, *Hōrinden yakuchū* (Tokyo: Uchiyama shoten, 2003), 382–83.

Chapter 8. Is Nirvāṇa the Same as Insentience? Chinese Struggles with an Indian Buddhist Ideal

I would like to thank the organizers and participants of the Indian Mythology and the Chinese Imagination conference at Tel Aviv University, March 25–26, 2009, for their comments and critiques. I would also like to thank Alexander von Rospatt, Elizabeth Horton Sharf, Jonathan Silk, Alberto Todeschini, and the anonymous reviewers of this volume for their astute criticisms and suggestions, which, for better or worse, I have not always followed.

1. For an anthropological reflection on the relationship between the attribution of agency on the one hand, and the construal of inside/outside relations on the other, see Alfred Gell, *Art and Agency* (Oxford: Oxford University Press, 1998).

2. See, for example, Merry Bullock, "Animism in Childhood Thinking: A New Look at an Old Question," *Developmental Psychology* 21, 2 (1985): 217–25; Alfonso Caramazza and Jennifer R. Shelton, "Domain-Specific Knowledge Systems in the Brain: The Animate-Inanimate Distinction," *Journal of Cognitive Neuroscience* 10, 1 (1998): 1–34; Susan Carey, *Conceptual Change in Childhood* (Cambridge, Mass.: MIT Press/Bradford Books, 1985); Rochel Gelman, "First Principles Organize Attention to and Learning About Relevant Data: Number and the Animate-Inanimate Distinction as Examples," *Cognitive Science* 14, 1 (1990): 79–106; Rochel Gelman, Frank Durgin, and Lisa Kaufman, "Distinguishing Between Animates and Inanimates: Not by Motion Alone," in *Causal Cognition: A Multidisciplinary Debate*, ed. Dan Sperber, David Premack, and Ann James Premack (New York: Clarendon, 1995), 150–84; Rochel Gelman, Elizabeth S. Spelke, and E. Meek, "What Preschoolers Know About Animate and Inanimate Objects," in *The Acquisition of Symbolic Skills*, ed. Don R. Rogers and John A. Sloboda (London: Plenum, 1983), 297–326; Susan A. Gelman and Paul Bloom, "Young Children Are Sensitive to How an Object Was Created When Deciding What to Name It," *Cognition* 76, 2 (2000): 91–103; Susan A. Gelman and John D. Coley, "The Importance of Knowing a Dodo Is a Bird: Categories and Inferences in 2–Year-Old Children," *Developmental Psychology* 26, 5 (1990): 796–804; Susan A. Gelman and John E. Opfer, "Development of the Animate-Inanimate Distinction," in *Blackwell Handbook of Childhood Cognitive Development*, ed. Usha Goswami (Oxford: Blackwell, 2002), 151–66; Susan A. Gelman and Anne Watson O'Reilly, "Children's Inductive Inferences Within Superordinate Categories: The Role of Language and Category Structure," *Child Development* 59, 4 (1988): 876–87; Susan A. Gelman and Henry M. Wellman, "Insides and Essences: Early Understandings of the Non-Obvious," *Cognition* 38, 3 (1991): 213–44; Cynthia R. Johnson and D. H. Rakison, "Early Categorization of Animate/Inanimate Concepts in Young Children with Autism," *Journal of Developmental and Physical Disabilities* 18, 2 (2006): 73–89; Benise S. K. Mak and Alonso H. Vera, "The Role of Motion in Children's Categorization of Objects," *Cognition* 71, 3 (1999): B11–21; Diane Poulin-Dubois, Anouk Lepage, and Doreen Ferland, "Infants' Concept of Animacy," *Cognitive Development* 11, 1 (1996): 19–36; David Premack, "The Infant's Theory of Self-Propelled Motion," *Cognition* 36, 1 (1990): 1–16; David H.

Rakison and Diane Poulin-Dubois, "Developmental Origin of the Animate-Inanimate Distinction," *Psychological Bulletin* 127, 2 (2001): 209–28; Daniel J. Simons and Frank C. Keil, "An Abstract to Concrete Shift in the Development of Biological Thought: The Insides Story," *Cognition* 56, 2 (1994): 129–53. On psychological essentialism, see especially the comprehensive overview in Susan A. Gelman, *The Essential Child: Origins of Essentialism in Everyday Thought* (Oxford: Oxford University Press, 2003).

3. See, for example, Simon Baron-Cohen, *Mindblindness: An Essay on Autism and Theory of Mind, Learning, Development, and Conceptual Change* (Cambridge, Mass.: MIT Press, 1995); George E. Butterworth, Paul L. Harris, Alan M. Leslie, and Henry M. Wellman, eds., *Perspectives on the Child's Theory of Mind* (Oxford: British Psychological Society and Oxford University Press, 1991); Alan M. Leslie, "*Pretending* and *Believing*: Issues in the Theory of ToMM," *Cognition* 50, 1–3 (1994): 211–38; Peter Mitchell, *Introduction to Theory of Mind: Children, Autism, and Apes* (London: Arnold, 1997); Henry M. Wellman, *The Child's Theory of Mind* (Cambridge Mass.: MIT Press, 1990). For a critique of the "theory of mind" approach to autism, see Peter R. Hobson, "Against the Theory of 'Theory of Mind,'" in *Perspectives on the Child's Theory of Mind*, ed. George E. Butterworth, Paul L. Harris, Alan M. Leslie, and Henry M. Wellman (Oxford: British Psychological Society and Oxford University Press, 1991), 33–51; and Peter R. Hobson, *Autism and the Development of Mind* (Hove, UK: Erlbaum, 1993).

4. Thomas Nagel, "What Is It Like to Be a Bat?," in *The Mind's I: Fantasies and Reflections on Self and Soul*, ed. Douglas R. Hofstadter and Daniel C. Dennett (New York: Basic Books, 1981), 392.

5. See, for example, Pascal Boyer, *The Naturalness of Religious Ideas: A Cognitive Theory of Religion* (Berkeley: University of California Press, 1994); idem, *Religion Explained: The Evolutionary Origins of Religious Thought* (New York: Basic Books, 2001). Critics of such theories question, among other things, the simplistic identification of religion with belief in supernatural agents.

6. For an extended discussion of the relationship between color cognition and the biological determinates behind color cognition, see Francisco J. Varela, Evan Thompson, and Eleanor Rosch, *The Embodied Mind: Cognitive Science and Human Experience* (Cambridge, Mass.: MIT Press, 1991), 157–71.

7. Bruno Latour, *We Have Never Been Modern* (Cambridge, Mass.: Harvard University Press, 1993).

8. The social scientific and philosophical literature on the topic is vast. See, for example, Debbora Battaglia, ed., *Rhetorics of Self-Making* (Berkeley: University of California Press, 1995); Michael Carrithers, Steven Collins, and Steven Lukes, eds., *The Category of the Person: Anthropology, Philosophy, History* (Cambridge: Cambridge University Press, 1985); Valentine E. Daniel, *Fluid Signs: Being a Person the Tamil Way* (Berkeley: University of California Press, 1984); Daniel C. Dennett, *The Intentional Stance* (Cambridge, Mass.: MIT Press, 1987); idem, *Consciousness Explained* (Boston: Little, Brown, 1991); Ian Hacking, *Rewriting the Soul: Multiple Personality and the Sciences of Memory* (Princeton, N.J.: Princeton University Press, 1995); Thomas Metzinger, *Being No One: The*

Self-Model Theory of Subjectivity (Cambridge, Mass.: MIT Press, 2003); Brian Morris, *Anthropology of the Self: The Individual in Cultural Perspective* (London: Pluto Press, 1994); Ulric Neisser and David A. Jopling, eds., *The Conceptual Self in Context: Culture, Experience, Self-Understanding* (Cambridge: Cambridge University Press, 1997); Charles Taylor, *Sources of the Self: The Making of the Modern Identity* (Cambridge, Mass.: Harvard University Press, 1989); Daniel M. Wegner, *The Illusion of Conscious Will* (Cambridge, Mass.: MIT Press, 2002); Geoffrey White and John Kirkpatrick, eds., *Person, Self, and Experience: Exploring Pacific Ethnopsychologies* (Berkeley: University of California Press, 1985).

9. Ned Block, "Inverted Earth," in *Action Theory and Philosophy of Mind, 1990*, ed. James E. Tomberlin, Philosophical Perspectives 4 (Atascadero, Calif.: Ridgeview, 1990), 53–79.

10. Daniel C. Dennett, "Quining Qualia," in *Consciousness in Contemporary Science*, ed. A. J. Marcel and E. Bisiach (Oxford: Clarendon, 1988), 42–77; Ned Block, "Troubles with Functionalism," in *Perception and Cognition: Issues in the Foundations of Psychology*, ed. C. W. Savage, Minnesota Studies in the Philosophy of Science, vol. 9 (Minneapolis: University of Minnesota Press, 1978), 261–325.

11. For an articulate defense of Buddhist scholasticism, along different lines, see Paul John Griffiths, "Scholasticism: The Possible Recovery of an Intellectual Practice," in *Scholasticism: Cross-Cultural and Comparative Perspectives*, ed. José Ignacio Cabezón (Albany: State University of New York Press, 1998), 201–35.

12. Nirvāṇa also has the related meaning of "to cool," as in to cool the fire [of delusion]; see Louis de la Vallée Poussin, *The Way to Nirvāṇa: Six Lectures on Ancient Buddhism as a Discipline of Salvation* (Cambridge: Cambridge University Press, 1917), 113.

13. For an overview of the controversy surrounding the interpretation of these two terms see Guy Richard Welbon, *The Buddhist Nirvana and Its Western Interpreters* (Chicago: University of Chicago Press, 1968), 208–20.

14. See the discussion in La Vallée Poussin, *The Way to Nirvāṇa*, 116–38.

15. *Alagaddūpama-sutta* (*Majjhima-nikāya* [MN] 22 i.140), trans. Bhikkhu Ñāṇamoli and Bhikkhu Bodhi, in *The Middle Length Discourses of the Buddha: A Translation of the Majjhima Nikāya* (Oxford: Pali Text Society, 1995), 234.

16. *Yamaka-sutta* (*Saṃyutta-nikāya* [SN] 22.85), trans. Bhikkhu Bodhi, in *The Connected Discourses of the Buddha: A New Translation of the Saṃyutta Nikāya* (Somerville, Mass.: Wisdom, 2000), vol. 1, 931–33.

17. The other six questions are: Is the universe eternal? Is it not eternal? Is it finite? Is it infinite? Is the body identical with the soul (*jīva*)? Is the body not identical with the soul? See, for example, *Poṭṭhapāda-sutta* (*Dīgha-nikāya* [DN] 9); *Cūla-māluṅkya-sutta* (MN 63) *Aggi-vacchagotta-sutta* (MN 72), and *Diṭṭhi-sutta* (*Aṅguttara-nikāya* [AN] 10.93). The question of the existence of the Tathāgata after death is handled separately in the *Khemātherī-sutta* (SN 44) and *Anurādhā-sutta* (SN 22.86).

18. On *nirodha* in non-Buddhist sources see Ian Whicher, "Nirodha, Yoga Praxis and the Transformation of the Mind," *Journal of Indian Philosophy* 25, 1 (1997): 1–67.

19. See, for example, *Mahāsaccaka-sutta* (MN 36, i.240 ff.).

20. The literature on the role of *śamatha* techniques and attainments in Buddhist path theory is vast; see esp. Johannes Bronkhorst, *The Two Traditions of Meditation in Ancient India* (Stuttgart: Franz Steiner, 1986); Paul John Griffiths, "Concentration or Insight: The Problematic of Therāvada Buddhist Meditation-Theory," *Journal of the American Academy of Religion* 49, 4 (1981): 605–24; and Lambert Schmithausen, "On Some Aspects of Descriptions or Theories of 'Liberating Insight' and 'Enlightenment' in Early Buddhism," in *Studien Zum Jainismus und Buddhismus*, ed. Klaus Bruhn and Albrecht Wezler (Wiesbaden: Franz Steiner, 1981), 199–250.

21. Griffiths cites AN 4.454, MN 1.209, and the *Visuddhimagga* to argue that the early tradition tended to equate *nirodha* with nirvāṇa; Paul John Griffiths, *On Being Mindless: Buddhist Meditation and the Mind-Body Problem* (La Salle, Ill.: Open Court, 1986), 29.

22. There was, admittedly, controversy on this point; Schmithausen notes that some sources assert (explicitly or implicitly) that *some* form of consciousness (*vijñāna*, *citta*) must remain in *nirodha*; see the detailed discussion in Lambert Schmithausen, *Ālayavijñāna: On the Origin and the Early Development of a Central Concept of Yogācāra Philosophy* (Tokyo: International Institute for Buddhist Studies of the International College for Postgraduate Buddhist Studies, 2007), vol. 1, 19 ff.

23. *Visuddhimagga* 23.30, Buddhaghosa, *The Path of Purification (Visuddhimagga)*, trans. Bhikkhu Ñyāṇamoli (Berkeley, Calif.: Shambhala, 1976), vol. 2, 828. See also in the same text: "But when Noble Ones who have already produced the eight attainments develop concentration thinking, 'We shall enter upon the attainment of cessation, and by being without consciousness for seven days we shall abide in bliss here and now by reaching the cessation that is nibbana', then the development of absorption concentration provides for them the benefit of cessation" (11.124, Buddhaghosa, *Visuddhimagga*, vol. 1, 407). The claim that *nirodha* is *phenomenologically* similar to or identical with nirvāṇa is odd, of course, given that neither state properly has a phenomenology per se. This underscores the conceptual ambiguities of these states; note how Buddhaghosa himself associates *nirodha* with the experience of bliss.

24. Griffiths, *On Being Mindless*. See also the extended discussions of *nirodha* in Collett Cox, *Disputed Dharmas: Early Buddhist Theories on Existence; An Annotated Translation of the Section on Factors Dissociated from Thought from Saṅghabhadra's Nyāyānusāra* (Tokyo: International Institute for Buddhist Studies, 1995), and Dan Lusthaus, *Buddhist Phenomenology: A Philosophical Investigation of Yogācāra Buddhism and the Ch'eng Wei-Shih Lun* (Richmond: RoutledgeCurzon, 2002), 123–53.

25. Buddhaghosa, *Visuddhimagga*, vol. 2, 830.

26. Cox, *Disputed Dharmas*, 118. The Sarvāstivādins still had other problems with *nirodha*, notably with the doctrine that a buddha spontaneously masters *nirodha* at the same time that he attains enlightenment. Since *nirodha* entails an interruption of the karmic stream, the Sarvāstivādins struggled to explain how interruption could be coextensive with the continuous series of thirty-four mind-moments that mark the attainment of enlightenment; see the discussion ibid., 116 ff.

27. On the connection between *nirodha* and the *ālayavijñāna* concept, see esp. Griffiths, *On Being Mindless*, 91–106, and Schmithausen, *Ālayavijñāna*.

28. In the Nyāyānusāra, for example, Saṅghabhadra mentions the Dārṣṭāntika argument that cessation cannot mean the cessation of mind (*xin*), but only feeling (*shou*) and conception (*xiang*); otherwise there would be no distinction between cessation and death (T. no. 1562, vol. 29, 403a21–24). Saṅghabhadra, of course, disagrees. See Cox, *Disputed Dharmas*, 114–22, 267; Griffiths, *On Being Mindless*, chap. 2; and Schmithausen, *Ālayavijñāna*, 18–27.

29. Buddhaghosa, *Visuddhimagga*, vol. 2, 829.

30. *Mahāvibhāṣāśāstra,* T. no. 1545, vol. 27, 779c29 ff.; *Nyāyānusāra,* p. 401c11–16, trans. Cox, *Disputed Dharmas*, 257; Vasubandhu, *Abhidharmakośabhāṣyam*, trans. Leo M. Pruden from the French translation of Louis de La Vallée Poussin (Berkeley, Calif.: Asian Humanities Press, 1988), vol. 1, 226, 229; *Cheng weishi lun*, T. no. 1585, vol. 31, 37c28ff., trans. Lusthaus, *Buddhist Phenomenology*, 150–51.

31. DN, iii.33–34, trans. Maurice Walshe, *Thus Have I Heard: The Long Discourses of the Buddha, Dīgha Nikāya* (London: Wisdom, 1987), 382, with changes. Cf. *Brahmajāla-sutta* i.28, trans. Walshe, *Thus Have I Heard*, 81.

32. *Abhidhamma vibhaṅga* 419, trans. Paṭhamakyaw Ashin Thiṭṭila, *The Book of Analysis (Vibhaṅga): The Second Book of the Abhidhamma Piṭaka* (Oxford: Pali Text Society, 1969), 537; *Visuddhimagga* 17.254, trans. Buddhaghosa, *Visuddhimagga*, vol. 2, 661; *Kathāvatthu* 4.11, trans. Shwe Zan Aung and Caroline A. F. Rhys Davids, *Points of Controversy, or, Subjects of Discourse, Being a Translation of the Kathā-vatthu* (London: Pali Text Society and Luzac, 1969), 153–55.

33. There are variations on the geography of the realm of form. The *Abhidharmakośabhāṣya*, for example, places the unconscious beings in a raised area within the Bṛhatphala Heaven (Vasubandhu, *Abhidharmakośabhāṣyam*, vol. 1, 222).

34. See, for example, *Abhidhamma vibhaṅga* 425; trans. Thiṭṭila, *The Book of Analysis*, 543.

35. Aung and Davids, *Points of Controversy*, 153–55.

36. Vasubandhu, *Abhidharmakośabhāṣyam*, vol. 1, 222.

37. The unconscious gods exist "there in the manner of an arrow fired by the force of the bowstring: as is the force from the bowstring, so is the height it reaches in the sky. In exactly the same way having been reborn there propelled by the force of the *jhāna*, as is the force of the *jhāna*, so is the length of time they remain there, but when the force of the *jhāna* is lost, then the physical aggregate disappears in that world and the relinking consciousness arises here in this world." *Sumaṅgalvilāsinī* (*Dīgha-nikāya-aṭṭhakathā*), 1. 118; trans. Rupert Gethin (personal communication).

38. The *Mahāvibhāṣāśāstra*, for example, devotes considerable space to this issue (pp. 784b14ff.). On the initial and terminal consciousness of the unconscious gods see also the discussion in the *Cheng weishi lun*, p. 37b8 ff. Additional references may be found in Lambert Schmithausen, "On the Problem of the Relation of Spiritual Practice and Philosophical Theory in Buddhism," in *German Scholars on India*, vol. 2, ed. Cultural

Department of the Delhi Embassy of the Federal Republic of Germany (Bombay: Nachiketa, 1976), 95 n. 526.

39. Vasubandhu, *Abhidharmakośabhāṣyam*, vol. 1, 221.

40. The Theravāda considered only the factors of form and *nibbāna* as belonging to this category; they were content to treat unconsciousness as an absence of something, rather than a presence of something that effects the absence. See Cox, *Disputed Dharmas*, 67–74.

41. *Nyāyānusāra*, p. 404a28–29, see the discussion in Cox, *Disputed Dharmas*, 275–76.

42. Cox, *Disputed Dharmas*, 115.

43. Ibid., 115–16. On the Yogācāra approach to the states without consciousness see also Lusthaus, *Buddhist Phenomenology*, 122–59.

44. *Sumaṅgalvilāsinī* (*Dīgha-nikāya-aṭṭhakathā*) 1,118; trans. Rupert Gethin (personal communication).

45. Vasubandhu, *Abhidharmakośabhāṣyam*, vol. 1, 223–24, with minor changes. Cf. the corresponding passage in Saṅghabhadra's *Nyāyānusāra*: "Holding that non-conception (*wu xiang*) is true liberation, and holding that the absorption of non-conception is the path of deliverance, [ordinary persons] cultivate this absorption in order to realize non-conception. No noble one would mistake something tainted (*āsrava*) to be true liberation or the true path of deliverance" (*Nyāyānusāra*, 401a19–21; trans. Cox, *Disputed Dharmas*, 247, with changes). The text goes on to say that the noble ones view the absorption of non-conception as a "deep pit" (*shenkeng*) to be avoided (401b5).

46. *Cheng weishi lun*, p. 37b3 ff.; cf. Swati Ganguly, *Treatise in Thirty Verses on Mere-Consciousness: A Critical English Translation of Hsüan-Tsang's Chinese Version of the Vijñaptimātratātriṃśikā with Notes from Dharmapāla's Commentary in Chinese* (Delhi: Motilal Banarsidass, 1992), 112, and Lusthaus, *Buddhist Phenomenology*, 147–48.

47. The *Abhidharmakośabhāṣya* argues that *pṛthagjana*s "cannot produce [*nirodha*] because they fear annihilation and because this absorption can only be produced through the power of the Path. In fact, it is the ascetic who has seen Nirvana who is determined to obtain it" (Vasubandhu, *Abhidharmakośabhāṣyam*, vol. 1, 226).

48. This contrast is explicit in the Yogācāra doctrine that the *manas*, which is responsible for the reification of the "self," is still active in *asaṃjñi-samāpatti* but has ceased in *nirodha*. See Lusthaus, *Buddhist Phenomenology*, 145–51.

49. The alternate reading of *Laozi* 49 is "The sage has no fixed mind; he considers the minds of the common people to be his own mind."

50. *Zhuangzi* 29/12/5–6, trans. Burton Watson in *The Complete Works of Chuang Tzu* (New York: Columbia University Press, 1968), 127; see also 30/12/43, trans. Watson,132. References to the Chinese text of the *Zhuangzi* are to the edition in the Harvard Yenching Concordance Series and are cited using the concordance format (page/chapter/line).

51. Robert H. Sharf, *Coming to Terms with Chinese Buddhism: A Reading of the Treasure Store Treatise* (Honolulu: University of Hawai'i Press, 2002), 90–93.

52. *Zhuangzi* 58/22/24.25, trans. Watson, 237.

53. T. no. 1858, vol. 45, 154b20–26, trans. Richard H. Robinson, *Early Mādhyamika in India and China* (Delhi: Motilal Banarsidass, 1976), 219, with changes. The term *wuxin* appears in the earlier translation of the *Aṣṭasāhasrikā-prajñāpāramitā-sūtra* by Lokakṣema (T. no. 224, vol. 8, 425c26), but the context is a Mādhyamika-style negation of the notions of *both* mind and no-mind. On the use of *wuxin* in various early sources, see esp. Urs App, "Treatise on No-Mind: A Chan Text from Dunhuang," *Eastern Buddhist* n.s. 28, 1 (1995): 83 n. 63; and Fukunaga Mitsuji, "'No-Mind' In *Chuang-Tzu* and in Ch'an Buddhism," *Zinbun* 12 (1969): 9–45.

54. On the meaning of these terms in the context of early Chan meditation techniques see Robert H. Sharf, "Mindfulness and Mindlessness in Early Chan," forthcoming in *Philosophy East & West*.

55. The following section draws directly from the discussion in Robert H. Sharf, "How to Think with Chan *Gong'an*," in *Thinking with Cases: Specialized Knowledge in Chinese Cultural History*, ed. Charlotte Furth, Judith Zeitlin, and Hsiung Ping-chen (Honolulu: University of Hawai'i Press, 2007), 210–22. See also the extended treatment of the subject in Lambert Schmithausen, *Plants in Early Buddhism and the Far Eastern Idea of the Buddha-Nature of Grasses and Trees* (Lumbini: Lumbini International Research Institute, 2009).

56. *Da banniepan jing*, T. no. 374, vol. 12, 581a22–23. The earlier six-fascicle version of the *Nirvāṇa-sūtra*, translated between 410 and 418, states that buddha-nature is eternal but *icchantika* do not possess it (*Da banniyuan jing*, T. no. 376, vol. 12, 881b24ff. and 893a9ff.). On Daosheng and the early debates concerning the universality of buddha-nature, see Whalen Lai, "The *Mahāparinirvāṇa Sūtra* and Its Earliest Interpreters in China: Two Prefaces by Tao-lang and Tao-sheng," *Journal of the American Oriental Society* 102, 1 (1982): 99–105; Walter Liebenthal, "The World Conception of Chu Tao-Sheng," *Monumenta Nipponica* 12, 1–2 (1956): 65–103, 241–68; Arthur Link, "Tao-sheng: A Biographical Essay" (Ph.D. dissertation, University of California, Berkeley, 1957); Liu Ming-Wood, "The Doctrine of the Buddha-Nature in the Mahāyāna *Mahāparinirvāna-sūtra*," *Journal of the International Association of Buddhist Studies* 5, 2 (1982): 63–94; idem, "The Problem of the *Icchantika* in the Mahāyāna *Mahāparinirvāṇa-sūtra*," *Journal of the International Association of Buddhist Studies* 7, 1 (1984): 57–81; Linda Penkower, "T'ien-t'ai During the T'ang Dynasty: Chan-jan and the Sinification of Buddhism" (Ph.D. dissertation, Columbia University, 1993), 393–96 n. 15; Tang Yongtong, *Han Wei liang Jin nanbeichao Fojiao shi* (Beijing: Zhonghua shuju, 1955), vol. 2, 601–76; Tokiwa Gishin and Yanagida Seizan, *Zekkanron: Eibun yakuchū, gembun kōtei, kokuyaku* (Kyoto: Zenbunka kenkyūjo, 1973), 178–93.

57. See the *Dacheng yizhang*, T. no. 1851, vol. 44, 472c18–26.

58. *Dacheng xuanlun*, T. 1853, vol. 45, 40a–41a. On Jizang's theory of buddha-nature, see Kamata Shigeo, *Chūgoku bukkyō shisōshi kenkyū* (Tokyo: Shunjūsha, 1968), 43–46; Aaron K. Koseki, "Chi-tsang's '*Ta-ch'eng-hsuan-lun*': The Two Truths and the Buddha-Nature" (Ph.D. dissertation, University of Wisconsin, 1977), 186–268; idem, "Prajñāpāramitā and the Buddhahood of the Non-Sentient World: The San-Lun Assimilation of

Buddha-Nature and Middle Path Doctrine," *Journal of the International Association of Buddhist Studies* 3, 1 (1980): 16–33; Liu Ming-Wood, *Madhyamaka Thought in China* (Leiden: Brill, 1994), 160–87; Schmithausen, *Plants in Early Buddhism*, 122 ff.; and Tokiwa Daijō, *Busshō no kenkyū* (Tokyo: Kokusho kankōkai, 1973), 217–19.

59. *Dacheng xuanlun*, p. 40b18–20 and 40c13–18; cf. Liu, *Madhyamaka Thought*, 186.

60. *Dacheng xuanlun*, p. 40c24–27.

61. *Jin'gang bei* (Adamantine Scalpel), T. no. 1932, vol. 46, 785b8–9; trans. Penkower, "T'ien-t'ai During the T'ang," 525–28, with minor changes. The *Jin'gang bei*, which was composed in 780 shortly before Zhanran's death, was the first full-length work dedicated to the doctrine of the buddha-nature of the insentient.

62. On the question of authorship and dating of the *Record of the Masters and Disciples of the Laṅkāvatāra*, see esp. Timothy H. Barrett, "The Date of the *Leng-chia shih-tzu chi*," *Journal of the Royal Asiatic Society* 3rd ser. 1, 2 (1991): 255–59 (Barrett believes the text could not have been written later than 716); and Bernard Faure, *The Will to Orthodoxy: A Critical Genealogy of Northern Chan Buddhism* (Stanford, Calif.: Stanford University Press, 1997), 160–76.

63. T. no. 2837, vol. 85, 1290a4–6 and 14–18; Yanagida Seizan, *Shoki no zenshi* 1, Zen no goroku 2 (Kyoto: Chikuma shobō, 1971), 287–88.

64. This text, associated with the Ox-Head lineage (Niutou zong), was likely composed by a later Ox-Head teacher sometime during the third quarter of the eighth century, i.e., just around the time that Zhanran was formulating his own position on the buddha-nature of the insentient. On the Ox-Head lineage in general and this text in particular, see John R. McRae, "The Ox-Head School of Chinese Ch'an Buddhism: From Early Ch'an to the Golden Age," in *Studies in Ch'an and Hua-yen*, ed. Robert M. Gimello and Peter N. Gregory (Honolulu: University of Hawai'i Press, 1983), 169–52. An edition of the *Treatise on Severing Discernment*, along with Japanese and English translations, can be found in Tokiwa and Yanagida, *Zekkanron*.

65. The first quotation may come from the *Avataṃsaka-sūtra* (T. no. 278 and 279), which contains numerous statements to the same effect. The second quotation is a slightly modified version of a sentence from *Vimalakīrti-sūtra* (T. no. 475, vol. 14, 542b12–13).

66. Tokiwa and Yanagida, *Zekkanron*, 91.

67. The Northern Chan master Shenxiu (605?–706), for example, takes a similar position in the *Zongjing lu* (Record of the Mirror of the Tradition), a text compiled by Yongming Yanshou (904–75) and published in 961 (T. no. 2016, vol. 48, 943a24–28).

68. I have not been able to identify the source of this verse; it appears repeatedly in discussions of the buddha-nature-of-the-insentient doctrine, including the *Zutang ji* records for Nanyang Huizhong, Dongshan Liangjie, and Dazhu Huihai; see Yanagida Seizan, *Sodōshū sakuin* (Kyoto: Kyōto daigaku jinbunkagaku kenkyūjo, 1984), 1.125.13; 2.65.3; and 4.47.6 respectively. (Citations from the *Zutang ji* are given using the concordance format: section.folio.line.)

69. *Shenhui yulu*, in Hu Shi, *Shenhui heshang yiji—fu Hu xiansheng zuihou de yanjiu* (Taibei: Hu Shi jinian guan, 1968), 139.

70. T. no. 2007, vol. 48, 344b9–10; cf. Philip B. Yampolsky, *The Platform Sutra of the Sixth Patriarch: The Text of the Tun-huang Manuscript with Translation, Introduction, and Notes* (New York: Columbia University Press, 1967), 177.

71. This wording is found, for example, in the editions found in the *Zutang ji* (1.85.11–12), the *Jingde chuandeng lu* (T. no. 2076, vol. 51, 223a17–18), and the 1291 "vulgate" edition of the *Platform Scripture* (T. no. 2008, vol. 48, 349a26–27).

72. While this text was not published until 1374, it agrees with the account of Huihai's teaching on the buddha-nature of the insentient found in the *Zutang ji* 4.47.6–11.

73. Hirano Sōjō, *Tongo yōmon* (Tokyo: Chikuma shobō, 1970), 138, 155, 175.

74. See the *Huangbo Duanji chanshi wanling lu*: "The Master ascended the hall and said: 'This very mind is buddha. It reaches upward to all the buddhas and downwards to things that slither on the ground; *everything that contains spirit* possesses buddha-nature and is equal with respect to the substance of the one mind. The reason that Bodhidharma came from India was only to transmit the dharma of one mind and to directly indicate that all beings are originally buddha'" (T. no. 2012, vol. 48, 386b2–5, italics mine; see also 381a28–29 for similar phrasing).

75. *Zutang ji* 1.124.5–14; cf. *Jingde chuandeng lu,* p. 438b6–11; see also the discussion in Schmithausen, *Plants in Early Buddhism*, 267–71.

76. T. no. 279, vol. 10, 30a6–7.

77. T. no. 220, vol. 7, 871c14–15.

78. *Zutang ji* 1.125.13–126.7 (this segment does not appear in the *Jingde chuandeng lu*). See the discussion in Liu, *Madhyamaka Thought*, 255.

79. The controversy took decidedly different turns in Japan: the issue is addressed, often in innovative ways, in the writings of Kūkai (774–835), Saichō (767–822), Annen (d. 889), Enchin (814–891), Ryōgen (912–985), Chūjin (1065–1138), Dōgen (1200–1253), and Nichiren (1222–1282), to name just a few. The controversy was also the focus of one of a series of spirited Hossō–Tendai debates held under imperial auspices in 963. Nor was the Japanese interest in the doctrine limited to exegetical works; it found its way into Japanese literature and performance arts as well. Sources on the buddha-nature-of-the-insentient doctrine in Japan include Paul Groner, *Ryōgen and Mount Hiei: Japanese Tendai in the Tenth Century* (Honolulu: University of Hawai'i Press, 2002), 337–39; William R. LaFleur, "Saigyō and the Buddhist Value of Nature, Part 1," *History of Religions* 13, 2 (1973): 93–128; idem, "Saigyō and the Buddhist Value of Nature, Part 2," *History of Religions* 13, 3 (1974): 227–48; Miyamoto Shōson, "'Sōmoku kokudo shikkai jōbutsu' no busshōronteki igi to sono sakusha," *Indogaku Bukkyōgaku kenkyū* 9, 2 (1961): 672–701; Fabio Rambelli, *Vegetal Buddhas: Ideological Effects of Japanese Buddhist Doctrines on the Salvation of Inanimate Beings* (Kyoto: Italian School of East Asian Studies, 2001); Sakamoto Yukio, "Hijō ni okeru busshō no umu ni tsuite—toku ni Tannen, Chōkan o chūshin to shite," *Indogaku Bukkyōgaku kenkyū* 7, 2 (1959): 21–30; idem, "On the 'Attainment of Buddhahood' by Trees and Plants," in *Proceedings of the IXth International Congress for the History of Religions (1958)* (Tokyo: Maruzen, 1960), 415–22; Donald H. Shively, "Buddhahood for the Nonsentient: A Theme in No Plays," *Harvard Journal of*

Asiatic Studies 20, 1–2 (1957): 135–61; Sueki Fumihiko, "Annen *Shinjō sōmoku jōbutsu shiki* ni tsuite," *Tōhōgaku* 80 (1990): 97–110; idem, "Annen: The Philosopher Who Japanized Buddhism," *Acta Asiatica: Bulletin of the Institute of Eastern Culture (Tōhōgakkai)* 66 (1994): 69–86; Yoshizu Yoshihide, "Mujō busshōsetsu no kōsatsu," *[Sōtōshū] Shūgaku kenkyū* 15 (March, 1973): 110–15.

80. *Chanzong wumen guan* case no. 37 (T. no. 2005, vol. 48, 297c5–6). For an extended analysis of the relationship between the buddha-nature-of-the-insentient controversy and the *gong'an* literature, see Sharf, "Chan *Gong'an*."

81. T. no. 2087, vol. 51, 942a21–24.

82. T. no. 2831, vol. 85, 1269c9–16; cf. App, "No-Mind," 94–98.

83. *Dunwu dasheng zhenglijue*, Pelliot 4646, folio 131 r–v; quoting from *Vajracchedikā*, T. no. 236, vol. 8, 754b24–25; cf. Paul Demiéville, *La concile de Lhasa: une controverse sur le quietisme entre bouddhistes de l'Inde et de la Chine au VIIIeme siècle de l'ère chrétienne* (Paris: Imprimerie Nationale, 1952), 62.

84. In terms of mediating the debate, I would note that Kamalaśīla and Moheyan were arguing from incommensurable epistemological positions. Moheyan is decidedly phenomenological in his approach, taking as authoritative what is immediately presented to consciousness, while Kamalaśīla places ultimate authority in scripture, reason, and tradition. As such, more often than not, they talk past one another.

Chapter 9. Karma and the Bonds of Kinship in Medieval Daoism: Reconciling the Irreconcilable

1. Erik Zürcher, "Buddhist Influence on Early Taoism: A Survey of Scriptural Evidence," *T'oung Pao* 66 (1980): 84–147.

2. Six Dynasties Daoist works start to mention the Eighteen Bureaus, and the *diyu* imported by Buddhism. The tortures perpetrated in these Buddhist hells are not yet so extensively described in Daoist works, but their eloquent names are listed as threats.

3. Michel Strickmann, *Mantras et mandarins: le bouddhisme tantrique en Chine* (Paris: Gallimard, 1996), 11. On karma in medieval China and related bibliography, see Livia Kohn, "Steal Holy Food and Come Back as a Viper: Conceptions of Karma and Rebirth in Medieval China," *Early Medieval China* 4 (1998): 1–34.

4. Stephen Teiser, *The Ghost Festival in Medieval China* (Princeton, N.J.: Princeton University Press, 1988), 198.

5. In that respect, Zhi Qian was inspired by two works translated a few decades earlier: the *Xiuxing benqi jing* (T. no. 184, vol. 3) and the *Zhong benqi jing* (T. no. 196, vol. 4). See Zürcher, "Buddhist Influence on Early Taoism."

6. Teiser, *The Ghost Festival*, 198.

7. *Lunheng jiaoshi* (Beijing: Zhonghua shuju, 1990), *juan* 6.

8. *Laozi xiang'er zhu jiaozheng*, ed. Rao Zongyi, 1956, rev. ed. (Shanghai: Shanghaigujichuban she, 1991), 24, trans. Stephen Bokenkamp, *Early Daoist Scriptures* (Berkeley: University of California Press, 1997), 108.

9. See Christine Mollier, "Visions of Evil: Demonology and Orthodoxy in Early Taoism," in *Daoism in History: Essays in Honour of Liu Ts'un-yan*, ed. Benjamin Penny (London: Routledge, 2006), 87–93.

10. The idea of registers of life and death where the names of each human being as well as their good and bad deeds are consigned goes back to the Han dynasty, as attested in funerary documents found in second-century CE tombs. The idea was adopted by Buddhism as shown in several versions of the *Sūtra of Amitābha* (translated in the second and third centuries) which mention "registers of names" in which deities consigned the bad deeds of people. Kuo Li-ying, *Confession et contrition dans le bouddhisme chinois de Ve au Xe siècle* (Paris: École Française d'Extrême-Orient, 1994), 91.

11. Fifth century, *Santian neijie jing*, Dz. 1205, ch.1. 6a, trans. Bokenkamp, *Early Daoist Scriptures*, 216.

12. They are divided into three groups: the first group concerns the highest practices; it advocates non-action, flexibility, and femininity. The second group recommends purity, quietness, good deeds, and renunciation of fame. The third group encourages measure, compassion, and absence of desire. See Ōfuchi Ninji, *Shoki no dōkyō* (Tokyo: Sōbunsha 1991), 251–57; Bokenkamp, *Early Daoist Scriptures*, 49.

13. Cf. Bokenkamp, *Early Daoist Scriptures*, 50.

14. The most ancient code of conduct of the early Way of the Celestial Master is the code of the "One Hundred Eighty Rules of Lord Lao," *Laojun yi bai bashi jie* (Dunhuang manuscripts Pelliot 4731 and Pelliot. 4562). It is hagiographically ascribed to the first Celestial Master, Zhang Daoling, but the extant version in the *Daozang* dates probably from the beginning of the fifth century. This code will remain the basis for all the Lingbao and Shangqing manuals of admonitions and prohibitions.

15. *Nüqing guilü*, Dz. 790, ch. 3, titled "Rules and Prohibitions of the Dao" (*Daolü jinji*), 1a–3b.

16. I.e., the sexual rites of *heqi* practiced by the adepts of the Tianshi dao as a means to conceive the "seed children" of the elected people.

17. Ge Hong emphasizes however, that a bad intention that is not followed by action does not generate a "reckoning," while harming someone else is punished by a reduction in lifespan.

18. *Baopuzi neipian*, ch. 6, 4b, Wang Ming ed., p. 125. Supposing that it is question of days, it would mean that the guilty person would have a very limited life expectation.

19. *Baopuzi*, ch. 7.

20. *Nüqing guilü*, Dz. 790, ch. 3, 9th admonition.

21. The work originates from the early Celestial Master organization, but the extant version would date from the mid-Tang dynasty. See Franciscus Verellen, "The Celestial Master Liturgical Agenda According to Chisong Zi's Petition Almanac," *Cahiers d'Extrême-Asie* 14 (2004): 291–343.

22. *Chisong zi zhangli*, Dz. 615, ch. 2, 31a–b.

23. See the Zhengyi, *Penal Code of the Mysterious Capital*, *Xuandu lüwen* (Dz. 188).

24. Dz. 335, ch. 9, 6b. See Christine Mollier, *Une apocalypse taoïste du début du Ve*

siècle: Le Livre des incantations divines des grottes abyssales, Mémoires de l'Institut des Hautes Études Chinoises 31 (Paris: Collège de France, 1990): 173–74.

25. *Taishang dongxuan lingbao sanyuan pinjie gongde qingzhong jing*; Dz. 456, 32b–38a. See Maeda Shigeki's translation, "Between Karmic Retribution and Entwining Infusion," in *Daoism in History: Essays in Honour of Liu Tsun-yan*, ed. Benjamin Penny (London: Routledge, 2006), 110–13.

26. Ge Xuan (Sir Immortal of the Left of the Great Bourne, Taiji zuoxian gong) is said to have received a majority of the founding texts of the Lingbao canon. See Stephen Bokenkamp, "Sources of the Ling-pao Scriptures," in *Tantric and Taoist Studies in Honour of R. A. Stein*, ed. Michel Strickmann (Brussels: Institut Belge des Hautes Études Chinoises, 1983), 437–38; Bokenkamp, *Early Daoist Scriptures*, 377–79; Robert Ford Campany, *To Live as Long as Heaven and Earth: A Translation and Study of Ge Hong's Traditions of Divine Transcendents* (Berkeley: University of California Press, 2002), 152–59.

27. It is listed fourteenth of the *Lingbao jing shumu* under the title *Falun zuifu* (*Scripture of the Wheel of the Law [Expounding] Sins and Blessings*). It has been edited in the extant Daoist Canon in the form of four independent texts which bear slightly different titles (Dz. 346, 348, 455, and 347). A three-*juan* version of this *Scripture of the Wheel of the Law* has been discovered at Dunhuang (mss. Stein 1605 and Stein 1906), but the opening section is missing. See Ōfuchi Ninji, "On Ku Ling-pao ching," *Acta Asiatica* 27 (1974): 50; Bokenkamp, "Sources of the Ling-pao Scriptures," 473.

28. Edited as *Lingbao Scripture of the Karmic Causation of Previous Existences* (*Lingbao benxing suyuan jing*), Dz. 1114, 3a belonging to the "new scriptures" revealed to Ge Xuan. See Ōfuchi Ninji, "On Ku Ling-pao ching," 43–44; Bokenkamp, "Sources of the Ling-Pao Scriptures," 484.

29. Dz. 336, *Taishang dongxuan lingbao yebao yinyuan jing*. See Yoshioka Yoshitoyo, *Dōkyō to Bukkyō* (Tokyo: Kokusho kankōkai, 1976), vol. 3, 148; Ōfuchi Ninji, *Dōkyō shi no kenkyū* (Okayama: Okayama Daigaku Kyōzaikai Shoseki-bu, 1964), 254–58. One finds another incomplete version of the work among the Dunhuang manuscripts. See Ōfuchi Ninji, *Tonkō dōkyō* (Tokyo: Fukutake shoten, 1978).

30. Sylvain Lévi, *Mahā-Karmavibhanga (La grande classification des actes)* (Paris: Leroux, 1932).

Chapter 10. This Foreign Religion of Ours: Lingbao Views of Buddhist Translation

1. Erik Zürcher, "Buddhist Influence on Early Taoism: A Survey of Scriptural Evidence," *T'oung-pao* 66, 1–3 (1980): 84–147.

2. Ibid., 143.

3. For more work on how Daoist responses to Buddhism might tell us something of more general Chinese responses to the foreign religion, see especially Kristofer Schipper, "Purity and Strangers: Shifting Boundaries in Medieval Taoism," *T'oung-pao* 80 (1994): 61–81; Kamitsuka Yoshiko, *Rikuchō dōkyō shisō no kenkyū* (Tokyo: Sōbunsha, 1999); Stephen R. Bokenkamp, *Ancestors and Anxiety: Daoism and the Birth of Rebirth in China*

(Berkeley: University of California Press, 2007); idem, "The *Vessantara-jātaka* in Buddhist and Daoist Translation," in *Daoism in History: Essays in Honour of Liu Ts'un-yan*, ed. Benjamin Penny (London: Routledge, 2006), 56–73; and idem, "The Silkworm and the Bodhi Tree: The Lingbao Attempt to Replace Buddhism in China and Our Attempt to Place Lingbao Daoism," in *Religion and Chinese Society*, vol. 1, *Ancient and Medieval China*, ed. John Lagerwey (Hong Kong: Chinese University Press, 2004), 317–39.

4. See Stephen R. Bokenkamp, "Sources of the Ling-pao Scriptures," in *Tantric and Taoist Studies in Honour of R. A. Stein*, ed. Michel Strickmann, vol. 2, Mélanges Chinois et Bouddhiques 21 (Bruxelles: Institut Belge des Hautes Études Chinoises, 1983), 468.

5. LB #16, Dz. 23, *Taishang zhutian lingshu duming miao jing*. Texts from the Daoist canon are cited in this chapter by the number assigned in Kristofer Schipper and Franciscus Verellen, *The Taoist Canon: A Historical Companion to the* Daozang (Chicago: University of Chicago Press, 2004), followed by chapter, page number, side, and line number as found in the string-bound edition of the *Zhengtong daozang*. The item number will be preceded by the abbreviation Dz. Other editions may be located through reference to volume 3 of *The Taoist Canon*. The scriptures that are part of the early Lingbao corpus will further be designated by their sequential number in the list in Bokenkamp, "Sources," 479–86. This number will be preceded by LB.

6. LB. #16, Dz. ch. 23, 3b, 5a–b, and 7a–b. The responses from the other directions are similar.

7. Modern scholarship has done much to clarify the identity of the regional dialects and languages from which the earliest Buddhist texts were likely translated into Chinese. For the purposes of this article, though, the actual identity of these languages makes no difference whatsoever, since the authors of the Lingbao texts, in constructing their imitation language, seem not to have closely modeled it on any living language. What is at issue here seems rather to be a creative adaptation of the Indic notion of the god Brahmā's creation of language. I will thus refer to the languages of South and Central-Asian Buddhism as "Sanskrit" or "the languages of Buddhism" without further attempts at distinction.

8. For a late third-century impression of the Buddhist religion and its practitioners, see Bokenkamp, *Ancestors and Anxiety*, 41ff.

9. See Ōfuchi Ninji, "On *Ku Ling-pao ching*," *Acta Asiatica* 27 (1974): 33–56; Bokenkamp, "Sources," 480–81; and Hans-Hermann Schmidt, "Taishang lingbao zhutian neiyin ziran yuzi," in *The Taoist Canon*, ed. Schipper and Verellen, vol. 1, 222. While Schmidt follows Ōfuchi in claiming that "the present version is incomplete," a check of *Rikuchō Tō Sō no kobunken shōin Dōkyō tenseki mokuroku, sakuin*, ed. Ōfuchi Ninji, Ishii Masako, and Ozaki Masaharu, rev. ed. (Tokyo: Kokusho kankōkai, 1999) reveals that the "missing citations" are in fact discussions of the scripture. There is thus no evidence to indicate that the canonical version of this text is incomplete. As we will see below, however, the scripture appears to have been altered, particularly those passages Buddhists have criticized.

10. LB #7, Dz. 97, *Taishang Lingbao zhutian neiyin ziran yuzi*.

11. See Hsieh Shu-wei, *Tianjie zhi wen: Wei Jin Nanbei chao Lingbao jingdian yanjiu* (Taibei: Taiwan shang wu yin shu guan, 2010), 125–66.

12. Dz. 97, ch. 3, 2b5–7.

13. "Hand towels" may seem a strange part of the scripture-copying process, but see the directions for constructing a scriptorium in the late sixth-century *Fengdao kejie yingshi* (Dz. 1125, ch. 1, 15b–16a) that specify the preparation of "clean cloths and wrappers"—to wipe implements and wrap the completed manuscripts, we presume. This passage is translated in Yoshioka Yoshitoyo, *Dōkyō to Bukkyō*, vol. 3 (Tokyo: Kokusho kankyōkai, 1976), 172–73, and Livia Kohn, *The Daoist Monastic Manual: A Translation of the* Fengdao kejie (New York: Oxford University Press, 2004), 92.

14. The procedures of early Buddhist translation teams are described in Erik Zürcher, *The Buddhist Conquest of China* (Leiden: Brill, 1959), 1, 31, and further explored in Daniel Boucher, "Gāndhārī and the Early Chinese Buddhist Translations Reconsidered: The Case of the Saddharmapuṇḍarīkasūtra," *Journal of the American Oriental Society* 118, 4 (October–December, 1998): 485–89.

15. Zürcher, "Buddhist Influence," 111. I have changed his Wade-Giles transcription to the pinyin form, but the hypothetical reconstructed Sanskrit is his.

16. An example might be found in Wang Chengwen, *Dunhuang gu Lingbao jing yu Jin Tang daojiao* (Beijing: Zhonghua, 2002), 776–89. To be fair, Wang is responding to contemporary Chinese views of religion. His main concern is to establish Daoism as part of "mainstream" culture and defend it against those who would denigrate it as a form of shamanism.

17. James Robson, "Signs of Power: Talismanic Writing in Chinese Buddhism," *History of Religions*, 48, 2 (November, 2008): 138. See also the definition found in the *HarperCollins Dictionary of Religion* that contains the following characterization: "Most talismans display divinatory diagrams and a highly stylized script understood to be heavenly writing." Jonathan Z. Smith, ed., *The HarperCollins Dictionary of Religion* (San Francisco: Harper, 1995), 45, "Chinese Religions."

18. *Zhen'gao*, Dz. 1016, ch. 1, 8b–9a. For a full exploration of this passage and its place in the history of Daoist celestial script, see Hsieh Shu-wei, "Writing from Heaven: Celestial Writing in Six Dynasties Daoism," Ph.D. dissertation, Indiana University, 2005, 250–62. On page 23 of this work, Hsieh shows that the idea of "sixty-four scripts" itself most likely first appeared in *Puyao jing* (T. no. 186), a translation of the *Lalitavistara Sutra* made by the Indo-Scythian Dharmarakṣa (Zhu Fahu) in 308 CE.

19. Zürcher uses "hierolalia" pejoratively to characterize the Hidden Language, "Buddhist Influence," 110. I take the word to refer to the sort of "speaking in tongues" performed by modern charismatic Christian groups. And indeed, given that the suffix *-lalia* generally denotes speech disorders or unusual speech, it is not surprising to find that Zürcher elsewhere uses the word to characterize shamanic verbal performances in imitation of the spoken languages of Buddhism. See Erik Zürcher, "Perspectives in the Study of Chinese Buddhism," *Journal of the Royal Asiatic Society of Great Britain and Ireland* 1 (1982): 166.

20. This can be demonstrated through the many discussions and analysis of the Hidden Language in later Daoist works. See, for instance, the scholarly glosses collected in Dz. 87,

Duren shangpin miaojing sizhu, 4.2b–30b and in the following series of commentaries in the canon (Dz. 88–95).

21. See Hsieh, *Writing from Heaven*, 329–33, and, for a further discussion of the canonical divisions, *Daojiao yishu*, Dz. 1129, ch. 2, 14b4–24a, and *Yunji qiqian*, Dz. 1032, ch. 6, 20a–23a.

22. The *Treatise Deriding the Dao* is collected in Dao Xuan's (fl. 624) *Guanghong mingji*. The three passages discussed here appear at (1) T. no. 2103, vol. 52, 146b12ff.; (2) T. no. 2103, vol. 52, 148a3 ff.; and (3) T. no. 2103, vol. 52, 152a16ff. For a general introduction to this text, see Charles D. Benn, "*Xiaodao lun*," in Fabrizio Pregadio, ed., *The Encyclopedia of Taoism* (London: Routledge, 2008), vol. 2, 1098–99.

23. While this locution is somewhat clumsy, I distinguish those terms in my sources that were *translated* into Chinese by presenting them in *pinyin* transcription and sometimes retranslating them into English. Those words that were *transliterated* into Chinese will be presented in Sanskrit transcription. The common practice of Buddhologists to render into Sanskrit transcription every Chinese term that can be provisionally identified with a Buddhist term (e.g., *ding* = *samādhi*) serves to misrepresent the Chinese Buddhist priesthood's knowledge of Sanskrit. See Robert Sharf, *Coming to Terms with Chinese Buddhism: A Reading of the* Treasure Store Treatise (Honolulu: University of Hawai'i Press, 2002), 7–21, for some of the concerns that prompt this procedure; and, for Chinese Buddhist scholiasts' glosses of a word that was commonly used to render *avadāna* by dealing with the etymology of the two Chinese graphs that translate it, while never once making reference to the meaning of any foreign term, see Stephen R. Bokenkamp, "Chinese Metaphor, Again: Reading—and Understanding—Imagery in the Chinese Poetic Tradition," *Journal of the American Oriental Society*, 109, 2 (1989): 211–21.

24. See the appendix at the end of this chapter for another supposed mention of the name *Guanyin*. For a discussion of the expurgation of texts, likely occurring in the late sixth or early seventh centuries, by which process the more noticeable Buddhist elements were replaced, see Bokenkamp, "Sources," 467–68, and "Stages of Transcendence: The *Bhūmi* Concept in Taoist Scripture," in *Chinese Buddhist Apocrypha*, ed. Robert E. Buswell (Honolulu: University of Hawai'i Press, 1990), 119–23, as well as Maeda Shigeki, "Tonkōhon to dōzōhon no sai ni tsuite: ko Reihōgyo o chūshin to shite," *Tōhō shūkyō* 84 (1994): 1–19, also collected in her *Shoki dōkyō kyōten no keisei* (Tokyo: Kyūko, 2004).

25. Cited in T. no. 2103, *Guanghong mingji*, vol. 52, 148a3–9. The passage extracted by Zhen Luan appears in Dz. 97, ch. 3, 19b–21a. The translation is my own. I have indicated passages and graphs apparently omitted by Zhen Luan with the mark [. . .]. Compare Livia Kohn, *Laughing at the Tao: Debates Among Buddhists and Taoists in Medieval China* (Princeton, N.J.: Princeton University Press, 1995), 95–97.

26. The graph *luo* has slipped into the text after *da*. This is presumably a copyist's error occasioned by the fact that the highest Lingbao heaven is called *Daluo*, "Grand Veil."

27. Here either Zhen Luan has misrepresented his source or a later copyist has altered the text so that the gloss accords with the eight graphs of the Hidden Language provided. I suspect the latter. As explained in the appendix, the presentation of these words is a

two-part process. According to Dz. 97, the hidden name of the Heavenly-Flying Perfected (Feitian zhenren) here is *Puti* not *Putai*.

28. *Luohan* is a common Buddhist transcription of *arhat* and so must be the product of an inattentive copyist. Zhen Luan would hardly have passed over this term without comment.

29. Dz. 97 has no mention of the Lady of the Moon. Instead, it states: "*Luoying* is the inner name of the celestial of the sun and moon." But Chen Jingyuan's (?–1094) collection of Tang and pre-Tang glosses on the *Book of Salvation*, the *Yuanshi wuliang duren shangpin miaojing sizhu*, contains the following version in the commentary of Li Shaowei (fl. 625?): "*Lüluo* is the name of the Lady of the Moon. Her byname is *Luoying*. Her appearance is like jade. She wears a green cape and blue robes, thus she is called *Lüluo* [green silk gauze]" (Dz. 87, ch. 4, 12a2–3). Dz. 97 has apparently been altered, keeping only the name *Luoying* but causing it to refer to another celestial being altogether. Interestingly, the verse in Dz. 97 still has the reference to a "green cape," a further confirmation that Li Shaowei's passage is the original one cited by Zhen Luan.

30. "Below" is missing from Dz. 97.

31. The *Taishō* edition has *tianxia* rather than *tiandi* at this point, an easy copyist's error.

32. Dz. 97 has "the chiliocosm will be unified and reside here," *daqian tongyi er cun yan,* where Zhen Luan has written *daqian dongran*. This might be a possible copyist error if the final two graphs of the Dz. 97 had become smudged or were omitted.

33. Criticizing discrepancies between scriptural catalogues and the Daoist notion of "unrevealed" scriptures collected in the heavens, Zhen Luan sneers "I have not heard of celestial beings descending, nor seen Daoists rising, so I don't know where these [new] scriptures might have come from" (*Guanghong mingji,* T. no. 2103, vol. 52, 151b12–13).

34. For a discussion and interesting hypothesis on early Chinese translations of this scripture, see Timothy H. Barrett, "Preliminary Considerations in the Search for a Daoist *Dhammapada*," in *Daoism in History: Essays in Honour of Liu Ts'un-yan*, ed. Benjamin Penny (London: Routledge, 2006), 41–55.

35. The translation is modified slightly from that of Charles Willemen, "The Prefaces to the Chinese *Dharmapadas, Fa-chu ching* and *Ch'u-yao ching*," *T'oung-pao* 59 (1973): 211.

36. The citation is to be found in the *Daodejing* 81.

37. Citing the "Appended Words" to the *Classic of Changes*. See Stephen Owen, *Readings in Chinese Literary Thought* (Cambridge, Mass.: Harvard University Press, 1992), 31–32.

38. Willemen, "Prefaces," 213, modified slightly based on the clearly edited version found in Sengyou's *Chu sanzang jiji*, T. no. 2145, vol. 55, 50a11–20.

39. See Zürcher, *Buddhist Conquest,* 1, 86–104.

40. The more historically important of these early discussions are explored in Owen, *Readings*, 19–72.

41. This characterization of writing by the goddess Wei Huacun is found in Dz. 1016, *Zhen'gao*, ch. 1, 8a8.

42. See Hsieh, "Writing from Heaven."

43. Xiao Tong (501–531), *Wen xuan* (Hong Kong: Shangwu, 1974), vol. 1, 350. For a full translation, see David R. Knechtges, *Wenxuan or Selections of Refined Literature* (Princeton, N.J.: Princeton University Press, 1996), vol. 3, 211–32, and, for analysis that differs from my own, see Owen, *Readings*, 96–98. Owen's points are useful. I would only counter that a "Daoist model of spiritual movement" goes far beyond the quiescence that he describes in this work.

44. For more on the multi-spirit body views of early China, see Stephen R. Bokenkamp, "What Daoist Body?" in *Purposes, Means, and Convictions in Daoism: A Berlin Symposium*, ed. Florian C. Reiter (Wiesbaden: Harrassowitz, 2007), 131–50.

45. For convenience' sake, I will treat the author of the Lingbao scriptures as singular, though the evidence seems to point to multiple authors over a relatively restricted period of time. For some of the issues involved here and a few of the alternative views on the composition of these texts, see Bokenkamp, "Silkworm."

46. In fact, the Lingbao scriptures, while borrowing whole passages from Buddhist texts, mention Buddhism only rarely.

47. Lb. #24, Dz. 532, *Taishang zhenren fu lingbao zhaijie weiyi zhujing yaojue* [short title: *Instructions on the Performance of Retreats*], 18b–19a.

48. See Stephen R. Bokenkamp, "*Tenkyō: Ko reihōgyō no senkyō hōhō,*" in *Dōkyō to kyōsei shisō*, ed. Tanaka Fumio and Terry Kleeman (Tokyo: Ogawa, 2009), 73–86.

49. These two similes are attributed to the third-century [*Da*] *loutan jing* by Daoshi in his *Fayuan zhulin*, T. no. 2122, vol. 53, 274a1–5. I have not found them in the received text.

50. Lb. #7, Dz. 97, ch. 4, 24a2–24b1, modified slightly by reference to Dunhuang ms. S. 6659, lines 340–49.

51. This description actually heads the third chapter of the work as it appears now in the Daoist canon. Lb. #7, Dz. 97, ch. 3, 1a–2b.

52. Lb. #7, Dz. 97, ch. 3, 6b2–7.

53. The graphs *na*[2] and *na* are cognate and interchangeable.

54. Lb. #7, Dz. 97, ch. 3, 7a–8a.

55. The canonical version of this scripture has *wu* rather than *yuan* at this point. The explanation below gives the reading *yuan*. It appears, then, that a copyist has mistaken the graph *yuan* for the simplified form *wu*[2].

56. The Jade Capitoline Mountain is in the Grand Veil Heaven, the highest heaven of the Lingbao cosmology.

57. This refers to the "six *qi* of Brahmā action," *fanxing liuqi*. These terms are interesting for the ways the Lingbao scriptures reconfigure the Hindu creator deity, Brahmā, as a type of inaugural *qi* and then associate him with the recurrent eschatology popular when these scriptures were written. The most concise gloss is given later in Dz. 97 by the Celestial Perfected himself: "The *qi* of Brahmā activity moves the pass of the six measures in correspondence with the numbers of heaven and earth. Once this number comes to its end, there is a transition between great kalpa cycles" (Dz. 97, ch. 3, 20b8–9). There may also be some contribution here from the Buddhist notion of Brahmā-heavens. (See Zürcher,

Buddhist Influence," 125–26, n. 76, for a description of these in Shangqing Daoist texts.) A full description of Lingbao eschatology would require another chapter at least as long as this one. For part of the story, see Stephen R. Bokenkamp, "Time After Time: Taoist Apocalyptic History and the Founding of the T'ang Dynasty," *Asia Major* 3rd ser. 7, pt. 1 (1994): 59–88.

58. "Seven treasure groves" refers by synecdoche to celestial realms full of trees formed of the seven most precious minerals and gemstones—gold, silver, amber, berylline, nacre, crystal, and carnelian, according to one list. See Edward H. Schafer, *The Golden Peaches of Samarkand: A Study of T'ang Exotics* (Berkeley: University of California Press, 1963), 227–49.

59. LB #7, Dz. 97, ch. 1, 15b–16b.

60. LB #7, DZ 97, ch. 1, 15b–16a.

61. LB #7, DZ 97, ch. 1, 16a–16b.

Bibliography

Abbreviations

Dz. *Zhengtong daozang* 正統道藏. Shanghai: Shanghai Yinshuguan, 1923–26. Citation is to number as given in Kristofer Schipper and Franciscus Verellen, *The Taoist Canon: A Historical Companion to the* Daozang (Chicago: University of Chicago Press, 2004), followed by chapter, page number, side, and line number as found in the string-bound edition of the *Zhengtong daozang*.

T. *Taishō shinshū daizōkyō* 大正新修大蔵經. Takakusu Junjirō 高楠順次郎 and Watanabe Kaigyoku 渡邊海旭, eds. Tokyo: Taishō issaikyō kankōkai, 1924–32. Citations are by Taisho number, followed by volume, page, and line number as necessary.

TZ. *Taishō shinshū daizōkyō tozōbu* 大正新修大蔵經圖像部. Takakusu Junjirō 高楠順次郎 and Watanabe Kaigyoku 渡邊海旭, eds. Tokyo: Taishō issaikyō kankōkai, 1932. Citations are by Taisho number followed by volume and page number as necessary. This is the iconographic supplement to the Taisho edition of the Buddhist canon.

X. *Wanxuzangjing* 卍續藏經. Taipei: Xinwenfeng, 1975.

Primary sources

Aggi-vacchagotta-sutta (*Majjhima-nikāya* 72), ed. V. Trenckner, R. Chalmers (London: Pali Text Society, 1888–1902).

Anurādho-sutta (*Saṃyutta-nikāya* 22), ed. L. Feer (London: Pali Text Society, 1884–98).

Ārya-Mahā-Māyūrī Vidyā-rājñī. Takubo Shūyo 田久保周譽, ed. Tokyo: Sankibo, 1972.

Asabashō 阿娑縛抄. TZ. no. 3190, vols. 8–9.

Avataṃsaka-sūtra (*Da fangguang fo huayan jing* 大方廣佛華嚴經), T nos.278 and 279, vol.9.

Ayuwang jing 阿育王經. T. no. 2043, vol. 47, pp. 131b–170a.

Ayuwang zhuan 阿育王傳. T. no. 2042, vol. 50, pp. 99a–131a.

Baopuzi neipian 抱朴子內篇. Ed. Wang Ming 王明. Beijing: Zhonghua Shuju, 1980.

Beifang Pishamen Tianwang sui jun hufa yigui 北方毗沙門天王隨軍護法儀軌. T. no. 1247.

Betsugyō 別行. T. no. 2476.

Biyan lu 碧巖錄. T. no. 2003.
Bukong juansuo shenbian zhenyan jing 不空羂索神變真言經. T. 1092.
Byakuhō kushō 白寶口抄. TZ. 3119, vols. 6–7.
Chanzong wumen guan 禪宗無門關, T. no.2005, vol. 48.
Cheng weishi lun 成唯識論, T. no.1585, vol. 31.
Chisong zi zhangli 赤松子章曆. Dz. 615.
Chuanfa zhengzong lun 傳法正宗論. T. no. 2080.
Cūla-māluṅkya-sutta (*Majjhima-nikāya* 63), ed. V. Trenckner, R. Chalmers, London: Pali Text Society, 1888–1902.
Da banniepan jing 大般涅槃經, T. no. 374, vol.12.
Da banniyuan jing 大般泥洹經, T. no. 376, vol. 12.
Da banruo boluomiduo jing 大般若波羅蜜多經, T. no. 220, vol. 7.
Dacheng xuanlun 大乘玄論, T. no. 1853, vol. 45.
Dacheng yizhang 大乘義章, T. no. 1851, vol. 44.
Dafang guangfo huayan jing 大方廣佛華嚴經. T. no. 278, vol. 9.
Daoxing banruo jing 道行般若經, T. no. 224, vol. 8.
Dai Nihon zokuzōkyō 大日本続蔵經*. Ed. Nakano Tatsue* 中野達慧*, Kyoto: Zōkyōshoin, 1905–12.*
Daijō butten 大乗仏典*, vol. 16: Shōtoku Taishi & Ganjin* 聖徳太子・鑑真*. Ed. Takasaki Naomichi* 高崎直道*. Tokyo: Chūō kōronsha* 中央公論社*, 1990.*
Da Piluzhena chengfo jing shu 大毘盧遮那成佛經疏. T. no. 1796, vol. 39.
Da Piluzhena chengfo shenbian jiachi jing 大毘盧遮那成佛神變加持經. T. no. 848, vol. 18.
Da Tang Xiyuji 大唐西域記. T. no. 2087, vol. 51.
Ditthi-sutta (Aṅguttara-nikāya 10), ed. R. Morris, E. Hardy (London: Pali Text Society, 1885–1900).
Dongyuan shen zhou jing 洞淵神咒經. Dz. 335.
Dunwu dasheng zhenglijue 頓悟大乘正理决 (Dunhuang manuscript), Pelliot no. 4646 and Stein no. 2672.
Fahua wenju ji 法華文句記. T. no. 1719, vol. 34.
Falun zuifu 法輪罪福. Dz. 346, 347, 348, and 455; Stein 1605 and Stein 1906.
Fayuan zhulin 法苑珠林. T. no. 2122, vol. 53.
Fengshen yanyi 封神演義 Author given as Xu Zhonglin 許仲琳, edited by Li Guoqing 李國慶. Beijing: Beijing tushuguan, 2001.
Fengshen yanyi: Xin zhengli ben 封神演義: 新整理本. Authors given as Xu Zhonglin 許仲琳, Li Yunxiang 李雲翔, and Zhong Bojing 鍾伯敬. Forward by Zhang Peiheng 章培恆. Nanjing: Jiangsu guji, 1991.
Fenyang Wude Chanshi yulu 汾陽無德禪師語錄. T no. 1992, vol. 47.
Foguang da cidian 佛光大辭典. General editor Ci Yi 慈怡. 8 vols. Gaoxiong: Foguang, 1988.
Fomu da kongque mingwang jing 佛母大孔雀明王經. T. no. 982, vol. 19.
Foshuo Baoxian tuoluoni jing 佛說寶賢陀羅尼經 T. no. 1285, vol. 21.

Foshuo dabei kongzhi jingang dajiao wang yigui jing 佛說大悲空智金剛大教王儀軌經, T. no. 892, vol. 18.

Foshuo da kongque zhou wang jing 佛說大孔雀呪王經. T. no. 985, vol. 19.

Foshuo pusa toushen taiehu qita yinyuan jing 佛說菩薩投身胎餓虎起塔因緣經. T. no. 2153, vol. 55.

Foshuo zao ta gongde jing 佛說造塔功德經.T. no. 699, vol. 16.

Fo suo xing zan jing 佛所行讚經. T. no. 192, vol. 4.

Fozu tongji 佛祖統紀. T. no. 2035, vol. 49.

Gaoseng Faxian zhuan 高僧法傳. T. no. 2085, vol. 51.

Gaoseng zhuan 高僧傳. T. no. 2059, vol. 50.

Gnod sbyin gar mkhan mchog gi rgyud. Tôh. no. 767. *DergéKanjur*, vol. WA, folios 81v.7–88v.7. Tr. by Dānagupta and Rab zhi Lo tsā ba.

Guang hongming ji 廣弘明集. T. no. 2103, vol. 52.

Hishō 祕鈔. T. no. 2489, vol. 85.

Hizō konpōshō 祕藏金寶鈔. T. no. 2485, vol. 85.

Honglou meng 紅樓夢. Cao Xueqin 曹雪芹 and Gao E 高鶚. Beijing: Zuojia, 1957. 3 vols.

Huangbo Duanji chanshi wanling lu 黃檗斷際禪師宛陵錄, T. no. 2012, vol. 48.

Ishiyama shichishū 石山七集. T. no. 2924, vol. 86.

Ji shenzhou sanbao gantong lu 集神州三寶感通錄. T. no. 2106, vol. 52.

Jin'gang bei 金剛錍, T. no. 1932, vol. 46.

Jingde chuandeng lu 景德傳燈錄. T. no. 2076, vol. 51.

Jizō bosatsu hosshin innen jūō kyō 地藏菩薩發心因緣十王經 in *Dai Nihonzokuzōkyō* 2b, 23, 4.

Kai Tian chuanxin ji 開天傳信記. By Zheng Qing 鄭綮 (?–899). Siku quanshu 四庫全書 edition.

Kakuzenshō 覺禪鈔. In *Dai Nihonbukkyō zensho* 大日本佛教全書, vols. 44–51; TZ. no. 3022, vols. 4–5.

Khemātherī-sutta (Saṃyutta-nikāya 44), ed. L. Feer (London: Pali Text Society, 1884–98).

Kongque wang zhou jing 孔雀王呪經. T. no. 984, vol. 19.

Laojun yi bai bashi jie 老君一百八十戒, Pelliot no. 4731 and Pelliot no. 4562.

Laozi xiang'er zhu jiaozheng 老子想爾注校證. Ed. Rao Zongyi (Jao Tsung-I) 饒宗頤. Shanghai: Shanghai Guji Chubanshe, 1991.

Lengqie shizi ji 楞伽師資記, T. no. 2837, vol. 85.

Liangshu 梁書. Taipei: Zhonghuashuju 中華書局,1966.

Liang Zhe jinshi zhi 兩浙金石志. Ruan Yuan 阮元. Collected in *Shike shiliao xinbian* 石刻史料新編. Taipei: Xinwenfeng 新文豐, 1986.

Liaozhai zhiyi huijiao huizhu huiping ben 聊齋志異會校會注會評本. Pu Songling 蒲松齡 (1640–1715), ed. Zhang Youhe 張友鶴. Shanghai: Shanghaiguji, 1986. 4 vols.

Lingbao benxing suyuan jing 靈寶本行宿緣經, Dz. 1114.

Lunheng jiaoshi 論衡校釋. Beijing: Zhonghua shuju, 1990.

Luofunu shuo jiuliao xiaoer jibing jing 囉嚩拏説救療小兒疾病經. T. no. 1330, vol. 21.

Mahāsaccaka-sutta (*Majjhima-nikāya* 36), ed. V. Trenckner, R. Chalmers (London: Pali Text Society, 1888–1902).

Mahāvibhāṣāśāstra (*Apidamo dapiposha lun* 阿毘達磨大毘婆沙論), T no. 1545, vol. 27.

Mahā yakṣa senāpati nartakapara kalpa (*Gnodsbyin gyi sdedpon chen po gar mkhanmchoggibrtag pa*). Tôh. no. 766. *DergéKanjur*, vol. WA, folios 69r.7-81v.7. Tr. by Dānagupta and Rabzhi Lo tsā ba.

Maṇibhadra nāma dhāraṇī (*'Phags pa nor bu bzangpo'igzungs*). Tôh. no. 764. *DergéKanjur*, vol. WA, folios 56r.1-56v.2. Tr. by Vidyākarasiṃha and Klu'i dbang po.

Maṇibhadra yakṣa sena kalpa (*Gnodsbyin nor bu bzangpo'irtog pa*). Tôh. no. 765. *DergéKanjur*, vol. WA, folios 56v.2–69r.6. Tr. by Mañjuśrī and Ba ri.

Mengxi bitan 夢溪筆談. Shen Kuo 沈括 (1029–1093). Taipei: Dingwen shuju 鼎文書局, 1977.

Mohe zhiguan 摩訶止觀, T. no. 1911, vol. 46.

Nanyue Sidachanshi lishi yuanwen 南嶽思大禪師立誓願文. T. no. 1933, vol. 46.

Nanzong dunjiao zuishang dasheng mohebanruoboluomi jing liuzu Huineng dashi yu Shaozhou Dafansi shifa tan jing 南宗頓教最上大乘摩訶般若波羅蜜經六祖惠能大師於韶州大梵寺施法壇經, T. no. 2007, vol. 48.

Nyāyānusāra (*Apidamo shunzhengli lun* 阿毘達磨順正理論), T. no. 1562, vol. 29.

Potthapada-sutta (Dīgha-nikāya 9), ed. T.W. Rhys Davids, J.E. Carpenter. London: Pali Text Society: 1890–1911.

Renwang huguo banruoboluomiduo jing tuoluoni niansong yigui 仁王護國般若波羅密多經陀羅尼念誦儀軌. T. no. 994, vol. 19.

Sanjiao yuanliu shengdi fozu sou shen daquan 三教源流聖帝佛祖搜神大全. Ming edition. Photographic reprint in vol. 3 of Wang Qiugui 王秋桂 and Li Fengmao 李豐楙, eds., *Zhongguo minjian xinyang ziliao huibian* 中國民間信仰資料彙編. Taibei: Xuesheng shuju, 1988.

Santian neijie jing 三天內解經. Dz. 1205.

Shan'e yinguo jing 善惡因果經. T. no. 2881, vol. 85.

Shaolin si zhi 少林寺志. Compiled by Ye Feng 葉封 et al. Revised by Shi Yizan 施奕簪 et al. 1748 edition.

Shiguo chunqiu 十國春秋. Wu Renchen 吳任臣 (Qing dynasty). Hong Kong: Dizhi wenhua, 1999.

Shijia shi pu 釋迦氏譜. T. no. 2041, vol. 50.

Shimen zhengtong 釋門正統. X. no. 1513.

Shin Nihon Koten bungaku taikei 新日本古典文学大系. Tokyo: Iwanami Shoten, 1989–98.

Shishi yaolan 釋氏要覽. T. no. 2127, vol. 54.

Shoson yōshō 諸尊要抄. T. no. 2484, vol. 85.

Song gaoseng zhuan 宋高僧傳. T. no. 2061, vol. 50.

Sumaṅgalavilāsinī (*Dīgha-nikāya-aṭṭhakathā*). Vol. 1, ed. T. W. Rhys Davids, and J. E. Carpenter. London: Pali Text Society, 1886; 2nd ed. 1968.

Taishang dongxuan lingbao yebao yinyuan jing 太上洞玄靈寶業報因緣經. *Dz. 336*.

Taishang dongxuan lingbao sanyuan pinjie gongde qingzhong jing 太上洞玄靈寶三元品戒功德輕重經. Dz. 456.

Taishang dongxuan lingbao benxing yinyuan jing 太上洞玄靈寶本行因緣經. Dz. 1115.

Taishang shuo zhuanlun wudao suming yinyuan jing 太上說轉輪五道宿命因緣經. Dz. 647.

Taishō issaikyō kankōkai 大正一切經刊行会. Ed. Takakusu Junjirō 高楠順次郎 and Watanabe Kaikoku 渡辺海旭. Tokyo: 1924–32.

Taizi ruiying benqi jing 太子瑞應本起經. T. no. 185, vol. 3.

Tōdai wajō tōseiden 唐大和上東征傳. Collected in *Youfang jichao* 遊方記抄. T. no. 2089, vol. 51.

Usuzōshi kuketsu 薄草子口決. T. no. 2535, vol.79.

Vajracchedikā (*Jin'gang banruo poluomi jing* 金剛般若波羅蜜經), T. no. 236, vol. 8.

Vimalakīrti-sūtra (*Weimojie suo shuo jing* 維摩詰所說經), T. no. 475, vol. 14.

Visuddhimagga, ed. H. C. Warren, rev. D. Kosambi. Cambridge Mass.: Harvard University Press, 1950.

Wudaihuiyao 五代會要. Wang Fu 王溥 (922–982). Shanghai: Shanghai guji, 1978.

Wugoujinguang da tuoluoni jing 無垢金光大陀羅尼經. T. no. 1024, vol. 19.

Wuliangshou jing yishu 無量壽經義疏. T. no. 1746, vol. 37.

Wuxin lun 無心論, T. no. 2831, vol. 85.

Wuyue beishi 吳越備史. Collected in *Biji xiaoshuo daguan* 筆記小說大觀, vol. 25. Taipei: Xinxing, 1978–84.

Xianyu jing 賢愚經. T. no. 202, vol. 4.

Xiuxing benqi jing 修行本起經. T. no. 184, vol. 3.

Xiyou ji 西遊記. Wu Cheng'en 吳承恩 (c. 1500–c. 1582). Beijing: Zuojia, 1954.

Xu gaoseng zhuan 續高僧傳. T. no. 2060, vol. 50.

Xuandu lüwen 玄都律文. Dz. 188.

Yanluo wang gongxingfa cidi 焰羅王供行法次第. T. no. 1290, vol. 21.

Yaoshi liuliguang rulai benyuan gongde jing 薬師瑠璃光如来本願功徳經. T. no. 450, vol. 14.

Yaoshi rulai benyuan jing 薬師如来本願經. T. no. 449, vol. 14.

*Yiqie jing yinyi*一切經音義. T. no. 2128, vol. 54.

*Yiqie rulai xinmimi quanshen sheli baoqieyin tuoloni jing*一切如來心秘密全身舍利寶篋印陀羅尼經. T. no. 1022A, 1022B, vol. 19.

*Yiqie rulai zhengfa mimi qieyinxin tuoloni jing*一切如來正法祕密篋印心陀羅尼經. T. no. 1023, vol. 19.

Yōson hō 要尊法. T. no. 2478, vol. 85.

Yuqieji yaojiu anan tuoluoni yankou gui yi jing 瑜伽集要救阿難陀羅尼焰口軌儀經. T. no. 1318, vol. 21.

Yuqie jiyao yan shishi qijiao anantuo an yuanyou 瑜伽集要焰施食起教阿難陀俺緣由. T. no. 1319, vol. 21.

Zhaolun 肇論, T. no. 1858, vol. 45.

Zhiguan fuxing chuan hongjue 止觀輔行傳弘決. T. no. 1912, vol. 46.

Zhong benqi jing 中本起經. T. no. 196, vol. 4.
Zhongguan lunshu 中觀論疏. T. no. 1824, vol. 42.
Zhuangzi 莊子, Harvard-Yenching Institute Sinological Index Series, Supplement no. 20 (Cambridge MA: Harvard University Press, 1956).
Zizhi tongjian 資治通鑒. Sima Guang 司馬光 (1019–1086). 294 vols.
Zongjing lu 宗鏡錄, T. no. 2016, vol. 48.
Zuishang mimi Nana tian jing 最上祕密那拏天經. T. no. 1288, vol. 21.
Zuo zhuan 左傳. Liang Kuan 梁寬. Taipei: Shangwu, 1973.
Zutang ji 祖堂集. In Yanagida Seizan 柳田聖山, ed. Sōdōshū 祖堂集. Kyoto: Chūun shuppansha, 1974.

Secondary Sources

App, Urs. "Treatise on No-Mind: A Chan Text from Dunhuang." *Eastern Buddhist* n.s. 28, 1 (1995): 70–107.
Archer, W. G. *The Loves of Krishna in Indian Painting and Poetry*. London: Allen and Unwin, 1957.
Asvaghosha. *The Buddha-Karita or Life of the Buddha*. Ed. and trans. Edward B. Cowell. 1894. Photographic reprint New Delhi: Cosmo, 1977.
Aung, Shwe Zan, and Caroline A. F. Rhys Davids. *Points of Controversy, or, Subjects of Discourse, Being a Translation of the Kathā-vatthu*. Attr. Moggaliputta Tissa. 1915. London: Pali Text Society and Luzac and Co., 1969.
Baron-Cohen, Simon. *Mindblindness: An Essay on Autism and Theory of Mind, Learning, Development, and Conceptual Change*. Cambridge, Mass.: MIT Press, 1995.
Barrett, Timothy H. "The Date of the *Leng-chia shih-tzu chi*." *Journal of the Royal Asiatic Society* 3rd ser. 1, 2 (1991): 255–59.
———. "Did I-Ching Go to India? Problems in Using I-Ching as a Source on South Asian Buddhism." *Buddhist Studies Review* 15, 2 (1998): 142–56.
———. "Preliminary Considerations in the Search for a Daoist *Dhammapada*." In *Daoism in History: Essays in Honour of Liu Ts'un-yan*, ed. Benjamin Penny. London: Routledge, 2006. 41–55.
Battaglia, Debbora, ed. *Rhetorics of Self-Making*. Berkeley: University of California Press, 1995.
Beal, Samuel. *Si-yu-ki: Buddhist Records of the Western World*. 1884. Reprint Delhi: Motilal Banarsidas, 2004.
Benn, Charles D. "*Xiaodao lun*." In Fabrizio Pregadio, ed., *The Encyclopedia of Taoism*. London: Routledge, 2008. 2: 1098–99.
Benveniste, Émile, and Paul Demiéville. "Notes sur le fragment sogdien du *Buddhadhyānasamādhisāgara-sūtra*." *Journal Asiatique* 223, 2 (1933): 193–248.
Berezkin, Rostislav. "Tang Dynasty Transformation Texts (*bianwen*) and Ming-Qing Precious Scrolls (*baojuan*): Legacy of Tang Narratives in Chinese Popular Literature." Manuscript. 2006.

Birnbaum, Raoul. *The Healing Buddha*. Boulder. Colo.: Shambhala, 1979.

Block, Ned. "Inverted Earth." In *Philosophical Perspectives* 4: *Action Theory and Philosophy of Mind*, ed. James E. Tomberlin. Atascadero, Calif.: Ridgeview, 1990. 53–79.

Bodhi, Bhikkhu. *The Connected Discourses of the Buddha: A New Translation of the Saṃyutta Nikāya*. 2 vols. Somerville, Mass.: Wisdom, 2000.

Bokenkamp, Stephen R. *Ancestors and Anxiety: Daoism and the Birth of Rebirth in China*. Berkeley: University of California Press, 2007.

———. "Chinese Metaphor, Again: Reading—and Understanding—Imagery in the Chinese Poetic Tradition." *Journal of the American Oriental Society* 109, 2 (1989): 211–21.

———. *Early Daoist Scriptures*. Berkeley: University of California Press, 1997.

———. "The Silkworm and the Bodhi Tree: The Lingbao Attempt to Replace Buddhism in China and Our Attempt to Place Lingbao Daoism." In *Religion and Chinese Society*, vol. 1, *Ancient and Medieval China*, ed. John Lagerwey. Hong Kong: Chinese University Press, 2004. 317–39.

———. "Sources of the Ling-pao Scriptures." In *Tantric and Taoist Studies in Honour of R. A. Stein*, ed. Michel Strickmann. Brussels: Institut Belge des Hautes Études Chinoises, 1983. 434–85.

———. "Stages of Transcendence: The *Bhūmi* Concept in Taoist Scripture." In *Chinese Buddhist Apocrypha*, ed. Robert E. Buswell. Honolulu: University of Hawai'i Press, 1990. 119–48.

———. "*Tenkyō: Ko reihōgyō no senkyō hōhō* 轉經: 古靈寶派の宣教方法." In *Dōkyō to kyōsei shisō* 道教と共生思想, ed. Tanaka Fumio 田中文雄 and Terry Kleeman. Tokyo: Ogawa, 2009. 73–86.

———. "The *Vessantara-jātaka* in Buddhist and Daoist Translation." In *Daoism in History: Essays in Honour of Liu Ts'un-yan*, ed. Benjamin Penny. London: Routledge, 2006. 56–73.

———. "What Daoist Body?" In *Purposes, Means, and Convictions in Daoism: A Berlin Symposium*, ed. Florian C. Reiter. Wiesbaden: Harrassowitz, 2007. 131–50.

Boucher, Daniel. "Buddhism and Language in Early-Medieval China." In *A Reader of Traditional Chinese Culture*, ed. Victor H. Mair, Paul R. Goldin, and Nancy Steinhardt. Honolulu: University of Hawai'i Press, 2005. 265–69.

———. "Gāndhārī and the Early Chinese Buddhist Translations Reconsidered: The Case of the *Saddharmapuṇḍarīkasūtra*." *Journal of the American Oriental Society* 118, 4 (1998): 471–506.

Boyer, Pascal. *The Naturalness of Religious Ideas: A Cognitive Theory of Religion*. Berkeley: University of California Press, 1994.

———. *Religion Explained: The Evolutionary Origins of Religious Thought*. New York: Basic Books, 2001.

Bronkhorst, Johannes. *The Two Traditions of Meditation in Ancient India*. Alt- und Neu-Indische Studien 28. Stuttgart: Franz Steiner, 1986.

Brose, Benjamin. "Crossing Ten Thousand Li of Waves: The Return of China's Lost Tiantai Texts." *Journal of International Association of Buddhist Studies* 29, 1 (2006/08): 21–62.

Bryant, Edwin F., ed. *Krishna: A Sourcebook*. Oxford: Oxford University Press, 2007.

Buddhaghosa. *The Path of Purification (Visuddhimagga)*. Trans. Bhikkhu Ñyāṇamoli. 2 vols. Berkeley, Calif.: Shambhala, 1976.

Bullock, Merry. "Animism in Childhood Thinking: A New Look at an Old Question." *Developmental Psychology* 21, 2 (1985): 217–25.

Butterworth, George E., Paul L. Harris, Alan M. Leslie, and Henry M. Wellman, eds. *Perspectives on the Child's Theory of Mind*. Oxford: British Psychological Society and Oxford University Press, 1991.

Campany, Robert Ford. *Strange Writing: Anomaly Accounts in Early Medieval China*. Albany: State University of New York Press, 1996.

———. *To Live as Long as Heaven and Earth: A Translation and Study of Ge Hong's Traditions of Divine Transcendents*. Berkeley: University of California Press, 2002.

Cao, Boyan 曹伯言, ed. *Hu Shi riji quanbian 4: 1923–1927* 胡適日記全編. Hefei 合肥: Anhui jiaoyu Chubanshe 安徽教育出版社, 2001.

Caramazza, Alfonso, and Jennifer R. Shelton. "Domain-Specific Knowledge Systems in the Brain: The Animate-Inanimate Distinction." *Journal of Cognitive Neuroscience* 10, 1 (1998): 1–34.

Carey, Susan. *Conceptual Change in Childhood*. Cambridge, Mass.: MIT Press/Bradford, 1985.

Carrithers, Michael, Steven Collins, and Steven Lukes, eds. *The Category of the Person: Anthropology, Philosophy, History*. Cambridge: Cambridge University Press, 1985.

Chan, Hok-Lam [Chen Xuelin]. *Legends of the Building of Old Peking*. Hong Kong: Chinese University Press, 2008.

Chang, K. C. *Art, Myth, and Ritual: The Path to Political Authority*. Cambridge, Mass.: Harvard University Press, 1988.

Chen, Jinhua. *Monks and Monarchs, Kinship and Kingship: Tanqian in Sui Buddhism and Politics*. Kyoto: Scuola Italiana di Studi sull'Asia Orientale (Italian School of East Asian Studies), 2002.

———. "Sarira and Scepter: Empress Wu's Political Use of Buddhist Relics." *Journal of the International Association of Buddhist Studies* 25, 1–2 (2002): 33–150.

Ch'en, Kenneth. *The Chinese Transformation of Buddhism*. Princeton, N.J.: Princeton University Press, 1973.

Chen, Xiaoyi 陳曉怡. "Nezha renwu ji gushi zhi yanjiu." 哪吒人物及故事之研究. Ph.D. dissertation, Fengjia University, 1994.

Chen, Xuelin 陳學霖 [Hok-Lam Chan]. *Liu Bowen Nezha cheng: Beijing jiancheng de chuanshou* 劉伯溫哪吒城 – 北京建城的傳說. Taibei: Sanmin, 1996.

Chou, Yi-liang. "Tantrism in China." *Harvard Journal of Asiatic Studies* 8, 3/4 (March 1945): 241–332.

Coomaraswamy, Ananda K. *Elements of Buddhist Iconography*. 3rd ed. New Delhi: Munshiram Manoharlal, [1935] 1979.

———. *Yakṣas: Essays in the Water Cosmology*. Ed. Paul Schroeder. Delhi: Indira Gandhi National Center for the Arts and Oxford University Press, 1993.

Cowell, Edward B., ed. *The Jātaka or Stories of the Buddha's Former Births*. 1895. Reprint New Delhi: Munshiram Manoharlal, 1990, vol. 3, trans. H. T. Francis and R. A. Neil.

Cox, Collett. *Disputed Dharmas: Early Buddhist Theories on Existence: An Annotated Translation of the Section on Factors Dissociated from Thought from Saṅghabhadra's Nyāyānusāra*. Studia Philologica Buddhica Monograph Series 11. Tokyo: International Institute for Buddhist Studies, 1995.

Crane, Ralph J. *Inventing India. A History of India in English-Language Fiction*. London: Macmillan, 1992.

Cronin, Richard. *Imagining India*. London: Macmillan, 1989.

Dang, Yan'ni 黨燕妮. "Pishamen Tianwang xinyang zai Dunhuang de liuchuan." 毗沙門天王信仰在敦煌的流傳. *Dunhuang yanjiu* 敦煌研究 3 (2005): 99–104.

Daniel, Valentine E. *Fluid Signs: Being a Person the Tamil Way*. Berkeley: University of California Press, 1984.

Davids, Caroline A. F. Rhys, trans. *The Book of the Kindred Sayings (Samyuta-Nikāya)*. 5 vols. 1917. Reprint Oxford: Pali Text Society, 1993.

Deeg, Max. *Das Gaoseng-Faxian-Zhuan als religionsgeschichtliche Quelle: Der älteste Bericht eines chinesischen buddhistischen Pilgermönchs über seine Reise nach Indien mit Übersetzung des Textes*. Wiesbaden: Harrassowitz, 2005.

——, ed. Special issue on early Chinese Buddhist translations. *Journal of the International Association of Buddhist* Studies 31, 1–2 (2008).

de Jong, J. W. *Textcritical Remarks on the Bodhisattvāvadānakalpalatā (Pallavas 42–108)*. Studia Philologica Buddhica Monograph Series 2. Tokyo: Reiyukai Library, 1979.

Demiéville, Paul. "Le Bouddhisme et la guerre." Reprinted in *Choix d'études Bouddhiques*. Leiden: Brill, 1973.

——. *Le concile de Lhasa: une controverse sur le quietisme entre bouddhistes de l'Inde et de la Chine au VIIIème siècle de l'ère chrétienne*. BIHEC 7. Paris: Imprimerie Nationale, 1952.

Dennett, Daniel C. *Consciousness Explained*. Boston: Little, Brown, 1991.

——. *The Intentional Stance*. Cambridge, Mass.: MIT Press, 1987.

Dimmitt, Cornelia, and J. A. B. van Buitenen, eds. and trans. *Classical Hindu Mythology: A Reader in the Sanskrit Purāṇas*. Philadelphia: Temple University Press, 1978.

Diyijie Nezha xueshu yantaohui lunwenji 第一屆哪吒學術研討會論文集. Edited by Guoli Zhongshan daxue qingdai xueshu yanjiu zhongxin 國立中山大學清代學術研究中心. Gaoxiong: Zhongshan daxue, 2003.

Dudbridge, Glen. "The General of the Five Paths in Tang and Pre-Tang China." *Cahiers d'Extrême-Asie* 9 (1996–97), 85–98.

——. *The Hsi-yu chi: A Study of Antecedents to the Sixteenth-Century Chinese Novel*. Cambridge: Cambridge University Press, 1970.

——. *The Legend of Miaoshan*. Oxford: Oxford University Press, 2004.

Duquenne, Robert. "Gaṇapati Rituals in Chinese." *Bulletin de l'École Française d'Extrême-Orient* 77, 1 (1988): 321–54.

Durt, Hubert. "The Meaning of Archaeology in Ancient Context: Notes on the Stūpas of Aśoka." *Buddhism and Science: Commemorative Volume, 80th Anniversary*. Seoul: Dongguk University Press, 1987. 1223–41.

Dutt, Manmatha Nath. *A Prose English Translation of the Harivamsha*. Calcutta: H.C. Dass, 1897.

Ecke, Gustav, and Paul Demiéville. *The Twin Pagodas of Zayton: A Study of Later Buddhist Sculpture in China*. Harvard-Yenching Monograph 2. Cambridge, Mass.: Harvard University Press, 1935.

Edgren, Soren. "The Printed Dhāraṇī Sūtra of A.D. 956." *Museum of Far Eastern Antiquities* (Ostasiastiska Museet) 44 (1972): 141–46.

Eliasberg, Danielle. "Quelques aspects du grand exorcisme No à Touen-houang." In *Contributions aux études de Touen-houang: Volume III*, ed. Michel Soymié. Paris: École Française d'Extrême-Orient, 1984. 237–53.

Elliott, Alan J. A. *Chinese Spirit-Medium Cults in Singapore*. 1955. Reprint London: Athlone, 1990.

Emmerick, R. E. *Tibetan Texts Concerning Khotan*. London Oriental Series 19. London: Oxford University Press, 1967.

Fan, Sheng 樊圣. "Yidipasi yu Nezha" 伊底帕斯与哪吒. *Taiwan Yijie* 39, 12 (1996): 57–61.

Faure, Bernard. "Bodhidharma as Textual and Religious Paradigm." *History of Religions* 25, 3 (1986): 123–32.

———. *Chan Insights and Oversights. An Epistemological Critique of the Chan Tradition*. Princeton, N.J.: Princeton University Press, 1993.

———. "The Elephant in the Room: The Cult of Secrecy in Japanese Tantrism." In *The Culture of Secrecy in Japanese Religion*, ed. Bernhard Scheid and Mark Teeuwen. London: Routledge, 2006. 255–68.

———. *The Rhetoric of Immediacy: A Cultural Critique of Chan/Zen Buddhism*. Princeton, N.J.: Princeton University Press, 1991.

———. *The Will to Orthodoxy: A Critical Genealogy of Northern Chan Buddhism*. Stanford, Calif.: Stanford University Press, 1997.

Filliozat, Jean. *Étude de démonologie indienne: Le Kumāratantra de Rāvaṇa et les textes parallèles indiens, tibétains, chinois, cambodgien et arabe*. Paris: Imprimerie Nationale, 1937.

Fraser, Sarah Elizabeth. *Performing the Visual: The Practice of Buddhist Wall Painting in China and Central Asia, 618–960*. Stanford, Calif.: Stanford University Press, 2004.

Frédéric, Louis. *Les Dieux du bouddhisme*. Paris: Flammarion, 2006.

Fukunaga Mitsuji 福永光司. "'No-Mind' in *Chuang-Tzu* and in Ch'an Buddhism." *Zinbun* 12 (1969): 9–45.

Ganguly, Swati. *Treatise in Thirty Verses on Mere-Consciousness: A Critical English Translation of Hsüan-Tsang's Chinese Version of the Vijñaptimātratātriṃśikā with Notes from Dharmapāla's Commentary in Chinese*. Delhi: Motilal Banarsidass, 1992.

Gaulier, Simone, Robert Jera-Bezard, and Monique Maillard. *Buddhism in Afghanistan and Central Asia*. Iconography of Religions 13, fasc. 14, pt. 2. Leiden: Brill, 1976.

Gell, Alfred. *Art and Agency*. Oxford: Oxford University Press, 1998.

Gelman, Rochel. "First Principles: Organize Attention to and Learning about Relevant Data: Number and the Animate-Inanimate Distinction as Examples." *Cognitive Science* 14, 1 (1990): 79–106.

Gelman, Rochel, Frank Durgin, and Lisa Kaufman. "Distinguishing Between Animates and Inanimates: Not by Motion Alone." In *Causal Cognition: A Multidisciplinary Debate*, ed. Dan Sperber, David Premack, and Ann James Premack. New York: Clarendon, 1995. 150–84.

Gelman, Rochel, Elizabeth S. Spelke, and E. Meek. "What Preschoolers Know About Animate and Inanimate Objects." In *The Acquisition of Symbolic Skills*, ed. Don R. Rogers and John A. Sloboda. London: Plenum, 1983. 297–326.

Gelman, Susan A. *The Essential Child: Origins of Essentialism in Everyday Thought*. Oxford: Oxford University Press, 2003.

Gelman, Susan A., and Paul Bloom. "Young Children Are Sensitive to How an Object Was Created When Deciding What to Name It." *Cognition* 76, 2 (2000): 91–103.

Gelman, Susan A., and John D. Coley. "The Importance of Knowing a Dodo Is a Bird: Categories and Inferences in 2–Year-Old Children." *Developmental Psychology* 26, 5 (1990): 796–804.

Gelman, Susan A., and John E. Opfer. "Development of the Animate-Inanimate Distinction." In *Blackwell Handbook of Childhood Cognitive Development*, ed. Usha Goswami. Oxford: Blackwell, 2002. 151–66.

Gelman, Susan A., and Anne Watson O'Reilly. "Children's Inductive Inferences Within Superordinate Categories: The Role of Language and Category Structure." *Child Development* 59, 4 (1988): 876–87.

Gelman, Susan A., and Henry M. Wellman. "Insides and Essences: Early Understandings of the Non-Obvious." *Cognition* 38, 3 (1991): 213–44.

Getty, Alice. *The Gods of Northern Buddhism: Their History, Iconography and Progressive Evolution Through the Northern Buddhist Countries*. 1928. Reprint New Delhi: Munshiram Manoharlal, 1978.

Gimello, Robert M. "Random Reflections on the 'Sinicization' of Buddhism." *Society for the Study of Chinese Religions Bulletin* 5 (1978): 52–89.

Goldman, Robert P. "Fathers, Sons and Gurus: Oedipal Conflict in the Sanskrit Epics." *Journal of Indian Philosophy*, 6, 3 (November 1978): 349–92.

——, trans. *The Rāmāyaṇa of Vālmīki: An Epic of Ancient India*. Vol. 1, *Bālakāṇḍa*. Princeton, N.J.: Princeton University Press, 1984.

Gonda, J. *Aspects of Early Viṣṇuism*. 1954. Reprint Delhi: Motilal Banarsidass, 1969.

Gong, Zhebing 宮哲兵. "Wuyue zhi di de sheli wenhua 吳越之地的舍利文化." In *Wuyue fojiao xueshu yantaohui* 吳越佛教研討會, ed. Hangzhou foxueyuan 杭州佛學院. Beijing: Zongjiao wenhua, 2004.

Granoff, Phyllis. "Tobatsu Bishamon: Three Japanese Statues in the United States and an Outline of the Rise of This Cult in East Asia." *East and West* n.s. 20, 1–2 (1970): 144–68.

Greene, Eric. "Another Look at Early Chan: Daoxuan, Bodhidharma, and the Three Levels Movement." *T'oung Pao* 94 (2008): 49–114.

Griffiths, Paul John. "Concentration or Insight: The Problematic of Therāvada Buddhist Meditation-Theory." *Journal of the American Academy of Religion* 49, 4 (1981): 605–24.

———. *On Being Mindless: Buddhist Meditation and the Mind-Body Problem*. La Salle, Ill.: Open Court, 1986.

———."Scholasticism: The Possible Recovery of an Intellectual Practice." In *Scholasticism: Cross-Cultural and Comparative Perspectives*, ed. José Ignacio Cabezón. Albany: State University of New York Press, 1998. 201–35.

Groner, Paul. *Ryōgen and Mount Hiei: Japanese Tendai in the Tenth Century*. Kuroda Institute Studies in East Asian Buddhism, 15. Honolulu: University of Hawai'i Press, 2002.

Grünwedel, Albert. *Alt-Kutscha: Archäologische und religionsgeschichtliche Forschungen an Tempera-Gemälden aus Buddhistischen Höhlen der ersten acht Jahrhunderte nach Christi Geburt*. Berlin: Otto Elsner, 1920.

Gu, Zhizong, trans. *Creation of the Gods*. 2 vols. Beijing: New World Press, 1992.

Guojia wenwuju 國家文物局, ed. *Zhongguo wenwu jinghua dacidian: qingtong juan* 中國文物精華大辭典：青銅卷. Shanghai: Shanghai Cishu Chubanshe 上海辭書出版社 and Shangwu yinshuguan 商務印書館, 1995.

Guo, Junye 郭俊葉. "Tuo ta Tianwang yu Nezha: Jiantan Dunhuang Pishamen Tianwang fu Nezha hui" 托塔天王與哪吒: 兼談敦煌毗沙門天王赴哪吒會圖. *Dunhuang yanjiu* 敦煌研究 109 (2008.3): 32–40.

Guo, Zizhang 郭子章, ed. *Ming zhou Ayuwangshan zhi* 明州阿育王山志. http://buddhistinformatics.ddbc.edu.tw/fosizhi/ui.html?book=g010

Gupta, Anand Swarup, ed. *The Kūrma Purāṇa*. Fort Ramnagar, Varanasi: All-India Kashiraj Trust, 1971.

Guy, John. "The Lost Temples of Nagapattinam and Quanzhou: A Study in Sino-Indian Relations." *Silk Road Art and Archeology* 3 (1993–94): 292–310.

———. "Tamil Merchant Guilds and the Quanzhou Trade." In *The Emporium of the World: Maritime Quanzhou, 1000–1400*, ed. Angela Schottenhammer. Leiden: Brill, 2001. 283–308.

Hacking, Ian. *Rewriting the Soul: Multiple Personality and the Sciences of Memory*. Princeton, N.J.: Princeton University Press, 1995.

Haesner, Chhaya. "Some Common Stylistic and Iconographic Features in the Buddhist Art of India and Central Asia." In *Investigating Indian Art: Proceedings of a Symposium on the Development of Early Buddhist and Hindu Iconography Held at the Museum of Indian Art, Berlin, in May 1986*, ed. Marianne Yaldiz and Wibke Lobo. Veröffentlichungen des Museums für Indische Kunst 8. Berlin: Museum für Indische Kunst, 1987. 105–20.

Hanan, Patrick. "The Early Chinese Short Story: A Critical Theory in Outline." *Harvard Journal of Asiatic Studies* 27 (1967): 168–207.

——. "The Making of *The Pearl-Sewn Shirt* and *The Courtesan's Jewel Box*." *Harvard Journal of Asiatic Studies* 33 (1973): 124–53.

——. "The Nature of Ling Meng-ch'u's Fiction." In *Chinese Narrative: Critical and Theoretical Essays*, ed. Andrew Plaks. Princeton, N.J.: Princeton University Press, 1977.

Hansen, Valerie. "Gods on Walls: A Case of Indian Influence on Chinese Lay Religion?" In *Religion and Society in T'ang and Sung China*, ed. Patricia Buckley Ebrey and Peter N. Gregory. Honolulu: University of Hawai'i Press, 1993. 75–113.

Hardy, Friedhelm. *Viraha-Bhakti: The Early History of Kṛṣṇa Devotion in South India*. Delhi: Oxford University Press, 1983.

Harle, J. C. *Gupta Sculpture: Indian Sculpture of the Fourth to the Sixth Centuries A.D.* New Delhi: Munshiram Manoharlal, 1996.

Hawley, John Stratton. *Krishna, the Butter Thief*. Princeton, N.J.: Princeton University Press, 1983.

——. "Krishna's Cosmic Victories." *Journal of the American Academy of Religion* 47, 2 (June 1979): 201–21.

Hiltebeitel, Alf, ed. *Criminal Gods and Demon Devotees: Essays on the Guardians of Popular Hinduism*. Albany: State University of New York Press, 1989.

Hirano, Sōjō 平野宗淨. *Tongo yōmon* 頓悟要門. Zen no goroku 禪の語錄 6. Tokyo: Chikuma shobō, 1970.

Ho, Kin-chung. "Nezha: Figure de l'enfant rebelle." *Études Chinoises* 7, 2 (Autumn 1988): 7–26.

Hobson, R. Peter. "Against the Theory of 'Theory of Mind.'" In *Perspectives on the Child's Theory of Mind*, ed. George E. Butterworth, Paul L. Harris, Alan M. Leslie, and Henry M. Wellman. Oxford: British Psychological Society and Oxford University Press, 1991. 33–51.

——. *Autism and the Development of Mind*. Essays in Developmental Psychology. Hove: Erlbaum, 1993.

Hoernle, A. F. Rudolf. *The Bower Manuscript: Facsimile Leaves, Nagari Transcript, Romanised Transliteration and English Translation with Notes*. 1908–12. Reprint New Delhi: Sharada Rani, 1983.

——. "A Note on the British Collection of Central Asian Antiquities." In *Actes du XIIe Congrès international des orientalistes. Rome, 1899*. Florence: Société Typographique Florentine, 1901–1902. 1: 151–85.

——. "Three Further Collections of Ancient Manuscripts from Central Asia." *Journal of the Asiatic Society of Bengal* 66 (1897): 213–60.

——. "The Weber Manuscripts." *Journal of the Asiatic Society of Bengal* 62 (1893): 1–40.

Hong, Shuling 洪淑苓. "Nezha xinyang yu nüxing shenmei yanjiu" 哪吒信仰與女性神媒研究. In *Diyijie Nezha xueshu yantaohui lunwenji*, ed. Guoli zhongshan daxue, 215–40.

Hsieh, Shu-wei (Xie Shiwei) 謝世維. *Tianjie zhi wen: Wei Jin Nanbei chao Lingbao jingdian yanjiu* 天界之文：魏晉南北朝靈寶經典研究. Taibei: Taiwan shang wu yin shu guan, 2010.

———. "Writing from Heaven: Celestial Writing in Six Dynasties Daoism." Ph.D. dissertation, Indiana University, 2005.

Hu, Shi 胡適. "The Indianization of China: A Case Study in Cultural Borrowing." In *Independence, Convergence, and Borrowing in Institutions, Thought, and Art*. Cambridge, Mass.: Harvard University Press, 1937. 219–47.

———. *Shenhui heshang yiji—fu Hu xiansheng zuihou de yanjiu* 神會和尚集—附胡先生最後的研究. Taibei: Hu Shi jinian guan, 1968.

Huang, Yi-hsun 黃繹勳. "Wuyue zhu wang (893–978) yu fojiao 吳越佛教諸王與佛教." *Chung-hwa Buddhist Journal* 17 (2004): 123–47.

Inden, Ronald B. *Imagining India*. Oxford: Blackwell, 1990.

Iriya, Yoshitaka 入矢義高. *Rakuyō garan ki* 洛陽伽藍記 (Record of the Monasteries of Luoyang). Tokyo: Heibonsha, 1990.

Iwamoto, Yutaka. *Sumāgadā avadāna kenkyū* スマーガダー＝アヴァダーナ研究 (A Study of the *Sumāgadhāvadāna*). *Bukkyō setsuwa kenkyū* 仏教説話研究, vol. 5. Tokyo: Keimei, 1979.

———. "The *Sumāgadhāvadāna*: A Buddhist Legend. Pt. 1. Revised Sanskrit-Text." *Tōkai Daigaku Bungakubu kiyō* 東海大学文学部紀要 1 (1959): 1–51.

Iyanaga, Nobumi. "Dākinī et l'Empereur: Mystique bouddhique de la royauté dans le Japon médiéval." *Versus: Quaderni di studi semiotici* 83/84 (1999): 41–111.

Johnson, Cynthia R., and D. H. Rakison. "Early Categorization of Animate/Inanimate Concepts in Young Children with Autism." *Journal of Developmental and Physical Disabilities* 18, 2, (2006): 73–89.

Jones, Andrew. "The Poetics of Uncertainty in Early Chinese Literature." *Sino-Platonic Papers* 4 (February 1987): 1–45.

Jordan, David K. *Gods, Ghosts and Ancestors: The Folk Religion of a Taiwanese Village*. Berkeley: University of California Press, 1972.

Kabanoff, Alexander. "The Kangi-ten (Gaṇapati) Cult in Medieval Japanese Mikkyō." In *Esoteric Buddhism in Japan*, ed. Ian Astley. Copenhagen: Seminar for Buddhist Studies, 1994. 99–126.

Kamata, Shigeo 鎌田茂雄. *Chūgoku bukkyō shisōshi kenkyū* 中國佛經思想史研究. Tokyo: Shunjūsha, 1968.

———. "Chūgoku zen shisōshi ni arawareta mujōbusshō shisō." *Shūgaku kenkyū* 4 (March 1962): 51–57.

Kamitsuka, Yoshiko 神塚淑子. *Rikuchō dōkyō shisō no kenkyū* 六朝道教思想の研究. Tokyo: Sōbunsha, 1999.

Kao, Karl S. Y., ed. *Classical Chinese Tales of the Supernatural and the Fantastic: Selections from the Third to the Tenth Century*. Bloomington: Indiana University Press, 1985.

Katz, Paul R. *Demon Hordes and Burning Boats: The Cult of Marshal Wen in Late Imperial Chekiang*. SUNY Series in Chinese Local Studies. Albany: State University of New York Press, 1995.

Kawamura, Kōshō 河村孝照. *Ubu no Budda ron* 有部の佛陀論. Tokyo: Sankibō Busshorin 山喜房仏書林, 1975.

Keown, Damien. *A Dictionary of Buddhism*. Oxford: Oxford University Press, 2003.

Kieschnick, John. *The Impact of Buddhism on Chinese Material Culture*. Princeton, N.J.: Princeton University Press, 2003.

Kinomiya, Yashuhiko 木宮泰彦. *Nisshi kōtsushi* 日支交通史, 2 vols. Tokyo: Kinshi Hōryūdō, 1926.

Kinsley, David. *Hindu Goddesses: Visions of the Divine Feminine in the Hindu Religious Tradition*. Berkeley: University of California Press, 1986.

Knechtges, David R. *Wenxuan or Selections of Refined Literature*. Princeton, N.J.: Princeton University Press, 1996.

Kohn, Livia. *The Daoist Monastic Manual: A Translation of the Fengdao kejie*. New York: Oxford University Press, 2004.

———. *Laughing at the Tao: Debates Among Buddhists and Taoists in Medieval China*. Princeton, N.J.: Princeton University Press, 1995.

———. "Steal Holy Food and Come Back as a Viper: Conceptions of Karma and Rebirth in Medieval China." *Early Medieval China* 4 (1998): 1–34.

Koseki, Aaron K. "Chi-tsang's *Ta-ch'eng-hsuan-lun*: The Two Truths and the Buddha-nature." Ph.D. dissertation, University of Wisconsin, 1977.

———. "Prajñāpāramitā and the Buddhahood of the Non-Sentient World: The San-Lun Assimilation of Buddha-Nature and Middle Path Doctrine." *Journal of the International Association of Buddhist Studies* 3, 1 (1980): 16–33.

Kramrisch, Stella. *Manifestations of Shiva*. Philadelphia: Philadelphia Museum of Art, 1981.

———. *The Presence of Śiva*. Princeton, N.J.: Princeton University Press, 1981.

Krishan, Yuvraj. *Gaṇeśa: Unravelling an Enigma*. Delhi: Motilal Banarsidass, 1999.

Kuo, Li-ying. *Confession et contrition dans le bouddhisme chinois de Ve au Xe siècle*. Paris: École Française d'Extrême-Orient, 1994.

La Vallée Poussin, Louis de. *The Way to Nirvāṇa: Six Lectures on Ancient Buddhism as a Discipline of Salvation*. Cambridge Cambridge University Press, 1917.

LaFleur, William R. "Saigyō and the Buddhist Value of Nature, Part 1." *History of Religions* 13, 2 (1973): 93–128.

———. "Saigyō and the Buddhist Value of Nature, Part 2." *History of Religions* 13, 3 (1974): 227–48.

Lai, Jiancheng 賴建成. *Wuyue fojiao zhi fazhan* 吳越佛教之發展. Taipei: Dongwu Chubanshe, 1990.

Lai, Whalen. "The *Mahāyānaparinirvāna Sūtra* and Its Earliest Interpreters in China: Two Prefaces by Tao-lang and Tao-sheng." *Journal of the American Oriental Society* 102, 1 (1982): 99–105.

Lamotte, Étienne. *Le traité de la grande vertu de sagesse de Nāgārjuna (Mahāprajñāpāramitāśāstra)*. Vols. 1–5. Louvain-la-Neuve: Institut Orientaliste, Université de Louvain, 1944–81.

Latour, Bruno. *We Have Never Been Modern*. Cambridge, Mass.: Harvard University Press, 1993.

Leslie, Alan M. "*Pretending* and *Believing*: Issues in the Theory of ToMM." *Cognition* 50, 1–3, (1994): 211–38.

Lévi, Sylvain M. "Catalogue géographique des yakṣa dans la Mahāmāyūrī." *Journal Asiatique* 5 (1915).

Li, Fengmao 李豐楙. "Wuying xinyang yu Zhongtan yuanshuai: qi yuanshi ji yanbian." 五營信仰與中壇元帥: 其原始及衍變. In *Diyijie Nezha xueshu yantaohui lunwenji*, ed. Guoli Zhongshan daxue. 549–94.

Li, Jining 李際寧. *Fojing banben* 佛經版本. Nanjing: Jiangsu guji Chubanshe 南京江蘇古籍出版社, 2002.

Li, Naiyang 李迺揚, ed. Baolin zhuan—*Chuandeng yuying ji* 寶林傳・傳燈玉英集. Kyoto 京都: Chūbun shuppansha 中文出版社, 1983.

Li, Qiao 李喬. *Zhongguo hangye shen chongbai* 中國行業神崇拜. Beijing: Zhongguo Huaqiao, 1990.

Li, Rongxi. *The Great Tang Dynasty Record of the Western Regions*. BDK English Tripitaka 79. Berkeley, Calif.: Numata Center, 1996.

Li, Xiaorong 李小榮. "Nazha gushi qiyuan bukao" 那吒故事起源補考, *Ming Qing xiaoshuo yanjiu* 65 (2002.3): 139–49.

Liebenthal, Walter. "The World Conception of Chu Tao-Sheng." *Monumenta Nipponica* 12, 1–2 (1956): 65–103; 241–268.

Lincoln, Bruce. *Death, War, and Sacrifice: Studies in Ideology and Practice*. Chicago: University of Chicago Press. 1991.

Link, Arthur. "Tao-sheng: A Biographical Essay." Ph.D. dissertation, University of California, Berkeley, 1957.

Liu, Cunren 柳存仁 [Liu Ts'un-Yan]. "Pishamen tianwang fuzi yu Zhongguo xiaoshuo zhi guanxi" 毗沙門天王父子與中國小說之關係. In volume 2 of his *Hefengtang wenji* 和風堂文集. Shanghai: Shanghai guji, 1991. 1045–94.

Liu, Ming-Wood. "The Doctrine of the Buddha-Nature in the Mahāyāna *Mahāparinirvāna-sūtra*." *Journal of the International Association of Buddhist Studies* 5, 2 (1982): 63–94.

——. *Madhyamaka Thought in China*. Leiden: Brill, 1994.

——. "The Problem of the *Icchantika* in the Mahāyāna *Mahaparinirvāna-sūtra*." *Journal of the International Association of Buddhist Studies* 7, 1 (1984): 57–81.

Liu, Shufen 劉淑芬. *Miezui yu duwang: Foding zunsheng tuoluoni jing chuang zhi yanjiu* 滅罪與度亡: 佛頂尊勝陀羅尼經幢之研究. Shanghai: Shanghai guji, 2008.

Liu, Ts'un-Yan. *Buddhist and Taoist Influences on Chinese Novels, Volume 1: The Authorship of the Feng Shen Yen I*. Wiesbaden: Kommissionsverlag, 1962.

Liu, Xinru. *Ancient India and Ancient China: Trade and Religious Exchange AD 1–600*. Oxford: Oxford University Press, 1988.

Liu, Yongzeng 劉永增. "*Xianyu jing* de jicheng niandai yu Dunhuang Mogaoku di 275 ku de kaizao." 《贤愚经》的集成年代与敦煌莫高窟第275窟的开凿. *Dunhuang yanjiu* 敦煌研究 70 (2001): 70–74.

Lu, Hsun. *A Brief History of Chinese Fiction*. Peking: Foreign Languages Press, 1976.

Luo, Shixian 羅時憲. "Tang Wudai zhi fanan yu Zhongguo" 唐五代之法難與中國. *Pumen Xuebao* 普門學報 50 (2009): 272–83.

Lusthaus, Dan. *Buddhist Phenomenology: A Philosophical Investigation of Yogācāra Buddhism and the Ch'eng Wei-Shih Lun*. Curzon Critical Studies in Buddhism 13. Richmond, Surrey: Routledge Curzon, 2002.

MacDonald, Ariane, ed. *Le Maṇḍala du Mañjuśrīmūlakalpa*. Paris: Adrien Maisonneuve, 1962.

Maeda, Shigeki 前田繁樹. "Between Karmic Retribution and Entwining Infusion." In *Daoism in History, Essays in Honour of Liu Ts'un-yan,* ed. Benjamin Penny. London: Routledge, 2006. 110–13.

———. *Shoki dōkyō kyōten no keisei* 初期道教經典の形成. Tokyo: Kyūko, 2004.

———. "Tonkōhon to dōzōhon no sai ni tsuite: ko Reihōgyo o chūshin to shite 敦煌本と道藏本の差異について—古靈寶經を中心として." *Tōhō shūkyō* 東方宗教 84 (1994): 1–19.

Mair, Victor. "Cheng Ch'iao's Understanding of Sanskrit: The Concept of Spelling in China." In *A Festschrift in Honour of Professor Jao Tsung-I on the Occasion of His Seventy-Fifth Anniversary*. Hong Kong: Chinese University of Hong Kong Press, 1993. 331–41.

———. "The Contributions of T'ang and Five Dynasties Transformation Texts (*pien-wen*) to Later Chinese Popular Literature." *Sino-Platonic Papers* 12 (August 1989): 1–71.

———, ed. *The Columbia Anthology of Traditional Chinese Literature*. New York: Columbia University Press, 1984.

———. "The Linguistic and Textual Antecedents of *The Sūtra of the Wise and the Foolish* (*Hsien-yü ching*): With an Appended Translation of 'Sudatta Raises a Monastery.'" *Sino-Platonic Papers* 38 (1993): 1–95.

———. "A Medieval, Central Asian Buddhist Theme in a Late Ming Taoist Tale by Feng Meng-lung." *Sino-Platonic Papers* 95 (May 1999): 1–27.

———. "The Narrative Revolution in Chinese Literature: Ontological Presuppositions." *Chinese Literature: Essays, Articles, Reviews* 5, 1 (July 1983; published July 1985): 1–27.

———. "The North(west)ern Peoples and the Recurrent Origins of the 'Chinese' State." In *The Teleology of the Modern Nation-State: Japan and China*, ed. Joshua A. Fogel. Philadelphia: University of Pennsylvania Press, 2005. 46–84.

———. *Painting and Performance: Chinese Picture Recitation and Its Indian Genesis*. Honolulu: University of Hawai'i Press, 1988.

———. "A Partial Bibliography for the Study of Indian Influence on Chinese Popular Literature." *Sino-Platonic Papers* 3 (March 1987).

———. "Records of Transformation Tableaux (*pien-hsiang*)." *T'oung Pao* 72 (1986): 3–43.

———. "Sariputra Defeats the Six Heterodox Masters: Oral-Visual Aspects of an Illustrated Transformation Scroll (P4524)." *Asia Major* 3rd ser. 8, 2 (1995): 1–52, 3 plates.

———. "Suen Wu-kung = Hanumat? The Progress of a Scholarly Debate." *Proceedings of the Second International Conference on Sinology*.Section on Literature. Taipei: Academia Sinica, 1989. 659–752.

———. *T'ang Transformation Texts: A Study of the Buddhist Contribution to the Rise of Vernacular Fiction and Drama in China*. Harvard-Yenching Institute Monograph Series 28. Cambridge, Mass.: Harvard University Council on East Asian Studies, 1989.

———. *Tun-huang Popular Narratives*. Cambridge: Cambridge University Press, 1983.

———. "What Is Geyi After All?" In *Philosophy and Religion in Early Medieval China*, ed. Alan Chan and Y. K. Lo. Albany: State University of New York Press Press, 2010.

———. "Xie He's 'Six Laws' of Painting and Their Indian Parallels." In *Chinese Aesthetics: The Ordering of Literature, the Arts, and the Universe in the Six Dynasties*, ed. Zong-qi Cai. Honolulu: University of Hawai'i Press, 2004. 81–122.

Mair, Victor, and Tsu-lin Mei. "The Sanskrit Origins of Recent Style Prosody." *Harvard Journal of Asiatic Studies* 51, 2 (December 1991): 375–470.

Mak, Benise S. K., and Alonso H. Vera. "The Role of Motion in Children's Categorization of Objects." *Cognition* 71, 3 (1999): B11–21.

Malamoud, Charles. *Le jumeau solaire*. Paris: Seuil, 2002

Masson, J. L. "The Childhood of Kṛṣṇa: Some Psychoanalytic Observations." *Journal of the American Oriental Society* 49, 4 (October–December 1974): 454–59.

Matchett, Freda. *Kṛṣṇa: Lord or Avatāra? The Relationship Between Kṛṣṇa and Viṣṇu*. Richmond: Curzon, 2001.

———. "The Taming of Kāliya: A Comparison of the Harivaṃśa, Viṣṇu-Purāṇa and Bhāgavata-Purāṇa Versions." *Religion* 16 (1986): 115–33.

Mather, Richard."Chinese and Indian Perceptions of Each Other Between the First and Seventh Centuries." *Journal of the American Oriental Society* 112, 1 (1992): 1–8.

McRae, John R. *The Northern School and the Formation of Early Ch'an Buddhism*. Honolulu: University of Hawai'i Press, 1986.

———. "The Northern School of Chinese Ch'an Buddhism." Ph.D. dissertation, Yale University, 1983.

———. "The Ox-Head School of Chinese Ch'an Buddhism: From Early Ch'an to the Golden Age." In *Studies in Ch'an and Hua-yen*, ed. Robert M. Gimello and Peter N. Gregory. Kuroda Institute Studies in East Asian Buddhism. Honolulu: University of Hawai'i Press, 1983. 169–252.

———. *Seeing Through Zen: Encounter, Transformation, and Genealogy in Chinese Zen Buddhism*. Berkeley: University of California Press, 2003.

———. "State Formation, Indigenization, and Buddhism in East Asian History: The Theoretical Foundation." *Indo tetsugaku bukkyōgaku kenkyū* インド哲學佛教學研究 13 (2006): 45–72.

Metzinger, Thomas. *Being No One: The Self-Model Theory of Subjectivity*. Cambridge, Mass.: MIT Press, 2003.

Meulenbeld, Mark R. E. "Civilized Demons: Ming Thunder Gods from Ritual to Literature." Ph.D. dissertation, Princeton University, 2007.

Mitchell, Peter. *Introduction to Theory of Mind: Children, Autism, and Apes*. London: Arnold, 1997.

Miyamoto, Shōson 宮本正尊. " 'Sōmoku kokudo shikkai jōbutsu' no busshōronteki igi to sono sakusha「草木國土悉皆成佛」の佛性論的意義とその作者." *Indogaku Bukkōgaku kenkyū* 9, 2 (1961): 672–701.

Mochizuki, Shinkō 望月信亨, ed. *Bukkyō daijiten* 佛教大辭典. 3rd ed., 10 vols. Kyoto: Sekai seiten kankô kyôkai, 1954–71.

Mollier, Christine. *Une apocalypse taoïste du début du Ve siècle: Le Livre des Incantations Divines des Grottes Abyssales*. Mémoires de l'Institut des Hautes Études Chinoises 31. Paris: Collège de France, 1990.

——. "Visions of Evil: Demonology and Orthodoxy in Early Taoism." In *Daoism in History: Essays in Honour of Liu Ts'un-yan*, ed. Benjamin Penny. London: Routledge, 2006. 87–93.

Monier-Williams, Monier. *A Sanskrit-English Dictionary, Etymologically and Philologically Arranged with Special Reference to Cognate Indo-European Languages*. 1899. Reprint Oxford: Clarendon Press, 1979.

Morris, Brian. *Anthropology of the Self: The Individual in Cultural Perspective*. London: Pluto Press, 1994.

Nagao, Kayoko 佳代子."Kan'yaku butten ni okeru 'kushōjin' no kaishaku" 漢訳仏典における倶生神の解釈. *Pāri-gaku bukkyō bunkagaku* パーリ学仏教文化学 13 (1999): 55–66.

——. "Kushōjin no tenkai" 倶生神の展開. *Bukkyō bunka* 仏教文化 10 (2000): 43–70.

Nagar, Shanti Lal. *Śiva-Mahāpurāṇa (An Exhaustive Introduction, Sanskrit Text, English Translation, with Photographs of Archaeological Evidence)*. 3 vols. Delhi: Parimal Publications, 2007.

Nagel, Thomas. *The View from Nowhere*. Oxford: Oxford University Press, 1986.

——. "What Is It Like to Be a Bat?" In *The Mind's I: Fantasies and Reflections on Self and Soul*, ed. Douglas R. Hofstadter and Daniel C. Dennett. New York: Basic Books, 1981. 391–403. Originally published in *Philosophical Review* 83 (1974): 435–50.

Nakamura, Teiri 中村禎里. *Kitsune no Nihon shi: Kodai · chūsei-hen* 狐の日本史—古代·中世篇. Tokyo: Nihon editā sukūru shuppanbu, 2001.

Ñāṇamoli, Bhikkhu, and Bhikkhu Bodhi. *The Middle Length Discourses of the Buddha: A Translation of the Majjhima Nikāya*. Oxford: Pali Text Society, 1995.

Nattier, Jan. *A Guide to the Earliest Chinese Buddhist Translations*. Tokyo: International Research Institute for Advanced Buddhology, Soka University, 2008.

——. "The *Heart Sūtra*: A Chinese Apocryphal Text?" *Journal of the International Association of Buddhist Studies* 15, 2 (1992): 153–223.

Neisser, Ulric, and David A. Jopling, eds. *The Conceptual Self in Context: Culture, Experience, Self-Understanding*. Emory Symposia in Cognition 7. Cambridge: Cambridge University Press, 1997.

Ng, Zhiru. *The Making of a Savior Bodhisattva: Dizang in Medieval China*. Studies in Medieval Buddhism 21. Honolulu: University of Hawai'i Press, 2007.

Nikaido, Yoshihirō 二階堂善弘. "Nata taishi kō" 那吒太子考. In *Dōkyō no rekishi to bunka* 道教の歴史と文化, ed. Yamada Toshiaki 山田利明 and Tanaka Fumio 田中文雄. Tokyo: Yūzankaku, 1998. 176–96.

O'Flaherty, Wendy Doniger. *Hindu Myths: A Sourcebook Translated from the Sanskrit*. Middlesex: Penguin, 1976.

——. *Śiva: The Erotic Ascetic*. Oxford: Oxford University Press, 1973, 1981.

Ōfuchi, Ninji 大淵忍爾. *Dōkyō shi no kenkyū* 道教史の研究. Okayama: Okayama Daigaku Kyōzaikai Shoseki-bu, 1964.

——. "On *Ku Ling-pao ching*." *Acta Asiatica* 27 (1974): 33–56.

——. *Shoki no dōkyō* 初期の道教. Tokyo: Sōbunsha, 1991.

——. *Tonkō dōkyō* 敦煌道教. Tokyo: Fukutake shoten, 1978.

Ōfuchi, Ninji, with Ishii Masako 石井昌子 and Ozaki Masaharu 尾崎正治, eds. *Rikuchō Tō Sō no kobunken shōin Dōkyō tenseki mokuroku, sakuin* 六朝唐宋古文獻所引, 道教典籍目錄—所引 (revised edition). Tokyo: Kokusho kankōkai, 1999.

Ohnuma, Reiko. *Heads, Eyes, Flesh, and Blood: Giving Away the Body in Buddhist Literature*. New York: Columbia University Press, 2006.

Okimoto, Katsumi 沖本克己. *Zoku kōsōden* Kōshōji-bon ni tsuite 『續高僧傳』興聖寺本について. http://iriz.hanazono.ac.jp/frame/k_room_f2.html/.

Ono, Genmyō 小野玄妙. *Kendara no Bukkyō bijutsu* 健駄邏の佛教美術 (Buddhist Art of Gandhāra). Tokyo: Heigo Shuppansha 丙午出版社, 1923.

Orzech, Charles. *Politics and Transcendent Wisdom: The Scripture of the Humane Kings in the Creation of Chinese Buddhism*. University Park: Pennsylvania State University Press, 1998.

Orzech, Charles D., Henrik H. Sørensen, and Richard K. Payne, eds. *Esoteric Buddhism and the Tantras in East Asia*. Leiden: Brill, 2011.

Osabe, Kazuo 長部和雄. *Tō Sō Mikkyōshi ronkō* 唐宋密教史論考. Kyoto, 1982.

Overmyer, Daniel L. *Precious Volumes: An Introduction to Chinese Sectarian Scriptures from the Sixteenth and Seventeenth Centuries*. Cambridge, Mass.: Harvard University Asia Center, 1999.

Owen, Stephen. *An Anthology of Chinese Literature: Beginnings to 1911*. New York: Norton, 1996.

——. *Readings in Chinese Literary Thought*. Cambridge, Mass.: Harvard University Press, 1992.

Pan, Jixing 潘吉星. "Lun Hanguo faxian de yinben 'Wugoujingguang da tuoluoni jing 論韓國發現的印本《無垢浄光大陀羅尼經》.'" *Kexue tongbao* 科學通報 42, 10 (1997): 1009–28.

Pelliot, Paul. "Autour d'une traduction Sanscrite du Tao Tö King." *T'oung Pao* 13, 3 (1912): 351–430.

——. Notes sur quelques artistes des six dynasties et des T'ang." *T'oung pao* 22 (1923).

Penkower, Linda. "T'ien-t'ai During the T'ang Dynasty: Chan-jan and the Sinification of Buddhism." Ph.D. dissertation, Columbia University, 1993.

Piṅgaḷi, Sūranna. *The Sound of the Kiss, or The Story That Must Never Be Told*. Trans. Velcheru Narayana Rao and David Shulman. New York: Columbia University Press, 2002.

Poulin-Dubois, Diane, Anouk Lepage, and Doreen Ferland. "Infants' Concept of Animacy." *Cognitive Development* 11, 1 (1996): 19–36.

Premack, David. "The Infant's Theory of Self-Propelled Motion." *Cognition* 36, 1 (1990): 1–16.

Prusek, Jaroslav. *Chinese History and Literature: Collection of Studies*. Prague: Academia, 1970.

Qiu, Dezai 仇德哉. *Taiwan miao shen zhuan* 台灣廟神傳. Douliu: Xintong, 1985.

Rakison, David H., and Diane Poulin-Dubois. «Developmental Origin of the Animate-Inanimate Distinction.» *Psychological Bulletin* 127, 2 (2001): 209–28.

Ramanujan, A. K. "The Indian 'Oedipus.'" In *Indian Literature: Proceedings of a Seminar*, ed. Arabinda Poddar. Simla: Indian Institute of Advanced Study, 1972. 127–37.

Rambelli, Fabio. *Vegetal Buddhas: Ideological Effects of Japanese Buddhist Doctrines on the Salvation of Inanimate Beings*. Italian School of East Asian Studies Occasional Papers Series, 9. Kyoto: Italian School of East Asian Studies, 2001.

Reischauer, Edwin O. *Ennin's Diary: The Record of a Pilgrimage to China in Search of the Law*. New York: Ronald Press, 1955.

Rhi, Ju-hyung. "Gandhāran Images of the 'Śrāvastī Miracle': An Iconographic Reassessment." Ph.D. dissertation, University of California, Berkeley, 1991.

Rhie, Marilyn Martin. *Early Buddhist Art of China and Central Asia*, vol. 2, *The Eastern China and Sixteen Kingdoms in China and Tumshuk, Kucha and Karashahr in Central Asia*. Leiden: Brill, 2002.

Robinson, Richard H. *Early Mādhyamika in India and China*. Delhi: Motilal Banarsidass, 1976.

Robson, James, "Signs of Power: Talismanic Writing in Chinese Buddhism." *History of Religions* 48, 2 (November 2008): 130–69.

Sakamoto, Yukio 阪本幸男. "Hijō ni okeru busshō no umu ni tsuite—toku ni Tannen, Chōkan o chūshin to shite 非情に於ける佛性の有無について— 特に湛然、澄觀を中心として." *Indogaku Bukkyōgaku kenkyū* 7, 2 (1959): 21–30.

———. "On the 'Attainment of Buddhahood' by Trees and Plants." In *Proceedings of the Ninth International Congress for the History of Religions*. Tokyo: Maruzen, 1960. 415–22.

Sangren, P. Steven. *Chinese Sociologies: An Anthropological Account of the Role of Alienation in Social Reproduction*. London School of Economics Monographs on Social Anthropology 72. London: Athlone, 2000.

Sasaki Ritsuko 佐々木律子. "Tonkō Bakkōkutsu dai 285 kutsu seiheki naiyō kaishaku shiron 敦煌莫高窟第二八五窟西壁 内容解釈試論." *Bijutsushi* 美術史 142 (1997): 121–38.

Sawada Mizuho 澤田瑞穂. *Jigoku-hen: Chūgoku no meikai setsu* 地獄變—中国の冥界說. Kyoto: Hōzōkan, 1968.

Schafer, Edward H. *The Golden Peaches of Samarkand: A Study of T'ang Exotics*. Berkeley: University of California Press, 1963.

——. *The Vermilion Bird: T'ang Images of the South*. Berkeley: University of California Press, 1967.

Schipper, Kristofer. "Purity and Strangers: Shifting Boundaries in Medieval Taoism." *T'oung-pao* 80 (1994): 61–81.

——. *The Taoist Canon: A Historical Companion to the* Daozang. Chicago: University of Chicago Press, 2004.

Schlingloff, Dieter. *Ein buddhistisches Yogalehrbuch,* Tafelband. Sanskrittexte aus den Turfanfunden. Vol. 7a. Berlin: Akademie-Verlag, 1966.

——. *Ein buddhistisches Yogalehrbuch,* Textband. Sanskrittexte aus den Turfanfunden. Vol. 7. Berlin: Akademie-Verlag, 1964.

——. *Ein buddhistisches Yogalehrbuch*, repr. (2 pts. in 1), with editions of the subsequently identified manuscripts. Ed. Jens-Uwe Hartmann and Hermann-Josef Röllicke. Munich: Iudicium, 2006.

Schmidt, Hans-Hermann. "Taishang lingbao zhutian neiyin ziran yuzi." In *The Taoist Canon: A Historical Companion to the* Daozang, ed. Kristofer Schipper and Franciscus Verellen, vol. 1. Chicago: University of Chicago Press, 2004.

Schmithausen, Lambert. *Ālayavijñāna: On the Origin and the Early Development of a Central Concept of Yogācāra Philosophy*. 2 vols. 1987. Reprint with addenda and corrigenda, Studia Philologica Buddhica Monograph Series 4a/b. Tokyo: International Institute for Buddhist Studies of the International College for Postgraduate Buddhist Studies, 2007.

——. "On Some Aspects of Descriptions or Theories of 'Liberating Insight' and 'Enlightenment' in Early Buddhism." In *Studien zum Jainismus und Buddhismus*, ed. Klaus Bruhn and Albrecht Wezler. Wiesbaden: Franz Steiner, 1981. 199–250.

——. "On the Problem of the Relation of Spiritual Practice and Philosophical Theory in Buddhism." In *German Scholars on India,* vol. 2, ed. Cultural Department of the Delhi Embassy of the Federal Republic of Germany. Bombay: Nachiketa, 1976. 235–50.

——. *Plants in Early Buddhism and the Far Eastern Idea of the Buddha-Nature of Grasses and Trees*. Lumbini: Lumbini International Research Institute, 2009.

Schopen, Gregory. "The Bhaiśajyagurusūtra and the Buddhism of Gilgit." Ph.D. dissertation, Australian National University, 1978.

Seaman, Gary, and Victor H. Mair, trans. "Romance of the Investiture of the Gods." Attributed to Lu Xixing. In *Hawai'i Reader in Traditional Chinese Culture*, ed. Victor H. Mair et al. Honolulu: University of Hawai'i Press, 2005. 467–89.

Seidel, Anna. "Danda." In *Hōbōgirin: Dictionnaire encyclopédique du bouddhisme d'après les sources chinoises et japonaises*, vol. 8. Paris: Maisonneuve, 2003. 1113–22.

Sen, Tansen. *Buddhism, Diplomacy, and Trade: The Realignment of Sino-Indian Relations 600–1400*. Asian Interactions and Comparisons. Honolulu: Association for Asian Studies and University of Hawai'i Press, 2003.

Shahar, Meir. *The Shaolin Monastery: History, Religion, and the Chinese Martial Arts*. Honolulu: University of Hawai'i Press, 2008.

Sharf, Robert H. *Coming to Terms with Chinese Buddhism: A Reading of the "Treasure*

Store Treatise." Kuroda Institute Studies in East Asian Buddhism. Honolulu: University of Hawai'i Press, 2002.

——. "How to Think with Chan *Gongans*." In *Thinking with Cases: Specialized Knowledge in Chinese Cultural History*, ed. Charlotte Furth, Judith Zeitlin, and Hsiung Ping-chen. Honolulu: University of Hawai'i Press, 2007. 205–43.

——. "Mindfulness and Mindlessness in Early Chan." *History of Religions*, forthcoming.

Sharma, Arvind. "The Significance of Viṣṇu Reclining on the Serpent." *Religion* 16 (1986): 101–14.

Shen, Hsueh-Man. "Realizing the Buddha's 'Dharma' Body During the Mofa Period: A Study of Liao Buddhist Relic Deposits." *Artibus Asiae* 61, 2 (2001): 263–303.

Shinkyō Uiguru Jichiku Bunbutsu Kanri Iinkai 新疆ウイグル自治区文物管理委員会 and Haijōken Kijiru Senbutsudō Bunbutsu Hokanjo 拝城県キジル千仏洞窟文物保管所, eds. *Chūgoku sekkutsu Kijiru sekkutsu* 中国石窟キジル石窟. Vol. 3. Tokyo: Heibonsha 平凡社, 1985.

Shinohara, Koichi "The Maitreyan Image in Shichen and Guanding's Biography of Zhiyi." In *From Benares to Beijing: Essays on Buddhism and Chinese Religion in Honour of Prof. Jan Yün-Hua*, ed. Koichi Shinohara and Gregory Schopen. Oakville, Ont.: Mosaic Press, 1991.

——. "Two Sources of Chinese Biographies: Stupa Inscriptions and Miracle Stories." In *Monks and Magicians: Religious Biographies in Asia*, ed. Phyllis Granoff and Koichi Shinohara. Oakville, Ont.: Mosaic Press, 1988.

Shively, Donald H. "Buddhahood for the Nonsentient: A Theme in No Plays." *Harvard Journal of Asiatic Studies* 20, 1–2 (1957): 135–61.

Siklós, Bulcsu. "The Evolution of the Buddhist Yama." In *The Buddhist Forum*, ed. Tadeusz Skorupski, vol. 4. London: SOAS, 1996.

Silk, Jonathan A. *Riven by Lust: Incest and Schism in Indian Buddhist Legend and Historiography*. Honolulu: University of Hawai'i Press, 2009.

Simons, Daniel J., and Frank C. Keil. "An Abstract to Concrete Shift in the Development of Biological Thought: The *Insides* Story." *Cognition* 56, 2 (1994): 129–53.

Smith, Jonathan Z., ed. *The HarperCollins Dictionary of Religion*. San Francisco: Harper, 1995.

Snodgrass, Adrian. *The Matrix and Diamond World Mandalas in Shingon Buddhism*. 2 vols. New Delhi: Aditya Prakashan 1988.

Soper, Alexander Coburn. "Aspects of Light Symbolism in Gandhāran Sculpture." *Artibus Asiae* 12 (1949): 252–83.

——. "Aspects of Light Symbolism in Gandhāran Sculpture: Continuation." *Artibus Asiae* 12 (1949): 314–30.

——. "Contributions to the Study of Sculpture and Architecture III: Japanese Evidence for the History of the Architecture and Iconography of Chinese Buddhism." *Monumenta Serica* 4 (1940): 638–78.

Sørensen, Henrik H. "The Spell of the Great, Golden Peacock Queen: The Origin,

Practices, and Lore of an Early Esoteric Buddhist Tradition in China." *Pacific World* 3rd ser., 8 (Fall 2006): 89–123.

Soymié, Michel. "Les dix jours de jeûne de Kṣitigarbha." In *Contributions aux études sur Touen-houang*, ed. Michel Soymié. Geneva: Droz, 1979. 135–59.

———. "Notes d'iconographie chinoise: les acolytes de Ti-tsang (1)." *Arts Asiatiques* 14 (1966): 45–73.

Stafford, Charles. *The Roads of Chinese Childhood: Learning and Identification in Angang*. Cambridge Studies in Social and Cultural Anthropology 97. Cambridge: Cambridge University Press, 1995.

Stein, Rolf A. "The Guardian of the Gate: An Example of Buddhist Mythology, from India to Japan." In *Asian Mythologies*, ed. Yves Bonnefoy and Wendy Doniger. Chicago: University of Chicago Press, 1991. 119–21.

Strickmann, Michel. *Chinese Magical Medicine*, ed. Bernard Faure. Asian Religions and Cultures. Stanford, Calif.: Stanford University Press, 2002.

———. *Mantras et mandarins: Le bouddhisme tantrique en Chine*. Paris: Gallimard, 1996.

Strong, John S. *The Legend and Cult of Upagupta: Sanskrit Buddhism in North India and Southeast Asia*. Princeton, N.J.: Princeton University Press, 1992; reprint Delhi: Motilal Banrsidass, 1994.

———. *The Legend of King Aśoka: A Study and Translation of the "Aśokāvadāna."* Princeton, N.J.: Princeton University Press, 1983.

———. *Relics of the Buddha*. Princeton, N.J.: Princeton University Press, 2004.

Sueki, Fumihiko 末木文美士. "Annen *Shinjō sōmoku jōbutsu shiki* ni tsuite 安然「斟定草木成佛私記」について." *Tōhōgaku* 80 (1990): 97–110.

———. "Annen: The Philosopher Who Japanized Buddhism." *Acta Asiatica: Bulletin of the Institute of Eastern Culture (Tōhōgakkai)* 66 (1994): 69–86.

Tachikawa, Musasi 立川武蔵, Ishiguro Atsushi 石黒淳, Hishida Kunio 菱田邦男, and Shima Iwao 島岩. *Hindū no kamigami* ヒンドゥーの神々. Tokyo: Serika Shobō せりか書房, 1980.

Tagare, Ganesh Vasudeo, trans. *The Bhāgavata-Purāṇa*. Ancient Indian Tradition and Mythology Series. 5 vols. Delhi: Motilal Banarsidass, 1976–78.

Takakusu, Junjiro. *A Record of the Buddhist Religion as Practiced in India and the Malay Archipelago (A.D. 671–695)*. Oxford: Clarendon, 1896.

Tan, Zhihui. "Daoxuan's Vision of Jetavana: Imagining a Utopian Monastery in Early Tang." Ph.D. dissertation, University of Arizona, 2002.

Tanaka, Ryōshō 田中良昭, *Hōrinden yakuchū* 宝林伝訳注. Tokyo: Uchiyama shoten 内山書店, 2003.

Tang, Yongtong 湯用彤. *Han Wei liang Jin nanbeichao Fojiao shi* 漢魏兩晉南北朝佛教史. 2 vols. Beijing: Zhonghua shuju, 1955. Originally published in Shanghai, 1938.

Taylor, Charles. *Sources of the Self: The Making of the Modern Identity*. Cambridge: Harvard University Press, 1989.

Teiser, Stephen F. *The Ghost Festival in Medieval China*. Princeton, N.J.: Princeton University Press, 1988, 1996.

———. *The Scripture on the Ten Kings and the Making of Purgatory in Medieval Chinese Buddhism*. Honolulu: University of Hawai'i Press, 1994.

Thiṭṭila, Paṭhamakyaw Ashin, trans. *The Book of Analysis (Vibhaṅga): The Second Book of the Abhidhamma Piṭaka*. Oxford: Pali Text Society, 1969.

Tokiwa, Daijo 常盤大定. *Busshō no kenkyū* 佛性の研究. Tokyo: Kokusho kankōkai, 1973.

Tokiwa, Gishin 常盤義伸 and Yanagida Seizan 柳田聖山. *Zekkanron: Eibun yakuchū, gembun kōtei, kokuyaku* 絕觀論：英文譯注·原文佼定·國譯. Kyoto: Zenbunka kenkyūjo, 1973.

Tokiwai, Gyōyū. *The Sumāgadhāvadāna: A Buddhist Legend*. Tokyo: Isshinden, 1969.

Tonkō Bunbutsu Kenkyūjo 敦煌文物研究所, ed. *Chūgoku sekkutsu Tonkō Bakkōkutsu* 中国石窟敦煌莫高窟 (Chinese Caves, Dunhuang Mogao Caves). Vol. 1. Tokyo: Heibonsha 平凡社, 1980.

Tsukinowa, Kenryū 月輪賢隆. *Butten no hihanteki kenkyū* 仏典の批判的研究. Kyoto: Hyakkaen 百華苑, 1971.

Unkō Sekkutsu Bunbutsu Hokanjo 雲岡石窟文物保管所, ed. *Chūgoku sekkutsu Unkō sekkutsu* 中国石窟雲岡石窟. Vol. 1. Tokyo: Heibonsha 平凡社, 1989.

Vaidya, P. L., ed. *Divyāvadānam*, Buddhist Sanskrit Texts 20. Dharbhanga, Bihar: Mithila Institute, 1959.

Van den Bosch, Lourens P. "Yama—The God on the Black Buffalo." In *Commemorative Figures*, ed. H. G. Kippenberg, L. P. van den Bosch, and L. Leertouwer. Visible Religion 1. Leiden: Brill, 1982. 21–61.

Van Gulik, Robert Hans. *Hayagrīva: The Mantrayānic Aspect of the Horse-Cult in China and Japan*. Leiden: Brill, 1935.

Vandier-Nicolas, Nicole, trans. and comm. *Sariputra et les Six maîtres d'erreur*. Fac-similé du Manuscrit Chinois 4524 de la Bibliothèque National Mission Pelliot en Asie Centrale, Série in-Quarto, V. Paris: Imprimerie Nationale, 1954.

Varela, Francisco J., Evan Thompson, and Eleanor Rosch. *The Embodied Mind: Cognitive Science and Human Experience*. Cambridge, Mass.: MIT Press, 1991.

Vasubandhu. *Abhidharmakośabhāṣyam*. 4 vols. Trans. Leo M. Pruden from the French translation of Louis de La Vallée Poussin. Berkeley, Calif.: Asian Humanities Press, 1988.

Verellen, Franciscus. "The Celestial Master Liturgical Agenda According to Chisong Zi's Petition Almanac." *Cahiers d'Extrême-Asie* 14 (2004): 291–344.

Waley, Arthur, trans. *Monkey*. 1943. New York: Grove, 1958.

Walshe, Maurice. *Thus Have I Heard: The Long Discourses of the Buddha, Dīgha Nikāya*. London: Wisdom, 1987.

Wang, Bangwei 王邦維. "Buddhist Nikāyas Through Ancient Chinese Eyes." In *Untersuchungen zur buddhistischen Literatur*. Sanskrit-Wörterbuch der buddhistischen Texte aus den Turfan-Funden, Beiheft 5. Göttingen: Vandenhoeck und Ruprecht, 1995. 166–203.

———. *Nanhai jigui neifa zhuan jiaozhu* 南海寄歸內法傳校注. Beijing: Zhonghua shuju, 2000.

Wang, Chengwen 王承文. *Dunhuang gu Lingbao jing yu Jin Tang daojiao* 敦煌古靈寶經與晉唐道教. Beijing: Zhonghua, 2002.

Wang, Li 王力. "'Baoqieyinjing ta' yu Wuyue guo dui ri wenhua jiaoliu 寶篋印經塔輿吳越國對日文化交流." *Zhejiang daxue xuebao* (*Renwen shehui kexue bao*) 浙江大學學報(人文社會科學報) 32, 5 (2002).

Wang, Shilun 王士倫. "Jinhua Wanfota taji qingli jianbao 金華萬佛塔塔基清理簡報." *Wenwu cankao ziliao* 文物參考資料 4 (1957), 41–46.

Wang, Xinxi 王心喜. "Qianshi Wuyueguo yu riben de jiaowang ji qi zai zhongri wenhua jiaoliusi shang de diwei 錢氏吳越國輿日本的交往及其在中日文化交流史上的地位." *Zhongguo wenhua yanjiu* 中國文化研究 2003 (Fall): 60–67.

Wang, Yi-T'ung. *A Record of Buddhist Monasteries in Lo-yang*. Princeton, N.J.: Princeton University Press, 1984.

Wang-Toutain, Françoise. *Le bodhisattva Kṣitigarbha en Chine du Ve au XIIIe siècle*. Paris: École Française d'Extrême-Orient, 1998.

Watson, Burton. *The Complete Works of Chuang Tzu*. New York: Columbia University Press, 1968.

Wayman, Alex. "Studies in Yama and Māra." *Indo-Iranian Journal* 3, 1 (1959): 44–73.

Wegner, Daniel M. *The Illusion of Conscious Will*. Cambridge, Mass.: MIT Press, 2002.

Welbon, Guy Richard. *The Buddhist Nirvana and Its Western Interpreters*. Chicago: University of Chicago Press, 1968.

Weller, Friedrich. "Bemerkungen zum soghdischen Dhyāna-texte." Part 1. *Monumenta Serika* 2 (1936–37): 340–404.

Wellman, Henry M. *The Child's Theory of Mind*. Cambridge, Mass.: MIT Press, 1990.

Wen, Yucheng 溫玉成. *Shaolin fanggu* 少林訪古. Tianjin: Baihua wenyi, 1999.

Wessels-Mevissen, Corinna. *The Gods of the Directions in Ancient India: Origins and Early Development in Art and Literature*. Monographien zur indischen Archäologie, Kunst und Philologie, vol. 14. Berlin: Dietrich Reimer, 2001.

Whicher, Ian. "Nirodha, Yoga Praxis and the Transformation of the Mind." *Journal of Indian Philosophy* 25, 1 (1997): 1–67.

White, Geoffrey, and John Kirkpatrick, eds. *Person, Self, and Experience: Exploring Pacific Ethnopsychologies*. Berkeley: University of California Press, 1985.

Whitfield, Roderick. *The Art of Central Asia*. Trans. into Japanese Ueno Aki 上野アキ as *Saiiki bijutsu: Daiei Hakubutsukan Stain korekushon* 西域美術：大英博物館スタイン・コレクション. Vol. 3, *Someori, Chōso, Hekiga* 染織・彫塑・壁画. Tokyo: Kōdansha 講談社, 1984.

Wilkinson, Endymion. *Chinese History: A Manual*. Harvard-Yenching Institute Monograph Series 52. Cambridge, Mass.: Harvard University Asia Center, 2000.

Willemen, Charles. *The Chinese Hevajratantra: The Scriptural Text of the Ritual of the Great King of the Teaching, the Adamantine One with Great Compassion and Knowledge of the Void*. Orientalia Gandensia 8. Leuven: Peeters, 1983.

———. "The Prefaces to the Chinese *Dharmapadas, Fa-chu ching* and *Ch'u-yao ching*." *T'oung-pao* 59 (1973): 203–19.

Williams, Joanna. "The Iconography of Khotanese Painting." *East and West* n.s. 23, 1–2 (1973): 109–54.

Wu, Wenliang 吴文良. *Quanzhou zongjiao shike* 泉州宗教石刻 (Religious stone-carvings from Quanzhou). Revised and enlarged by Wu Youxiong 吴幼雄. Beijing: Kexue, 2005.

Xiao, Dengfu 蕭登福. "Nezha suyuan" 哪吒溯源. In Guoli Zhongshan daxue, *Diyijie Nezha xueshu yantaohui lunwenji*, 1–66.

Xinjiang Weiwu'er Zizhiqu Bowuguan 新疆维吾尔自治区博物馆, ed. *Xinjiang shiku, Tulufan Bozikelike shiku* 新疆石窟吐鲁番伯孜克里克石窟. Urumchi: Xinjiang Renmin Chubanshe 新疆人民出版社; Shanghai: Shanghai Renmin Meishu Chubanshe 上海人民美术出版社, 1990.

Xu, Dishan 許地山. "Fanju tili jiqi zai Hanjushang de diandian didi" 梵劇體例及其在漢劇上底點點滴滴. In *Zhongguo xiju qiyuan* 中國戲劇起源, ed. Xia Xieshi 夏寫時 et al. Shanghai: Zhishi Chubanshe, 1990. 86–118.

Yamabe, Nobuyoshi. "Could Turfan Be the Birthplace of Visualization Sutras?" In *Tulufanxue yanjiu: Dierjie Tulufanxue Guoji Xueshu Yantaohui lunwenji* 吐鲁番学研究：第二届吐鲁番学国际学术研讨会论文集, ed. Xinjiang Tulufan Diqu Wenwuju 新疆吐鲁番地区文物局. Shanghai: Shanghai Cishu Chubanshe, 2006. 419–30.

———. "An Examination of the Mural Paintings of Toyok Cave 20 in Conjunction with the Origin of the *Amitayus Visualization Sutra*." *Orientations* 30, 4 (1999): 38–44.

———. "An Examination of the Mural Paintings of Visualizing Monks in Toyok Cave 42: In Conjunction with the Origin of Some Chinese Texts on Meditation." In *Turfan Revisited: The First Century of Research into the Arts and Cultures of the Silk Road*, ed. Desmond Durkin-Meisterernst et al. Berlin: Dietrich Reimer, 2004.

———. "The *Ocean Sūtra* as a Cross-Cultural Product: An Analysis of Some Stories on the Buddha's 'Hidden Organ.'" In *"The Way of Buddha" 2003: The 100th Anniversary of the Otani Mission and the 50th of the Researh Society for Central Asian Cultures*, ed. Irisawa Takashi. Kyoto: Ryukoku University, 2010.

———. "Practice of Visualization and the *Visualization Sūtra*: An Examination of Mural Paintings at Toyok, Turfan." *Pacific World: Journal of the Institute of Buddhist Studies* 3rd ser., 4 (2002): 123–52.

———. "The Significance of the *'Yogalehrbuch'* for the Investigation into the Origin of Chinese Meditation Texts." *Bukkyō bunka* 佛教文化 9 (1999): 1–74.

———. "'The Sūtra on the Ocean-Like Samādhi of the Visualization of the Buddha': The Interfusion of the Chinese and Indian Cultures in Central Asia as Reflected in a Fifth-Century Apocryphal Sūtra." Ph.D. dissertation, Yale University, 1999.

Yampolsky, Philip B. *The Platform Sutra of the Sixth Patriarch: The Text of the Tun-huang Manuscript with Translation, Introduction, and Notes*. New York: Columbia University Press, 1967.

Yan, Yaozhong 嚴耀中. *Han chuan mijiao* 漢傳密教 (Chinese Tantric Buddhism). Shanghai: Xuelin, 1999.

Yanagida, Seizan 柳田聖山. *Sodōshū sakuin* 祖堂集索引. 3 vols. Kyoto: Kyōto daigaku jinbunkagaku kenkyūjo, 1984.

——. *Shoki no zenshi* 初期の禪史 1. Zen no goroku 禪の語錄 2. Kyoto: Chikuma shobō, 1971.

Yang, Qinzhang 楊欽章. "Quanzhou yindujiao pishinu shen xingxiang shike" 泉州印度教毗濕奴神形象石刻. *Shijie zongjiao yanjiu* 世界宗教研究 (1988.1): 96–105.

——. "Quanzhou yindujiao diaoke yuanyuan kao" 泉州印度教雕刻淵源考. *Shijie zongjiao yanjiu* 世界宗教研究 (1982.2): 87–94.

Ye, Derong 叶德荣. *Zong tong yu fa tong: Yi Songshan Shaolin si wei zhongxin* 宗統與法統以嵩山少林寺為中心. Guangzhou: Guangdong renmin, 2010.

Yiengpruksawan, Mimi Hall. "One Millionth of a Buddha: The *Hyakumantō Darani* in the Scheide Library." *Princeton University Library Chronicle* 48, 3 (1987): 224–38.

Yin Yuzhen 銀玉珍, and Zhu Geji 諸葛計, eds. *Wuyue shishi biannian* 吳越史事編年. Hangzhou: Zhejiang guji Chubanshe 浙江古籍出版社, 1987.

Yoshikawa, Isao 吉河功. *Sekizō hōkyōin-tō no seiritsu* 石造宝印塔の成立. Tokyo: Daiichi Shobō 第一書房, 2000.

Yoshioka, Yoshitoyo 吉岡義豐. *Dōkyō to Bukkyō* 道教と佛教. Tokyo: Kokusho kankōkai, 1976.

Yoshizu, Yoshihide 吉津宜英. "Mujō busshōsetsu no kōsatsu 無情佛性說の考察." [Sōtōshū] Shūgaku kenkyū 15 (March 1973): 110–15.

Young, Stuart H. "Conceiving the Indian Buddhist Patriarchs in China." Ph.D. dissertation, Princeton University, 2008.

Yu, Anthony C., trans. *The Journey to the West*. Chicago: University of Chicago Press, 1977–83.

Zacchetti, Stefano. *In Praise of Light: A Critical Synoptic Edition with an Annotated Translation of Chapters 1–3 Dharmarakṣa's* Guang zan jin 光讚經. Tokyo: International Research Institute for Advanced Buddhology, Soka University, 2005.

Zeng, Guodong 曾國棟. "Xinying Taizigong de lishi yanjiu" 新營太子宮的歷史研究. In *Nezha xueshu yantaohui lunwenji*, ed. Guoli Zhongshan daxue, *Diyijie*. 117–45.

Zhang, Xiumin 張秀民, "Wudai Wuyueguodeyinshua 五代吳越國的印刷." *Wenwu* 文物 12 (1978): 74–76

Zhao, Henry. *The Uneasy Narrator: Chinese Fiction from the Traditional to the Modern*. Oxford: Oxford University Press, 1995.

Zhao, Li. "Verification of the Original Locations of the Murals from Caves in Kizil Kept in the Museum für Indische Kunst, Berlin." In *Turfan Revisited: The First Century of Research into the Arts and Cultures of the Silk Road*, ed. Desmond Durkin-Meisterernst et al. Berlin: Dietrich Reimer, 2004. 418–23.

Zhiru. *The Making of a Savior Bodhisattva: Dizang in Medieval China*. Honolulu: University of Hawai'i Press, 2007.

Zhongguo Meishu Quanji Bianji Weiyuanhui 中國美術全集編輯委員會, ed. *Zhongguo Meishu Quanji: Huihua bian* 中國美術全集繪畫編. Vol. 16. Xinjiang shiku bihua 新疆石窟壁畫. Beijing: Wenwu Chubanshe 文物出版社, 1989.

Zhongtai shan bowuguan 中台山博物館, ed. *Diyong tianbao: Zhejiang sheng bowuguan zhenpin tezhan* 地涌天寶: 浙江省博物館博物館珍品特展. Nantou 南投: Wen xin wenhua shiye gufen youxian gongsi 文心文化事業股份有限公司, 2009.

Zhou, Feng 周峰, ed. *Wuyue shoufu Hangzhou* 吳越首府杭州. Hangzhou: Zhejiang Renmin Chubanshe 浙江人民出版社, 1988.

Zürcher, Erik. *The Buddhist Conquest of China*. Leiden: Brill, 1959.

———. "Buddhist Influence on Early Taoism: A Survey of Scriptural Evidence." *T'oung Pao* 66 (1980): 84–147.

Zengaku shisōshi 禅学思想史 (History of the Thought of Zen Training), vol. 1. Tokyo: Genkōsha 玄黄社, 1923.

Zhejiangsheng wenwu guanli weiyuanhui 浙江省文物管理委員會, ed. *Jinhua Wanfota chutu wenwu* 金華萬佛塔出土文物. Beijing: Wenwu Chubanshe, 1958.

Zhejiang sheng wenwu kaogu yanjiusuo 浙江省文物考古研究所, ed. *Leifeng yi zhen* 雷鋒遺珍. Beijing: Wenwu Chubanshe 文物出版社, 2002.

———. *Leifengtayizhi* 雷鋒塔遺址. Beijing: Wenwu Chubanshe 文物出版社, 2005.

Contributors

Stephen R. Bokenkamp is Professor of Chinese, Department of Religious Studies, Arizona State University.

Bernard Faure is Kao Professor in Japanese Religion, Department of Religion, Columbia University.

John Kieschnick is Robert H. N. Ho Family Foundation Professor of Buddhist Studies, Department of Religious Studies, Stanford University.

Victor H. Mair is Professor of Chinese Language and Literature, Department of East Asian Languages and Civilizations, University of Pennsylvania.

John R. McRae, formerly Professor of East Asian Buddhism at Indiana and Komazawa Universities, died during the preparation of this book.

Christine Mollier is Director of Research at the French National Center for Scientific Research (CNRS/CRCAO), Paris.

Meir Shahar is Associate Professor of Chinese Studies in the Department of East Asian Studies, Tel Aviv University.

Robert Sharf is D. H. Chen Distinguished Professor of Buddhist Studies, Department of East Asian Languages and Cultures, University of California, Berkeley.

Nobuyoshi Yamabe is Professor of Bioethics and Foreign Languages, Tokyo University of Agriculture.

Ye Derong is an independent scholar specializing in Chinese Buddhism.

Shi Zhiru is Associate Professor of Religious Studies, Pomona College.

Index